INTRODUCTORY MICROECONOMICS

Kruger Brentt
Publishers

INTRODUCTORY MICROECONOMICS

VOLUME-2

Margaret Anderson
Bryan Clark
Matthew Qiu

Kruger Brentt
Publishers

2023

Kruger Brentt Publishers UK. LTD.
Company Number 9728962

Regd. Office: 68 St Margarets Road, Edgware, Middlesex HA8 9UU

ISBN: 978-1-78715-198-7

Disclaimer:

Every possible effort has been made to ensure that the information contained in this book is accurate at the time of going to press, and the publisher and author cannot accept responsibility for any errors or omissions, however caused. No responsibility for loss or damage occasioned to any person acting, or refraining from action, as a result of the material in this publication can be accepted by the editor, the publisher or the author. The Publisher is not associated with any product or vendor mentioned in the book. The contents of this work are intended to further general scientific research, understanding and discussion only. Readers should consult with a specialist where appropriate.

Every effort has been made to trace the owners of copyright material used in this book, if any. The author and the publisher will be grateful for any omission brought to their notice for acknowledgement in the future editions of the book.

For information on all our publications visit our website at http://krugerbrentt.com/

PREFACE

The science of economics was born with the publication of Adam Smith's an Inquiry into the Nature and Causes of Wealth of Nations in the year 1776. Adam Smith is known as the father of Economics. At its birth, the name of economics was 'Political Economy'. Towards the end of the 19th century there was a definite change from use of word 'Political Economy' to 'Economics'. The word 'Economics' was derived from two Greek words oikou (a house) and nomos (to manage). Thus, the word economics was used to mean home management with limited funds available in the most economical manner possible. Lionel Robbins defines economics as a science of scarcity. Prof. Robbins in his book Nature and Significance of Economic Science states, "Economics is the science which studies human behaviour as a relationship between ends and scarce means which have alternative uses". Paul A. Samuelson defines economics as "the study of how men and society choose, withor without the use of money, to employ scarce productive resources which could have alternative uses, to produce various commodities over time and distribute them for consumption now and in future among various people and groups of society." This definition emphasises growth over time. It is modern and wider in scope. The definition takes into account consumption, production, distribution and exchange ofgoods. Hence, it is most satisfactory definition of economics.

Traditionally, the subject matter of economics has been studied under two broad branches: Microeconomics and Macroeconomics. In microeconomics, we study the behaviour of individual economic agents in the markets for different goods and services and try to figure out how prices and quantities of goods and services are determined through the interaction of individuals in these markets. In macroeconomics, on the other hand, we try to get an understanding of the economy as a whole by focusing our attention on aggregate measures such as total output, employment and aggregate price level. Here, we are interested in finding out how the levels of these aggregate measures are determined and how the levels of these aggregate measures change over time.

The present book contains 28-chapters namely welcome to economics!, a world of scarcity and choice, a pluralist approach to defining economics, concepts of demand and supply, labor and financial markets, elasticity an overview, consumer choices, challenging utilitarianism's impact, modern consumption: an institutional analysis, the cost and the industry structure, perfect competition in economics, the monopoly and its kind, competition in monopolists and oligopoly, the growth of big business, pricing and costs: the evidence, the megacorp: principle of economics, policy on monopoly and antitrust, negative externalities and environmental protection, public goods and positive externalities, economic inequality and poverty, major issues in labor markets: unions, discrimination, immigration, knowledge, risk, and insurance, financial markets and business, introduction to public economy, money and the firm's theory, introduction to international trade, globalization and protectionism and the globalization and trade economics: a pluralistic approach. This book covers the scope and sequence of most introductory microeconomics courses.The text includes many current examples, which are handled in a politically equitable way. The outcome is a balanced approach to the theory and application of economics concept. This book provides clear, accurate coverage of advanced microeconomic concepts while illustrating how theory applies to practical situations. This book is useful for undergraduate as well as postgraduate students of economics, commerce, marketing, management, finance, banking and for everybody interested in microeconomics.

We are grateful to all those persons as well as various books, manuals, periodicals, magazines, journals etc. that helped in the preparation of this book. In spite of the best efforts, it is possible that some errors may have occurred into the compilation and editing of the book. Further queries, constructive suggestions and criticisms for the improvement of the book are always welcomed and shall be thankfully acknowledged.

Margaret Anderson

Bryan Clark

Matthew Qiu

CONTENTS

Contents

CHAPTER 16

THE MEGACORP: PRINCIPLE OF ECONOMICS

16.1 THE TECHNOLOGY'S IMPERATIVES

In chapter "Costs and Prices" you learned (or will learn) that modern businesses are treated as going concerns–that is, organizations which are expected to continue to exist into the foreseeable future. This idea, reflected in accounting practices developed in the second half of the 19th century, is central to how heterodox economists understand the nature of the modern business enterprise. Its historical roots are explored in more detail in chapter "The Rise of the Big Business," but here we want to focus on a particular cause, technological advance, and its implications.

In his classic, The New Industrial State (1967), economist John Kenneth Galbraith compared the Ford Motor Company in the year of its founding, 1903, to the same business at the introduction of the first Mustang in 1964. In 1903 the company employed around 125 people, worked with approximately $150,000 in capital, and required only months of negotiations, preparation, and production to bring an automobile to the market. It would be an understatement to say that, six decades later, the process was more involved. The Mustang was the result of several years of preparation, millions of dollars on engineering and 'styling', and tens of millions on tooling for production. At the time, Ford employed over 300,000 people.

Galbraith argued that the essential cause of this massive increase in preparation, capital, and labor was the tremendous advance in technology (which he defined as "the application of scientific or other organized knowledge to practical tasks"). Increasingly sophisticated technology requires specialization–of machinery and the materials it will work on, as well as of workers. All of which, of course, requires more capital (that is, money). It also means that increasingly specialized workers, machines, and so on must be more carefully managed; and that a commitment to produce something must be made much further in advance of actually having something to sell. As Galbraith explained, the Dodge brothers' machine shop, responsible for machining the engine and chassis of the original Ford automobiles, could have hypothetically been asked to accommodate significant changes in the car's design with only a few hours delay. The factories which built the Mustang, on the other hand, were effectively locked into making Mustangs for well over a year. Finally, and most importantly, there is the technological imperative of planning. As Galbraith argued, the large financial and material commitments necessary to design a product and prepare for its production require that each part of the process works today so that, in the distant future, when all the parts are brought together, the job is done correctly. This means that the business enterprise will require specialists in predicting (and shaping) future market conditions, specialists in materials acquisition, specialists in education to ensure a competent workforce, and so on–all to ensure that what the organization set out to do some months or years or decades earlier actually gets done and, with some luck, proves successful. Without that capacity, the confidence to set out on such a sophisticated enterprise would never have existed in the first place.

Figure 3. A 1964 Ford Mustang in Wimbledon White, photographed at the 50th anniversary of the Mustang at the Charlotte Motor Speedway. (Source: Sicnag, Wikimedia, CC-BY-2.0)

What bearing, then, does this have on our theories of how businesses behave and how markets operate? We'll start with the general points: first, the small firm of the perfect competition model will not do in an age of increasingly sophisticated technology. Both the complexity of specialized knowledge and its management through a large organization suggest that a large business enterprise will be the norm. Second, that complexity of knowledge and organization suggests that the modern business enterprise ought to be considered in more dimensions that simply its cost curves and a goal of maximizing profits. The politics and culture of organization become relevant to understanding what Galbraith called the **technostructure**–that is, the whole of those people who participate in the group decision-making that directs the business enterprise through time.

Does the internet move us closer to perfect competition?

A common refrain in recent years argues that information technology–in particular, the internet–contradicts the tendency toward big business. Recall that the model of perfect competition doesn't suggest that firms must be absolutely tiny–say, having no more than a handful of employees. Rather, it simply considers situations in which firms are small *relative to the size of the market.* Many have argued that the internet has made global markets out of local markets; and, as a result, firms that used to be considered large are now small *relative to* the whole world of competitors. Yet, within the tech sector, as in most other industries, concentration and big business appear to be the norm. Large business like IBM have long dominated traditional computing, before the World Wide Web, and relatively newer firms like Google and Facebook continue to expand control over much of the newer, web-based markets. Of course, Amazon, Paypal, eBay, AirBnB, and Uber have allowed for a proliferation of small merchants, taxi drivers, and hotels; but with these large corporations looming over the markets they've created, have we really returned to the traditional competitive product markets of past centuries–or are we looking at the competitive (one might say, 'divide and conquer') *labor* markets that characterized the rise of big business in the late ١٨٠٠'s?

Third, if planning is the central concern of the modern business enterprise, then we have to reconsider how we see firms relating to their markets. In previous chapters, you have studied the basic neoclassical models of market structure and how firms respond to particular market conditions. The implicit assumption in these models is that firms react to markets. Yet, if long term planning is to be done effectively it would seem obvious that businesses cannot take the markets as given and respond accordingly. Instead, they will have to actively shape those markets to ensure stable, predictable conditions into the future.

This third point has a particular bearing on our theories of prices and competition. History shows that businesses often try to avoid competition in terms of price. You can probably imagine why this is, given the complexity of modern technologies and the magnitude of investments necessary to get a business off the ground. Where starting a new business or a new product line for an existing business requires huge sums of money and years of planning, it is simply a must that the investors and management are reasonably sure that it will be able to sell the product profitably in the relatively distant future. The business enterprise's problem in this scenario is that competitors may be making the same investments; and, in an attempt to make sure those investments don't go to waste due to weak sales, they may try to grab market share by lowering their prices. If everyone in the market pursues the same strategy, what do you think the result would be?

Stiff competition based on prices is relatively rare in established markets for a simple reason: it tends to be mutually destructive to most or all competitors who engage in it. In fact, when prominent businesses engage in that sort of scenario–as, for instance, the fast food giants occasionally have in recent years–it is often considered newsworthy, usually showing up in the headlines of the business press as a 'price war'. A century ago, the term 'cut throat competition,' which includes aggressive price cuts and other efforts to drive competitors out of the market, was common. Clearly, both of the terms suggest that price competition can be a violent thing–something, one would hope at least, that should be avoided if at all possible.

In summary, then, heterodox economists typically see the modern business enterprise as a going concern, engaged in long term planning which includes managing and shaping both technological and market conditions. In this view firms don't maximize profits so much as they seek to survive through time. If it is appropriate to say that businesses tend to maximize anything, it would be growth through time rather than profits specifically. Likewise, outright price competition is a relatively rare occurrence in mature markets today. Though most businesses will take competition into consideration when setting their prices, it would be a better description of the real world to say that competition occurs mainly through other practices, like advertising and branding, product innovations, or more cost-effective production practices. That is to say that businesses compete chiefly through their investments, not their prices.

16.2 BUSINESS MODELS, PLURAL: GOALS AND APPROACHES OF MEGACORP

As a professor of mine, James Sturgeon, is fond of saying, there's more than one way to make money: You could...

- Steal
- Extort
- Accept a bribe
- Speculate on the financial or real estate markets
- Inherit
- Con
- Or, perhaps failing all of the above, you could earn it

For our purposes here, this can be interpreted as a rather cheeky way of saying that different businesses have different **business models**–that is, different ways of making money in a market (or several markets). And, while they might all be treated with the utmost abstraction as combining inputs to produce outputs of greater value, heterodox economists are inclined to believe that not every way of making money is the same.

Breaking down all of the means by which modern businesses make money is far beyond the scope of this chapter (though the odds are good that the reader is taking this course to fulfill a requirement for a business degree for which she or he will be spending plenty of time doing just that). Instead, we'll borrow from Karl Marx's extensive work on how capitalist economies function to create a simplified picture, Figure 4, of what a business enterprise does. And from there, we'll look to institutional economics to understand qualitative difference in how businesses generate their earnings.

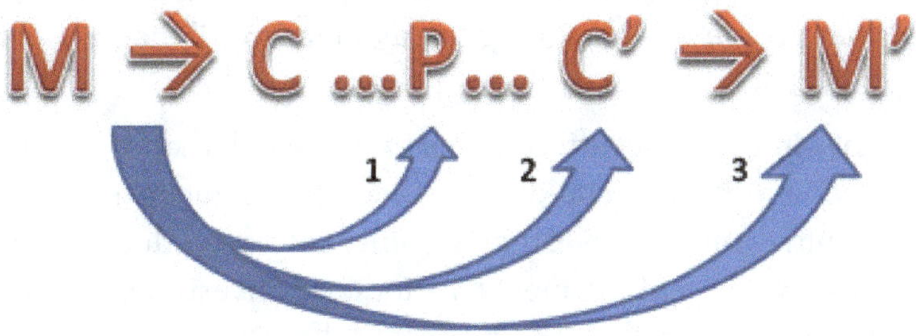

Figure 4. The Business Enterprise in a Monetary Production Economy.

In Figure 4, M represents an amount of money and C represents a commodity (for instance the lumber and other building materials a construction company may use to build a house). P represents the production process that converts the commodity C (building materials) into some other commodity C' (for instance, a house) to be sold for some amount of money M'. This process can be treated as a shorthand depiction of what any business does, with the requirement that if the business is to remain in business M' must be greater than M. Take a moment to review the chapter "Cost and Industry Structure," specifically the definitions of firm and production therein. How does Figure 4 differ?

The difference may not be obvious, but it is important. In the neoclassical tradition in economics–indeed, in the classical tradition which Marx was critiquing–production by businesses is treated as a C→ C' process. That is, all business activity is part of converting commodity inputs into commodity outputs which are of greater value, ultimately, to consumers. Clearly, Figure 4 is more than that: it treats money and commodities as distinct things. This allows us to look at the step-by-step process by which money is converted into commodities, production creates new commodities, and money is created by sale of those new commodities. The whole process of turning money into commodity inputs and ultimately selling commodity outputs for money we'll call **monetary production**. The full implications of these distinctions for Marxian (or radical political) economics would require its own course. For now, we can use this shorthand description of how a business enterprise works to think about different types of business models.

The three numbered arrows in Figure 4 represent three different ways that managers, engineers, markers, and others within a business enterprise can influence the process of monetary production. The first arrow, following M to P, indicates something close to the traditional way of thinking of a business: money is invested into a production process that turns inputs into outputs for sale. This could include building a new factory or setting up a research and development (R&D) team to design new products and more efficient production practices. What is significant here is that the focus is on producing something–turning stuff C into stuff C', presumably with the hope that people will be willing to pay more for C' than was paid for the C necessary to produce it.

The second arrow indicates a different business model–that is, another way the monetary production process could be influenced to make money. Here, you will notice, the initial money invested is going not to production, P, but to the produced commodity, C'. This is meant to indicate investments made to change the perceived value of the product the business sells. Of course, one way to do this is to improve the product itself, which would be indicated by the first arrow. With arrow 2, however, we're dealing with changing the perceived value of the product without actually changing the product itself; and you've probably already guessed the most salient way this can be done: advertising.

Here, the founder of institutional economics, Thorstein Veblen, is worth quoting at length:

> The end sought by the systematic advertising of the larger business concerns is...a monopoly of custom and prestige.... The great end of consistent advertising is to establish such differential monopolies resting on popular conviction.... The cost, as well as the pecuniary value and the magnitude, of this organized fabrication of popular convictions is indicated by such statements as that the proprietors of a certain well-known household remedy, reputed among medical authorities to be of entirely dubious value, have for a series of years found their profits in spending several million dollars annually in advertisements. This case is by no means unique.
>
> It has been said, no doubt in good faith and certainly with some reason, that advertising as currently carried on gives the body of consumers valuable information and guidance as to the ways and means whereby their wants can be satisfied and their purchasing power can be best utilized. To the extent to which this holds true, advertising is a service to the community. But there is a large reservation to be

made on this head. Advertising is competitive; the greater part of it aims to divert purchases, etc., from one channel to another channel of the same general class. And to the extent to which the efforts of advertising in all its branches are spent on this *competitive disturbance of trade*, they are, on the whole, of *slight if any immediate service to the community*. (Veblen 1904, pp. 55-7, Public Domain, emphasis added)

Veblen's inimitable prose may be a bit irksome to read, but reference to the italicized bits above should be enough to understand the argument. 'Custom and prestige,' and the 'fabrication of popular conviction' suggest that businesses are competing through persuasion rather than production of something of value. The second paragraph, then, considers whether these activities are actually of value to society (or perhaps, in neoclassical terms, whether or not they're 'welfare enhancing'). For the most part, they are decidedly not. They may create a pecuniary (that is, money) value for the business–the perception of C' is improved and M' increases as a result. But, to society in general they amount to little more than a needless shifting of buying habits and consumption patterns. As Professor Sturgeon notes, there's more than one way to make money.

We should pause to consider the usefulness of this model. Separating money from commodities in the monetary production process has allowed us to consider different business activities as essentially different things. The abstract firm in standard neoclassical theory might lead us to treat anything that makes a business more money as part of the production process (C…P…C'), suggesting that advertising was just another commodity in the production process improving the value of the product to be sold. By implication, then, the advertising added value to society. Yet, treating production and advertising as two different activities allowed room for the argument that, in fact, the advertising was generally wasteful.

Distinguishing Arrow 1 from Arrow 2: The Pharmaceutical Industry

A contemporary example should indicate the importance of distinguishing between arrows 1 and 2. The price of pharmaceutical drugs continues to be a controversial topic in the United States, and it's no surprise why: according to the OECD, pharmaceutical spending has risen from an average of $159 per person (or 0.87% of all spending in the US) in 1985 to $1,112 per person (or 2.04% of total spending) in 2014. Moreover, a 2016 Reuters article found that the prices of 4 of the top 10 most widely used drugs more than doubled in just the previous 5 years.

A number of factors are important to explaining these rapid price increases, including an aging population in the US and an exceedingly complex distribution and insurance system for pharmaceuticals. But, let's focus on the common explanation given by the producers themselves: high prices are necessary to recover the high costs of research and development (much of which leads to dead-end investments that don't produce effective drugs that can be brought to market) and the clinical trials necessary for regulatory approval. Clearly, this is in line with the general framework of heterodox economic theory. Pharmaceutical companies are engaging in long-run planning, including significant investments into better products (that is, investments into P in Figure 1), and prices are a reflection of those investments.

But, what's more, our monetary production model can help us find a fuller explanation of the nature and extent of those investments. Consider estimates from Gagnon and Lexchin (2008) on promotional expenditures by the industry. The authors found that, for 2004, the industry devoted about 24% of its sales revenue to promotion, versus about 13% to research and development. Looking specifically to promotion directed at physicians, the authors estimate that approximately $61,000 was spent per physician in the US. To be sure, there are other estimates lower than those made by Gagnon and Lexchin. Just the same, it is clear that pharmaceutical enterprises are investing heavily not only in developing new drugs, but in promoting their use as well.

Moreover, the pharmaceutical industry provides us with a somewhat unique opportunity to clearly distinguish investments in C' (arrow 2 in figure 1) from investments in P (arrow 1). Because these drugs are systematically evaluated for their effectiveness in treating specific illnesses, data exist to indicate how well supposedly-arrow 1 investments are improving the product. On this matter, Gagnon (2013) finds that fewer and fewer new molecular entities (truly new drugs, without precedent in drugs already in use) are being developed, and only a small minority of new drugs represent substantial therapeutic advances over existing treatments. The proliferation of 'me-too' drugs, which are new products to be marketed if not actually better treatments for illnesses, suggests that the business model in this industry is focused less on improvements in P and more on inflating C'. That is, arrow 2 appears to dominate, with arrow 1 a secondary concern, in the normal business models of this industry.

Finally, there is arrow 3, a direct line from an initial sum of money to a greater amount of money, bypassing all the troublesome in-between steps of producing and selling a good or service. This sort of business model takes many forms and is becoming increasingly popular in the capitalism of today. The traditional exemplar is the financial firm–or, say, the stock broker–which has no direct ties to actually producing something, but rather only to trading in the ownership rights of those producers.

The full role and consequences of financial firms and markets cannot be covered here. What's of interest presently is business activity that can turn a profit without being concerned with producing something for sale, or even simply with persuading people to buy a product. You may have heard about the causes of the Great Recession of 2008-09 being chiefly linked to business models in finance, insurance, and real estate (the so-called FIRE sector). The problem, many believe, is in the opacity and complexity of a system in which mortgage contracts representing an agreement to pay for a house over time were packaged together into derivative contracts to be sold to investors, then resold, repackaged, and so on. Indeed to make a system even more complex, many financial firms were making side bets that the contracts they themselves were selling would in fact not pay out. Many articles, books, and documentaries have been produced retelling that story, and The Big Short is an effective and accurate dramatization of some of those events. For now, it is enough to say that the businesses engaged in those activities were largely concerned with turning money into more money by persuading others that these contracts built on contracts (built on contracts...) were worth more than they were. These were arrow 3 business activities, having little to do with the actual business of housing people.

A century earlier, Veblen had described similar practices in the stock markets, where the goal is to, induce a discrepancy between the putative and the actual earning-capacity, by expedients well known and approved for the purpose. Partial information, as well as misinformation, sagaciously given out at a critical juncture, will go far toward producing a favorable temporary discrepancy of this kind. (Veblen, 1904, p. 156, Public Domain)

It was, more recently, precisely this type of behavior which ultimately caused the deepest recession since the Great Depression (which, incidentally, had also been caused by this type of behavior). As a result, many of the largest banks and other financial institutions in the US and abroad have been made to pay fines in the 10's of billions of dollars. Whether these fines will be enough to make this business model unattractive in the future is debatable–but it seems unlikely.

16.3 ENHANCING MARKET STABILITY

The previous sections dealt mainly with the nature of the modern business enterprise as an individual organization. But, of course, no business is created in a vacuum, and no business can operate in complete isolation. This section will look at the economic, social, and political nature of markets to better understand how real businesses fit into a heterodox understanding of the economy.

Any business model–including those discussed above and beyond–is a plan for how to successfully operate a business within one or more markets. A good business plan will have to consider, among other things, the competition, the potential customer base, rules and regulations, and the necessary infrastructure to produce and distribute the product, whatever it may be. Established businesses will have worked out their business models over time, will have built (or had built for them) the necessary infrastructure (for instance, roads or communications protocols), and will typically have helped define the rules and regulations that dictate which individual and competitive activities are permissible and which are not. This is to say that markets themselves are defined by (and the way business enterprises behave in these markets is guided by) their infrastructure and their corporate and market governance structures.

Definitions

Infrastructure: the common structures, facilities, and systems necessary for organizations to operate. These may include physical infrastructure like highways, bridges, electrical grids, and sewage systems; as well as systems like the complex networks of computers tied together through communications lines and protocols we know as the internet.

Corporate governance: the rules and practices defining how and by whom a business is directed as well as how members of the business will interact with each other and those outside of the business. These are both formal rules like accounting practices or the corporate hierarchy of who reports to whom, as well as informal norms, traditions, and relationships.

Market governance: the rules and practices defining how business enterprises will behave in a market, including especially how they will interact with their competitors. These may include formal agreements–for instance, a consent decree by which a business agrees not to engage in an activity the government considers anticompetitive, or a joint venture operation between two energy companies to explore a potential source of crude oil. Probably more important, though, are the various informal arrangements by which certain types of competition and cooperation between businesses are allowed while others are not. A side note: these shared rules and infrastructure are not fixed in time–they evolve, whether by unintended consequence or intentional change. Moreover, they are socially constructed, which means there is a political element to all of them. Although we're focusing for now on the private, business side of the matter, it should be remembered that there is almost always a government role in the development, regulation, and sometimes prohibition of these structures. Finally, a fourth component, property rights, is worth adding. Property rights are legal norms defining who can own what, what can be done with that property, and therefore how businesses can generate earnings and who has claims on those earnings. While property is often considered simply a natural right, the actual content of property rights is a complex, perpetually evolving, and highly contested subject.

These attributes of the organization of businesses and the markets in which they operate are all geared toward essentially the same thing: stability. As an earlier section explained, most parts of the modern economy involve sophisticated and usually large-scale technologies. For this and other reasons long term planning is necessary for production to go forward; and long term planning requires predictable outcomes. Hence, markets and businesses must be organized to promote stability. In particular, as a previous section explains, businesses require predictability in prices.

Now, consider the neoclassical models of previous chapters. In each of these some, perhaps natural, equilibration process is used–that is, a process by which firm's, consumers, and ultimately markets move toward an equilibrium, toward stability. The utility maximizing consumer seeks an optimal combination of consumers goods, the profit maximizing firm seeks an optimal level of production, and the market, through competition and price bidding, moves toward the equilibrium price and output.

Many heterodox economists reject each of these models, in part because of the unrealistic mechanisms by which equilibrium is reached. For instance, as chapter "Costs and Prices" demonstrates, few markets in the modern US economy are characterized by the sort of price adjustments that the standard market model relies on to reach a stable equilibrium. Moreover, considerable evidence suggests that competition–especially price competition–actually promotes instability. And it is for this reason that the concept of market governance is so important. Without a workable set of norms concerning acceptable and unacceptable forms of competition and cooperation, most markets would never reach equilibrium. Instead, price competition and chicanery would wreak havoc on businesses and consumers alike.

16.4 COLLEGE TEXTBOOKS ARE VERY EXPENSIVE.

In this concluding section of the chapter we'll look at a question you've probably asked yourself: why do college textbooks cost so much? The question is particularly interesting for economic theory. Nationally, textbooks prices have risen more than three times the prices of other goods and services in the economy–an increase from the 1977 to 2015 of 1,041%, reports ABC News. As of September 2016, the average undergraduate student will be spending just shy of $1,300 a year on textbooks and supplies. That's no small sum.

Standard analysis would look for low elasticities of demand and lack of competition to explain high prices. Question: as a student, is your demand for college textbooks elastic or inelastic? Why? Likely, you answered 'very inelastic' since you have little choice in buying a textbook that is required for a course. (In fact a 2014 Student PIRG survey found that two thirds of students had foregone buying at least one textbook due to cost. Not surprisingly, almost all of those students indicated concern that the decision would impact their grades negatively.)

As for competition in the textbook publishing business, it may not surprise you to learn that, like in most other markets, there are only a handful of large corporations controlling the bulk of the college textbook supply. International corporations, which in many cases have existed for over a century, dominate the global market for these products, bringing in billions of dollars in revenue each year. While not a pure monopoly, it would seem that this industry is closer to our neoclassical monopoly model than to perfect competition. The outcome of this captive-market situation, as you've seen in a previous chapter, is clear: fewer students purchase textbooks than would like, and they pay higher prices than would exist under more competitive conditions.

But, then, is competition the solution? Certainly, the industry meets the definition of high concentration, suggesting that textbook publishing is far from the ideal model of perfect competition. Publishers appear to enjoy significant market power, especially in setting their own prices, rather than taking the competitive market price as given. But, if we accept that these large corporations are not price takers in the markets for their books, we still have to answer: how–that is, for what reasons–do they determine the prices they will charge? And this is where the business model becomes important.

The mainstream assumption that firms, always and everywhere, maximize profits suggests that output is being set according to marginal costs and marginal revenues, and that the high inelasticity of demand allows publishers to raise prices well above the actual costs of production. Firms produce to maximize profits, and a lack of competition allows them to take monopoly rents through higher prices.

But, consider the heterodox position–that business enterprises generally want to survive and grow, and that competition occurs chiefly through investments, not prices. This view suggests that it's not so much that publishers wish to get every last dollar of profit to be had (that is, to maximize profits), nor that they will raise prices to whatever the students (that is, demanders) are willing to pay. Rather, these producers are seeking to make the investments necessary to survive (to make a profit) in their markets. The prices they charge, then, may seem like price gouging, but may really just be the results of the markups necessary to cover the costs of those investments. (However, the more recent focus among publicly traded companies on keeping stock prices up may drive them toward price gouging over simply pricing to cover full costs.)

And this is where we come back to the original question: is competition the solution? From the perspective of heterodox economics, the high price of college textbooks reflects the high cost of investing in new textbook editions–in computer software tools to complement the text (and ensure the student pays for the online access), in test banks and slideshows to aid the instructor using the text, and so on. And what compels publishers to make these investments? Largely, competition. If a publisher neglected to develop new editions, it could not compete with the used textbook markets. If a publisher fell behind in developing software and supplements for instructors, the other publishers would have a competitive advantage in pitching their texts to instructors. Perhaps surprisingly, the conclusion is that prices are high, not so much from a lack of price competition, but because of a particular dynamic in investment competition. It is–or so one could argue–a lack of appropriate planning across the industry as a whole that keeps publishers grasping at market share by investing in anything and everything that might help sell their textbooks...and the student pays the price.

The Courts and Property Rights

In a previous breakout box it was mentioned that a proper understanding of market structure would require, among other things, an understanding of the specific property rights relevant to production, exchange, and consumption processes of the market. A recent US Supreme Court case offers a good illustration of that very point.

John Wiley & Sons, Inc. is a global publishing company with thousands of employees and a market cap (total value of outstanding shares) in the billions of dollars. In 2008 Wiley sued Supap Kirtsaeng for copyright infringement. Kirtsaeng, a Thailand native who had studied in the US, had discovered that foreign edition textbooks could be imported into the US to be sold at lower prices than the texts' American-edition prices. Wiley believed that this was a violation of their property rights which included the right to prevent importation of their copyrighted works.

While two lower courts sided with the publisher's position on the control that copyright afforded them, the US Supreme Court did not. They argued in their ruling that the 'first-sale doctrine', allowing those who obtained a textbook legally to re-sell it, limited Wiley's right to control the importation of their books. As an economist-in-training, how do you think things would be different if the Supreme Court had ruled in favor of Wiley? Would prices continue to rise, plateau, or come down? Would this change the direction of investment in the publishing industry? How would students, faculties, and higher education more generally be affected?

CHAPTER 17
POLICY ON MONOPOLY AND ANTITRUST

Monopoly and Antitrust Policy: An Overview

The previous chapters on the theory of the firm identified three important lessons: First, that competition, by providing consumers with lower prices and a variety of innovative products, is a good thing; second, that large-scale production can dramatically lower average costs; and third, that markets in the real world are rarely perfectly competitive. As a consequence, government policymakers must determine how much to intervene to balance the potential benefits of large-scale production against the potential loss of competition that can occur when businesses grow in size, especially through mergers.

For example, in 2011, AT&T and T-Mobile proposed a merger. At the time, there were only four major mobile phone service providers. The proposal was blocked by both the Justice Department and the FCC.

The two companies argued that the merger would benefit consumers, who would be able to purchase better telecommunications services at a cheaper price because the newly created firm would be able to produce more efficiently by taking advantage of economies of scale and eliminating duplicate investments. However, a number of activist groups like the Consumer Federation of America and Public Knowledge expressed fears that the merger would reduce competition and lead to higher prices for consumers for decades to come. In December 2006, the federal government allowed the merger to proceed. By 2009, the new post-merger AT&T was the eighth largest company by revenues in the United States, and by that measure the largest telecommunications company in the world. Economists have spent – and will still spend – years trying to determine whether the merger of AT&T and BellSouth, as well as other smaller mergers of telecommunications companies at about this same time, helped consumers, hurt them, or did not make much difference.

This chapter discusses public policy issues about competition. How can economists and governments determine when mergers of large companies like AT&T

and BellSouth should be allowed and when they should be blocked? The government also plays a role in policing anticompetitive behavior other than mergers, like prohibiting certain kinds of contracts that might restrict competition. In the case of natural monopoly, however, trying to preserve competition probably will not work very well, and so government will often resort to regulation of price and/or quantity of output. In recent decades, there has been a global trend toward less government intervention in the price and output decisions of businesses.

17.1 MERGERS OF CORPORATES

A corporate merger occurs when two formerly separate firms combine to become a single firm. When one firm purchases another, it is called an acquisition. An acquisition may not look just like a merger, since the newly purchased firm may continue to be operated under its former company name. Mergers can also be lateral, where two firms of similar sizes combine to become one. However, both mergers and acquisitions lead to two formerly separate firms being under common ownership, and so they are commonly grouped together.

Regulations for Merger Approval

Since a merger combines two firms into one, it can reduce the extent of competition between firms. Therefore, when two U.S. firms announce a merger or acquisition where at least one of the firms is above a minimum size of sales (a threshold that moves up gradually over time, and was at $70.9 million in 2013), or certain other conditions are met, they are required under law to notify the U.S. Federal Trade Commission (FTC). The left-hand panel of Figure 1 (a) shows the number of mergers submitted for review to the FTC each year from 1999 to 2012. Mergers were very high in the late 1990s, diminished in the early 2000s, and then rebounded somewhat in a cyclical fashion. The right-hand panel of Figure 1 (b) shows the distribution of those mergers submitted for review in 2012 as measured by the size of the transaction. It is important to remember that this total leaves out many small mergers under $50 million, which only need to be reported in certain limited circumstances. About a quarter of all reported merger and acquisition transactions in 2012 exceeded $500 million, while about 11 percent exceeded $1 billion. In 2014, the FTC took action against mergers likely to stifle competition in markets worth 18.6 billion in sales.

The laws that give government the power to block certain mergers, and even in some cases to break up large firms into smaller ones, are called **antitrust laws**. Before a large merger happens, the antitrust regulators at the FTC and the U.S. Department of Justice can allow the merger, prohibit it, or allow it if certain conditions are met. One common condition is that the merger will be allowed if the firm agrees to sell off certain parts. For example, in 2006, Johnson & Johnson bought the Pfizer's "consumer health" division, which included well-known brands like Listerine mouthwash and

Sudafed cold medicine. As a condition of allowing the merger, Johnson & Johnson was required to sell off six brands to other firms, including Zantac® heartburn relief medication, Cortizone anti-itch cream, and Balmex diaper rash medication, to preserve a greater degree of competition in these markets.

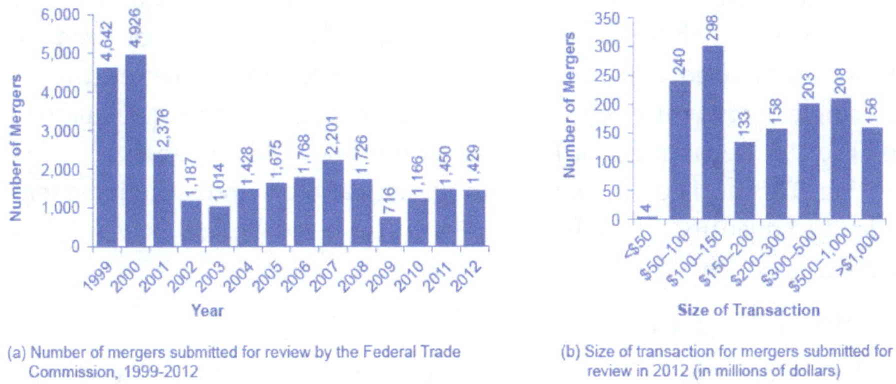

Figure 1. Number and Size of Mergers. (a) The number of mergers in 1999 and 2000 were relatively high compared to the annual numbers seen from 2001–2012. While 2001 and 2007 saw a high number of mergers, these were still only about half the number of mergers in 1999 and 2000. (b) In 2012, the greatest number of mergers submitted for review was for transactions between $100 and $150 million.

The U.S. government approves most proposed mergers. In a market-oriented economy, firms have the freedom to make their own choices. Private firms generally have the freedom to:

- expand or reduce production
- set the price they choose
- open new factories or sales facilities or close them
- hire workers or to lay them off
- start selling new products or stop selling existing ones

If the owners want to acquire a firm or be acquired, or to merge with another firm, this decision is just one of many that firms are free to make. In these conditions, the managers of private firms will sometimes make mistakes. They may close down a factory which, it later turns out, would have been profitable. They may start selling a product that ends up losing money. A merger between two companies can sometimes lead to a clash of corporate personalities that makes both firms worse off. But the fundamental belief behind a market-oriented economy is that firms, not governments, are in the best position to know if their actions will lead to attracting more customers or producing more efficiently.

Indeed, government regulators agree that most mergers are beneficial to consumers. As the Federal Trade Commission has noted on its website (as of November, 2013): "Most mergers actually benefit competition and consumers by allowing firms to operate more efficiently." At the same time, the FTC recognizes, "Some [mergers] are likely to lessen competition. That, in turn, can lead to higher prices, reduced availability of goods or services, lower quality of products, and less innovation. Indeed, some mergers create a concentrated market, while others enable a single firm to raise prices." The challenge for the antitrust regulators at the FTC and the U.S. Department of Justice is to figure out when a merger may hinder competition. This decision involves both numerical tools and some judgments that are difficult to quantify. The following Clear it Up helps explain how antitrust laws came about.

What is U.S. antitrust law?

In the closing decades of the 1800s, many industries in the U.S. economy were dominated by a single firm that had most of the sales for the entire country. Supporters of these large firms argued that they could take advantage of economies of scale and careful planning to provide consumers with products at low prices. However, critics pointed out that when competition was reduced, these firms were free to charge more and make permanently higher profits, and that without the goading of competition, it was not clear that they were as efficient or innovative as they could be.

In many cases, these large firms were organized in the legal form of a "trust," in which a group of formerly independent firms were consolidated together by mergers and purchases, and a group of "trustees" then ran the companies as if they were a single firm. Thus, when the U.S. government passed the Sherman Antitrust Act in 1890 to limit the power of these trusts, it was called an antitrust law. In an early demonstration of the law's power, the U.S. Supreme Court in 1911 upheld the government's right to break up Standard Oil, which had controlled about 90% of the country's oil refining, into 34 independent firms, including Exxon, Mobil, Amoco, and Chevron. In 1914, the Clayton Antitrust Act outlawed mergers and acquisitions (where the outcome would be to "substantially lessen competition" in an industry), price discrimination (where different customers are charged different prices for the same product), and tied sales (where purchase of one product commits the buyer to purchase some other product). Also in 1914, the Federal Trade Commission (FTC) was created to define more specifically what competition was unfair. In 1950, the Celler-Kefauver Act extended the Clayton Act by restricting vertical and conglomerate mergers. In the twenty-first century, the FTC and the U.S. Department of Justice continue to enforce antitrust laws.

The Four-Firm Concentration Ratio

Regulators have struggled for decades to measure the degree of monopoly power in an industry. An early tool was the **concentration ratio**, which measures what share of the total sales in the industry are accounted for by the largest firms, typically the top four to eight firms. For an explanation of how high market concentrations can create inefficiencies in an economy, refer to Monopoly.

Say that the market for replacing broken automobile windshields in a certain city has 18 firms with the market shares shown in Table 1, where the market share is each firm's proportion of total sales in that market. The four-firm concentration ratio is calculated by adding the market shares of the four largest firms: in this case, 16 + 10 + 8 + 6 = 40. This concentration ratio would not be considered especially high, because the largest four firms have less than half the market.

Table 1. Calculating Concentration Ratios from Market Shares

If the market shares in the market for replacing automobile windshields are:	
Smooth as Glass Repair Company	16% of the market
The Auto Glass Doctor Company	10% of the market
Your Car Shield Company	8% of the market
Seven firms that each have 6% of the market	42% of the market, combined
Eight firms that each have 3% of the market	24% of the market, combined
Then the four-firm concentration ratio is 16 + 10 + 8 + 6 = 40.	

The concentration ratio approach can help to clarify some of the fuzziness over deciding when a merger might affect competition. For instance, if two of the smallest firms in the hypothetical market for repairing automobile windshields merged, the four-firm concentration ratio would not change—which implies that there is not much worry that the degree of competition in the market has notably diminished. However, if the top two firms merged, then the four-firm concentration ratio would become 46 (that is, 26 + 8 + 6 + 6). While this concentration ratio is modestly higher, the four-firm concentration ratio would still be less than half, so such a proposed merger might barely raise an eyebrow among antitrust regulators.

The Herfindahl - Hirshman Index

A four-firm concentration ratio is a simple tool, which may reveal only part of the story. For example, consider two industries that both have a four-firm concentration ratio of 80. However, in one industry five firms each control 20% of the market, while in the other industry, the top firm holds 77% of the market and all the other firms have 1% each. Although the four-firm concentration ratios are identical, it would be reasonable to worry more about the extent of competition in the second case—where the largest firm is nearly a monopoly—than in the first.

Another approach to measuring industry concentration that can distinguish between these two cases is called the **Herfindahl-Hirschman Index (HHI)**. The HHI, as it is often called, is calculated by summing the squares of the market share of each firm in the industry, as the following Work it Out shows.

Calculating HHI

Step 1. Calculate the HHI for a monopoly with a market share of 100%. Because there is only one firm, it has 100% market share. The HHI is 1002 = 10,000.

Step 2. For an extremely competitive industry, with dozens or hundreds of extremely small competitors, the value of the HHI might drop as low as 100 or even less. Calculate the HHI for an industry with 100 firms that each have 1% of the market. In this case, the HHI is $100(1^2) = 100$.

Step 3. Calculate the HHI for the industry shown in Table 1. In this case, the HHI is $16^2 + 10^2 + 8^2 + 7^{(62)} + 8^{(32)} = 744$.

Step 4. Note that the HHI gives greater weight to large firms.

Step 5. Consider the example given earlier, comparing one industry where five firms each have 20% of the market with an industry where one firm has 77% and the other 23 firms have 1% each. The two industries have the same four-firm concentration ratio of 80. But the HHI for the first industry is 5(202) = 2,000, while the HHI for the second industry is much higher at $77^2 + 23^{(12)} = 5{,}952$.

Step 6. Note that the near-monopolist in the second industry drives up the HHI measure of industrial concentration.

Step 7. Review Table 2 which gives some examples of the four-firm concentration ratio and the HHI in various U.S. industries in 2009. (You can find market share data from multiple industry sources. Data in the table are from: Verizon (for wireless), The Wall Street Journal (for automobiles), IDC Worldwide (for computers) and the U.S. Bureau of Transportation Statistics (for airlines).)

Table 2. Examples of Concentration Ratios and HHIs in the U.S. Economy, 2009

U.S. Industry	Four-Firm Ratio	HHI
Wireless	91	2,311
Largest five: Verizon, AT&T, Sprint, T-Mobile, MetroPCS		
Automobiles	63	1,121
Largest five: GM, Toyota, Ford, Honda, Chrysler		
Computers	74	1,737
Largest five: HP, Dell, Acer, Apple, Toshiba		
Airlines	44	536
Largest five: Southwest, American, Delta, United, U.S. Airways		

In the 1980s, the FTC followed these guidelines: If a merger would result in an HHI of less than 1,000, the FTC would probably approve it. If a merger would result in an HHI of more than 1,800, the FTC would probably challenge it. If a merger would result in an HHI between 1,000 and 1,800, then the FTC would scrutinize the plan and make a case-by-case decision. However, in the last several decades, the antitrust enforcement authorities have moved away from relying as heavily on measures of concentration ratios and HHIs to determine whether a merger will be allowed, and instead carried out more case-by-case analysis on the extent of competition in different industries.

New Directions for Antitrust

Both the four-firm concentration ratio and the Herfindahl-Hirschman index share some weaknesses. First, they begin from the assumption that the "market" under discussion is well-defined, and the only question is measuring how sales are divided in that market. Second, they are based on an implicit assumption that competitive conditions across industries are similar enough that a broad measure of concentration in the market is enough to make a decision about the effects of a merger. These assumptions, however, are not always correct. In response to these two problems, the antitrust regulators have been changing their approach in the last decade or two.

Defining a market is often controversial. For example, Microsoft in the early 2000s had a dominant share of the software for computer operating systems. However, in the total market for all computer software and services, including everything from games to scientific programs, the Microsoft share was only about 14% in 2014. A narrowly defined market will tend to make concentration appear higher, while a broadly defined market will tend to make it appear smaller.

There are two especially important shifts affecting how markets are defined in recent decades: one centers on technology and the other centers on **globalization**. In addition, these two shifts are interconnected. With the vast improvement in communications technologies, including the development of the Internet, a consumer can order books or pet supplies from all over the country or the world. As a result, the degree of competition many local retail businesses face has increased. The same effect may operate even more strongly in markets for business supplies, where so-called "business-to-business" websites can allow buyers and suppliers from anywhere in the world to find each other.

Globalization has changed the boundaries of markets. As recently as the 1970s, it was common for measurements of concentration ratios and HHIs to stop at national borders. Now, many industries find that their competition comes from the global market. A few decades ago, three companies, General Motors, Ford, and Chrysler, dominated the U.S. auto market. By 2014, however, these three firms were making less than half of U.S. auto sales, and facing competition from well-known car manufacturers such as Toyota, Honda, Nissan, Volkswagen, Mitsubishi, and Mazda. When HHIs are calculated with a global perspective, concentration in most major industries—including cars—is lower than in a purely domestic context.

Because attempting to define a particular market can be difficult and controversial, the Federal Trade Commission has begun to look less at market share and more at the data on actual competition between businesses. For example, in February 2007, Whole Foods Market and Wild Oats Market announced that they wished to merge. These were the two largest companies in the market that the government defined as "premium natural and organic supermarket chains." However, one could also argue that they were two relatively small companies in the broader market for all stores that sell groceries or specialty food products.

Rather than relying on a market definition, the government antitrust regulators looked at detailed evidence on profits and prices for specific stores in different cities, both before and after other competitive stores entered or exited. Based on that evidence, the Federal Trade Commission decided to block the merger. After two years of legal battles, the merger was eventually allowed in 2009 under the conditions that Whole Foods sell off the Wild Oats brand name and a number of individual stores, to preserve competition in certain local markets. For more on the difficulties of defining markets, refer to Monopoly.

This new approach to antitrust regulation involves detailed analysis of specific markets and companies, instead of defining a market and counting up total sales. A common starting point is for antitrust regulators to use statistical tools and real-world evidence to estimate the demand curves and supply curves faced by the firms that are proposing the merger. A second step is to specify how competition occurs in this specific industry. Some possibilities include competing to cut prices, to raise output, to build a brand name through advertising, and to build a reputation for good service or high quality. With these pieces of the puzzle in place, it is then possible to build a statistical model that estimates the likely outcome for consumers if the two firms are allowed to merge. Of course, these models do require some degree of subjective judgment, and so they can become the subject of legal disputes between the antitrust authorities and the companies that wish to merge.

Concepts and Summary

A corporate merger involves two private firms joining together. An acquisition refers to one firm buying another firm. In either case, two formerly independent firms become one firm. Antitrust laws seek to ensure active competition in markets, sometimes by preventing large firms from forming through mergers and acquisitions, sometimes by regulating business practices that might restrict competition, and sometimes by breaking up large firms into smaller competitors.

A four-firm concentration ratio is one way of measuring the extent of competition in a market. It is calculated by adding the market shares—that is, the percentage of total sales—of the four largest firms in the market. A Herfindahl-Hirschman Index (HHI) is another way of measuring the extent of competition in a market. It is calculated by taking the market shares of all firms in the market, squaring them, and then summing the total.

The forces of globalization and new communications and information technology have increased the level of competition faced by many firms by increasing the amount of competition from other regions and countries.

17.2 CONTROLLING ANTICOMPETITIVE ACTION

The U.S. antitrust laws reach beyond blocking mergers that would reduce competition to include a wide array of anticompetitive practices. For example, it is illegal for competitors to form a cartel to collude to make pricing and output decisions, as if they were a monopoly firm. The Federal Trade Commission and the U.S. Department of Justice prohibit firms from agreeing to fix prices or output, rigging bids, or sharing or dividing markets by allocating customers, suppliers, territories, or lines of commerce.

In the late 1990s, for example, the antitrust regulators prosecuted an international cartel of vitamin manufacturers, including the Swiss firm Hoffman-La Roche, the German firm BASF, and the French firm Rhone-Poulenc. These firms reached agreements on how much to produce, how much to charge, and which firm would sell to which customers. The high-priced vitamins were then bought by firms like General Mills, Kellogg, Purina-Mills, and Proctor and Gamble, which pushed up the prices more. Hoffman-La Roche pleaded guilty in May 1999 and agreed both to pay a fine of $500 million and to have at least one top executive serve four months of jail time.

Under U.S. antitrust laws, monopoly itself is not illegal. If a firm has a monopoly because of a newly patented invention, for example, the law explicitly allows a firm to earn higher-than-normal profits for a time as a reward for innovation. If a firm achieves a large share of the market by producing a better product at a lower price, such behavior is not prohibited by antitrust law.

Restrictive Practices

Antitrust law includes rules against **restrictive practices**—practices that do not involve outright agreements to raise price or to reduce the quantity produced, but that might have the effect of reducing competition. Antitrust cases involving restrictive practices are often controversial, because they delve into specific contracts or agreements between firms that are allowed in some cases but not in others.

For example, if a product manufacturer is selling to a group of dealers who then sell to the general public it is illegal for the manufacturer to demand a **minimum resale price maintenance agreement**, which would require the dealers to sell for at least a certain minimum price. A minimum price contract is illegal because it would restrict competition among dealers. However, the manufacturer is legally allowed to "suggest" minimum prices and to stop selling to dealers who regularly undercut the suggested price. If you think this rule sounds like a fairly subtle distinction, you are right.

An exclusive dealing agreement between a manufacturer and a dealer can be legal or illegal. It is legal if the purpose of the contract is to encourage competition between dealers. For example, it is legal for the Ford Motor Company to sell its cars to only Ford dealers, for General Motors to sell to only GM dealers, and so on. However, exclusive deals may also limit competition. If one large retailer obtained the exclusive rights to be the sole distributor of televisions, computers, and audio equipment made by a number of companies, then this exclusive contract would have an anticompetitive effect on other retailers.

Tying sales happen when a customer is required to buy one product only if the customer also buys a second product. Tying sales are controversial because they force consumers to purchase a product that they may not actually want or need. Further, the additional, required products are not necessarily advantageous to the customer. Suppose that to purchase a popular DVD, the store required that you also purchase a portable TV of a certain model. These products are only loosely related, thus there is no reason to make the purchase of one contingent on the other. Even if a customer was interested in a portable TV, the tying to a particular model prevents the customer from having the option of selecting one from the numerous types available in the market. A related, but not identical, concept is called bundling, where two or more products are sold as one. Bundling typically offers an advantage for the consumer by allowing them to acquire multiple products or services for a better price. For example, several cable companies allow customers to buy products like cable, internet, and a phone line through a special price available through bundling. Customers are also welcome to purchase these products separately, but the price of bundling is usually more appealing.

In some cases, tying sales and bundling can be viewed as anticompetitive. However, in other cases they may be legal and even common. It is common for people to purchase season tickets to a sports team or a set of concerts so that they can be guaranteed tickets to the few contests or shows that are most popular and likely to sell out. Computer software manufacturers may often bundle together a number of different programs, even when the buyer wants only a few of the programs. Think about the software that is included in a new computer purchase, for example.

Recall from the chapter on Monopoly that predatory pricing occurs when the existing firm (or firms) reacts to a new firm by dropping prices very low, until the new firm is driven out of the market, at which point the existing firm raises prices again. This pattern of pricing is aimed at deterring the entry of new firms into the market. But in practice, it can be hard to figure out when pricing should be considered predatory. Say that American Airlines is flying between two cities, and a new airline starts flying between the same two cities, at a lower price. If American Airlines cuts its price to match the new entrant, is this predatory pricing? Or is it just market competition at work? A commonly proposed rule is that if a firm is selling for less than its average variable cost—that is, at a price where it should be shutting down—then there is evidence for predatory pricing. But calculating in the real world what costs are variable and what costs are fixed is often not obvious, either.

The Microsoft antitrust case embodies many of these gray areas in restrictive practices, as the next Clear it Up shows.

Did Microsoft® engage in anticompetitive and restrictive practices?

The most famous restrictive practices case of recent years was a series of lawsuits by the U.S. government against Microsoft—lawsuits that were encouraged by some of Microsoft's competitors. All sides admitted that Microsoft's Windows program had a near-monopoly position in the market for the software used in general computer operating systems. All sides agreed that the software had many satisfied customers. All sides agreed that the capabilities of computer software that was compatible with Windows—both software produced by Microsoft and that produced by other companies—had expanded dramatically in the 1990s. Having a monopoly or a near-monopoly is not necessarily illegal in and of itself, but in cases where one company controls a great deal of the market, antitrust regulators look at any allegations of restrictive practices with special care.

The antitrust regulators argued that Microsoft had gone beyond profiting from its software innovations and its dominant position in the software market for operating systems, and had tried to use its market power in operating systems software to take over other parts of the software industry. For example, the government argued that Microsoft had engaged in an anticompetitive form of exclusive dealing by threatening computer makers that, if they did not leave another firm's software off their machines (specifically, Netscape's Internet browser), then Microsoft would not sell them its operating system software. Microsoft was accused by the government antitrust regulators of tying together its Windows operating system software, where it had a monopoly, with its Internet Explorer browser software, where it did not have a monopoly, and thus using this bundling as an anticompetitive tool. Microsoft was also accused of a form of predatory pricing; namely, giving away certain additional software products for free as part of Windows, as a way of driving out the competition from other makers of software.

In April 2000, a federal court held that Microsoft's behavior had crossed the line into unfair competition, and recommended that the company be broken into two competing firms. However, that penalty was overturned on appeal, and in November 2002 Microsoft reached a settlement with the government that it would end its restrictive practices.

The concept of restrictive practices is continually evolving, as firms seek new ways to earn profits and government regulators define what is permissible and what is not. A situation where the law is evolving and changing is always somewhat troublesome, since laws are most useful and fair when firms know what they are in advance. In addition, since the law is open to interpretation, competitors who are losing out in the market can accuse successful firms of anticompetitive restrictive practices, and try to win through government regulation what they have failed to accomplish in the market. Officials at the Federal Trade Commission and the Department of Justice are, of course, aware of these issues, but there is no easy way to resolve them.

Concepts and Summary

Firms are blocked by antitrust authorities from openly colluding to form a cartel that will reduce output and raise prices. Companies sometimes attempt to find other ways around these restrictions and, consequently, many antitrust cases involve restrictive practices that can reduce competition in certain circumstances, like tie-in sales, bundling, and predatory pricing.

17.3 MANAGEMENT OF NATURAL MONOPOLIS

Most true monopolies today in the U.S. are regulated, natural monopolies. A natural monopoly poses a difficult challenge for competition policy, because the structure of costs and demand seems to make competition unlikely or costly. A natural monopoly arises when average costs are declining over the range of production that satisfies market demand. This typically happens when fixed costs are large relative to variable costs. As a result, one firm is able to supply the total quantity demanded in the market at lower cost than two or more firms—so splitting up the natural monopoly would raise the average cost of production and force customers to pay more.

Public utilities, the companies that have traditionally provided water and electrical service across much of the United States, are leading examples of natural monopoly. It would make little sense to argue that a local water company should be broken up into several competing companies, each with its own separate set of pipes and water supplies. Installing four or five identical sets of pipes under a city, one for each water company, so that each household could choose its own water provider, would be terribly costly. The same argument applies to the idea of having many competing companies for delivering electricity to homes, each with its own set of wires. Before the advent of wireless phones, the argument also applied to the idea of many different phone companies, each with its own set of phone wires running through the neighborhood.

The Choices in Regulating a Natural Monopoly

So what then is the appropriate competition policy for a natural monopoly? Figure 1 illustrates the case of natural monopoly, with a market demand curve that cuts through the downward-sloping portion of the average cost curve. Points A, B, C, and F illustrate four of the main choices for regulation. Table 5 outlines the regulatory choices for dealing with a natural monopoly.

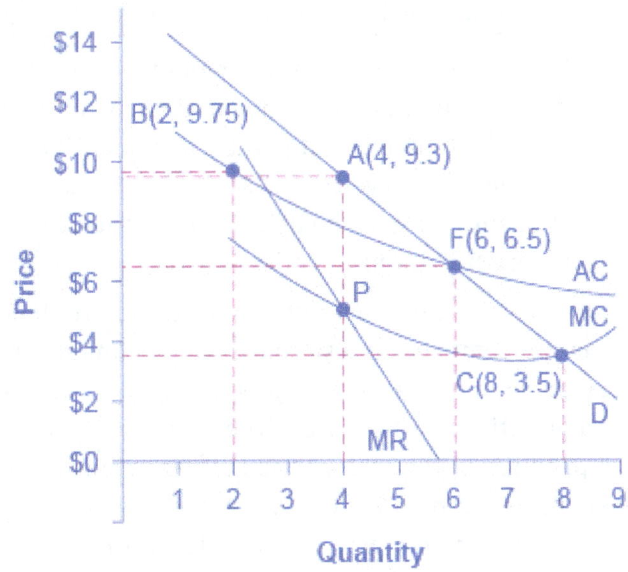

Figure 1. Regulatory Choices in Dealing with Natural Monopoly. A natural monopoly will maximize profits by producing at the quantity where marginal revenue (MR) equals marginal costs (MC) and by then looking to the market demand curve to see what price to charge for this quantity. This monopoly will produce at point A, with a quantity of 4 and a price of 9.3. If antitrust regulators split this company exactly in half, then each half would produce at point B, with average costs of 9.75 and output of 2. The regulators might require the firm to produce where marginal cost crosses the market demand curve at point C. However, if the firm is required to produce at a quantity of 8 and sell at a price of 3.5, the firm will suffer from losses. The most likely choice is point F, where the firm is required to produce a quantity of 6 and charge a price of 6.5.

Table 5. Regulatory Choices in Dealing with Natural Monopoly. (*Total Revenue is given by multiplying price and quantity. However, some of the price values in this table have been rounded for ease of presentation.)

Quantity	Price	Total Revenue*	Marginal Revenue	Total Cost	Marginal Cost	Average Cost
1	14.7	14.7	–	11.0	–	11.00
2	12.4	24.7	10.0	19.5	8.5	9.75
3	10.6	31.7	7.0	25.5	6.0	8.50
4	9.3	37.2	5.5	31.0	5.5	7.75
5	8.0	40.0	2.8	35.0	4.0	7.00
6	6.5	39.0	–1.0	39.0	4.0	6.50
7	5.0	35.0	–4.0	42.0	3.0	6.00
8	3.5	28.0	–7.0	45.5	3.5	5.70
9	2.0	18.0	–10.0	49.5	4.0	5.5

The first possibility is to leave the natural monopoly alone. In this case, the monopoly will follow its normal approach to maximizing profits. It determines the quantity where MR = MC, which happens at point P at a quantity of 4. The firm then looks to point A on the demand curve to find that it can charge a price of 9.3 for that profit-maximizing quantity. Since the price is above the average cost curve, the natural monopoly would earn economic profits.

A second outcome arises if antitrust authorities decide to divide the company, so that the new firms can compete. As a simple example, imagine that the company is cut in half. Thus, instead of one large firm producing a quantity of 4, two half-size firms each produce a quantity of 2. Because of the declining average cost curve (AC), the average cost of production for each of the half-size companies each producing 2, as shown at point B, would be 9.75, while the average cost of production for a larger firm producing 4 would only be 7.75. Thus, the economy would become less productively efficient, since the good is being produced at a higher average cost. In a situation with a downward-sloping average cost curve, two smaller firms will always have higher average costs of production than one larger firm for any quantity of total output. In addition, the antitrust authorities must worry that splitting the natural monopoly into pieces may be only the start of their problems. If one of the two firms grows larger than the other, it will have lower average costs and may be able to drive its competitor out of the market. Alternatively, two firms in a market may discover subtle ways of coordinating their behavior and keeping prices high. Either way, the result will not be the greater competition that was desired.

A third alternative is that regulators may decide to set prices and quantities produced for this industry. The regulators will try to choose a point along the market demand curve that benefits both consumers and the broader social interest. Point

C illustrates one tempting choice: the regulator requires that the firm produce the quantity of output where marginal cost crosses the demand curve at an output of 8, and charge the price of 3.5, which is equal to marginal cost at that point. This rule is appealing because it requires price to be set equal to marginal cost, which is what would occur in a perfectly competitive market, and it would assure consumers a higher quantity and lower price than at the monopoly choice A. In fact, efficient allocation of resources would occur at point C, since the value to the consumers of the last unit bought and sold in this market is equal to the marginal cost of producing it.

Attempting to bring about point C through force of regulation, however, runs into a severe difficulty. At point C, with an output of 8, a price of 3.5 is below the average cost of production, which is 5.7, and so if the firm charges a price of 3.5, it will be suffering losses. Unless the regulators or the government offer the firm an ongoing public subsidy (and there are numerous political problems with that option), the firm will lose money and go out of business.

Perhaps the most plausible option for the regulator is point F; that is, to set the price where AC crosses the demand curve at an output of 6 and a price of 6.5. This plan makes some sense at an intuitive level: let the natural monopoly charge enough to cover its average costs and earn a normal rate of profit, so that it can continue operating, but prevent the firm from raising prices and earning abnormally high monopoly profits, as it would at the monopoly choice A. Of course, determining this level of output and price with the political pressures, time constraints, and limited information of the real world is much harder than identifying the point on a graph. For more on the problems that can arise from a centrally determined price, see the discussion of price floors and price ceilings in Demand and Supply.

Cost-Plus versus Price Cap Regulation

Indeed, regulators of public utilities for many decades followed the general approach of attempting to choose a point like F in Figure 1. They calculated the average cost of production for the water or electricity companies, added in an amount for the normal rate of profit the firm should expect to earn, and set the price for consumers accordingly. This method was known as **cost-plus regulation**.

Cost-plus regulation raises difficulties of its own. If producers are reimbursed for their costs, plus a bit more, then at a minimum, producers have less reason to be concerned with high costs—because they can just pass them along in higher prices. Worse, firms under cost-plus regulation even have an incentive to generate high costs by building huge factories or employing lots of staff, because what they can charge is linked to the costs they incur.

Thus, in the 1980s and 1990s, some regulators of public utilities began to use **price cap regulation**, where the regulator sets a price that the firm can charge over the next few years. A common pattern was to require a price that declined slightly over time. If the firm can find ways of reducing its costs more quickly than the price caps, it can make a high level of profits. However, if the firm cannot keep up with the price caps or suffers bad luck in the market, it may suffer losses. A few years down the road, the regulators will then set a new series of price caps based on the firm's performance.

Price cap regulation requires delicacy. It will not work if the price regulators set the price cap unrealistically low. It may not work if the market changes dramatically so that the firm is doomed to incurring losses no matter what it does—say, if energy prices rise dramatically on world markets, then the company selling natural gas or heating oil to homes may not be able to meet price caps that seemed reasonable a year or two ago. But if the regulators compare the prices with producers of the same good in other areas, they can, in effect, pressure a natural monopoly in one area to compete with the prices being charged in other areas. Moreover, the possibility of earning greater profits or experiencing losses—instead of having an average rate of profit locked in every year by cost-plus regulation—can provide the natural monopoly with incentives for efficiency and innovation.

With natural monopoly, market competition is unlikely to take root, so if consumers are not to suffer the high prices and restricted output of an unrestricted monopoly, government regulation will need to play a role. In attempting to design a system of price cap regulation with flexibility and incentive, government regulators do not have an easy task.

Concepts and Summary

In the case of a natural monopoly, market competition will not work well and so, rather than allowing an unregulated monopoly to raise price and reduce output, the government may wish to regulate price and/or output. Common examples of regulation are public utilities, the regulated firms that often provide electricity and water service.

Cost-plus regulation refers to government regulation of a firm which sets the price that a firm can charge over a period of time by looking at the firm's accounting costs and then adding a normal rate of profit. Price cap regulation refers to government regulation of a firm where the government sets a price level several years in advance. In this case, the firm can either make high profits if it manages to produce at lower costs or sell a higher quantity than expected or suffer low profits or losses if costs are high or it sells less than expected.

17.4 The Great Deregulatory Test

Governments at all levels across the United States have regulated prices in a wide range of industries. In some cases, like water and electricity that have natural monopoly characteristics, there is some room in economic theory for such regulation. But once politicians are given a basis to intervene in markets and to choose prices and quantities, it is hard to know where to stop.

Doubts about Regulation of Prices and Quantities

Beginning in the 1970s, it became clear to policymakers of all political leanings that the existing price regulation was not working well. The United States carried out a great policy experiment—the deregulation discussed in Monopoly—removing government controls over prices and quantities produced in airlines, railroads, trucking, intercity bus travel, natural gas, and bank interest rates. The Clear it Up discusses the outcome of deregulation in one industry in particular—airlines.

What are the results of airline deregulation?

Why did the pendulum swing in favor of deregulation? Consider the airline industry. In the early days of air travel, no airline could make a profit just by flying passengers. Airlines needed something else to carry and the Postal Service provided that something with airmail. And so the first U.S. government regulation of the airline industry happened through the Postal Service, when in 1926 the Postmaster General began giving airlines permission to fly certain routes based on the needs of mail delivery—and the airlines took some passengers along for the ride. In 1934, the Postmaster General was charged by the antitrust authorities with colluding with the major airlines of that day to monopolize the nation's airways. In 1938, the Civil Aeronautics Board (CAB) was created to regulate airfares and routes instead. For 40 years, from 1938 to 1978, the CAB approved all fares, controlled all entry and exit, and specified which airlines could fly which routes. There was zero entry of new airlines on the main routes across the country for 40 years, because the CAB did not think it was necessary.

In 1978, the Airline Deregulation Act took the government out of the business of determining airfares and schedules. The new law shook up the industry. Famous old airlines like Pan American, Eastern, and Braniff went bankrupt and disappeared. Some new airlines like People Express were created—and then vanished.

The greater competition from deregulation reduced airfares by about one-third over the next two decades, saving consumers billions of dollars a year. The average flight used to take off with just half its seats full; now it is two-thirds full, which is far more efficient. Airlines have also developed hub-and-spoke systems, where planes all fly into a central hub city at a certain time and then depart. As a result, one can fly between any of the spoke cities with just one connection—and there is greater service to more cities than before deregulation. With lower fares and more service, the number of air passengers doubled from the late 1970s to the start of the 2000s—an increase that, in turn, doubled the number of jobs in the airline industry. Meanwhile, with the watchful oversight of government safety inspectors, commercial air travel has continued to get safer over time.

The U.S. airline industry is far from perfect. For example, a string of mergers in recent years has raised concerns over how competition might be compromised.

One difficulty with government price regulation is what economists call **regulatory capture**, in which the firms supposedly being regulated end up playing a large role in setting the regulations that they will follow. When the airline industry was being regulated, for example, it suggested appointees to the regulatory board, sent lobbyists to argue with the board, provided most of the information on which the board made decisions, and offered well-paid jobs to at least some of the people leaving the board. In this situation, consumers can easily end up being not very well represented by the regulators. The result of regulatory capture is that government price regulation can often become a way for existing competitors to work together to reduce output, keep prices high, and limit competition.

The Effects of Deregulation

Deregulation, both of airlines and of other industries, has its negatives. The greater pressure of competition led to entry and exit. When firms went bankrupt or contracted substantially in size, they laid off workers who had to find other jobs. Market competition is, after all, a full-contact sport.

A number of major accounting scandals involving prominent corporations such as Enron, Tyco International, and WorldCom led to the Sarbanes-Oxley Act in 2002. Sarbanes-Oxley was designed to increase confidence in financial information provided by public corporations to protect investors from accounting fraud.

The Great Recession which began in late 2007 and which the U.S. economy is still struggling to recover from was caused at least in part by a global financial crisis, which began in the United States. The key component of the crisis was the creation and subsequent failure of several types of unregulated financial assets, such as collateralized mortgage obligations (CMOs, a type of mortgage-backed security), and credit default swaps (CDSs, insurance contracts on assets like CMOs that provided a payoff even if the holder of the CDS did not own the CMO). Many of these assets were rated very safe by private credit rating agencies such as Standard & Poors, Moody's, and Fitch.

The collapse of the markets for these assets precipitated the financial crisis and led to the failure of Lehman Brothers, a major investment bank, numerous large commercial banks, such as Wachovia, and even the Federal National Mortgage

Corporation (Fannie Mae), which had to be nationalized—that is, taken over by the federal government. One response to the financial crisis was the **Dodd-Frank Act**, which attempted major reforms of the financial system. The legislation's purpose, as noted on dodd-frank.com is:

> To promote the financial stability of the United States by improving accountability and transparency in the financial system, to end "too big to fail," to protect the American taxpayer by ending bailouts, [and] to protect consumers from abusive financial services practices. . .

We will explore the financial crisis and the Great Recession in more detail in the macroeconomic chapters of this book, but for now it should be clear that many Americans have grown disenchanted with deregulation, at least of financial markets.

All market-based economies operate against a background of laws and regulations, including laws about enforcing contracts, collecting taxes, and protecting health and the environment. The government policies discussed in this chapter—like blocking certain anticompetitive mergers, ending restrictive practices, imposing price cap regulation on natural monopolies, and deregulation—demonstrate the role of government to strengthen the incentives that come with a greater degree of competition.

More than Cooking, Heating, and Cooling

What did the Federal Trade Commission (FTC) decide on the Kinder Morgan / El Paso Corporation merger? After careful examination, federal officials decided there was only one area of significant overlap that might provide the merged firm with strong market power. The FTC approved the merger, provided Kinder Morgan divest itself of the overlap area. Tallgrass purchased Kinder Morgan Interstate Gas Transmission, Trailblazer Pipeline Co. LLC, two processing facilities in Wyoming, and Kinder Morgan's 50 percent interest in the Rockies Express Pipeline to meet the FTC requirements. The FTC was attempting to strike a balance between potential cost reductions resulting from economies of scale and concentration of market power.

Did the price of natural gas decrease? Yes, rather significantly. In 2010, the wellhead price of natural gas was $4.48 per thousand cubic foot; in 2012 the price had fallen to just $2.66. Was the merger responsible for the large drop in price? The answer is uncertain. The larger contributor to the sharp drop in price was the overall increase in the supply of natural gas. More and more natural gas was able to be recovered by fracturing shale deposits, a process called fracking. Fracking, which is controversial for environmental reasons, enabled the recovery of known reserves of natural gas that previously were not economically feasible to tap. Kinder Morgan's control of 80,000-plus miles of pipeline likely made moving the gas from wellheads to end users smoother and allowed for an even greater benefit from the increased supply.

CONCEPTS AND SUMMARY

The U.S. economy experienced a wave of deregulation in the late 1970s and early 1980s, when a number of government regulations that had set prices and quantities produced in a number of industries were eliminated. Major accounting scandals in the early 2000s and, more recently, the Great Recession have spurred new regulation to prevent similar occurrences in the future. Regulatory capture occurs when the industries being regulated end up having a strong influence over what regulations exist.

CHAPTER

NEGATIVE EXTERNALITIES AND ENVIRONMENTAL PROTECTION 18

18.1 THE POLLUTION ECONOMICS

From 1970 to 2012, the U.S. population increased by one-third and the size of the U.S. economy more than doubled. Since the 1970s, however, the United States, using a variety of anti-pollution policies, has made genuine progress against a number of pollutants. Table 1 lists the change in carbon dioxide emissions by users of energy (from residential to industrial) according to the U.S. Energy Information Administration (EIA). The table shows that emissions of certain key air pollutants declined substantially from 2007 to 2012; they dropped 730 million metric tons (MMT) a year—a 12% reduction. This seems to indicate that progress has been made in the United States in reducing overall carbon dioxide emissions, which cause greenhouse gases.

Table 1. U.S. Carbon Dioxide (CO2) Emissions from Fossil Fuels Consumed 2007–2012, Million Metric Tons (MMT) per Year. (Source: EIA Monthly Energy Review)

	Primary Fossil Fuels			Purchased Electric Power	Total Primary Fossil Fuels
End-use Sector	Coal	Petroleum	Natural Gas		
Residential	(0)	(14)	(31)	(134)	(179)
Commercial	(2)	(2)	(7)	(126)	(136)
Industrial	(40)	(62)	31	(118)	(191)
Transportation	0	(228)	5	(1)	(224)
Power	(464)	(36)	(122)	–	–
Change 2007–2012	(508)	(342)	121	(378)	(730)

Despite the gradual reduction in emissions from fossil fuels, many important environmental issues remain. Along with the still high levels of air and water pollution, other issues include hazardous waste disposal, destruction of wetlands and other wildlife habitats, and the impact on human health from pollution.

Externalities

Private markets, such as the cell phone industry, offer an efficient way to put buyers and sellers together and determine what goods are produced, how they are produced, and who gets them. The principle that voluntary exchange benefits both buyers and sellers is a fundamental building block of the economic way of thinking. But what happens when a voluntary exchange affects a third party who is neither the buyer nor the seller?

As an example, consider a concert producer who wants to build an outdoor arena that will host country music concerts a half-mile from your neighborhood. You will be able to hear these outdoor concerts while sitting on your back porch—or perhaps even in your dining room. In this case, the sellers and buyers of concert tickets may both be quite satisfied with their voluntary exchange, but you have no voice in their market transaction. The effect of a market exchange on a third party who is outside or "external" to the exchange is called an **externality**. Because externalities that occur in market transactions affect other parties beyond those involved, they are sometimes called **spillovers.**

Externalities can be negative or positive. If you hate country music, then having it waft into your house every night would be a **negative externality.** If you love country music, then what amounts to a series of free concerts would be a **positive externality**.

POLLUTION AS A NEGATIVE EXTERNALITY

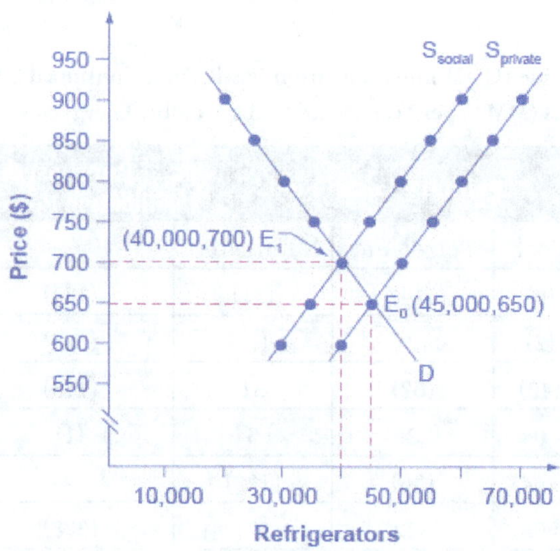

Figure 1. Taking Social Costs into Account: A Supply Shift. If the firm takes only its own costs of production into account, then its supply curve will be Sprivate, and the market equilibrium will occur at E0. Accounting for additional external costs of $100 for every unit produced, the firm's supply curve will be Ssocial. The new equilibrium will occur at E1.

Pollution is a negative externality. Economists illustrate the social costs of production with a demand and supply diagram. The social costs include the private costs of production incurred by the company and the external costs of pollution that are passed on to society. Figure 1 shows the demand and supply for manufacturing refrigerators. The demand curve (D) shows the quantity demanded at each price. The supply curve (Sprivate) shows the quantity of refrigerators supplied by all the firms at each price if they are taking only their private costs into account and they are allowed to emit pollution at zero cost. The market equilibrium (E0), where quantity supplied and quantity demanded are equal, is at a price of $650 and a quantity of 45,000. This information is also reflected in the first three columns of Table 2.

Table 2. A Supply Shift Caused by Pollution Costs

Price	Quantity Demanded	Quantity Supplied before Considering Pollution Cost	Quantity Supplied after Considering Pollution Cost
$600	50,000	40,000	30,000
$650	45,000	45,000	35,000
$700	40,000	50,000	40,000
$750	35,000	55,000	45,000
$800	30,000	60,000	50,000
$850	25,000	65,000	55,000
$900	20,000	70,000	60,000

However, as a by-product of the metals, plastics, chemicals and energy that are used in manufacturing refrigerators, some pollution is created. Let's say that, if these pollutants were emitted into the air and water, they would create costs of $100 per refrigerator produced. These costs might occur because of injuries to human health, property values, wildlife habitat, reduction of recreation possibilities, or because of other negative impacts. In a market with no anti-pollution restrictions, firms can dispose of certain wastes absolutely free. Now imagine that firms which produce refrigerators must factor in these external costs of pollution—that is, the firms have to consider not only the costs of labor and materials needed to make a refrigerator, but also the broader costs to society of injuries to health and other values caused by pollution. If the firm is required to pay $100 for the additional external costs of pollution each time it produces a refrigerator, production becomes more costly and the entire supply curve shifts up by $100.

As illustrated in the fourth column of Table 2 and in Figure 1, the firm will need to receive a price of $700 per refrigerator and produce a quantity of 40,000—and the firm's new supply curve will be S_{social}. The new equilibrium will occur at E_1, taking the additional external costs of pollution into account results in a higher price, a lower quantity of production, and a lower quantity of pollution. The following Work It Out feature will walk you through an example, this time with musical accompaniment.

Identifying the Equilibrium Price and Quantity

Table 3 shows the supply and demand conditions for a firm that will play trumpets on the streets when requested. Output is measured as the number of songs played.

Table 3. Supply and Demand Conditions for a Trumpet-Playing Firm

Price	Quantity Demanded	Quantity Supplied without paying the costs of the externality	Quantity Supplied after paying the costs of the externality
$20	0	10	8
$18	1	9	7
$15	2.5	7.5	5.5
$12	4	6	4
$10	5	5	3
$5	7.5	2.5	0.5

Step 1. Determine the negative externality in this situation. To do this, you must think about the situation described and consider all parties that might be impacted. A negative externality might be the increase in noise pollution in the area where the firm is playing.

Step 2. Identify the equilibrium price and quantity when only private costs are taken into account, and then when social costs are taken into account. Remember that equilibrium is where the quantity demanded is equal to the quantity supplied.

Step 3. Look down the columns to where the quantity demanded (the second column) is equal to the "quantity supplied without paying the costs of the externality" (the third column). Then refer to the first column of that row to determine the equilibrium price. In this case, the equilibrium price and quantity when only private costs are taken into account would be at a price of $10 and a quantity of five.

Step 4. Identify the equilibrium price and quantity when the additional external costs are taken into account. Look down the columns of quantity demanded (the second column) and the "quantity supplied after paying the costs of the externality" (the fourth column) then refer to the first column of that row to determine the equilibrium price. In this case, the equilibrium will be at a price of $12 and a quantity of four.

Step 5. Consider how taking the externality into account affects the equilibrium price and quantity. Do this by comparing the two equilibrium situations. If the firm is forced to pay its additional external costs, then production of trumpet songs becomes more costly, and the supply curve will shift up.

Remember that the supply curve is based on choices about production that firms make while looking at their marginal costs, while the demand curve is based on the benefits that individuals perceive while maximizing utility. If no externalities existed, private costs would be the same as the costs to society as a whole, and private benefits would be the same as the benefits to society as a whole. Thus, if no externalities existed, the interaction of demand and supply will coordinate social costs and benefits.

However, when the externality of pollution exists, the supply curve no longer represents all social costs. Because externalities represent a case where markets no longer consider all social costs, but only some of them, economists commonly refer to externalities as an example of **market failure**. When there is market failure, the private market fails to achieve efficient output, because either firms do not account for all costs incurred in the production of output and/or consumers do not account for all benefits obtained (a positive externality). In the case of pollution, at the market output, social costs of production exceed social benefits to consumers, and the market produces too much of the product.

We can see a general lesson here. If firms were required to pay the social costs of pollution, they would create less pollution but produce less of the product and charge a higher price. In the next module, we will explore how governments require firms to take the social costs of pollution into account.

Concepts and Summary

Economic production can cause environmental damage. This trade-off arises for all countries, whether high-income or low-income, and whether their economies are market-oriented or command-oriented.

An externality occurs when an exchange between a buyer and seller has an impact on a third party who is not part of the exchange. An externality, which is sometimes also called a spill over, can have a negative or a positive impact on the third party. If those parties imposing a negative externality on others had to take the broader social cost of their behaviour into account, they would have an incentive to reduce the production of whatever is causing the negative externality. In the case of a positive externality, the third party is obtaining benefits from the exchange between a buyer and a seller, but they are not paying for these benefits. If this is the case, then markets would tend to under produce output because suppliers are not aware of the additional demand from others. If the parties that are generating benefits to others would be somehow compensated for these external benefits, they would have an incentive to increase production of whatever is causing the positive externality.

18.2 RULES OF COMMAND AND CONTROL

When the United States started passing comprehensive environmental laws in the late 1960s and early 1970s, a typical law specified how much pollution could be emitted out of a smokestack or a drainpipe and imposed penalties if that limit was exceeded. Other laws required the installation of certain equipment—for example, on automobile tailpipes or on smokestacks—to reduce pollution. These types of laws, which specify allowable quantities of pollution and which also may detail which pollution-control technologies must be used, fall under the category of **command-and-control regulation.** In effect, command-and-control regulation requires that firms increase their costs by installing anti-pollution equipment; firms are thus required to take the social costs of pollution into account.

Command-and-control regulation has been highly successful in protecting and cleaning up the U.S. environment. In 1970, the Environmental Protection Agency (EPA) was created to oversee all environmental laws. In the same year, the Clean Air Act was enacted to address air pollution. Just two years later, in 1972, Congress passed and the president signed the far-reaching Clean Water Act. These command-and-control environmental laws, and their amendments and updates, have been largely responsible for America's cleaner air and water in recent decades. However, economists have pointed out three difficulties with command-and-control environmental regulation.

First, command-and-control regulation offers no incentive to improve the quality of the environment beyond the standard set by a particular law. Once the command-and-control regulation has been satisfied, polluters have zero incentive to do better.

Second, command-and-control regulation is inflexible. It usually requires the same standard for all polluters, and often the same pollution-control technology as well. This means that command-and-control regulation draws no distinctions between firms that would find it easy and inexpensive to meet the pollution standard—or to reduce pollution even further—and firms that might find it difficult and costly to meet the standard. Firms have no reason to rethink their production methods in fundamental ways that might reduce pollution even more and at lower cost.

Third, command-and-control regulations are written by legislators and the EPA, and so they are subject to compromises in the political process. Existing firms often argue (and lobby) that stricter environmental standards should not apply to them, only to new firms that wish to start production. Consequently, real-world environmental laws are full of fine print, loopholes, and exceptions.

Although critics accept the goal of reducing pollution, they question whether command-and-control regulation is the best way to design policy tools for accomplishing that goal. A different approach is the use of market-oriented tools, which are discussed in the next section.

Concepts and Summary

Command-and-control regulation sets specific limits for pollution emissions and/or specific pollution-control technologies that must be used. Although such regulations have helped to protect the environment, they have three shortcomings: they provide no incentive for going beyond the limits they set; they offer limited flexibility on where and how to reduce pollution; and they often have politically-motivated loopholes.

18.3 ENVIRONMENTAL TOOLS BASED ON THE MARKET

Market-oriented environmental policies create incentives to allow firms some flexibility in reducing pollution. The three main categories of market-oriented approaches to pollution control are pollution charges, marketable permits, and better-defined property rights. All of these policy tools, discussed below, address the shortcomings of command-and-control regulation—albeit in different ways.

Pollution Charges

A pollution charge is a tax imposed on the quantity of pollution that a firm emits. A pollution charge gives a profit-maximizing firm an incentive to figure out ways to reduce its emissions—as long as the marginal cost of reducing the emissions is less than the tax.

For example, consider a small firm that emits 50 pounds per year of small particles, such as soot, into the air. Particulate matter, as it is called, causes respiratory illnesses and also imposes costs on firms and individuals.

Figure 1 illustrates the marginal costs that a firm faces in reducing pollution. The marginal cost of pollution reduction, like most most marginal cost curves increases with output, at least in the short run. Reducing the first 10 pounds of particulate emissions costs the firm $300. Reducing the second 10 pounds would cost $500; reducing the third ten pounds would cost $900; reducing the fourth 10 pounds would cost $1,500; and the fifth 10 pounds would cost $2,500. This pattern for the costs of reducing pollution is common, because the firm can use the cheapest and easiest method to make initial reductions in pollution, but additional reductions in pollution become more expensive.

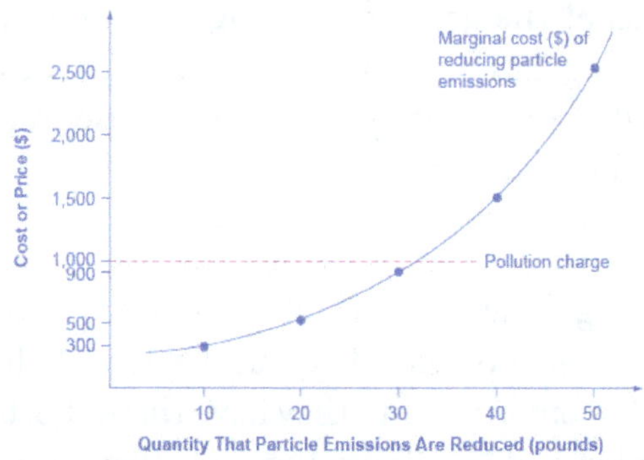

Figure 1. A Pollution Charge. If a pollution charge is set equal to $1,000, then the firm will have an incentive to reduce pollution by 30 pounds because the $900 cost of these reductions would be less than the cost of paying the pollution charge.

Imagine the firm now faces a pollution tax of $1,000 for every 10 pounds of particulates emitted. The firm has the choice of either polluting and paying the tax, or reducing the amount of particulates they emit and paying the cost of abatement as shown in the figure. How much will the firm pollute and how much will the firm abate? The first 10 pounds would cost the firm $300 to abate. This is substantially less than the $1,000 tax, so they will choose to abate. The second 10 pounds would cost $500 to abate, which is still less than the tax, so they will choose to abate. The third 10 pounds would cost $900 to abate, which is slightly less than the $1,000 tax. The fourth 10 pounds would cost $1,500, which is much more costly than paying the tax. As a result, the firm will decide to reduce pollutants by 30 pounds, because the marginal cost of reducing pollution by this amount is less than the pollution tax. With a tax of $1,000, the firm has no incentive to reduce pollution more than 30 pounds.

A firm that has to pay a pollution tax will have an incentive to figure out the least expensive technologies for reducing pollution. Firms that can reduce pollution cheaply and easily will do so to minimize their pollution taxes, whereas firms that will incur high costs for reducing pollution will end up paying the pollution tax instead. If the pollution tax applies to every source of pollution, then no special favoritism or loopholes are created for politically well-connected producers.

For an example of a pollution charge at the household level, consider two ways of charging for garbage collection. One method is to have a flat fee per household, no matter how much garbage a household produces. An alternative approach is to have several levels of fees, depending on how much garbage the household produces—and to offer lower or free charges for recyclable materials. As of 2006 (latest statistics available), the EPA had recorded over 7,000 communities that have implemented "pay as you throw" programs. When people have a financial incentive to put out less garbage and to increase recycling, they find ways of doing so.

A number of environmental policies are really pollution charges, although they often do not travel under that name. For example, the federal government and many state governments impose taxes on gasoline. We can view this tax as a charge on the air pollution that cars generate as well as a source of funding for maintaining roads. Indeed, gasoline taxes are far higher in most other countries than in the United States.

Similarly, the refundable charge of five or 10 cents that only 10 states have for returning recyclable cans and bottles works like a pollution tax that provides an incentive to avoid littering or throwing bottles in the trash. Compared with command-and-control regulation, a pollution tax reduces pollution in a more flexible and cost-effective way.

Marketable Permits

When a city or state government sets up a marketable permit program (e.g. cap-and-trade), it must start by determining the overall quantity of pollution it will allow as it tries to meet national pollution standards. Then, a number of permits allowing only this quantity of pollution are divided among the firms that emit that pollutant. These permits to pollute can be sold or given to firms free.

Now, add two more conditions. Imagine that these permits are designed to reduce total emissions over time. For example, a permit may allow emission of 10 units of pollution one year, but only nine units the next year, then eight units the year after that, and so on down to some lower level. In addition, imagine that these are marketable permits, meaning that firms can buy and sell them.

To see how marketable permits can work to reduce pollution, consider the four firms listed in Table 6. The table shows current emissions of lead from each firm. At the start of the marketable permit program, each firm receives permits to allow this level of pollution. However, these permits are shrinkable, and next year the permits allow the firms to emit only half as much pollution. Let's say that in a year, Firm Gamma finds it easy and cheap to reduce emissions from 600 tons of lead to 200 tons, which means that it has permits that it is not using that allow emitting 100 tons of lead. Firm Beta reduces its lead pollution from 400 tons to 200 tons, so it does not need to buy any permits, and it does not have any extra permits to sell. However, although Firm Alpha can easily reduce pollution from 200 tons to 150 tons, it finds that it is cheaper to purchase permits from Gamma rather than to reduce its own emissions to 100. Meanwhile, Firm Delta did not even exist in the first period, so the only way it can start production is to purchase permits to emit 50 tons of lead.

The total quantity of pollution will decline. But the buying and selling of the marketable permits will determine exactly which firms reduce pollution and by how much. With a system of marketable permits, the firms that find it least expensive to do so will reduce pollution the most.

Table 6. How Marketable Permits Work

	Firm Alpha	Firm Beta	Firm Gamma	Firm Delta
Current emissions—permits distributed free for this amount	200 tons	400 tons	600 tons	0 tons
How much pollution will these permits allow in one year?	100 tons	200 tons	300 tons	0 tons
Actual emissions one year in the future	150 tons	200 tons	200 tons	50 tons
Buyer or seller of marketable permit?	Buys permits for 50 tons	Doesn't buy or sell permits	Sells permits for 100 tons	Buys permits for 50 tons

Another application of marketable permits occurred when the Clean Air Act was amended in 1990. The revised law sought to reduce sulfur dioxide emissions from electric power plants to half of the 1980 levels out of concern that sulfur dioxide was causing acid rain, which harms forests as well as buildings. In this case, the marketable permits the federal government issued were free of charge (no pun intended) to electricity-generating plants across the country, especially those that were burning coal (which produces sulfur dioxide). These permits were of the "shrinkable" type; that is, the amount of pollution allowed by a given permit declined with time.

Better-Defined Property Rights

A clarified and strengthened idea of property rights can also strike a balance between economic activity and pollution. Ronald Coase (1910–2013), who won the 1991 Nobel Prize in economics, offered a vivid illustration of an externality: a railroad track running beside a farmer's field where the railroad locomotive sometimes gives off sparks and sets the field ablaze. Coase asked whose responsibility it was to address this spillover. Should the farmer be required to build a tall fence alongside the field to block the sparks? Or should the railroad be required to put some gadget on the locomotive's smokestack to reduce the number of sparks?

Coase pointed out that this issue cannot be resolved until property rights are clearly defined—that is, the legal rights of ownership on which others are not allowed to infringe without paying compensation. Does the farmer have a property right not to have a field burned? Does the railroad have a property right to run its own trains on its own tracks? If neither party has a property right, then the two sides may squabble endlessly, nothing will be done, and sparks will continue to set the field aflame. However, if either the farmer or the railroad has a well-defined legal responsibility, then that party will seek out and pay for the least costly method of reducing the risk that sparks will hit the field. The property right determines whether the farmer or the railroad pays the bills.

The property rights approach is highly relevant in cases involving endangered species. The U.S. government's endangered species list includes about 1,000 plants and animals, and about 90% of these species live on privately owned land. The protection of these endangered species requires careful thinking about incentives and property rights. The discovery of an endangered species on private land has often triggered an automatic reaction from the government to prohibit the landowner from using that land for any purpose that might disturb the imperiled creatures. Consider the incentives of that policy: If you admit to the government that you have an endangered species, the government effectively prohibits you from using your land. As a result, rumors abounded of landowners who followed a policy of "shoot, shovel, and shut up" when they found an endangered animal on their land. Other landowners have deliberately cut trees or managed land in a way that they knew would discourage endangered animals from locating there.

How effective are market-oriented environmental policy tools?

Environmentalists sometimes fear that market-oriented environmental tools are an excuse to weaken or eliminate strict limits on pollution emissions and instead to allow more pollution. It is true that if pollution charges are set very low or if marketable permits do not reduce pollution by very much then market-oriented tools will not work well. But command-and-control environmental laws can also be full of loopholes or have exemptions that do not reduce pollution by much, either. The advantage of market-oriented environmental tools is not that they reduce pollution by more or less, but because of their incentives and flexibility, they can achieve any desired reduction in pollution at a lower cost to society.

A more productive policy would consider how to provide private landowners with an incentive to protect the endangered species that they find and to provide a habitat for additional endangered species. For example, the government might pay landowners who provide and maintain suitable habitats for endangered species or who restrict the use of their land to protect an endangered species. Again, an environmental law built on incentives and flexibility offers greater promise than a command-and-control approach, which tries to oversee millions of acres of privately owned land.

Applying Market-Oriented Environmental Tools

Market-oriented environmental policies are a tool kit. Specific policy tools will work better in some situations than in others. For example, marketable permits work best when a few dozen or a few hundred parties are highly interested in trading, as in the cases of oil refineries that trade lead permits or electrical utilities that trade sulfur dioxide permits. However, for cases in which millions of users emit small amounts of pollution—such as emissions from car engines or unrecycled soda cans—and have no strong interest in trading, pollution charges will typically offer a better choice. Market-oriented environmental tools can also be combined. Marketable permits can be viewed as a form of improved property rights. Or the government could combine marketable permits with a pollution tax on any emissions not covered by a permit.

Concepts and Summary

Examples of market-oriented environmental policies, also referred to as cap and trade programs, include pollution charges, marketable permits, and better-defined property rights. Market-oriented environmental policies include taxes, markets, and property rights so that those who impose negative externalities must face the social cost.

18.4 THE ADVANTAGES AND DISADVANTAGES OF US ENVIRONMENTAL LAWS

Government economists have estimated that U.S. firms may pay more than $200 billion per year to comply with federal environmental laws. That is big bucks. Is the money well spent?

Benefits and Costs of Clean Air and Clean Water

The benefits of a cleaner environment can be divided into four areas: (1) people may stay healthier and live longer; (2) certain industries that rely on clean air and water, such as farming, fishing, and tourism, may benefit; (3) property values may be higher; and (4) people may simply enjoy a cleaner environment in a way that does not need to involve a market transaction. Some of these benefits, such as gains to tourism or farming, are relatively easy to value in economic terms. It is harder to assign a monetary value to others, such as the value of clean air for someone with asthma. It seems impossible to put a clear-cut monetary value on still others, such as the satisfaction you might feel from knowing that the air is clear over the Grand Canyon, even if you have never visited the Grand Canyon.

Although estimates of environmental benefits are not precise, they can still be revealing. For example, a study by the Environmental Protection Agency looked at the costs and benefits of the Clean Air Act from 1970 to 1990. It found that total costs over that time period were roughly $500 billion—a huge amount. However, it also found that a middle-range estimate of the health and other benefits from cleaner air was $22 trillion—about 44 times higher than the costs. A more recent study by the EPA estimated that the environmental benefits to Americans from the Clean Air Act will exceed their costs by a margin of four to one. The EPA estimated that "in 2010 the benefits of Clean Air Act programs will total about $110 billion. This estimate represents the value of avoiding increases in illness and premature death which would have prevailed." Saying that overall benefits of environmental regulation have exceeded costs in the past, however, is very different from saying that every environmental regulation makes sense. For example, studies suggest that when breaking down emission reductions by type of contaminants, the benefits of air pollution control outweigh the costs primarily for particulates and lead, but when looking at other air pollutants, the costs of reducing them may be comparable to or greater than the benefits. Just because some environmental regulations have had benefits much higher than costs does not prove that every individual regulation is a sensible idea.

ECOTOURISM: MAKING ENVIRONMENTALISM PAY

The definition of ecotourism is a little vague. Does it mean sleeping on the ground, eating roots, and getting close to wild animals? Does it mean flying in a helicopter to shoot anesthetic darts at African wildlife? Or a little of both? The definition may be fuzzy, but tourists who hope to appreciate the ecology of their destination—"eco tourists"—are the impetus to a big and growing business. The International Ecotourism Society estimates that international tourists interested in seeing nature or wildlife will take 1.56 billion trips by 2020.

Realizing the attraction of ecotourism, the residents of low-income countries may come to see that preserving wildlife habitats is more lucrative than, say, cutting down forests or grazing livestock to survive. In South Africa, Namibia, and Zimbabwe, for example, a substantial expansion of both rhinoceros and elephant populations is broadly credited to ecotourism, which has given local communities an economic interest in protecting them. Some of the leading ecotourism destinations include: Costa Rica and Panama in Central America; the Caribbean; Malaysia, and other South Pacific destinations; New Zealand; the Serengeti in Tanzania; the Amazon rain forests; and the Galapagos Islands. In many of these countries and regions, governments have enacted policies whereby revenues from ecotourism are shared with local communities, to give people in those local communities a kind of property right that encourages them to conserve their local environment.

Ecotourism needs careful management, so that the combination of eager tourists and local entrepreneurs does not destroy what the visitors are coming to see. But whatever one's qualms are about certain kinds of ecotourism—such as the occasional practice of rich tourists shooting elderly lions with high-powered rifles—it is worth remembering that the alternative is often that low-income people in poor countries will damage their local environment in their effort to survive.

Marginal Benefits and Marginal Costs

We can use the tools of marginal analysis to illustrate the marginal costs and the marginal benefits of reducing pollution. Figure 1 illustrates a theoretical model of this situation. When the quantity of environmental protection is low so that pollution is extensive—for example, at quantity Qa—there are usually a lot of relatively cheap and easy ways to reduce pollution, and the marginal benefits of doing so are quite high.

At Qa, it makes sense to allocate more resources to fight pollution. However, as the extent of environmental protection increases, the cheap and easy ways of reducing pollution begin to decrease, and more costly methods must be used. The marginal cost curve rises. Also, as environmental protection increases, the largest marginal benefits are achieved first, followed by reduced marginal benefits. As the quantity of environmental protection increases to, say, Qb, the gap between marginal benefits and marginal costs narrows. At point Qc the marginal costs will exceed the marginal benefits. At this level of environmental protection, society is not allocating resources efficiently, because too many resources are being given up to reduce pollution.

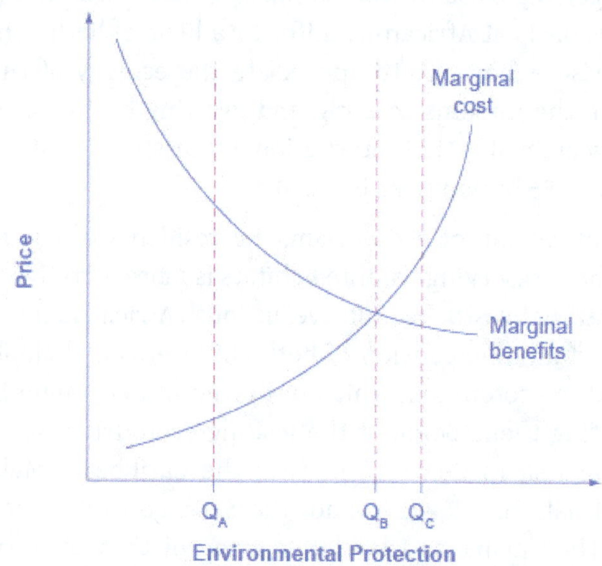

Figure 1. Marginal Costs and Marginal Benefits of Environmental Protection. Reducing pollution is costly—resources must be sacrificed. The marginal costs of reducing pollution are generally increasing, because the least expensive and easiest reductions can be made first, leaving the more expensive methods for later. The marginal benefits of reducing pollution are generally declining, because the steps that provide the greatest benefit can be taken first, and steps that provide less benefit can wait until later.

As society draws closer to Qb, some might argue that it becomes more important to use market-oriented environmental tools to hold down the costs of reducing pollution. Their objective would be to avoid environmental rules that would provide the quantity of environmental protection at Qc, where marginal costs exceed marginal benefits. The following Clear It Up feature delves into how the EPA measures its policies - and the monetary value of our lives.

What's a life worth?

The U.S. Environmental Protection Agency (EPA) must estimate the value of saving lives by reducing pollution against the additional costs. In measuring the benefits of government environmental policies, the EPA's National Center for Environmental Economics (NCEE) values a statistical human life at $7.4 million (in 2006 U.S. dollars).

Economists value a human life on the basis of studies of the value that people actually place on human lives in their own decisions. For example, some jobs have a higher probability of death than others, and these jobs typically pay more to compensate for the risk. Examples are ocean fishery as opposed to fish farming, and ice trucking in Alaska as opposed to truck driving in the "lower forty-eight" states.

Government regulators use estimates such as these when deciding what proposed regulations are "reasonable," which means deciding which proposals have high enough benefits to justify their cost. For example, when the U.S. Department of Transportation makes decisions about what safety systems should be required in cars or airplanes, it will approve rules only where the estimated cost per life saved is $3 million or less.

Resources spent on life-saving regulations create tradeoff. A study by W. Kip Viscusi of Vanderbilt University estimated that when a regulation costs $50 million, it diverts enough spending in the rest of the economy from health care and safety expenditures that it costs a life. This finding suggests that any regulation that costs more than $50 million per life saved actually costs lives, rather than saving them.

Concepts and Summary

We can make a strong case, taken as a whole, that the benefits of U.S. environmental regulation have outweighed the costs. As the extent of environment regulation increases, additional expenditures on environmental protection will probably have increasing marginal costs and decreasing marginal benefits. This pattern suggests that the flexibility and cost savings of market-oriented environmental policies will become more important.

18.5 WORLD ENVIRONMENTAL PROBLEMS

Many countries around the world have become more aware of the benefits of environmental protection. Yet even if most nations individually took steps to address their environmental issues, no nation acting alone can solve certain environmental problems which spill over national borders. No nation by itself can reduce emissions of carbon dioxide and other gases by enough to solve the problem of global warming—not without the cooperation of other nations. Another issue is the challenge of preserving **biodiversity**, which includes the full spectrum of animal and plant genetic material. Although a nation can protect biodiversity within its own borders, no nation acting alone can protect biodiversity around the world. Global warming and biodiversity are examples of **international externalities.**

Bringing the nations of the world together to address environmental issues requires a difficult set of negotiations between countries with different income levels and different sets of priorities. If nations such as China, India, Brazil, Mexico, and others are developing their economies by burning vast amounts of fossil fuels or by stripping their forest and wildlife habitats, then the world's high-income countries acting alone will not be able to reduce greenhouse gases. However, low-income countries, with some understandable exasperation, point out that high-income countries do not have much moral standing to lecture them on the necessities of putting environmental protection ahead of economic growth. After all, high-income countries have historically been the primary contributors to greenhouse warming by burning **fossil fuels**—and still are today. It is hard to tell people who are living in a low-income country, where adequate diet, health care, and education are lacking, that they should sacrifice an improved quality of life for a cleaner environment.

Can rich and poor countries come together to address global environmental spillovers? At the initiative of the European Union and the most vulnerable developing nations, the Durban climate conference in December 2011 launched negotiations to develop a new international climate change agreement that covers all countries. The agreement will take the form of an agreed upon outcome with legal force applicable to all parties. According to the EU, the goal is to adopt the plan in 2015 and implement it in 2020. For the agreement to work, the two biggest emitters of greenhouse gases—China and the United States—will have to sign on.

If high-income countries want low-income countries to reduce their emissions of greenhouse gases, then the high-income countries may need to pay some of the costs. Perhaps some of these payments will happen through private markets; for example, some tourists from rich countries will pay handsomely to vacation near the natural treasures of low-income countries. Perhaps some of the transfer of resources can happen through making modern pollution-control technology available to poorer countries.

The practical details of what such an international system might look like and how it would operate across international borders are forbiddingly complex. But it seems highly unlikely that some form of world government will impose a detailed system of environmental command-and-control regulation around the world. As a result, a decentralized and market-oriented approach may be the only practical way to address international issues such as global warming and biodiversity.

Concepts and Summary

Certain global environmental issues, such as global warming and biodiversity, spill over national borders and will need to be addressed with some form of international agreement.

18.6THE TRADE OFF BETWEEN ECONOMIC OUTPUT AND ENVIRONMENTAL PROTECTION

The tradeoff between economic output and the environment can be analyzed with a **production possibility frontier (PPF)** such as the one shown in Figure 1. At one extreme, at a choice like P, a country would be selecting a high level of economic output but very little environmental protection. At the other extreme, at a choice like T, a country would be selecting a high level of environmental protection but little economic output. According to the graph, an increase in environmental protection involves an opportunity cost of less economic output. No matter what their preferences, all societies should wish to avoid choices like M, which are productively inefficient. Efficiency requires that the choice should be on the production possibility frontier.

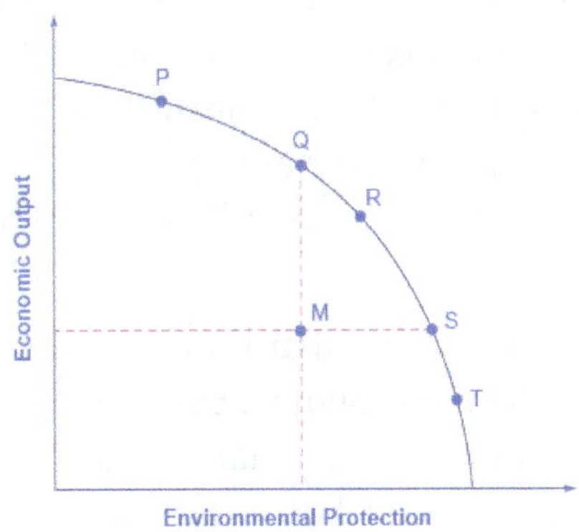

Figure 1. The Tradeoff between Economic Output and Environmental Protection. Each society will have to weigh its own values and decide whether it prefers a choice like P with more economic output and less environmental protection, or a choice like T with more environmental protection and less economic output.

Economists do not have a great deal to say about the choice between P, Q, R, S and T in Figure 1, all of which lie along the production possibility frontier. Countries with low per capita **gross domestic product (GDP)**, such as China, place a greater emphasis on economic output—which in turn helps to produce nutrition, shelter, health, education, and desirable consumer goods. Countries with higher income levels, where a greater share of people have access to the basic necessities of life, may be willing to place a relatively greater emphasis on environmental protection.

However, economists are united in their belief that an inefficient choice such as M is undesirable. Rather than choosing M, a nation could achieve either greater economic output with the same environmental protection, as at point Q, or greater environmental protection with the same level of output, as at point S. The problem with command-and-control environmental laws is that they sometimes involve a choice like M. Market-oriented environmental tools offer a mechanism either for providing either the same environmental protection at lower cost, or providing a greater degree of environmental protection for the same cost.

Keystone XL

So how would an economist respond to claims of environmental damage caused by the Keystone XL project? Clearly the environmental cost of oil spills would be considered a negative externality, but how many external costs would arise? And are these costs "too high" when measured against any potential for economic benefit?

As this chapter indicates, in deciding whether construction of the pipeline is a good idea, an economist would want to know not only about the marginal benefits resulting from the additional pipeline construction, but also the potential marginal costs—and especially the marginal external costs of the pipeline. Typically these come in the form of environmental impact statements, which are usually required for these kinds of projects. The most recent impact statement, released in March 2013 by the Nebraska Department of State, considered the possibility of fewer miles of pipeline going over the aquifer system and avoiding completely environmentally fragile areas; it indicated that "most resources" would not be harmed by construction of the pipeline.

As of press time, the Obama Administration has not approved construction of the Keystone XL project. While the economic benefits of additional oil in the United States may be fairly easily quantified, the social costs are not. It seems that, in a period of economic expansion, people want to err on the side of caution and estimate the marginal costs to be greater than the marginal benefits of additional oil generation. Those estimates may change, however, if the price of gasoline continues to rise.

Concepts and Summary

Depending on their different income levels and political preferences, countries are likely to make different choices about allocative efficiency—that is, the choice between economic output and environmental protection along the production possibility frontier. However, all countries should prefer to make a choice that shows productive efficiency—that is, the choice is somewhere on the production possibility frontier rather than inside it. Revisit Choice in a World of Scarcity for more on these terms.

CHAPTER 19
PUBLIC GOODS AND POSITIVE EXTERNALITIES

19.1 DETAILS OF WHY THE PRIVATE SECTOR IS UNDER INVESTING IN INNOVATION

Market competition can provide an incentive for discovering new technology because a firm can earn higher profits by finding a way to produce products more cheaply or to create products with characteristics consumers want. As Gregory Lee, CEO of Samsung said, "Relentless pursuit of new innovation is the key principle of our business and enables consumers to discover a world of possibilities with technology." An innovative firm knows that it will usually have a temporary edge over its competitors and thus an ability to earn above-normal profits before competitors can catch up.

In certain cases, however, **competition** can discourage new **technology**, especially when other firms can quickly copy a new idea. Consider a pharmaceutical firm deciding to develop a new drug. On average, it can cost $800 million and take more than a decade to discover a new drug, perform the necessary safety tests, and bring the drug to market. If the research and development (R&D) effort fails—and every R&D project has some chance of failure—then the firm will suffer losses and could even be driven out of business. If the project succeeds, then the firm's competitors may figure out ways of adapting and copying the underlying idea, but without having to pay the costs themselves. As a result, the innovative company will bear the much higher costs of the R&D and will enjoy at best only a small, temporary advantage over the competition.

Many inventors over the years have discovered that their inventions brought them less profit than they might have reasonably expected.

- Eli Whitney (1765–1825) invented the cotton gin, but then southern cotton planters built their own seed-separating devices with a few minor changes in Whitney's design. When Whitney sued, he found that the courts in southern states would not uphold his patent rights.

- Thomas Edison (1847–1931) still holds the record for most patents granted to an individual. His first invention was an automatic vote counter, and despite the social benefits, he could not find a government that wanted to buy it.
- Gordon Gould came up with the idea behind the laser in 1957. He put off applying for a patent and, by the time he did apply, other scientists had laser inventions of their own. A lengthy legal battle resulted, in which Gould spent $100,000 on lawyers, before he eventually received a patent for the laser in 1977. Compared to the enormous social benefits of the laser, Gould received relatively little financial reward.
- In 1936, Turing delivered a paper titled, "On Computable Numbers, with an Application to the Entscheidungsproblem," in which he presented the notion of a universal machine (later called the "Universal Turing Machine," and then the "Turing machine") capable of computing anything that is computable. The central concept of the modern computer was based on Turing's paper.

A variety of studies by economists have found that the original inventor receives one-third to one-half of the total economic benefits from innovations, while other businesses and new product users receive the rest.

The Positive Externalities of New Technology

Will private firms in a market economy under invest in research and technology? If a firm builds a factory or buys a piece of equipment, the firm receives all the economic benefits that result from the investments. However, when a firm invests in new technology, the private benefits, or profits, that the firm receives are only a portion of the overall social benefits. The social benefits of an innovation take into account the value of all the positive externalities of the new idea or product, whether enjoyed by other companies or society as a whole, as well as the private benefits received by the firm that developed the new technology. As you learned in Environmental Protection and Negative Externalities, positive externalities are beneficial spillovers to a third party, or parties.

Consider the example of the Big Drug Company, which is planning its R&D budget for the next year. Economists and scientists working for Big Drug have compiled a list of potential research and development projects and estimated rates of return. (The rate of return is the estimated payoff from the project.) Figure 1 shows how the calculations work. The downward-sloping $D_{Private}$ curve represents the firm's demand for financial capital and reflects the company's willingness to borrow to finance research and development projects at various interest rates. Suppose that this firm's investment in research and development creates a spillover benefit to other firms and households. After all, new innovations often spark other creative endeavors that society also values. If we add the spillover benefits society enjoys to the firm's private demand for financial capital, we can draw DSocial that lies above DPrivate.

If there was a way for the firm to fully monopolize those social benefits by somehow making them unavailable to the rest of us, the firm's private demand curve would be the same as society's demand curve. According to Figure 1 and Table 1, if the going rate of interest on borrowing is 8%, and the company can receive the private benefits of innovation only, then the company would finance $30 million. Society, at the same rate of 8%, would find it optimal to have $52 million of borrowing. Unless there is a way for the company to fully enjoy the total benefits, then it will borrow less than the socially optimal level of $52 million.

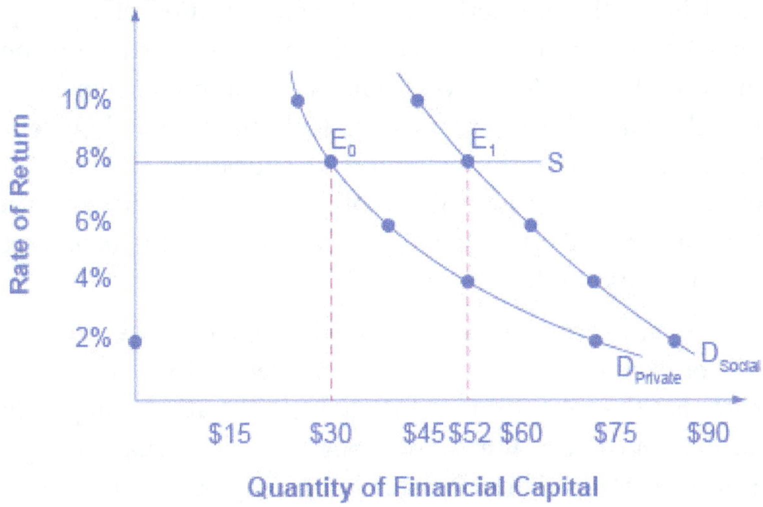

Figure 1. Positive Externalities and Technology. Big Drug faces a cost of borrowing of ٪۸. If the firm receives only the private benefits of investing in R&D, then its demand curve for financial capital is shown by $D_{Private}$, and the equilibrium will occur at $30 million. Because there are spillover benefits, society would find it optimal to have $52 million of investment. If the firm could keep the social benefits of its investment for itself, its demand curve for financial capital would be D_{Social} and it would be willing to borrow ۵۲$ million.

Table 1. Return and Demand for Capital

Rate of Return	DPrivate (in millions)	DSocial (in millions)
2%	$72	$84
4%	$52	$72
6%	$38	$62
8%	$30	$52
10%	$26	$44

Big Drug's original demand for financial capital ($D_{Private}$) is based on the profits received by the firm. However, other pharmaceutical firms and health care companies may learn new lessons about how to treat certain medical conditions and are then able to create their own competing products. The social benefit of the drug takes into account the value of all the positive externalities of the drug. If Big Drug were able to gain this social return instead of other companies, its **demand** for financial capital would shift to the demand curve D_{Social}, and it would be willing to borrow and invest $52 million. However, if Big Drug is receiving only 50 cents of each dollar of social benefits, the firm will not spend as much on creating new products. The amount it would be willing to spend would fall somewhere in between $D_{Private}$ and D_{Social}.

Why Invest in Human Capital?

The investment in anything, whether it is the construction of a new power plant or research in a new cancer treatment, usually requires a certain upfront cost with an uncertain future benefit. The investment in education, or human capital, is no different. Over the span of many years, a student and her family invest significant amounts of time and money into that student's education. The idea is that higher levels of educational attainment will eventually serve to increase the student's future productivity and subsequent ability to earn. Once the numbers are crunched, does this investment pay off for the student?

Almost universally, economists have found that the answer to this question is a clear "Yes." For example, several studies of the return to education in the United States estimate that the rate of return to a college education is approximately 10%. Data in Table 2, from the U.S. Bureau of Labor Statistics' Usual Weekly Earnings of Wage and Salary Workers, Third Quarter 2014, demonstrate that median weekly earnings are higher for workers who have completed more education. While these rates of return will beat equivalent investments in Treasury bonds or savings accounts, the estimated returns to education go primarily to the individual worker, so these returns are private rates of return to education.

Table 2. Usual Weekly Earnings of Wage and Salary Workers, Third Quarter 2014. (Source: http://www.bls.gov/news.release/pdf/wkyeng.pdf)

	Less than a High School Degree	High School Degree, No College	Bachelor's Degree
Median Weekly Earnings (full-time workers over the age of 25)	$488	$668	$1,101

What does society gain from investing in the education of another student? After all, if the government is spending taxpayer dollars to subsidize public education, society should expect some kind of return on that spending. Again, economists like George Psacharopoulos have found that, across a variety of nations, the social rate of return on schooling is also positive. After all, positive externalities exist from investment in education. While not always easy to measure, according to Walter McMahon, the positive externalities to education typically include better health outcomes for the population, lower levels of crime, a cleaner environment and a more stable, democratic government. For these reasons, many nations have chosen to use taxpayer dollars to subsidize primary, secondary, and higher education. Education clearly benefits the person who receives it, but a society where most people have a good level of education provides positive externalities for all.

Examples of Positive Externalities

Although technology may be the most prominent example of a positive externality, it is not the only one. For example, being vaccinated against disease is not only a protection for the individual, but it has the positive spillover of protecting others who may become infected. When a number of homes in a neighborhood are modernized, updated, and restored, not only does it increase the value of those homes, but the value of other properties in the neighborhood may increase as well.

The appropriate public policy response to a positive externality, like a new technology, is to help the party creating the positive externality receive a greater share of the social benefits. In the case of vaccines, like flu shots, an effective policy might be to provide a subsidy to those who choose to get vaccinated.

Figure 2 shows the market for flu shots. The market demand curve DMarket for flu shots reflects only the marginal private benefits (MPB) that the vaccinated individuals receive from the shots. Assuming that there are no spillover costs in the production of flu shots, the market supply curve is given by the marginal private cost (MPC) of producing the vaccinations.

The equilibrium quantity of flu shots produced in the market, where MPB is equal to MPC, is Q_{Market} and the price of flu shots is P_{Market}. However, spillover benefits exist in this market because others, those who chose not to purchase a flu shot, receive a positive externality in a reduced chance of contracting the flu. When we add the spillover benefits to the marginal private benefit of flu shots, the marginal social benefit (MSB) of flu shots is given by D_{Social}. Because the MPB is greater than MSB, we see that the socially optimal level of flu shots is greater than the market quantity (Q_{Social} exceeds Q_{Market}) and the corresponding price of flu shots, if the market were to produce Q_{Social}, would be at P_{Social}. Unfortunately, the marketplace does not recognize the positive externality and flu shots will go under produced and under consumed.

So how can government try to move the market level of output closer to the socially desirable level of output? One policy would be to provide a subsidy, like a voucher, to any citizen who wishes to get vaccinated. This voucher would act as "income" that could be used to purchase only a flu shot and, if the voucher was exactly equal to the per-unit spillover benefits, would increase market equilibrium to a quantity of Q_{Social} and a price of P_{Social} where MSB equals MSC. Suppliers of the flu shots would receive payment of P_{Social} per vaccination, while consumers of flu shots would redeem the voucher and only pay a price of $P_{Subsidy}$. When the government uses a subsidy in this way, the socially optimal quantity of vaccinations is produced.

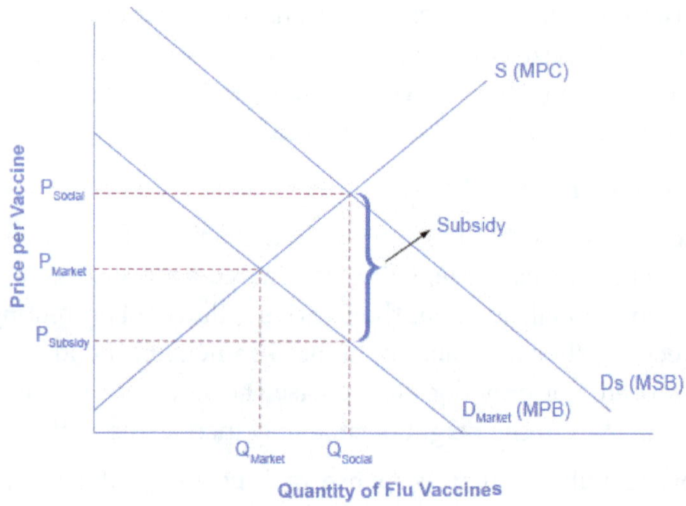

Figure 2. The Market for Flu Shots with Spillover Benefits (A Positive Externality). The market demand curve does not reflect the positive externality of flu vaccinations, so only QMarket will be exchanged. This outcome is inefficient because the marginal social benefit exceeds the marginal social cost. If the government provides a subsidy to consumers of flu shots, equal to the marginal social benefit minus the marginal private benefit, the level of vaccinations can increase to the socially optimal quantity of QSocial.

Concepts and Summary

Competition creates pressure to innovate. However, if new inventions can be easily copied, then the original inventor loses the incentive to invest further in research and development. New technology often has positive externalities; that is, there are often spillovers from the invention of new technology that benefit firms other than the innovator. The social benefit of an invention, once these spillovers are taken into account, typically exceeds the private benefit to the inventor. If inventors could receive a greater share of the broader social benefits for their work, they would have a greater incentive to seek out new inventions.

19.2 HOW GOVERNMENTS CAN ENCOURAGE INNOVATION

A number of different government policies can increase the incentives to innovate, including: guaranteeing intellectual property rights, government assistance with the costs of research and development, and cooperative research ventures between universities and companies.

Intellectual Property Rights

One way to increase new technology is to guarantee the innovator an exclusive right to that new product or process. Intellectual property rights include patents, which give the inventor the exclusive legal right to make, use, or sell the invention for a limited time, and copyright laws, which give the author an exclusive legal right over works of literature, music, film/video, and pictures. For example, if a pharmaceutical firm has a patent on a new drug, then no other firm can manufacture or sell that drug for twenty-one years, unless the firm with the patent grants permission. Without a patent, the pharmaceutical firm would have to face competition for any successful products, and could earn no more than a normal rate of profit. With a patent, a firm is able to earn monopoly profits on its product for a period of time—which offers an incentive for research and development. In general, how long can "a period of time" be? The Clear it Up discusses patent and copyright protection timeframes for some works you might have heard of.

How long is Mickey Mouse protected from being copied?

All patents and copyrights are scheduled to end someday. In 2003, copyright protection for Mickey Mouse was scheduled to run out. Once the copyright had expired, anyone would be able to copy Mickey Mouse cartoons or draw and sell new ones. In 1998, however, Congress passed the Sonny Bono Copyright Term Extension Act. For copyrights owned by companies or other entities, it increased or extended the copyright from 75 years to 95 years after publication. For copyrights owned by individuals, it increased or extended the copyright coverage from 50 years to 70 years after death. Along with protecting Mickey for another 20 years, the copyright extension affected about 400,000 books, movies, and songs.

Figure 1 illustrates how the total number of patent applications filed with the U.S. Patent and Trademark Office, as well as the total number of patents granted, surged in the mid-1990s with the invention of the Internet, and is still going strong today.

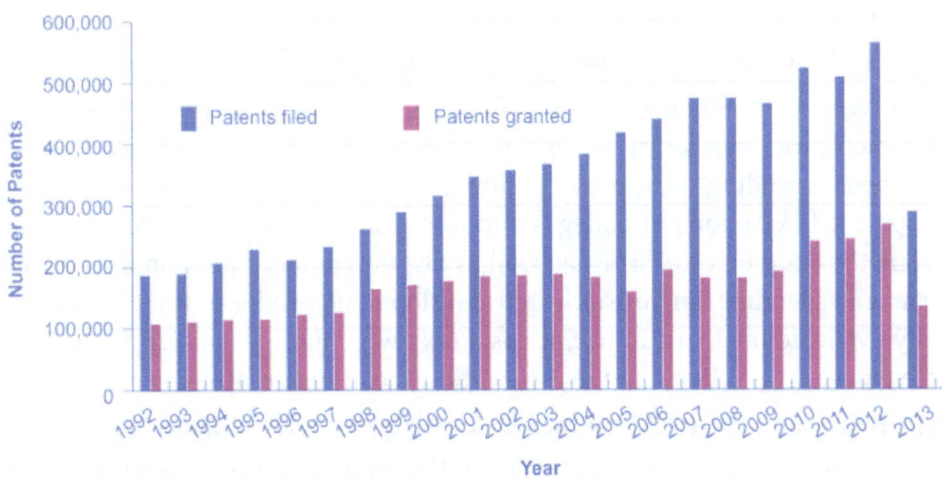

Figure 1. Patents Filed and Granted, 1981–2012. The number of applications filed for patents increased substantially from the mid-1990s into the first years of the 2000s, due in part to the invention of the Internet, which has led to many other inventions and to the 1998 Copyright Term Extension Act. (Source: http://www.uspto.gov/web/offices/ac/ido/oeip/taf/us_stat.htm)

While patents provide an incentive to innovate by protecting the innovator, they are not perfect. For example:

- In countries that already have patents, economic studies show that inventors receive only one-third to one-half of the total economic value of their inventions.
- In a fast-moving high-technology industry like biotechnology or semiconductor design, patents may be almost irrelevant because technology is advancing so quickly.
- Not every new idea can be protected with a patent or a copyright—for example, a new way of organizing a factory or a new way of training employees.
- Patents may sometimes cover too much or be granted too easily. In the early 1970s, Xerox had received over 1,700 patents on various elements of the photocopy machine. Every time Xerox improved the photocopier, it received a patent on the improvement.
- The 21-year time period for a patent is somewhat arbitrary. Ideally, a patent should cover a long enough period of time for the inventor to earn a good return, but not so long that it allows the inventor to charge a monopoly price permanently.

Because patents are imperfect and do not apply well to all situations, alternative methods of improving the rate of return for inventors of new technology are desirable. Some of these possible alternative policies are described in the following sections.

Policy #1: Government Spending on Research and Development

If the private sector does not have sufficient incentive to carry out research and development, one possibility is for the government to fund such work directly. Government spending can provide direct financial support for research and development (R&D) done at colleges and universities, nonprofit research entities, and sometimes by private firms, as well as at government-run laboratories. While government spending on research and development produces technology that is broadly available for firms to use, it costs taxpayers money and can sometimes be directed more for political than for scientific or economic reasons.

The first column of Table 5 shows the sources of total U.S. spending on research and development; the second column shows the total dollars of R&D funding by each source. The third column shows that, relative to the total amount of funding, 26% comes from the federal government, about 67% of R&D is done by industry, and less than 3% is done by universities and colleges. (The percentages below do not add up to exactly 100% due to rounding.)

Table 5. U.S. Research and Development Expenditures, 2011.

Sources of R&D Funding	Amount ($ billions)	Percent of the Total
Federal government	$133.6	32%
Industry	$249	60.2%
Universities and colleges	$12.5	3%
Nonprofits	$15.1	3.6%
Nonfederal government	$3.8	0.91%
Total	$414	

In the 1960s the federal government paid for about two-thirds of the nation's R&D. Over time, the U.S. economy has come to rely much more heavily on industry-funded R&D. The federal government has tried to focus its direct R&D spending on areas where private firms are not as active. One difficulty with direct government support of R&D is that it inevitably involves political decisions about which projects are worthy. The scientific question of whether research is worthwhile can easily become entangled with considerations like the location of the congressional district in which the research funding is being spent.

Policy #2: Tax Breaks for Research and Development

A complementary approach to supporting R&D that does not involve the government's close scrutiny of specific projects is to give firms a reduction in taxes depending on how much research and development they do. The federal government refers to this policy as the research and experimentation (R&E) tax credit. According to the Treasury Department: ". . . the R&E Credit is also a cost-effective policy for stimulating additional private sector investment. Most recent studies find that each dollar of foregone tax revenue through the R&E Tax Credit causes firms to invest at least a dollar in R&D, with some studies finding a benefit to cost ratio of 2 or 2.96."

Policy #3 Cooperative Research

State and federal governments support research in a variety of ways. For example, United for Medical Research, a coalition of groups that seek funding for the National Institutes of Health, (which is supported by federal grants), states: "NIH-supported research added $69 billion to our GDP and supported seven million jobs in 2011 alone." The United States remains the leading sponsor of medical-related research spending $117 billion in 2011. Other institutions, such as the National Academy of Scientists and the National Academy of Engineers, receive federal grants for innovative projects. The Agriculture and Food Research Initiative (AFRI) at the United States Department of Agriculture awards federal grants to projects that apply the best science to the most important agricultural problems, from food safety to childhood obesity.

Cooperation between government-funded universities, academies, and the private sector can spur product innovation and create whole new industries.

Concepts and Summary

Public policy with regard to technology must often strike a balance. For example, patents provide an incentive for inventors, but they should be limited to genuinely new inventions and not extend forever.

Government has a variety of policy tools for increasing the rate of return for new technology and encouraging its development, including: direct government funding of R&D, tax incentives for R&D, protection of intellectual property, and forming cooperative relationships between universities and the private sector.

19.3 PUBLIC GOODS: KIND OF GOOD

Even though new technology creates positive externalities so that perhaps one-third or one-half of the social benefit of new inventions spills over to others, the inventor still receives some private return. What about a situation where the positive externalities are so extensive that private firms could not expect to receive any of the social benefit? This kind of good is called a **public good**. Spending on national defense is a good example of a public good. Let's begin by defining the characteristics of a public good and discussing why these characteristics make it difficult for private firms to supply public goods. Then we will see how government may step in to address the issue.

The Definition of a Public Good

Economists have a strict definition of a public good, and it does not necessarily include all goods financed through taxes. To understand the defining characteristics of a public good, first consider an ordinary private good, like a piece of pizza. A piece of pizza can be bought and sold fairly easily because it is a separate and identifiable item. However, public goods are not separate and identifiable in this way.

Instead, public goods have two defining characteristics: they are nonexcludable and nonrivalrous. The first characteristic, that a public good is **nonexcludable**, means that it is costly or impossible to exclude someone from using the good. If Larry buys a private good like a piece of pizza, then he can exclude others, like Lorna, from eating that pizza. However, if national defense is being provided, then it includes everyone. Even if you strongly disagree with America's defense policies or with the level of defense spending, the national defense still protects you. You cannot choose to be unprotected, and national defense cannot protect everyone else and exclude you.

The second main characteristic of a public good, that it is **nonrivalrous**, means that when one person uses the public good, another can also use it. With a private good like pizza, if Max is eating the pizza then Michelle cannot also eat it; that is, the two people are rivals in consumption. With a public good like national defense, Max's consumption of national defense does not reduce the amount left for Michelle, so they are nonrivalrous in this area.

A number of government services are examples of public goods. For instance, it would not be easy to provide fire and police service so that some people in a neighborhood would be protected from the burning and burglary of their property, while others would not be protected at all. Protecting some necessarily means protecting others, too.

Positive externalities and public goods are closely related concepts. Public goods have positive externalities, like police protection or public health funding. Not all goods and services with positive externalities, however, are public goods. Investments in education have huge positive spillovers but can be provided by a private company. Private companies can invest in new inventions such as the Apple iPad and reap profits that may not capture all of the social benefits. Patents can also be described as an attempt to make new inventions into private goods, which are excludable and rivalrous, so that no one but the inventor is allowed to use them during the length of the patent.

The Free Rider Problem of Public Goods

Private companies find it difficult to produce public goods. If a good or service is nonexcludable, like national defense, so that it is impossible or very costly to exclude people from using this good or service, then how can a firm charge people for it?

When individuals make decisions about buying a public good, a free rider problem can arise, in which people have an incentive to let others pay for the public good and then to "free ride" on the purchases of others. The free rider problem can be expressed in terms of the prisoner's dilemma game, which is discussed as a representation of oligopoly in Monopolistic Competition and Oligopoly. Say that two people are thinking about contributing to a public good: Rachel and Samuel. When either of them contributes to a public good, such as a local fire department, their personal cost of doing so is $4 and the social benefit of that person's contribution is $6. Because society's benefit of $6 is greater than the cost of $4, the investment is a good idea for society as a whole. The problem is that, while Rachel and Samuel pay for the entire cost of their contribution to the public good, they receive only half of the benefit, because the benefit of the public good is divided equally among the members of society. This sets up the prisoner's dilemma illustrated in Table 6.

Table 6. Contributing to a Public Good as a Prisoner's Dilemma

	Samuel (S) Contribute	Samuel (S) Do Not Contribute
Rachel (R) Contribute	R pays $4, receives $6, net gain +$2 S pays $4, receives $6, net gain +$2	R pays $4, receives $3, net gain –$1 S pays $0, receives $3, net gain +$3
Rachel (R) Do Not Contribute	R pays $0, receives $3, net gain +$3 S pays $4, receives $3, net gain –$1	R pays $0, receives $0 S pays $0, receives $0

If neither Rachel nor Samuel contributes to the public good, then there are no costs and no benefits of the public good. Suppose, however, that only Rachel contributes, while Samuel does not. Rachel incurs a cost of $4, but receives only $3 of benefit (half of the total $6 of benefit to society), while Samuel incurs no cost, and yet he also receives $3 of benefit. In this outcome, Rachel actually loses $1 while Samuel gains $3. A similar outcome, albeit with roles reversed, would occur if Samuel had contributed, but Rachel had not. Finally, if both parties contribute, then each incurs a cost of $4 and each receives $6 of benefit (half of the total $12 benefit to society). There is a dilemma with the Prisoner's Dilemma, though. See the Work it Out feature.

The Problem with the Prisoner's Dilemma

The difficulty with the prisoner's dilemma arises as each person thinks through his or her strategic choices.

Step 1. Rachel reasons in this way: If Samuel does not contribute, then I would be a fool to contribute. However, if Samuel does contribute, then I can come out ahead by not contributing.

Step 2. Either way, I should choose not to contribute, and instead hope that I can be a free rider who uses the public good paid for by Samuel.

Step 3. Samuel reasons the same way about Rachel.

Step 4. When both people reason in that way, the public good never gets built, and there is no movement to the option where everyone cooperates—which is actually best for all parties.

The Role of Government in Paying for Public Goods

The key insight in paying for public goods is to find a way of assuring that everyone will make a contribution and to prevent free riders. For example, if people come together through the political process and agree to pay taxes and make group decisions about the quantity of public goods, they can defeat the free rider problem by requiring, through the law, that everyone contributes.

However, government spending and taxes are not the only way to provide public goods. In some cases, markets can produce public goods. For example, think about radio. It is nonexcludable, since once the radio signal is being broadcast, it would be very difficult to stop someone from receiving it. It is nonrivalrous, since one person listening to the signal does not prevent others from listening as well. Because of these features, it is practically impossible to charge listeners directly for listening to conventional radio broadcasts.

Radio has found a way to collect revenue by selling advertising, which is an indirect way of "charging" listeners by taking up some of their time. Ultimately, consumers who purchase the goods advertised are also paying for the radio service, since the cost of advertising is built into the product cost. In a more recent development, satellite radio companies, such as SirusXM, charge a regular subscription fee for streaming music without commercials. In this case, however, the product is excludable—only those who pay for the subscription will receive the broadcast.

Some public goods will also have a mixture of public provision at no charge along with fees for some purposes, like a public city park that is free to use, but the government charges a fee for parking your car, for reserving certain picnic grounds, and for food sold at a refreshment stand.

In other cases, social pressures and personal appeals can be used, rather than the force of law, to reduce the number of free riders and to collect resources for the public good. For example, neighbors sometimes form an association to carry out beautification projects or to patrol their area after dark to discourage crime. In low-income countries, where social pressure strongly encourages all farmers to participate, farmers in a region may come together to work on a large irrigation project that will benefit all. Many fundraising efforts, including raising money for local charities and for the endowments of colleges and universities, also can be viewed as an attempt to use social pressure to discourage free riding and to generate the outcome that will produce a public benefit.

Common Resources and the "Tragedy of the Commons"

There are some goods that do not fall neatly into the categories of private good or public good. While it is easy to classify a pizza as a private good and a city park as a public good, what about an item that is nonexcludable and rivalrous, such as the queen conch?

In the Caribbean, the queen conch is a large marine mollusk found in shallow waters of sea grass. These waters are so shallow, and so clear, that a single diver may harvest many conch in a single day. Not only is conch meat a local delicacy and an important part of the local diet, but the large ornate shells are used in art and can be crafted into musical instruments. Because almost anyone with a small boat, snorkel, and mask, can participate in the conch harvest, it is essentially nonexcludable. At the same time, fishing for conch is rivalrous; once a diver catches one conch it cannot be caught by another diver.

Goods that are nonexcludable and rivalrous are called **common resources**. Because the waters of the Caribbean are open to all conch fishermen, and because any conch that *you* catch is conch that *I* cannot catch, common resources like the conch tend to be overharvested.

The problem of overharvesting common resources is not a new one, but ecologist Garret Hardin put the tag "Tragedy of the Commons" to the problem in a 1968 article in the magazine *Science*. Economists view this as a problem of property rights. Since nobody owns the ocean, or the conch that crawl on the sand beneath it, no one individual has an incentive to protect that resource and responsibly harvest it. To address the issue of overharvesting conch and other marine fisheries, economists typically advocate simple devices like fishing licenses, harvest limits, and shorter fishing seasons. When the population of a species drops to critically low numbers, governments have even banned the harvest until biologists determine that the population has returned to sustainable levels. In fact, such is the case with the conch, the harvesting of which has been effectively banned in the United States since 1986.

Positive Externalities in Public Health Programs

One of the most remarkable changes in the standard of living in the last several centuries is that people are living longer. Thousands of years ago, human life expectancy is believed to have been in the range of 20 to 30 years. By 1900, average life expectancy in the United States was 47 years. By 2015, life expectancy is 79 years. Most of the gains in life expectancy in the history of the human race happened in the twentieth century.

The rise in life expectancy seems to stem from three primary factors. First, systems for providing clean water and disposing of human waste helped to prevent the transmission of many diseases. Second, changes in public behavior have advanced health. Early in the twentieth century, for example, people learned the importance of boiling bottles before using them for food storage and baby's milk, washing their hands, and protecting food from flies. More recent behavioral changes include reducing the number of people who smoke tobacco and precautions to limit sexually transmitted diseases. Third, medicine has played a large role. Immunizations for diphtheria, cholera, pertussis, tuberculosis, tetanus, and yellow fever were developed between 1890 and 1930. Penicillin, discovered in 1941, led to a series of other antibiotic drugs for bringing infectious diseases under control. In recent decades, drugs that reduce the risks of high blood pressure have had a dramatic effect in extending lives.

These advances in public health have all been closely linked to positive externalities and public goods. Public health officials taught hygienic practices to mothers in the early 1900s and encouraged less smoking in the late 1900s. Many public sanitation systems and storm sewers were funded by government because they have the key traits of public goods. In the twentieth century, many medical discoveries came out of government or university-funded research. Patents and intellectual property rights provided an additional incentive for private inventors. The reason for requiring immunizations, phrased in economic terms, is that it prevents spillovers of illness to others—as well as helping the person immunized.

The Benefits of Voyager I Live On

While we applaud the technology spillovers of NASA's space projects, we should also acknowledge that those benefits are not shared equally. Economists like **Tyler Cowen**, a professor at George Mason University, are seeing more and more evidence of a widening gap between those who have access to rapidly improving technology, and those who do not. According to Cowen author of the recent book, *Average Is Over: Powering America Beyond the Age of the Great Stagnation*, this inequality in access to technology and information is going to deepen the inequality in skills, and ultimately, in wages and global standards of living.

Concepts and Summary

A public good has two key characteristics: it is nonexcludable and nonrivalrous. Nonexcludable means that it is costly or impossible for one user to exclude others from using the good. Nonrivalrous means that when one person uses the good, it does not prevent others from using it. Markets often have a difficult time producing public goods because free riders will attempt to use the public good without paying for it. The free rider problem can be overcome through measures to assure that users of the public good pay for it. Such measures include government actions, social pressures, and specific situations where markets have discovered a way to collect payments.

CHAPTER

ECONOMIC INEQUALITY AND POVERTY 20

20.1 POVERTY LINE DRAWING

Comparisons of high and low incomes raise two different issues: economic inequality and poverty. Poverty is measured by the number of people who fall below a certain level of income—called the poverty line—that defines the income needed for a basic standard of living. Income inequality compares the share of the total income (or wealth) in society that is received by different groups; for example, comparing the share of income received by the top 10% to the share of income received by the bottom 10%.

In the United States, the official definition of the poverty line traces back to a single person: Mollie Orshansky. In 1963, Orshansky, who was working for the Social Security Administration, published an article called "Children of the Poor" in a highly useful and dry-as-dust publication called the Social Security Bulletin. Orshansky's idea was to define a poverty line based on the cost of a healthy diet.

Her previous job had been at the U.S. Department of Agriculture, where she had worked in an agency called the Bureau of Home Economics and Human Nutrition. One task of this bureau had been to calculate how much it would cost to feed a nutritionally adequate diet to a family. Orshansky found that the average family spent one-third of its income on food. She then proposed that the poverty line be the amount needed to buy a nutritionally adequate diet, given the size of the family, multiplied by three.

The current U.S. poverty line is essentially the same as the Orshansky poverty line, although the dollar amounts are adjusted each year to represent the same buying power over time. The U.S. poverty line in 2015 ranged from $11,790 for a single individual to $25,240 for a household of four people.

Figure 1 shows the U.S. poverty rate over time; that is, the percentage of the population below the poverty line in any given year. The poverty rate declined through the 1960s, rose in the early 1980s and early 1990s, but seems to have been slightly lower since the mid-1990s. However, in no year in the last four decades has the poverty rate been less than 11% of the U.S. population—that is, at best about one American in nine is below the poverty line. In recent years, the poverty rate appears to have peaked at 15.9% in 2011 before dropping to 14.5% in 2013. Table 1 compares poverty rates for different groups in 2011. As you will see when we delve further into these numbers, poverty rates are relatively low for whites, for the elderly, for the well-educated, and for male-headed households. Poverty rates for females, Hispanics, and African Americans are much higher than for whites. While Hispanics and African Americans have a higher percentage of individuals living in poverty than others, most people in the United States living below the poverty line are white.

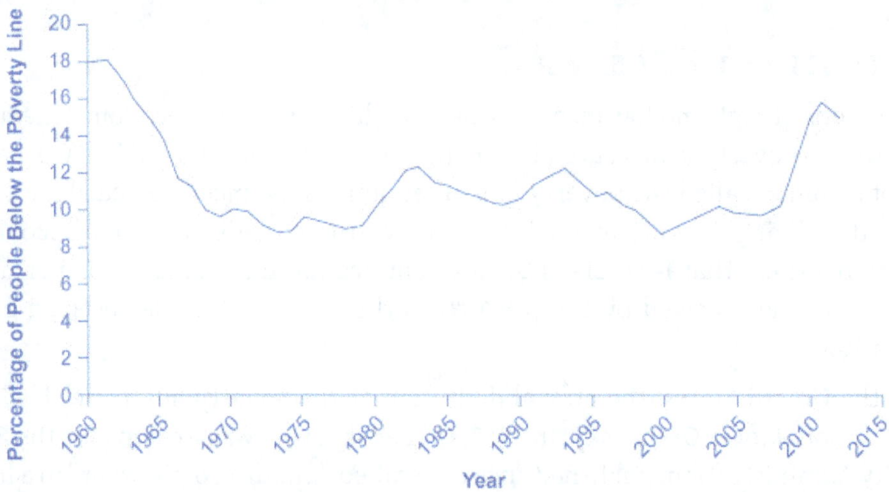

Figure 1. The U.S. Poverty Rate since 1960. The poverty rate fell dramatically during the 1960s, rose in the early 1980s and early 1990s, and, after declining in the 1990s through mid-2000s, rose to 15.9% in 2011, which is close to the 1960 levels. In 2013, the poverty dropped slightly to 14.5%. (Source: U.S. Census Bureau)

Table 1. Poverty Rates by Group, 2013

Group	Poverty Rate
Females	15.8%
Males	13.1%
White	9.6%
Black	27.1%
Hispanic	23.5%
Under age 18	19.9%
Ages 18–24	20.6%
Ages 25–34	15.9%

Ages 35–44	12.2%
Ages 45–54	10.9%
Ages 55–59	10.7%
Ages 60–64	10.8%
Ages 65 and older	9.5%

The concept of a poverty line raises many tricky questions. In a vast country like the United States, should there be a national poverty line? After all, according to the Federal Register, the median household income for a family of four was $102,552 in New Jersey and $57,132 in Mississippi in 2013, and prices of some basic goods like housing are quite different between states. The poverty line is based on cash income, which means it does not take into account government programs that provide assistance to the poor in a non-cash form, like **Medicaid** (health care for low-income individuals and families) and food aid. Also, low-income families can qualify for federal housing assistance. (These and other government aid programs will be discussed in detail later in this chapter.)

Should the poverty line be adjusted to take the value of such programs into account? Many economists and policymakers wonder whether the concept of what poverty means in the twenty-first century should be rethought. The following Clear It Up feature explains the poverty lines set by the World Bank for low-income countries around the world.

How is poverty measured in low-income countries?

The World Bank sets two poverty lines for low-income countries around the world. One poverty line is set at an income of $1.25/day per person; the other is at $2/day. By comparison, the U.S. 2015 poverty line of $20,090 annually for a family of three works out to $18.35 per person per day.

Clearly, many people around the world are far poorer than Americans, as Table 2 shows. China and India both have more than a billion people; Nigeria is the most populous country in Africa; and Egypt is the most populous country in the Middle East. In all four of those countries, in the mid-2000s, a substantial share of the population subsisted on less than $2/day. Indeed, about half the world lives on less than $2.50 a day, and 80 percent of the world lives on less than $10 per day. (Of course, the cost of food, clothing, and shelter in those countries can be very different from those costs in the United States, so the $2 and $2.50 figures may mean greater purchasing power than they would in the United States.)

Table 2. Poverty Lines for Low-Income Countries, mid-2000s. (Source: http://data.worldbank.org/indicator/SI.POV.DDAY)

Country	Share of Population below $1.25/Day	Share of Population below $2.00/Day
Brazil (in 2009)	6.1%	10.8%
China (in 2009)	11.8%	27.2%
Egypt (in 2008)	1.7%	15.4%
India (in 2010)	32.7%	68.8%
Mexico (in 2010)	0.7%	4.5%
Nigeria (in 2010)	68.0%	84.5%

Any poverty line will be somewhat arbitrary, and it is useful to have a poverty line whose basic definition does not change much over time. If Congress voted every few years to redefine what poverty means, then it would be difficult to compare rates over time. After all, would a lower poverty rate mean that the definition had been changed, or that people were actually better off? Government statisticians at the U.S. Census Bureau have ongoing research programs to address questions like these.

Concepts and Summary

Wages are influenced by supply and demand in labor markets, which can lead to very low incomes for some people and very high incomes for others. Poverty and income inequality are not the same thing. Poverty applies to the condition of people who cannot afford the necessities of life. Income inequality refers to the disparity between those with higher and lower incomes. The poverty rate is what percentage of the population lives below the poverty line, which is determined by the amount of income that it takes to purchase the necessities of life. Choosing a poverty line will always be somewhat controversial.

20.2 THE TRAP OF POVERTY

Can you give people too much help, or the wrong kind of help? When people are provided with food, shelter, healthcare, income, and other necessities, assistance may reduce their incentive to work. Consider a program to fight poverty that works in this reasonable-sounding manner: the government provides assistance to the poor, but as the poor earn income to support themselves, the government reduces the level of assistance it provides. With such a program, every time a poor person earns $100, the person loses $100 in government support. As a result, the person experiences no net gain for working. Economists call this problem the **poverty trap**.

Consider the situation faced by a single-parent family. A single mother (earning $8 an hour) with two children, as illustrated in Figure 1.1 First, consider the labor-leisure budget constraint faced by this family in a situation without government assistance. On the horizontal axis is hours of leisure (or time spent with family responsibilities) increasing in quantity from right to left. Also on the horizontal axis is the number of hours at paid work, going from zero hours on the right to the maximum of 2,500 hours on the left. On the vertical axis is the amount of income per year rising from low to higher amounts of income. The budget constraint line shows that at zero hours of leisure and 2,500 hours of work, the maximum amount of income is $20,000 ($8 × 2,500 hours). At the other extreme of the budget constraint line, an individual would work zero hours, earn zero income, but enjoy 2,500 hours of leisure. At point A on the budget constraint line, by working 40 hours a week, 50 weeks a year, the utility-maximizing choice is to work a total of 2,000 hours per year and earn $16,000.

Now suppose that a government antipoverty program guarantees every family with a single mother and two children $18,000 in income. This is represented on the graph by a horizontal line at $18,000. With this program, each time the mother earns $1,000, the government will deduct $1,000 of its support. Table 3 shows what will happen at each combination of work and government support.

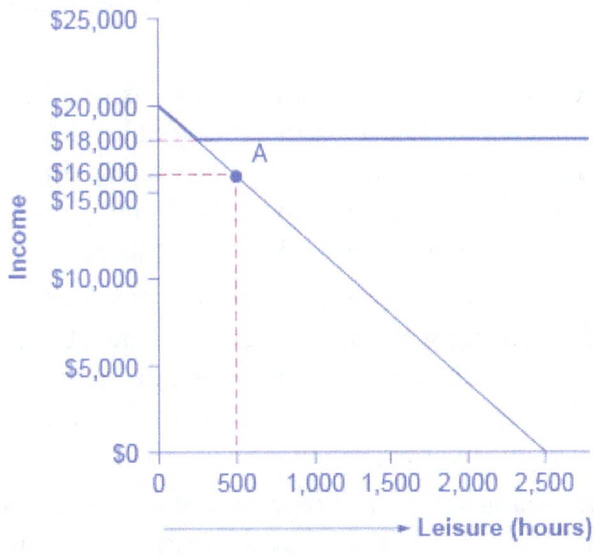

Figure 1.1 The Poverty Trap in Action. The original choice is 500 hours of leisure, 2,000 hours of work at point A, and income of $16,000. With a guaranteed income of $18,000, this family would receive $18,000 whether it provides zero hours of work or 2,000 hours of work. Only if the family provides, say, 2,300 hours of work does its income rise above the guaranteed level of $18,000—and even then, the marginal gain to income from working many hours is small.

Table 3. Total Income at Various Combinations of Work and Support

Amount Worked (hours)	Total Earnings	Government Support	Total Income
0	0	$18,000	$18,000
500	$4,000	$14,000	$18,000
1,000	$8,000	$10,000	$18,000
1,500	$12,000	$6,000	$18,000
2,000	$16,000	$2,000	$18,000
2,500	$20,000	0	$20,000

The new budget line, with the antipoverty program in place, is the horizontal and heavy line that is flat at $18,000. If the mother does not work at all, she receives $18,000, all from the government. If she works full time, giving up 40 hours per week with her children, she still ends up with $18,000 at the end of the year. Only if she works 2,300 hours in the year—which is an average of 44 hours per week for 50 weeks a year—does household income rise to $18,400. Even in this case, all of her year's work means that household income rises by only $400 over the income she would receive if she did not work at all. She would need to work 50 hours a week to reach $20,000.

Indeed, the poverty trap is even stronger than this simplified example shows, because a working mother will have extra expenses like clothing, transportation, and child care that a nonworking mother will not face, making the economic gains from working even smaller. Moreover, those who do not work fail to build up job experience and contacts, which makes working in the future even less likely.

The bite of the poverty trap can be reduced by designing an antipoverty program so that, instead of reducing government payments by $1 for every $1 earned, payments are reduced by some smaller amount instead. The bite of the poverty trap can also be reduced by imposing requirements for work as a condition of receiving benefits and setting a time limit on benefits.

Figure 2 illustrates a government program that guarantees $18,000 in income, even for those who do not work at all, but then reduces this amount by 50 cents for each $1 earned. The new, higher budget line in Figure 2 shows that, with this program, additional hours of work will bring some economic gain. Because of the reduction in government income when an individual works, an individual earning $8.00 will really net only $4.00 per hour. The vertical intercept of this higher budget constraint line is at $28,000 ($18,000 + 2,500 hours × $4.00 = $28,000). The horizontal intercept is at the point on the graph where $18,000 and 2500 hours of leisure is set. Table 4 shows the total income differences with various choices of labor and leisure.

However, this type of program raises other issues. First, even if it does not eliminate the incentive to work by reducing government payments by $1 for every $1 earned, enacting such a program may still reduce the incentive to work. At least some people who would be working 2,000 hours each year without this program might decide to work fewer hours but still end up with more income—that is, their choice on the new budget line would be like S, above and to the right of the original choice P. Of course, others may choose a point like R, which involves the same amount of work as P, or even a point to the left of R that involves more work.

The second major issue is that when the government phases out its support payments more slowly, the antipoverty program costs more money. Still, it may be preferable in the long run to spend more money on a program that retains a greater incentive to work, rather than spending less money on a program that nearly eliminates any gains from working.

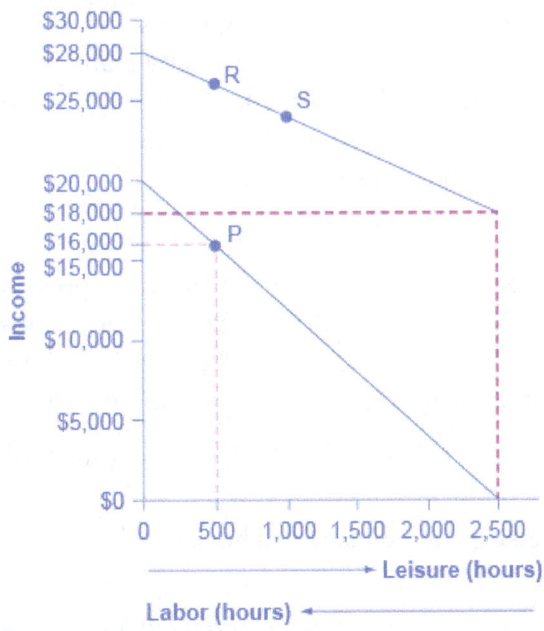

Figure 2. Loosening the Poverty Trap: Reducing Government Assistance by 50 Cents for Every $1 Earned.

On the original labor-leisure opportunity set, the lower budget set shown by the smaller dashed line in the figure, the preferred choice P is 500 hours of leisure and $16,000 of income. Then, the government created an antipoverty program that guarantees $18,000 in income even to those who work zero hours, shown by the larger dashed line. In addition, every $1 earned means phasing out 50 cents of benefits. This program leads to the higher budget set shown in the diagram. The hope is that this program will provide incentives to work the same or more hours, despite receiving income assistance. However, it is possible that the recipients will choose a point on the new budget set like S, with less work, more leisure, and greater income, or a point like R, with the same work and greater income.

Table 4. The Labor-Leisure Tradeoff with Assistance Reduced by 50 Cents for Every Dollar Earned

Amount Worked (hours)	Total Earnings	Government Support	Total Income
0	0	$18,000	$18,000
500	$4,000	$16,000	$20,000
1,000	$8,000	$14,000	$22,000
1,500	$12,000	$12,000	$24,000
2,000	$16,000	$10,000	$26,000
2,500	$20,000	$8,000	$28,000

The next module will consider a variety of government support programs focused specifically on the poor, including welfare, SNAP (food supplement), Medicaid, and the earned income tax credit (EITC). Although these programs vary from state to state, it is generally a true statement that in many states from the 1960s into the 1980s, if poor people worked, their level of income barely rose—or did not rise at all—after the reduction in government support payments was factored in. The following Work It Out feature shows how this happens.

Calculating a Budget Constraint Line

Jason earns $9.00 an hour, and a government antipoverty program provides a floor of $10,000 guaranteed income. The government reduces government support by $0.50 for each $1.00 earned. What are the horizontal and vertical intercepts of the budget constraint line? Assume the maximum hours for work or leisure is 2,500 hours.

Step 1. Determine the amount of the government guaranteed income. In this case, it is $10,000.

Step 2. Plot that guaranteed income as a horizontal line on the budget constraint line.

Step 3. Determine what Jason earns if he has no income and enjoys 2,500 hours of leisure. In this case, he will receive the guaranteed $10,000 (the horizontal intercept).

Step 4. Calculate how much Jason's salary will be reduced by due to the reduction in government income. In Jason's case, it will be reduced by one half. He will, in effect, net only $4.50 an hour.

Step 5. If Jason works 1,000 hours, at a maximum what income will Jason receive? Jason will get the government assistance of $10,000. He will net only $4.50 for every hour he chooses to work. If he works 1,000 hours at $4.50, his earned income is $4,500 plus the government income of $10,000. Thus the total maximum income (the vertical intercept) is $10,000 + $4,500 = $14,500.

Concepts and Summary

A poverty trap occurs when government-support payments for the poor decline as the poor earn more income. As a result, the poor do not end up with much more income when they work, because the loss of government support largely or completely offsets any income that is earned by working. The bite of the poverty trap can be reduced by phasing out government benefits more slowly, as well as by imposing requirements for work as a condition of receiving benefits and a time limit on benefits.

20.3 THE SAFETY NET

The U.S. government has implemented a number of programs to assist those below the poverty line and those who have incomes just above the poverty line, who are referred to as the **near-poor**. Such programs are called the **safety net**, in recognition of the fact that they offer some protection for those who find themselves without jobs or income.

Temporary Assistance for Needy Families

From the Great Depression of the 1930s until 1996, the United States' most visible antipoverty program was **Aid to Families with Dependent Children (AFDC)**, which provided cash payments to mothers with children who were below the poverty line. This program was often just called "welfare." In 1996, Congress passed and President Bill Clinton signed into law the Personal Responsibility and Work Opportunity Reconciliation Act, more commonly called the "welfare reform act." The new law replaced AFDC with **Temporary Assistance for Needy Families (TANF)**.

TANF brought several dramatic changes in how welfare operated. Under the old AFDC program, states set the level of welfare benefits that they would pay to the poor, and the federal government guaranteed it would chip in some of the money as well. The federal government's welfare spending would rise or fall depending on the number of poor people, and on how each state set its own welfare contribution.

Under TANF, however, the federal government gives a fixed amount of money to each state. The state can then use the money for almost any program with an antipoverty component: for example, the state might use the money to give cash to poor families, or to reduce teenage pregnancy, or even to raise the high school graduation rate. However, the federal government imposed two key requirements. First, if states are to keep receiving the TANF grants, they must impose work requirements so that most of those receiving TANF benefits are working (or attending school). Second, no one can receive TANF benefits with federal money for more than a total of five years over his or her lifetime. The old AFDC program had no such work requirements or time limits.

TANF attempts to avoid the poverty trap by requiring that welfare recipients work and by limiting the length of time they can receive benefits. In its first few years, the program was quite successful. The number of families receiving payments in 1995, the last year of AFDC, was 4.8 million. By 2012, according to the Congressional Research Service, the average number of families receiving payments under TANF was 1.8 million—a decline of more than half.

TANF benefits to poor families vary considerably across states. For example, again according to the Congressional Research Service, in 2011 the highest monthly payment in Alaska to a single mother with two children was $923, while in Mississippi the highest monthly payment to that family was $170. These payments reflect differences in states' cost of living. Total spending on TANF was approximately $16.6 billion in 1997. As of 2012, spending was at $12 billion, an almost 28% decrease, split about evenly between the federal and state governments. When you take into account the effects of inflation, the decline is even greater. Moreover, there seemed little evidence that poor families were suffering a reduced standard of living as a result of TANF—although, on the other side, there was not much evidence that poor families had greatly improved their total levels of income, either.

The Earned Income Tax Credit (EITC)

The **earned income tax credit (EITC)**, first passed in 1975, is a method of assisting the working poor through the tax system. The EITC is one of the largest assistance program for low-income groups, and projections for 2013 expected 26 million households to take advantage of it at an estimated cost of $50 billion. In 2013, for example, a single parent with two children would have received a tax credit of $5,372 up to an income level of $17,530. The amount of the tax break increases with the amount of income earned, up to a point. The earned income tax credit has often been popular with both economists and the general public because of the way it effectively increases the payment received for work.

What about the danger of the poverty trap that every additional $1 earned will reduce government support payments by close to $1? To minimize this problem, the earned income tax credit is phased out slowly. According to the Tax Policy Center, for a single-parent family with two children in 2013, the credit is not reduced at all (but neither is it increased) as earnings rise from $13,430 to $17,530. Then, for every $1 earned above $17,530, the amount received from the credit is reduced by 21.06 cents, until the credit phases out completely at an income level of $46,227.

Figure 2.1 illustrates that the earned income tax credits, child tax credits, and the TANF program all cost the federal government money—either in direct outlays or in loss of tax revenues. CTC stands for the government tax cuts for the child tax credit.

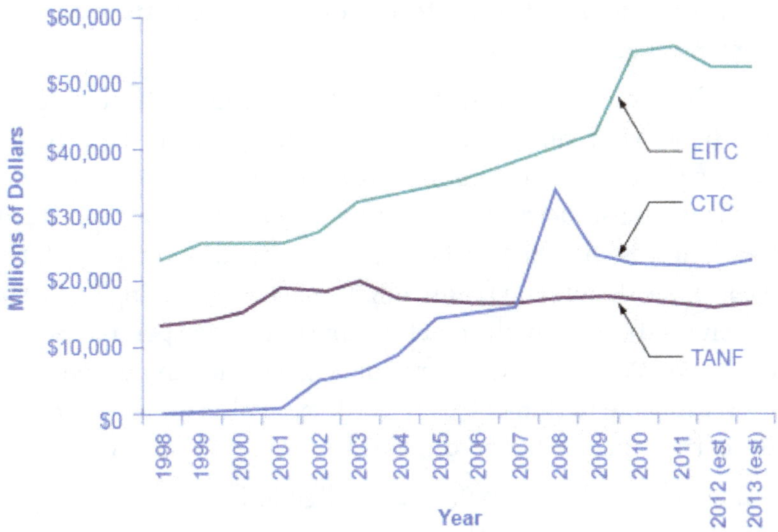

Figure 2.1. Real Federal Spending on CTC, EITC, and TANF, 1975-2013. EITC increased from more than $20 billion in 2000 to over an estimated $50 billion by 2013, far exceeding estimated 2013 outlays in the CTC (Child Tax Credits) and TANF of over $20 billion and $10 billion, respectively. (Source: Office of Management and Budget)

In recent years, the EITC has become a hugely expensive government program for providing income assistance to the poor and near-poor, costing about $60 billion in 2012. In that year, the EITC provided benefits to about 27 million families and individuals and, on average, is worth about $2,296 per family (with children), according to the Tax Policy Center. One reason that the TANF law worked as well as it did is that the EITC was greatly expanded in the late 1980s and again in the early 1990s, which increased the returns to work for low-income Americans.

Supplemental Nutrition Assistance Program (SNAP)

Often called "food stamps," Supplemental Nutrition Assistance Program (SNAP) is a federally funded program, started in 1964, in which each month poor people receive a card like a debit card that they can use to buy food. The amount of food aid for which a household is eligible varies by income, number of children, and other factors but, in general, households are expected to spend about 30% of their own net income on food, and if 30% of their net income is not enough to purchase a nutritionally adequate diet, then those households are eligible for SNAP.

SNAP can contribute to the poverty trap. For every $100 earned, the government assumes that a family can spend $30 more for food, and thus reduces its eligibility for food aid by $30. This decreased benefit is not a complete disincentive to work—but combined with how other programs reduce benefits as income increases, it adds to the problem. SNAP, however, does try to address the poverty trap with its own set of work requirements and time limits.

Why give debit cards and not just cash? Part of the political support for SNAP comes from a belief that since the cards must be spent on food, they cannot be "wasted" on other forms of consumption. From an economic point of view, however, the belief that cards must increase spending on food seems wrong-headed. After all, say that a poor family is spending $2,500 per year on food, and then it starts receiving $1,000 per year in SNAP aid. The family might react by spending $3,500 per year on food (income plus aid), or it might react by continuing to spend $2,500 per year on food, but use the $1,000 in food aid to free up $1,000 that can now be spent on other goods. So it is reasonable to think of SNAP cards as an alternative method, along with TANF and the earned income tax credit, of transferring income to the working poor.

Indeed, anyone eligible for TANF is also eligible for SNAP, although states can expand eligibility for food aid if they wish to do so. In some states, where TANF welfare spending is relatively low, a poor family may receive more in support from SNAP than from TANF. In 2014, about 40 million people received food aid at an annual cost of about $76 billion, with an average monthly benefit of about $287 per person per month. SNAP participation increased by 70% between 2007 and 2011, from 26.6 million participants to 45 million. According to the Congressional Budget Office, this dramatic rise in participation was caused by the Great Recession of 2008–2009 and rising food prices.

The federal government deploys a range of income security programs that are funded through departments such as Health and Human Services, Agriculture, and Housing and Urban Development (HUD) (see Figure 2.2). According to the Office of Management and Budget, collectively, these three departments provided an estimated $62 billion of aid through programs such as supplemental feeding programs for women and children, subsidized housing, and energy assistance. The federal government also transfers funds to individual states through special grant programs.

The safety net includes a number of other programs: government-subsidized school lunches and breakfasts for children from low-income families; the **Special Supplemental Food Program for Women, Infants and Children (WIC)**, which provides food assistance for pregnant women and newborns; the Low Income Home Energy Assistance Program, which provides help with home heating bills; housing assistance, which helps pay the rent; and Supplemental Security Income, which provides cash support for the disabled and the elderly poor.

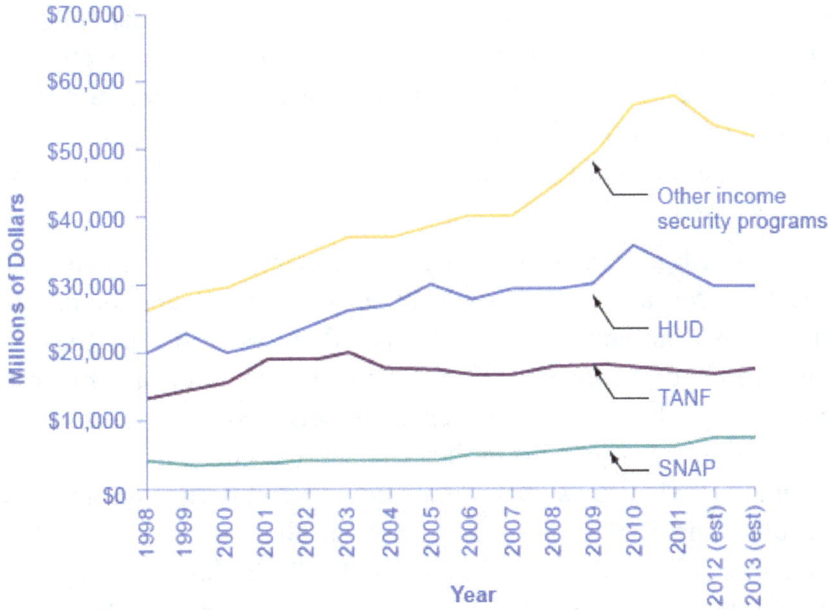

Figure 2.2. Expenditure Comparison of TANF, SNAP, HUD, and Other Income Security Programs, 1988–2013 (est.). Total expenditures on income security continued to rise between 1988 and 2010, while payments for TANF have increased from $13 billion in 1998 to an estimated $17.3 billion in 2013. SNAP has seen relatively small increments. These two programs comprise a relatively small portion of the estimated $106 billion dedicated to income security in 2013. Note that other programs and housing programs increased dramatically during the 2008 and 2010 time periods. (Source: Table 12.3 Section 600 Income Security, https://www.whitehouse.gov/sites/default/files/omb/budget/fy2013/assets/hist.pdf)

Medicaid

Medicaid was created by Congress in 1965 and is a joint health insurance program entered into by both the states and the federal government. The federal government helps fund Medicaid, but each state is responsible for administering the program, determining the level of benefits, and determining eligibility. It provides medical insurance for certain low-income people, including those below the poverty line, with a focus on families with children, the elderly, and the disabled. About one-third of Medicaid spending is for low-income mothers with children. While an increasing share of the program funding in recent years has gone to pay for nursing home costs for the elderly poor. The program ensures that a basic level of benefits is provided to Medicaid participants, but because each state sets eligibility requirements and provides varying levels of service, the program differs from state to state.

In the past, a common problem has been that many low-paying jobs pay enough to a breadwinner so that a family could lose its eligibility for Medicaid, yet the job does not offer health insurance benefits. A poor parent considering such a job might choose not to work rather than lose health insurance for his or her children. In this way, health insurance can become a part of the poverty trap. Many states recognized this problem in the 1980s and 1990s and expanded their Medicaid coverage to include not just the poor, but the near-poor earning up to 135% or even 185% of the poverty line. Some states also guaranteed that children would not lose coverage if their parents worked.

These expanded guarantees cost the government money, of course, but they also helped to encourage those on welfare to enter the labor force. As of 2014, approximately 69.7 million people participated in Medicaid. Of those enrolled, almost half are children. Healthcare expenditures, however, are highest for the elderly population, which comprises approximately 25% of participants. As Figure 3 (a) indicates, the largest number of households that enroll in Medicaid are those with children. Lower-income adults are the next largest group enrolled in Medicaid at 28%. The blind and disabled are 16% of those enrolled, and seniors are 9% of those enrolled. Figure 3 (b) shows how much actual Medicaid dollars are spent for each group. Out of total Medicaid spending, more is spent on seniors (20%) and the blind and disabled (44%). So, 64% of all Medicaid spending goes to seniors, the blind, and disabled. Children receive 21% of all Medicaid spending, followed by adults at 15%.

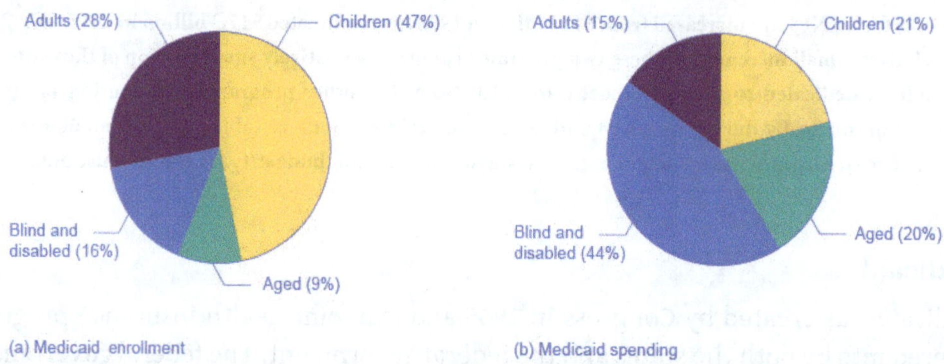

Figure 3. Medicaid Enrollment and Spending. Part (a) shows the Medicaid enrollment by different populations, with children comprising the largest percentage at 47%, followed by adults at 28%, and the blind and disabled at 16%. Part (b) shows that Medicaid spending is principally for the blind and disabled, followed by the elderly. Although children are the largest population covered by Medicaid, expenditures on children are only at 21%.

Concepts and Summary

The group of government programs that assist the poor are called the safety net. In the United States, prominent safety net programs include Temporary Assistance to Needy Families (TANF), the Supplemental Nutrition Assistance Program (SNAP), the earned income tax credit (EITC), Medicaid, and the Special Supplemental Food Program for Women, Infants, and Children (WIC).

20.4 MEASUREMENT AND CAUSES OF INCOME INEQUALITY

Poverty levels can be subjective based on the overall income levels of a country; typically poverty is measured based on a percentage of the median income. Income inequality, however, has to do with the distribution of that income, in terms of which group receives the most or the least income. Income inequality involves comparing those with high incomes, middle incomes, and low incomes—not just looking at those below or near the poverty line. In turn, measuring income inequality means dividing up the population into various groups and then comparing the groups, a task that can be carried out in several ways, as the next Clear It Up feature shows.

How do you separate poverty and income inequality?

Poverty can change even when inequality does not move at all. Imagine a situation in which income for everyone in the population declines by 10%. Poverty would rise, since a greater share of the population would now fall below the poverty line. However, inequality would be the same, because everyone suffered the same proportional loss. Conversely, a general rise in income levels over time would keep inequality the same, but reduce poverty.

It is also possible for income inequality to change without affecting the poverty rate. Imagine a situation in which a large number of people who already have high incomes increase their incomes by even more. Inequality would rise as a result—but the number of people below the poverty line would remain unchanged.

Why did inequality of household income increase in the United States in recent decades? Indeed, a trend toward greater income inequality has occurred in many countries around the world, although the effect has been more powerful in the U.S. economy. Economists have focused their explanations for the increasing inequality on two factors that changed more or less continually from the 1970s into the 2000s. One set of explanations focuses on the changing shape of American households; the other focuses on greater inequality of wages, what some economists call "winner take all" **labor markets**. We will begin with how we measure inequality, and then consider the explanations for growing inequality in the United States.

Measuring Income Distribution by Quintiles

One common way of measuring income inequality is to rank all households by income, from lowest to highest, and then to divide all households into five groups with equal numbers of people, known as **quintiles**. This calculation allows for measuring the distribution of income among the five groups compared to the total. The first quintile is the lowest fifth or 20%, the second quintile is the next lowest, and so on. Income inequality can be measured by comparing what share of the total income is earned by each quintile.

U.S. income distribution by quintile appears in Table 7. In 2011, for example, the bottom quintile of the income distribution received 3.2% of income; the second quintile received 8.4%; the third quintile, 14.3%; the fourth quintile, 23.0%; and the top quintile, 51.14%. The final column of Table 7 shows what share of income went to households in the top 5% of the income distribution: 22.3% in 2011. Over time, from the late 1960s to the early 1980s, the top fifth of the income distribution typically received between about 43% to 44% of all income. The share of income that the top fifth received then begins to rise. According to the Census Bureau, much of this increase in the share of income going to the top fifth can be traced to an increase in the share of income going to the top 5%. The quintile measure shows how income inequality has increased in recent decades.

Table 7. Share of Aggregate Income Received by Each Fifth and Top 5% of Households, 1967–2013. (Source: U.S. Census Bureau, Table 2)

Year	Lowest Quintile	Second Quintile	Third Quintile	Fourth Quintile	Highest Quintile	Top 5%
1967	4.0	10.8	17.3	24.2	43.6	17.2
1970	4.1	10.8	17.4	24.5	43.3	16.6
1975	4.3	10.4	17.0	24.7	43.6	16.5
1980	4.2	10.2	16.8	24.7	44.1	16.5
1985	3.9	9.8	16.2	24.4	45.6	17.6
1990	3.8	9.6	15.9	24.0	46.6	18.5
1995	3.7	9.1	15.2	23.3	48.7	21.0
2000	3.6	8.9	14.8	23.0	49.8	22.1
2005	3.4	8.6	14.6	23.0	50.4	22.2
2010	3.3	8.5	14.6	23.4	50.3	21.3
2013	3.2	8.4	14.4	23.0	51	22.2

It can also be useful to divide the income distribution in ways other than quintiles; for example, into tenths or even into percentiles (that is, hundredths). A more detailed breakdown can provide additional insights. For example, the last column of Table 7 shows the income received by the top 5% percent of the income distribution. Between 1980 and 2013, the share of income going to the top 5% increased by 5.7 percentage points (from 16.5% in 1980 to 22.2% in 2013). From 1980 to 2013 the share of income going to the top quintile increased by 7.0 percentage points (from 44.1% in 1980 to 51% in 2013). Thus, the top 20% of householders (the fifth quintile) received over half (51%) of all the income in the United States in 2013.

Lorenz Curve

The data on income inequality can be presented in various ways. For example, you could draw a bar graph that showed the share of income going to each fifth of the income distribution. Figure 1 presents an alternative way of showing inequality data in what is called a Lorenz curve. The Lorenz curve shows the cumulative share of population on the horizontal axis and the cumulative percentage of total income received on the vertical axis.

Figure 3.1. The Lorenz Curve. A Lorenz curve graphs the cumulative shares of income received by everyone up to a certain quintile. The income distribution in 1980 was closer to the perfect equality line than the income distribution in 2011—that is, the U.S. income distribution became more unequal over time.

Every Lorenz curve diagram begins with a line sloping up at a 45-degree angle, shown as a dashed line in Figure 3.1. The points along this line show what perfect equality of the income distribution looks like. It would mean, for example, that the bottom 20% of the income distribution receives 20% of the total income, the bottom 40% gets 40% of total income, and so on. The other lines reflect actual U.S. data on inequality for 1980 and 2011.

The trick in graphing a Lorenz curve is that you must change the shares of income for each specific quintile, which are shown in the first column of numbers in Table 8, into cumulative income, shown in the second column of numbers. For example, the bottom 40% of the cumulative income distribution will be the sum of the first and second quintiles; the bottom 60% of the cumulative income distribution will be the sum of the first, second, and third quintiles, and so on. The final entry in the cumulative income column needs to be 100%, because by definition, 100% of the population receives 100% of the income.

Table 8. Calculating the Lorenz Curve

Income Category	Share of Income in 1980 (%)	Cumulative Share of Income in 1980 (%)	Share of Income in 2013 (%)	Cumulative Share of Income in 2013 (%)
First quintile	4.2	4.2	3.2	3.2
Second quintile	10.2	14.4	8.4	11.6
Third quintile	16.8	31.2	14.4	26.0
Fourth quintile	24.7	55.9	23.0	49.0
Fifth quintile	44.1	100.0	51.0	100.0

In a Lorenz curve diagram, a more unequal distribution of income will loop farther down and away from the 45-degree line, while a more equal distribution of income will move the line closer to the 45-degree line. The greater inequality of the U.S. income distribution between 1980 and 2013 is illustrated in Figure 1 because the Lorenz curve for 2013 is farther from the 45-degree line than the Lorenz curve for 1980. The Lorenz curve is a useful way of presenting the quintile data that provides an image of all the quintile data at once. The next Clear It Up feature shows how income inequality differs in various countries compared to the United States.

How does economic inequality vary around the world?

The U.S. economy has a relatively high degree of income inequality by global standards. As Table 9 shows, based on a variety of national surveys done for a selection of years in the last five years of the 2000s (with the exception of Germany, and adjusted to make the measures more comparable), the U.S. economy has greater inequality than Germany (along with most Western European countries). The region of the world with the highest level of income inequality is Latin America, illustrated in the numbers for Brazil and Mexico. The level of inequality in the United States is lower than in some of the low-income countries of the world, like China and Nigeria, or some middle-income countries like the Russian Federation. However, not all poor countries have highly unequal income distributions; India provides a counterexample.

Table 9. Income Distribution in Select Countries. (Source: U.S. data from U.S. Census Bureau Table 2. Other data from The World Bank Poverty and Inequality Data Base, http://databank.worldbank.org/data/views/reports/tableview.aspx#)

Country	Survey Year	First Quintile	Second Quintile	Third Quintile	Fourth Quintile	Fifth Quintile
United States	2013	3.2%	8.4%	14.4%	23.0%	51.0%
Germany	2000	8.5%	13.7%	17.8%	23.1%	36.9%

Country	Survey Year	First Quintile	Second Quintile	Third Quintile	Fourth Quintile	Fifth Quintile
Brazil	2009	2.9%	7.1%	12.4%	19.0%	58.6%
Mexico	2010	4.9%	8.8%	13.3%	20.2%	52.8%
China	2009	4.7%	9.7%	15.3%	23.2%	47.1%
India	2010	8.5%	12.1%	15.7%	20.8%	42.8%
Russia	2009	6.1%	10.4%	14.8%	21.3%	47.1%
Nigeria	2010	4.4%	8.3%	13.0%	20.3%	54.0%

Causes of Growing Inequality: The Changing Composition of American Households

In 1970, 41% of married women were in the labor force, but by 2015, according to the Bureau of Labor Statistics, 56.7% of married women were in the labor force. One result of this trend is that more households have two earners. Moreover, it has become more common for one high earner to marry another high earner. A few decades ago, the common pattern featured a man with relatively high earnings, such as an executive or a doctor, marrying a woman who did not earn as much, like a secretary or a nurse. Often, the woman would leave paid employment, at least for a few years, to raise a family. However, now doctors are marrying doctors and executives are marrying executives, and mothers with high-powered careers are often returning to work while their children are quite young. This pattern of households with two high earners tends to increase the proportion of high-earning households.

According to data in the National Journal, even as two-earner couples have increased, so have single-parent households. Of all U.S. families, 13.1% were headed by single mothers; the poverty rate among single-parent households tends to be relatively high.

These changes in family structure, including the growth of single-parent families who tend to be at the lower end of the income distribution, and the growth of two-career high-earner couples near the top end of the income distribution, account for roughly half of the rise in income inequality across households in recent decades.

Causes of Growing Inequality: A Shift in the Distribution of Wages

Another factor behind the rise in U.S. income inequality is that earnings have become less equal since the late 1970s. In particular, the earnings of high-skilled labor relative to low-skilled labor have increased. Winner-take-all labor markets result from changes in technology, which have increased global demand for "stars,"—whether the best CEO, doctor, basketball player, or actor. This global demand pushes salaries far above productivity differences versus educational differences. One way to measure this change is to take the earnings of workers with at least a four-year college bachelor's degree (including those who went on and completed an advanced degree) and divide them by the earnings of workers with only a high school degree. The result is that those in the 25–34 age bracket with college degrees earned about 1.67 times as much as high school graduates in 2010, up from 1.59 times in 1995, according to U.S. Census data. Winner-take-all labor market theory argues that the salary gap between the median and the top 1 percent is not due to educational differences.

Economists use the demand and supply model to reason through the most likely causes of this shift. According to the National Center for Education Statistics, in recent decades, the supply of U.S. workers with college degrees has increased substantially; for example, 840,000 four-year bachelor's degrees were conferred on Americans in 1970; in 2009–2010, 1,602,480 such degrees were conferred—an increase of about 90%. In Figure 3.2, this shift in supply to the right, from S_0 to S_1, should result in a lower equilibrium wage for high-skilled labor. Thus, the increase in the price of high-skilled labor must be explained by a greater demand, like the movement from D_0 to D_1. Evidently, combining both the increase in supply and in demand has resulted in a shift from E_0 to E_1, and a resulting higher wage.

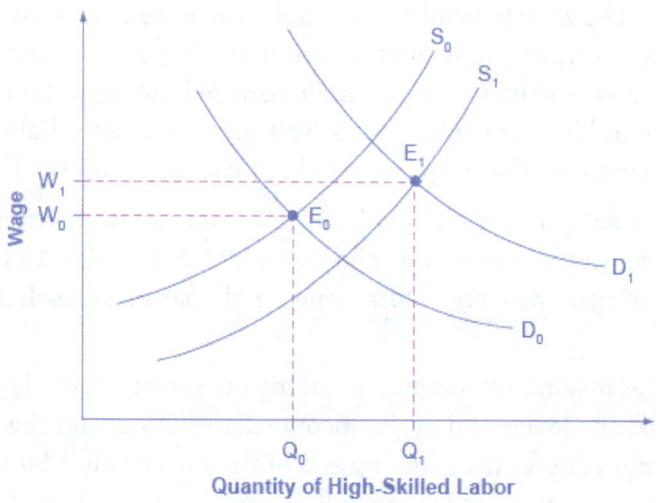

Figure 3.2. Why Would Wages Rise for High-Skilled Labor?

The proportion of workers attending college has increased in recent decades, so the supply curve for high-skilled labor has shifted to the right, from S_0 to S_1. If the demand for high-skilled labor had remained at D_0, then this shift in supply would have led to lower wages for high-skilled labor. However, the wages for high-skilled labor, especially if there is a large global demand, have increased even with the shift in supply to the right. The explanation must lie in a shift to the right in demand for high-skilled labor, from D_0 to D_1. The figure shows how a combination of the shift in supply, from S_0 to S_1, and the shift in demand, from D_0 to D_1, led to both an increase in the quantity of high-skilled labor hired and also to a rise in the wage for such labor, from W_0 to W_1.

What factors would cause the demand for high-skilled labor to rise? The most plausible explanation is that while the explosion in new information and communications technologies over the last several decades has helped many workers to become more productive, the benefits have been especially great for high-skilled workers like top business managers, consultants, and design professionals. The new technologies have also helped to encourage **globalization**, the remarkable increase in international trade over the last few decades, by making it more possible to learn about and coordinate economic interactions all around the world. In turn, the rising impact of foreign trade in the U.S. economy has opened up greater opportunities for high-skilled workers to sell their services around the world. And lower-skilled workers have to compete with a larger supply of similarly skilled workers around the globe.

The market for high-skilled labor can be viewed as a race between forces of supply and demand. Additional education and on-the-job training will tend to increase the supply of high-skilled labor and to hold down its relative wage. Conversely, new technology and other economic trends like globalization tend to increase the demand for high-skilled labor and push up its relative wage. The greater inequality of wages can be viewed as a sign that demand for skilled labor is increasing faster than supply. On the other hand, if the supply of lower skilled workers exceeds the demand, then average wages in the lower quintiles of the income distribution will decrease. The combination of forces in the high-skilled and low-skilled labor markets leads to increased income disparity.

Concepts and Summary

Measuring inequality involves making comparisons across the entire distribution of income, not just the poor. One way of doing this is to divide the population into groups, like quintiles, and then calculate what share of income is received by each group. An alternative approach is to draw Lorenz curves, which compare the cumulative income actually received to a perfectly equal distribution of income. Income inequality in the United States increased substantially from the late 1970s and early 1980s into the 2000s. The two most common explanations cited by economists are changes in the structure of households that have led to more two-earner couples and single-parent families, and the effect of new information and communications technology on wages.

20.5 GOVT. ACTIONS TO REDUCE INCOME INEQUITY

No society should expect or desire complete equality of income at a given point in time, for a number of reasons. First, most workers receive relatively low earnings in their first few jobs, higher earnings as they reach middle age, and then lower earnings after retirement. Thus, a society with people of varying ages will have a certain amount of income inequality. Second, people's preferences and desires differ. Some are willing to work long hours to have income for large houses, fast cars and computers, luxury vacations, and the ability to support children and grandchildren.

These factors all imply that a snapshot of inequality in a given year does not provide an accurate picture of how people's incomes rise and fall over time. Even if some degree of economic inequality is expected at any point in time, how much inequality should there be? There is also the difference between income and wealth, as the following Clear It Up feature explains.

How do you measure wealth versus income inequality?

Income is a flow of money received, often measured on a monthly or an annual basis; wealth is the sum of the value of all assets, including money in bank accounts, financial investments, a pension fund, and the value of a home. In calculating wealth all debts must be subtracted, such as debt owed on a home mortgage and on credit cards. A retired person, for example, may have relatively little income in a given year, other than a pension or Social Security. However, if that person has saved and invested over time, the person's accumulated wealth can be quite substantial.

In the United States, the wealth distribution is more unequal than the income distribution, because differences in income can accumulate over time to make even larger differences in wealth. However, the degree of inequality in the wealth distribution can be measured with the same tools we use to measure the inequality in the income distribution, like quintile measurements. Data on wealth are collected once every three years in the Survey of Consumer Finance.

Even if they cannot answer the question of how much inequality is too much, economists can still play an important role in spelling out policy options and tradeoffs. If a society decides to reduce the level of economic inequality, it has three main sets of tools: redistribution from those with high incomes to those with low incomes; trying to assure that a ladder of opportunity is widely available; and a tax on inheritance.

Redistribution

Redistribution means taking income from those with higher incomes and providing income to those with lower incomes. Earlier in this chapter, we considered some of the key government policies that provide support for the poor: the welfare program

TANF, the earned income tax credit, SNAP, and Medicaid. If a reduction in inequality is desired, these programs could receive additional funding.

The programs are paid for through the federal income tax, which is a progressive tax system designed in such a way that the rich pay a higher percent in income taxes than the poor. Data from household income tax returns in 2009 shows that the top 1% of households had an average income of $1,219,700 per year in pre-tax income and paid an average federal tax rate of 28.9%. The effective income tax, which is total taxes paid divided by total income (all sources of income such as wages, profits, interest, rental income, and government transfers such as veterans' benefits), was much lower. The effective tax paid by the top 1% of householders was 20.4%, while the bottom two quintiles actually paid negative effective income taxes, because of provisions like the earned income tax credit. News stories occasionally report on a high-income person who has managed to pay very little in taxes, but while such individual cases exist, according to the Congressional Budget Office, the typical pattern is that people with higher incomes pay a higher average share of their income in federal income taxes.

Of course, the fact that some degree of redistribution occurs now through the federal income tax and government antipoverty programs does not settle the questions of how much redistribution is appropriate, and whether more redistribution should occur.

The Ladder of Opportunity

Economic inequality is perhaps most troubling when it is not the result of effort or talent, but instead is determined by the circumstances under which a child grows up. One child attends a well-run grade school and high school and heads on to college, while parents help out by supporting education and other interests, paying for college, a first car, and a first house, and offering work connections that lead to internships and jobs. Another child attends a poorly run grade school, barely makes it through a low-quality high school, does not go to college, and lacks family and peer support. These two children may be similar in their underlying talents and in the effort they put forth, but their economic outcomes are likely to be quite different.

Public policy can attempt to build a ladder of opportunities so that, even though all children will never come from identical families and attend identical schools, each child has a reasonable opportunity to attain an economic niche in society based on their interests, desires, talents, and efforts. Some of those initiatives include those shown in Table 13.

Table 13. Public Policy Initiatives

Children	College Level	Adults
• Improved day care	• Widespread loans and grants for those in financial need	• Opportunities for retraining and acquiring new skills
• Enrichment programs for preschoolers	• Public support for a range of institutions from two-year community colleges to large research universities	• Prohibiting discrimination in job markets and housing on the basis of race, gender, age, and disability
• Improved public schools	–	–
• After school and community activities	–	–
• Internships and apprenticeships	–	–

The United States has often been called a land of opportunity. Although the general idea of a ladder of opportunity for all citizens continues to exert a powerful attraction, specifics are often quite controversial. Society can experiment with a wide variety of proposals for building a ladder of opportunity, especially for those who otherwise seem likely to start their lives in a disadvantaged position. Such policy experiments need to be carried out in a spirit of open-mindedness, because some will succeed while others will not show positive results or will cost too much to enact on a widespread basis.

Inheritance Taxes

There is always a debate about inheritance taxes. It goes like this: On the one hand, why should people who have worked hard all their lives and saved up a substantial nest egg not be able to give their money and possessions to their children and grandchildren? In particular, it would seem un-American if children were unable to inherit a family business or a family home. On the other hand, many Americans are far more comfortable with inequality resulting from high-income people who earned their money by starting innovative new companies than they are with inequality resulting from high-income people who have inherited money from rich parents.

The United States does have an **estate tax**—that is, a tax imposed on the value of an inheritance—which suggests a willingness to limit how much wealth can be passed on as an inheritance. However, according to the Center on Budget and Policy Priorities, in 2015 the estate tax applied only to those leaving inheritances of more than $5.43 million and thus applies to only a tiny percentage of those with high levels of wealth.

The Trade off between Incentives and Income Equality

Government policies to reduce poverty or to encourage economic equality, if carried to extremes, can injure incentives for economic output. The poverty trap, for example, defines a situation where guaranteeing a certain level of income can eliminate or reduce the incentive to work. An extremely high degree of redistribution, with very high taxes on the rich, would be likely to discourage work and entrepreneurship. Thus, it is common to draw the tradeoff between economic output and equality, as shown in Figure 1 (a). In this formulation, if society wishes a high level of economic output, like point A, it must also accept a high degree of inequality. Conversely, if society wants a high level of equality, like point B, it must accept a lower level of economic output because of reduced incentives for production.

This view of the tradeoff between economic output and equality may be too pessimistic, and Figure 3.3 (b) presents an alternate vision. Here, the tradeoff between economic output and equality first slopes up, in the vicinity of choice C, suggesting that certain programs might increase both output and economic equality. For example, the policy of providing free public education has an element of redistribution, since the value of the public schooling received by children of low-income families is clearly higher than what low-income families pay in taxes. A well-educated population, however, is also an enormously powerful factor in providing the skilled workers of tomorrow and helping the economy to grow and expand. In this case, equality and economic growth may complement each other.

Moreover, policies to diminish inequality and soften the hardship of poverty may sustain political support for a market economy. After all, if society does not make some effort toward reducing inequality and poverty, the alternative might be that people would rebel against market forces. Citizens might seek economic security by demanding that their legislators pass laws forbidding employers from ever laying off workers or reducing wages, or laws that would impose price floors and price ceilings and shut off international trade. From this viewpoint, policies to reduce inequality may help economic output by building social support for allowing markets to operate.

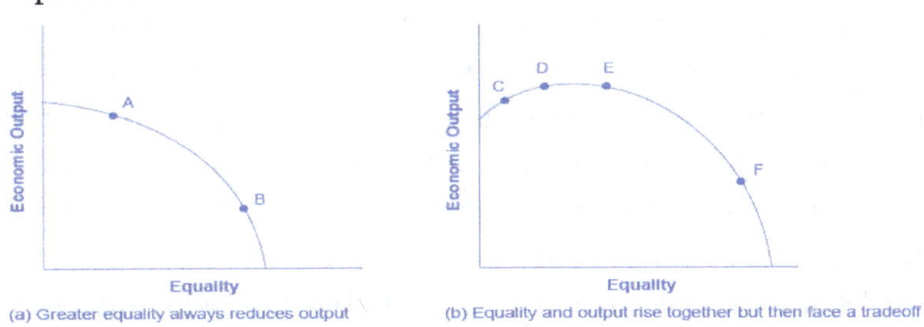

(a) Greater equality always reduces output (b) Equality and output rise together but then face a tradeoff

Figure 3.3. The Tradeoff between Incentives and Economic Equality. (a) Society faces a trade-off where any attempt to move toward greater equality, like moving from choice A to B, involves a reduction in economic

output. (b) Situations can arise like point C, where it is possible both to increase equality and also to increase economic output, to a choice like D. It may also be possible to increase equality with little impact on economic output, like the movement from choice D to E. However, at some point, too aggressive a push for equality will tend to reduce economic output, as in the shift from E to F.

The tradeoff in Figure 1 (b) then flattens out in the area between points D and E, which reflects the pattern that a number of countries that provide similar levels of income to their citizens—the United States, Canada, the nations of the European Union, Japan, Australia—have different levels of inequality. The pattern suggests that countries in this range could choose a greater or a lesser degree of inequality without much impact on economic output. Only if these countries push for a much higher level of equality, like at point F, will they experience the diminished incentives that lead to lower levels of economic output. In this view, while a danger always exists that an agenda to reduce poverty or inequality can be poorly designed or pushed too far, it is also possible to discover and design policies that improve equality and do not injure incentives for economic output by very much—or even improve such incentives.

Occupy Wall Street

The Occupy movement took on a life of its own over the last few months of 2011, bringing to light issues faced by many people on the lower end of the income distribution. The contents of this chapter indicate that there is a significant amount of income inequality in the United States. The question is: What should be done about it?

The Great Recession of 2008–2009 caused unemployment to rise and incomes to fall. Many people attribute the recession to mismanagement of the financial system by bankers and financial managers—those in the 1% of the income distribution—but those in lower quintiles bore the greater burden of the recession through unemployment. This seemed to present the picture of inequality in a different light: the group that seemed responsible for the recession was not the group that seemed to bear the burden of the decline in output. A burden shared can bring a society closer together; a burden pushed off onto others can polarize it.

On one level, the problem with trying to reduce income inequality comes down to whether you still believe in the American Dream. If you believe that one day you will have your American Dream—a large income, large house, happy family, or whatever else you would like to have in life—then you do not necessarily want to prevent anyone else from living out their dream. You certainly would not want to run the risk that someone would want to take part of your dream away from you. So there is some reluctance to engage in a redistributive policy to reduce inequality.

However, when those for whom the likelihood of living the American Dream is very small are considered, there are sound arguments in favor of trying to create greater balance. As the text indicated, a little more income equality, gained through long-term programs like increased education and job training, can increase overall economic output. Then everyone is made better off. And the 1% will not seem like such a small group any more.

Concepts and Summary

Policies that can affect the level of economic inequality include redistribution between rich and poor, making it easier for people to climb the ladder of opportunity; and estate taxes, which are taxes on inheritances. Pushing too aggressively for economic equality can run the risk of decreasing economic incentives. However, a moderate push for economic equality can increase economic output, both through methods like improved education and by building a base of political support for market forces.

CHAPTER

MAJOR ISSUES IN LABOR MARKETS: UNIONS, DISCRIMINATION, IMMIGRATION

21

21.1 LABOUR UNIONS

A **labor union** is an organization of workers that negotiates with employers over wages and working conditions. A labor union seeks to change the balance of power between employers and workers by requiring employers to deal with workers collectively, rather than as individuals. Thus, negotiations between unions and firms are sometimes called **collective bargaining**.

The subject of labor unions can be controversial. Supporters of labor unions view them as the workers' primary line of defense against efforts by profit-seeking firms to hold down wages and benefits. Critics of labor unions view them as having a tendency to grab as much as they can in the short term, even if it means injuring workers in the long run by driving firms into bankruptcy or by blocking the new technologies and production methods that lead to economic growth. We will start with some facts about union membership in the United States.

Facts about Union Membership and Pay

According to the U.S. Bureau of Labor and Statistics, about 11.1% of all U.S. workers belong to unions. Following are some of the facts provided by the bureau for 2014:

- 12.0% of U.S. male workers belong to unions; 10.5% of female workers do
- 11.1% of white workers, 13.4 % of black workers, and 9.8 % of Hispanic workers belong to unions
- 12.5% of full-time workers and 6.0% of part-time workers are union members
- 4.2% of workers ages 16–24 belong to unions, as do 14% of workers ages 45-54

Occupations in which relatively high percentages of workers belong to unions are the federal government (26.9% belong to a union), state government (31.3%), local government (41.7%); transportation and utilities (20.6%); natural resources, construction, and maintenance (16.3%); and production, transportation, and material moving (14.7%)

Occupations that have relatively low percentages of unionized workers are agricultural workers (1.4%), financial services (1.1%), professional and business services (2.4%), leisure and hospitality (2.7%), and wholesale and retail trade (4.7%)

In summary, the percentage of workers belonging to a union is higher for men than women; higher for blacks than for whites or Hispanics; higher for the 45–64 age range; and higher among workers in government and manufacturing than workers in agriculture or service-oriented jobs. Table 2 lists the largest U.S. labor unions and their membership.

Table 2. The Largest American Unions in 2013. (Source: U.S. Department of Labor, Bureau of Labor Statistics)

Union	Membership
National Education Association (NEA)	3.2 million
Service Employees International Union (SEIU)	2.1 million
American Federation of Teachers (AFT)	1.5 million
International Brotherhood of Teamsters (IBT)	1.4 million
The American Federation of State, County, and Municipal Workers (AFSCME)	1.3 million
United Food and Commercial Workers International Union	1.3 million
United Steelworkers	1.2 million
International Union, United Automobile, Aerospace and Agricultural Implement Workers of America (UAW)	990,000
International Association of Machinists and Aerospace Workers	720,000
International Brotherhood of Electrical Workers (IBEW)	675,000

In terms of pay, benefits, and hiring, U.S. unions offer a good news/bad news story. The good news for unions and their members is that their members earn about 20% more than nonunion workers, even after adjusting for factors such as years of work experience and education level. The bad news for unions is that the share of U.S. workers who belong to a labor union has been steadily declining for 50 years, as shown in Figure 1. About one-quarter of all U.S. workers belonged to a union in the mid-1950s, but only 11.1% of U.S. workers are union members today. If you leave out workers employed by the government (which includes teachers in public schools), only 6.6% of the workers employed by private firms now work for a union.

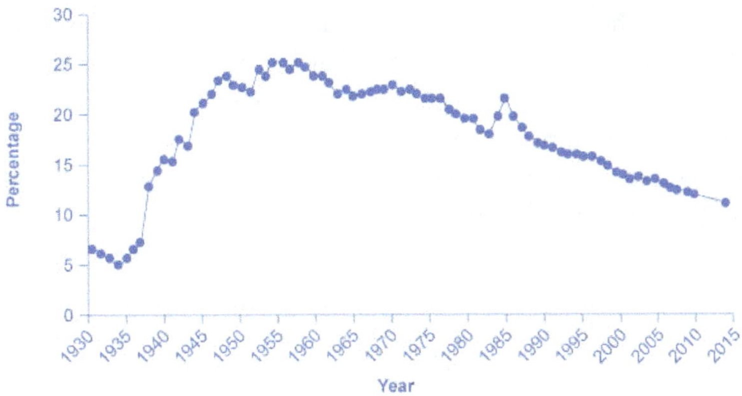

Figure 1. Percentage of Wage and Salary Workers Who Are Union Members. The share of wage and salary workers who belong to unions rose sharply in the ١٩٣٠s and ١٩٤٠s, but has tailed off since then to ٪١١,١ of all workers in ٢٠١٤.

The following section analyzes the higher pay union workers receive compared the pay rates for nonunion workers. The following section analyzes declining union membership levels. An overview of these two issues will allow us to discuss many aspects of how unions work.

Higher Wages for Union Workers

Why might union workers receive higher pay? What are the limits on how much higher pay they can receive? To analyze these questions, let's consider a situation where all firms in an industry must negotiate with a single union, and no **firm** is allowed to hire nonunion labor. If no labor union existed in this market, then equilibrium (E) in the labor market would occur at the intersection of the demand for labor (D) and the supply of labor (S) in Figure 2. The union can, however, threaten that, unless firms agree to the wages they demand, the workers will strike. As a result, the labor union manages to achieve, through negotiations with the firms, a union wage of Wu for its members, above what the equilibrium wage would otherwise have been.

This labor market situation resembles what a **monopoly firm** does in selling a product, but in this case a union is a monopoly selling labor to firms. At the higher union wage Wu, the firms in this industry will hire less labor than they would have hired in equilibrium. Moreover, an excess supply of workers want union jobs, but firms will not be hiring for such jobs.

From the union point of view, workers who receive higher wages are better off. However, notice that the quantity of workers (Qd) hired at the union wage Wu is smaller than the quantity Qe that would have been hired at the original equilibrium wage. A sensible union must recognize that when it pushes up the wage, it also reduces the incentive of firms to hire. This situation does not necessarily mean that union workers are fired. Instead, it may be that when union workers move on to other jobs or retire, they are not always replaced. Or perhaps when a firm expands production, it expands employment somewhat less with a higher union wage than it would have done with the lower equilibrium wage. Or perhaps a firm decides to purchase inputs from nonunion producers, rather than producing them with its own highly paid unionized workers. Or perhaps the firm moves or opens a new facility in a state or country where unions are less powerful.

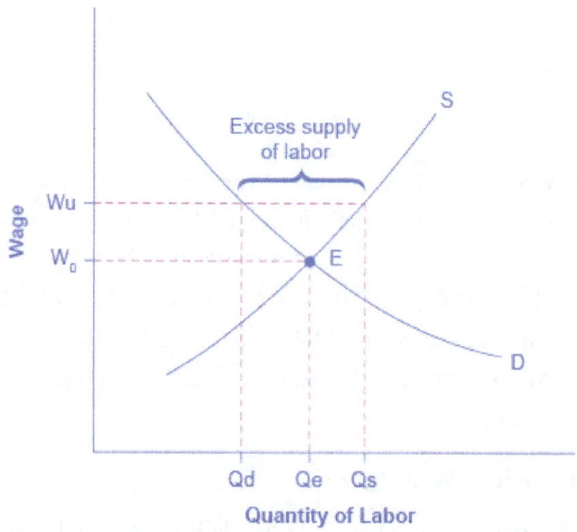

Figure 2. Union Wage Negotiations. Without a union, the equilibrium at E would have involved the wage We and the quantity of labor Qe. However, the union is able to use its bargaining power to raise the wage to Wu. The result is an excess supply of labor for union jobs. That is, a quantity of labor supplied, Qs is greater than firms' quantity demanded for labor, Qd.

From the firm's point of view, the key question is whether the higher wage of union workers is matched by higher productivity. If so, then the firm can afford to pay the higher union wages and, indeed, the demand curve for "unionized" labor could actually shift to the right. This could reduce the job losses as the equilibrium employment level shifts to the right and the difference between the equilibrium and the union wages will have been reduced. If worker unionization does not increase productivity, then the higher union wage will cause lower profits or losses for the firm.

Union workers might have higher productivity than nonunion workers for a number of reasons. First, higher wages may elicit higher productivity. Second, union workers tend to stay longer at a given job, a trend that reduces the employer's costs for training and hiring and results in workers with more years of experience. Many unions also offer job training and apprenticeship programs.

In addition, firms that are confronted with union demands for higher wages may choose production methods that involve more physical capital and less labor, resulting in increased labor productivity. Table 3 provides an example. Assume that a firm can produce a home exercise cycle with three different combinations of labor and manufacturing equipment. Say that labor is paid $16 an hour (including benefits) and the machines for manufacturing cost $200 each. Under these circumstances, the total cost of producing a home exercise cycle will be lowest if the firm adopts the plan of 50 hours of labor and one machine, as the table shows. Now, suppose that a union negotiates a wage of $20 an hour including benefits. In this case, it makes no difference to the firm whether it uses more hours of labor and fewer machines or less labor and more machines, though it might prefer to use more machines and to hire fewer union workers. (After all, machines never threaten to strike—but they do not buy the final product or service either.) In the final column of the table, the wage has risen to $24 an hour. In this case, the firm clearly has an incentive for using the plan that involves paying for fewer hours of labor and using three machines. If management responds to union demands for higher wages by investing more in machinery, then union workers can be more productive because they are working with more or better physical capital equipment than the typical nonunion worker. However, the firm will need to hire fewer workers.

Table 3. Three Production Choices to Manufacture a Home Exercise Cycle

Hours of Labor	Number of Machines	Cost of Labor + Cost of Machine $16/ hour	Cost of Labor + Cost of Machine $20/hour	Cost of Labor + Cost of Machine $24/hr
30	3	$480 + $600 = $1,080	$600 + $600 = $1,200	$720 + $600 = $1,320
40	2	$640 + $400 = $1,040	$800 + $400 = $1,200	$960 + $400 = $1,360
50	1	$800 + $200 = $1,000	$1,000 + $200 = $1,200	$1,200 + $200 = $1,400

In some cases, unions have discouraged the use of labor-saving physical capital equipment—out of the reasonable fear that new machinery will reduce the number of union jobs. For example, in 2002, the union representing longshoremen who unload ships and the firms that operate shipping companies and port facilities staged a work stoppage that shut down the ports on the western coast of the United States. Two key issues in the dispute were the desire of the shipping companies and port operators to use handheld scanners for record-keeping and computer-operated cabs for loading and unloading ships—changes which the union opposed, along with overtime pay. President Obama threatened to use the Labor Management Relations Act of 1947—commonly known as the **Taft-Hartley Act**—where a court can impose an 80-day "cooling-off period" in order to allow time for negotiations to proceed without the threat of a work stoppage. Federal mediators were called in, and the two sides agreed to a deal in February 2015. The ultimate agreement allowed the new technologies, but also kept wages, health, and pension benefits high for workers. In the past, presidential use of the Taft-Hartley Act sometimes has made labor negotiations more bitter and argumentative but, in this case, it seems to have smoothed the road to an agreement.

In other instances, unions have proved quite willing to adopt new technologies. In one prominent example, during the 1950s and 1960s, the United Mineworkers union demanded that mining companies install labor-saving machinery in the mines. The mineworkers' union realized that over time, the new machines would reduce the number of jobs in the mines, but the union leaders also knew that the mine owners would have to pay higher wages if the workers became more productive, and mechanization was a necessary step toward greater productivity.

In fact, in some cases union workers may be more willing to accept new technology than nonunion workers, because the union workers believe that the union will negotiate to protect their jobs and wages, whereas nonunion workers may be more concerned that the new technology will replace their jobs. In addition, union workers, who typically have higher job market experience and training, are likely to suffer less and benefit more than non-union workers from the introduction of new technology. Overall, it is hard to make a definitive case that union workers as a group are always either more or less welcoming to new technology than are nonunion workers.

The Decline in U.S. Union Membership

- The proportion of U.S. workers belonging to unions has declined dramatically since the early 1950s. Economists have offered a number of possible explanations:
- The shift from manufacturing to service industries
- The force of globalization and increased competition from foreign producers
- A reduced desire for unions because of the workplace protection laws now in place
- U.S. legal environment that makes it relatively more difficult for unions to organize workers and expand their membership
- Let's discuss each of these four explanations in more detail.

A first possible explanation for the decline in the share of U.S. workers belonging to unions involves the patterns of job growth in the manufacturing and service sectors of the economy shown in Figure 3. The U.S. economy had about 15 million manufacturing jobs in 1960. This total rose to 19 million by the late 1970s and then declined to 17 million in 2013. Meanwhile, the number of jobs in service industries and in government combined rose from 35 million in 1960 to over 118 million by 2013, according to the Bureau of Labor Statistics. Because over time unions were stronger in manufacturing than in service industries, the growth in jobs was not happening where the unions were. It is interesting to note that several of the biggest unions in the country are made up of government workers, including the **American Federation of State, County and Municipal Employees (AFSCME)**; the **Service Employees International Union**; and the **National Education Association**. The membership of each of these unions is listed in Table 2. Outside of government employees, however, unions have not had great success in organizing the service sector.

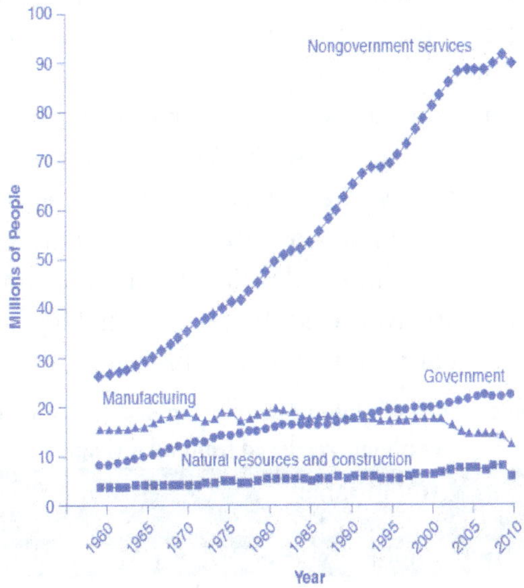

Figure 3. The Growth of Service Jobs. Jobs in services have increased dramatically in the last few decades. Jobs in government have increased modestly. Jobs in manufacturing have not changed much, although they have trended down in recent years. Source: U.S. Department of Labor, Bureau of Labor Statistics.

A second explanation for the decline in the share of unionized workers looks at import competition. Starting in the 1960s, U.S. carmakers and steelmakers faced increasing competition from Japanese and European manufacturers. As sales of imported cars and steel rose, the number of jobs in U.S. auto manufacturing fell. This industry is heavily unionized. Not surprisingly, membership in the United Auto Workers, which was 975,000 in 1985, had fallen to roughly 390,000 by 2015. Import competition not only decreases the employment in sectors where unions were once strong, but also decreases the bargaining power of unions in those sectors. However, as we have seen, unions that organize public-sector workers, who are not threatened by import competition, have continued to see growth.

A third possible reason for the decline in the number of union workers is that citizens often call on their elected representatives to pass laws concerning work conditions, overtime, parental leave, regulation of pensions, and other issues. Unions offered strong political support for these laws aimed at protecting workers but, in an ironic twist, the passage of those laws then made many workers feel less need for unions.

These first three possible reasons for the decline of unions are all somewhat plausible, but they have a common problem. Most other developed economies have experienced similar economic and political trends, such as the shift from manufacturing to services, globalization, and increasing government social benefits and regulation of the workplace. Clearly there are cultural differences between countries as to their acceptance of unions in the workplace. The share of the population belonging to unions in other countries is very high compared with the share in the United States. Table 4 shows the proportion of workers in a number of the world's high-income economies who belong to unions. The United States is near the bottom, along with France and Spain. The last column shows union coverage, defined as including those workers whose wages are determined by a union negotiation even if the workers do not officially belong to the union. In the United States, union membership is almost identical to union coverage. However, in many countries, the wages of many workers who do not officially belong to a union are still determined by collective bargaining between unions and firms.

Table 4. International Comparisons of Union Membership and Coverage in 2012. (Source, CIA World Factbook, retrieved from www.cia.gov)

Country	Union Density: Percentage of Workers Belonging to a Union	Union Coverage: Percentage of Workers Whose Wages Are Determined by Union Bargaining
Austria	37%	99%
France	9%	95%
Germany	26%	63%
Japan	22%	23%
Netherlands	25%	82%
Spain	11.3%	81%
Sweden	82%	92%
United Kingdom	29%	35%
United States	11.1%	12.5%

These international differences in union membership suggest a fourth reason for the decline of union membership in the United States: perhaps U.S. laws are less friendly to the formation of unions than such laws in other countries. The close connection between union membership and a friendly legal environment is apparent in the history of U.S. unions. The great rise in union membership in the 1930s followed the passage of the National Labor-Management Relations Act of 1935, which specified that workers had a right to organize unions and that management had to give them a fair chance to do so. The U.S. government strongly encouraged the formation of unions during the early 1940s in the belief that unions would help to coordinate the all-out production efforts needed during World War II. However, after World War II came the passage of the Taft-Hartley Act of 1947, which gave states the power to allow workers to opt out of the union in their workplace if they so desired. This law made the legal climate less encouraging to those seeking to form unions, and union membership levels soon started declining.

The procedures for forming a union differ substantially from country to country. For example, the procedures in the United States and those in Canada are strikingly different. When a group of workers wish to form a union in the United States, they announce this fact and an election date is set when the employees at a firm will vote in a secret ballot on whether to form a union. Supporters of the union lobby for a "yes" vote, and the management of the firm lobbies for a "no" vote—often even hiring outside consultants for assistance in swaying workers to vote "no." In Canada, by contrast, a union is formed when a sufficient proportion of workers (usually about 60%) sign an official card saying that they want a union. There is no separate "election date." The management of Canadian firms is limited by law in its ability to lobby against the union. In addition, though it is illegal to discriminate and fire workers based on their union activity in the United States, the penalties are slight, making this a not so costly way of deterring union activity. In short, forming unions is easier in Canada—and in many other countries—than in the United States.

In summary, union membership in the United States is lower than in many other high-income countries, a difference that may be due to different legal environments and cultural attitudes toward unions.

Concepts and Summary

A labor union is an organization of workers that negotiates as a group with employers over compensation and work conditions. Union workers in the United States are paid more on average than other workers with comparable education and experience. Thus, either union workers must be more productive to match this higher pay or the higher pay will lead employers to find ways of hiring fewer union workers than they otherwise would. American union membership has been falling for decades. Some possible reasons include the shift of jobs to service industries; greater competition from globalization; the passage of worker-friendly legislation; and U.S. laws that are less favorable to organizing unions.

21.2 EMPLOYMENT DISCRIMINATION

Discrimination involves acting on the belief that members of a certain group are inferior solely because of a factor such as race, gender, or religion. There are many types of discrimination but the focus here will be on discrimination in labor markets, which arises if workers with the same skill levels—as measured by education, experience, and expertise—receive different pay receive different pay or have different job opportunities because of their race or gender.

Earnings Gaps by Race and Gender

A possible signal of labor market discrimination is when one group is paid less than another. Figure 3.1 shows the average wage of black workers as a ratio of the average wage of white workers and the average wage of female workers as a ratio of the average wage of male workers. Research by the economists Francine Blau and Laurence Kahn shows that the gap between the earnings of women and men did not move much in the 1970s, but has declined since the 1980s. According to the U.S. Census, the gap between the earnings of blacks and whites diminished in the 1970s, but has not changed in 50 years. In both gender and race, an earnings gap remains.

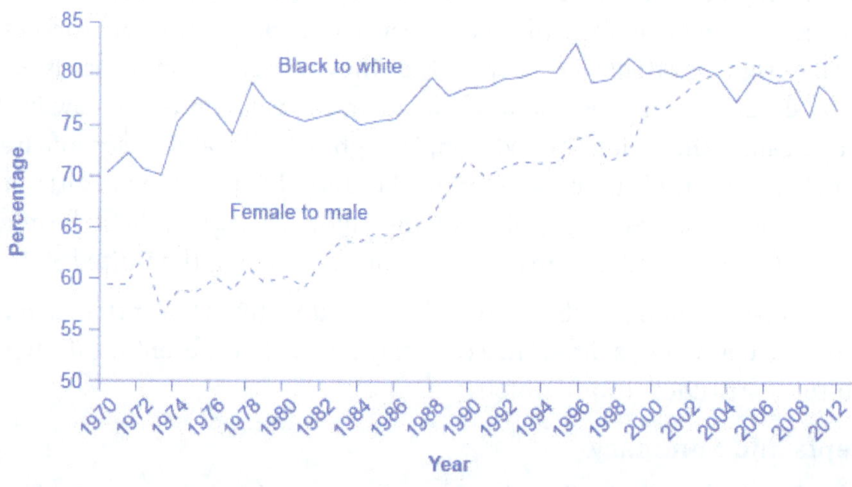

Figure 3.1. Wage Ratios by Sex and Race. The ratio of wages for black workers to white workers rose substantially in the late 1960s and through the 1970s, but has not changed much since then. The ratio of wages for female to male workers changed little through the 1970s, but has risen substantially since the 1980s. In both cases, a gap remains between the average wages of black and white workers and between the average wages of female and male workers. Source: U.S. Department of Labor, Bureau of Labor Statistics.

An earnings gap between average wages, in and of itself, does not prove that discrimination is occurring in the labor market. We need to apply the same productivity characteristics to all parties (employees) involved. Gender discrimination in the labor market occurs when women are paid less than men despite having comparable levels of education, experience, and expertise. (Read the Clear It Up about the sex-discrimination suit brought against Wal-Mart.) Similarly, racial discrimination in the labor market exists when racially diverse employees are paid less than their coworkers of the majority race despite having comparable levels of education, experience, and expertise. To bring a successful gender discrimination lawsuit, a female employee must prove that she is paid less than a male employee who holds a similar job, with similar educational attainment, and with similar expertise. Likewise, someone who wants to sue on the grounds of racial discrimination must prove that he or she is paid less than an employee of another race who holds a similar job, with similar educational attainment, and with similar expertise.

What was the sex-discrimination case against Wal-Mart?

In one of the largest class-action sex-discrimination cases in U.S. history, 1.2 million female employees of Wal-Mart claimed that the company engaged in wage and promotion discrimination. In 2011, the Supreme Court threw out the case on the grounds that the group was too large and too diverse for the case to be considered a class action suit. Lawyers for the women regrouped and are now suing in smaller groups. Part of the difficulty for the female employees is that the court said that pay and promotion decisions were made by local managers and were not necessarily policies of the company as a whole. Consequently, female Wal-Mart employees in Texas are arguing that their new suit will challenge the management of a "discrete group of regional district and store managers." They claim these managers made biased pay and promotion decisions. However, in 2013, a smaller California class action suit against the company was again rejected by a federal district court.

On other issues, Wal-Mart made the news again in 2013 when the National Labor Relations Board found Wal-Mart guilty of illegally penalizing and firing workers who took part in labor protests and strikes. Wal-Mart has already paid $11.7 million in back wages and compensation damages to women in Kentucky who were denied jobs due to their sex.

Investigating the Female/Male Earnings Gap

As a result of changes in law and culture, women began to enter the paid workforce in substantial numbers in the mid- to late-twentieth century. By 2014, 58.1% of adult women held jobs while 72.0% of adult men did. Moreover, along with entering the workforce, women began to ratchet up their education levels. In 1971, 44% of undergraduate college degrees went to women; by 2014, women received 56% of bachelor's degrees. In 1970, women received 5.4% of the degrees from law schools and 8.4% of the degrees from medical schools. By 2014, women were receiving 47% of the law degrees and 48.0% of the medical degrees. These gains in education and experience have reduced the female/male wage gap over time. However, concerns remain about the extent to which women have not yet assumed a substantial share of the positions at the top of the largest companies or in the U.S. Congress.

There are factors that can lower women's average wages. Women are likely to bear a disproportionately large share of household responsibilities. A mother of young children is more likely to drop out of the labor force for several years or work on a reduced schedule than is the father. As a result, women in their 30s and 40s are likely, on average, to have less job experience than men. In the United States, childless women with the same education and experience levels as men are typically paid comparably. However, women with families and children are typically paid about 7% to 14% less than other women of similar education and work experience. (Meanwhile, married men earn about 10% to 15% more than single men with comparable education and work experience.)

The different patterns of family responsibilities possibly could be called discrimination, but it is primarily rooted in America's social patterns of discrimination, which involve the roles that fathers and mothers play in child-rearing, rather than discrimination by employers in hiring and salary decisions.

Investigating the Black/White Earnings Gap

Blacks experienced blatant labor market discrimination during much of the twentieth century. Until the passage of the **Civil Rights Act of 1964**, it was legal in many states to refuse to hire a black worker, regardless of the credentials or experience of that worker. Moreover, blacks were often denied access to educational opportunities, which in turn meant that they had lower levels of qualifications for many jobs. At least one economic study has shown that the 1964 law is partially responsible for the narrowing of the gap in black–white earnings in the late 1960s and into the 1970s; for example, the ratio of total earnings of black male workers to white male workers rose from 62% in 1964 to 75.3% in 2013, according to the Bureau of Labor Statistics.

However, the earnings gap between black and white workers has not changed as much as the earnings gap between men and women has in the last half century. The remaining racial gap seems related both to continuing differences in education levels and to the presence of discrimination. Table 6 shows that the percentage of blacks who complete a four-year college degree remains substantially lower than the percentage of whites who complete college. According to the U.S. Census, both whites and blacks have higher levels of educational attainment than Hispanics and lower levels than Asians. The lower average levels of education for black workers surely explain part of the earnings gap. In fact, black women who have the same levels of education and experience as white women receive, on average, about the same level of pay. One study shows that white and black college graduates have identical salaries immediately after college; however, the racial wage gap widens over time, an outcome that suggests the possibility of continuing discrimination. Another study conducted a field experiment by responding to job advertisements with fictitious resumes with either very African American sounding names or very white sounding names and found out that white names received 50 percent more callbacks for interviews. This is suggestive of discrimination in job opportunities. Further, as the following Clear It Up feature explains, there is evidence to support that discrimination in the housing market is connected to employment discrimination.'

Table 6. Educational Attainment by Race and Ethnicity in 2012. (Source: http://www.census.gov/hhes/socdemo/education/data/cps/2014/tables.html)

	White	Hispanic	Black	Asian
Completed four years of high school or more	89.0%	65.0%	84.2%	88.9%
Completed four years of college or more	29.0%	14.0%	17.0%	52.0%

How is discrimination in the housing market connected to employment discrimination?

In a recent study by the Housing and Urban Development (HUD) department, black homebuyers who ask to look at homes for sale are shown 18 percent fewer homes compared to white homebuyers. Asians are shown 19 percent fewer properties. Additionally, Hispanics experience more discrimination in renting apartments and undergo stiffer credit checks than white renters. In a 2012 study conducted by the U.S. Department of Housing and Urban Development and the nonprofit Urban Institute, Hispanic testers who contacted agents about advertised rental units were given information about 12 percent fewer units available and were shown seven percent fewer units than white renters. The $9 million study, based on research in 28 metropolitan areas, concluded that blatant "door slamming" forms of discrimination are on the decline but that the discrimination that does exist is harder to detect, and as a result, more difficult to remedy. According to the *Chicago Tribune*, HUD Secretary Shaun Donovan told reporters, "Just because it's taken on a hidden form doesn't make it any less harmful. You might not be able to move into that community with the good schools."

The lower levels of education for black workers can also be a result of discrimination—although it may be pre-labor market discrimination, rather than direct discrimination by employers in the labor market. For example, if discrimination in housing markets causes black families to live clustered together in certain poorer neighborhoods, then the black children will continue to have lower educational attainment then their white counterparts and, consequently, not be able to obtain the higher paying jobs that require higher levels of education. Another element to consider is that in the past, when blacks were effectively barred from many high-paying jobs, getting additional education could have seemed somewhat pointless, because the educational degrees would not pay off. Even though labor market discrimination has been legally abolished, it can take some time to establish a culture and a tradition of valuing education highly. Additionally, a legacy of past discrimination may contribute to an attitude that blacks will have a difficult time succeeding in academic subjects. In any case, the impact of social discrimination in labor markets is more complicated than seeking to punish a few bigoted employers.

Competitive Markets and Discrimination

Gary Becker (b. 1930), who won the Nobel Prize in economics in 1992, was one of the first to analyze discrimination in economic terms. Becker pointed out that while competitive markets can allow some employers to practice discrimination, it can also provide profit-seeking firms with incentives not to discriminate. Given these incentives, Becker explored the question of why discrimination persists.

If a business is located in an area with a large minority population and refuses to sell to minorities, it will cut into its own profits. If some businesses run by bigoted employers refuse to pay women and/or minorities a wage based on their productivity, then other profit-seeking employers can hire these workers. In a **competitive market**, if the owners of a business care more about the color of money than about the color of skin, they will have an incentive to make buying, selling, hiring, and promotion decisions strictly based on economic factors.

The power of markets to offer at least a degree of freedom to oppressed groups should not be underestimated. In many countries, cohesive minority groups like Jews and emigrant Chinese have managed to carve out a space for themselves through their economic activities, despite legal and social discrimination against them. Many immigrants, including those who come to the United States, have taken advantage of economic freedom to make new lives for themselves. However, history teaches that market forces alone are unlikely to eliminate discrimination. After all, discrimination against African Americans persisted in the market-oriented U.S. economy during the century between President Abraham Lincoln's Emancipation Proclamation, which freed the slaves in 1863, and the passage of the Civil Rights Act of 1964—and has continued since then, too.

So why does discrimination persist in competitive markets? Gary Becker sought to explain this persistence. Discriminatory impulses can emerge at a number of levels: among managers, among workers, and among customers. Consider the situation of a manager who is not personally prejudiced, but who has many workers or customers who are prejudiced. If that manager treats minority groups or women fairly, the manager may find it hurts the morale of prejudiced co-workers or drives away prejudiced customers. In such a situation, a policy of nondiscrimination could reduce the firm's profits. After all, a business firm is part of society, and a firm that does not follow the societal norms is likely to suffer. Market forces alone are unlikely to overwhelm strong social attitudes about discrimination.

Public Policies to Reduce Discrimination

A first public policy step against discrimination in the labor market is to make it illegal. For example, the Equal Pay Act of 1963 said that men and women who do equal work at a company must be paid the same. The Civil Rights Act of 1964 prohibits employment discrimination based on race, color, religion, sex, or national origin. The Age Discrimination in Employment Act of 1967 prohibited discrimination on the basis of age against individuals who are 40 years of age or older. The Civil Rights Act of 1991 provides monetary damages in cases of intentional employment discrimination. The Pregnancy Discrimination Act of 1978 was aimed at prohibiting discrimination against women in the workplace who are planning to get pregnant, are pregnant, or are returning after pregnancy. Passing a law, however, is only part of the answer, since discrimination by prejudiced employers may be less important than broader social patterns.

These laws against discrimination have reduced the gender wage gap. A study by the Department of Labor in 2007 compared salaries of men and women who have similar educational achievement, work experience, and occupation and found that the gender wage gap is only 5%.

In the case of the earnings gap between blacks and whites (and also between Hispanics and whites), probably the single largest step that could be taken at this point in U.S. history to close the earnings gap would be to reduce the gap in educational achievement. Part of the answer to this issue involves finding ways to improve the performance of schools, which is a highly controversial topic in itself. In addition, the education gap is unlikely to close unless black and Hispanic families and peer groups strengthen their culture of support for educational achievement.

Affirmative action is the name given to active efforts by government or businesses that give special rights to minorities in hiring and promotion to make up for past discrimination. Affirmative action, in its limited and not especially controversial form, means making an effort to reach out to a broader range of minority candidates for jobs. In its more aggressive and controversial form, affirmative action required government and companies to hire a specific number or percentage of minority employees. However, the U.S. Supreme Court has ruled against state affirmative action laws. Today, affirmative action policies are applied only to federal contractors who have lost a discrimination lawsuit. This type of redress is enforced by the federal Equal Employment Opportunity Commission (EEOC).

An Increasingly Diverse Workforce

Racial and ethnic diversity is on the rise in the U.S. population and work force. As Figure 2 shows, while the white Americans composed 78% of the population in 2012, the U.S. Bureau of the Census projects that whites will be 69% of the U.S.

population by 2060. The proportion of U.S. citizens who are of Hispanic background is predicted to rise substantially. Moreover, in addition to expected changes in the population, diversity is being increased in the workforce as the women who entered the workforce in the 1970s and 1980s are now moving up the promotion ladders within their organizations.

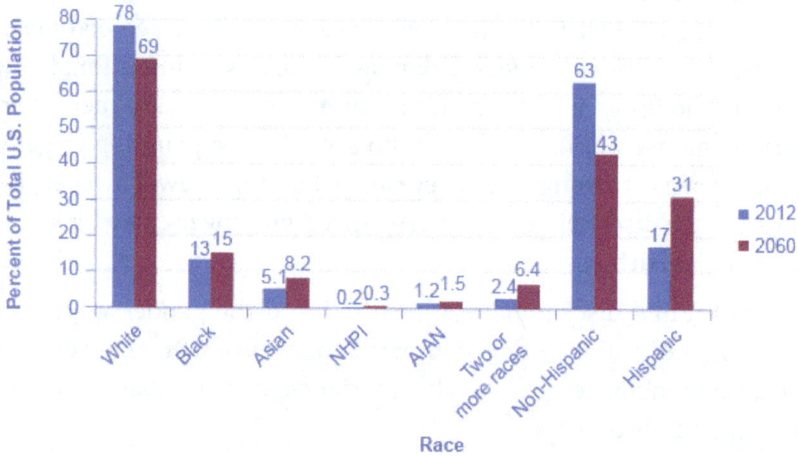

Figure 3.2. Projected Changes in America's Racial and Ethnic Diversity. This figure shows projected changes in the ethnic makeup of the U.S. population by 2060. Note that "NHPI" stands for Native Hawaiian and Other Pacific Islander. "AIAN" stands for American Indian and Alaska Native. Source: US Department of Commerce

Fortune-telling is not economics, but it still can be clarifying to speculate about the future. Optimists argue that the growing proportions of minority workers will knock over remaining discriminatory barriers. The economy will benefit as an increasing proportion of workers from traditionally disadvantaged groups have a greater opportunity to fulfill their potential. Pessimists worry that the social tensions between men and women and between ethnic groups will rise and that workers will be less productive as a result. Anti-discrimination policy, at its best, seeks to help society move toward the more optimistic outcome.

Concepts and Summary

Discrimination occurs in a labor market when workers with the same economic characteristics, such as education, experience, and skill, are paid different amounts because of race, gender, religion, age, or disability status. In the United States, female workers on average earn less than male workers, and black workers on average earn less than white workers. There is controversy over the extent to which these earnings gaps can be explained by discrimination or by differences in factors like education and job experience. Free markets can allow discrimination to occur; but the threat of a loss of sales or a loss of productive workers can also create incentives for a firm not to discriminate. A range of public policies can be used to reduce earnings gaps between men and women or between white and other racial/ethnic groups: requiring equal pay for equal work, and attaining more equal educational outcomes.

21.3 IMMIGRATION

Most Americans would be outraged if a law prevented them from moving to another city or another state. However, when the conversation turns to crossing national borders and are about other people arriving in the United States, laws preventing such movement often seem more reasonable. Some of the tensions over immigration stem from worries over how it might affect a country's culture, including differences in language, and patterns of family, authority, or gender relationships. Economics does not have much to say about such cultural issues. Some of the worries about immigration do, however, have to do with its effects on wages and income levels, and how it affects government taxes and spending. On those topics, economists have insights and research to offer.

Historical Patterns of Immigration

Supporters and opponents of immigration look at the same data and see different patterns. Those who express concern about immigration levels to the United States point to graphics like Figure 3.4 which shows total inflows of immigrants decade by decade through the twentieth century. Clearly, the level of immigration has been high and rising in recent years, reaching and exceeding the towering levels of the early twentieth century. However, those who are less worried about immigration point out that the high immigration levels of the early twentieth century happened when total population was much lower. Since the U.S. population roughly tripled during the twentieth century, the seemingly high levels in immigration in the 1990s and 2000s look relatively smaller when they are divided by the population.

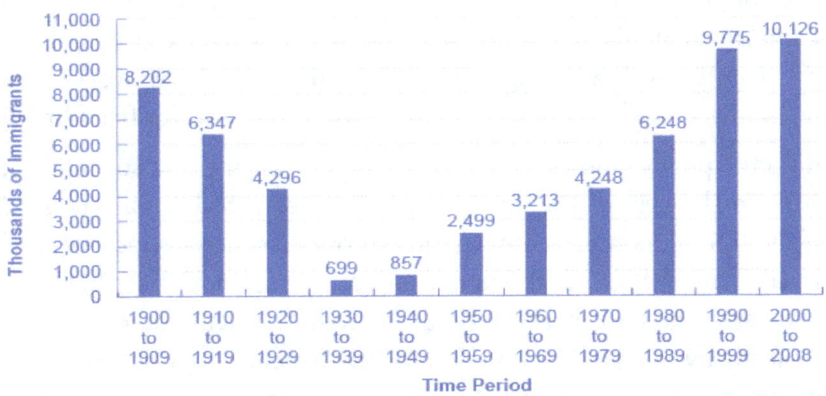

Figure 3.4. Immigration Since 1900. The number of immigrants in each decade declined between 1900 and the 1940s, but has risen sharply in recent decades. (Source: U.S. Department of Homeland Security, Yearbook of Immigration Statistics: 2011, Table 1)

Where have the immigrants come from? Immigrants from Europe were more than 90% of the total in the first decade of the twentieth century, but less than 20% of the total by the end of the century. By the 2000s, about half of U.S. immigration came from the rest of the Americas, especially Mexico, and about a quarter came from various countries in Asia.

Economic Effects of Immigration

A surge of immigration can affect the economy in a number of different ways. In this section, we will consider how immigrants might benefit the rest of the economy, how they might affect wage levels, and how they might affect government spending at the federal and local level.

To understand the economic consequences of immigration, consider the following scenario. Imagine that the immigrants entering the United States matched the existing U.S. population in age range, education, skill levels, family size, occupations, and so on. How would immigration of this type affect the rest of the U.S. economy? Immigrants themselves would be much better off, because their standard of living would be higher in the United States. Immigrants would contribute to both increased production and increased consumption. Given enough time for adjustment, the range of jobs performed, income earned, taxes paid, and public services needed would not be much affected by this kind of immigration. It would be as if the population simply increased a little.

Now, consider the reality of recent immigration to the United States. Immigrants are not identical to the rest of the U.S. population. About one-third of immigrants over the age of 25 lack a high school diploma. As a result, many of the recent immigrants end up in jobs like restaurant and hotel work, lawn care, and janitorial work. This kind of immigration represents a shift to the right in the supply of unskilled labor for a number of jobs, which will lead to lower wages for these jobs. The middle- and upper-income households that purchase the services of these unskilled workers will benefit from these lower wages. However, low-skilled U.S. workers who must compete with low-skilled immigrants for jobs will tend to suffer from immigration.

The difficult policy questions about immigration are not so much about the overall gains to the rest of the economy, which seem to be real but small in the context of the U.S. economy, as they are about the disruptive effects of immigration in specific labor markets. One disruptive effect, as just noted, is that immigration weighted toward low-skill workers tends to reduce wages for domestic low-skill workers. A study by Michael S. Clune found that for each 10% rise in the number of employed immigrants with no more than a high school diploma in the labor market, high school students reduced their annual number of hours worked by 3%. The effects on wages of low-skill workers are not large—perhaps in the range of decline of about

1%. These effects are likely kept low, in part, because of the legal floor of federal and state minimum wage laws. In addition, immigrants are also thought to contribute to increased demand for local goods and services which can stimulate the local low skilled labor market. It is also possible that employers, in face of abundant low-skill workers may choose production processes which are more labor intensive than otherwise would have been. These various factors would explain the small negative wage effect observed among the native low-skill workers as a result of immigration.

Another potential disruptive effect is the impact on the budgets of state and local government. Many of the costs imposed by immigrants are costs that arise in state-run programs, like the cost of public schooling and of welfare benefits. However, many of the taxes that immigrants pay are federal taxes like income taxes and Social Security taxes. Many immigrants do not own property (such as homes and cars), so they do not pay property taxes, which are one of the main sources of state and local tax revenue. Though they do pay sales taxes, which are state and local, and the landlords of property they rent pay property taxes. According to the nonprofit Rand Corporation, the effects of immigration on taxes are generally positive at the federal level, but they are negative at the state and local levels in places where there are many low-skilled immigrants.

Proposals for Immigration Reform

The Congressional Jordan Commission of the 1990s proposed reducing overall levels of immigration and refocusing U.S. immigration policy to give priority to immigrants with a higher level of skills. In the labor market, focusing on high-skilled immigrants would help prevent any negative effects on the wages of low-skilled workers. For government budgets, higher-skilled workers find jobs more quickly, earn higher wages, and pay more in taxes. Several other immigration-friendly countries, notably Canada and Australia, have immigration systems where those with high levels of education or job skills have a much better chance of obtaining permission to immigrate. For the United States, high tech companies regularly ask for a more lenient immigration policy to admit a greater quantity of highly skilled workers. In addition, a current immigration issue deals with the so-called "DREAM Act" legislation not yet passed by Congress, which would offer a path to citizenship for illegal immigrants brought to the United States before the age of 16. However, some state legislatures, such as California, have passed their own Dream Acts.

If the United States decided to reduce immigration substantially, the economic losses would likely be small relative to the overall economy. If the United States decided to increase immigration substantially, the U.S. economy certainly is large enough to afford some additional assistance to low-wage workers or to local governments that might be adversely affected by immigration. Whether immigration levels are increased, decreased, or left the same, the quality of the debate over immigration policy would be improved by an explicit recognition of who receives economic benefits from immigration and who bears its costs.

Collective Bargaining in Wisconsin

Should we end collective bargaining rights for government employees? In an effort to reduce the budget deficit, a contentious Wisconsin law prohibited most public employees from collectively bargaining on anything except wages. Legislators in Wisconsin argued that public safety is so important that public safety workers should be exempted from this. They could not risk firefighters and police going on strike. All firms and employees know that pensions and benefits are expensive; and there was a $3.6 billion budget deficit in Wisconsin that Governor Walker and legislators wanted to decrease. A lingering question is: should the unions have been more willing to shoulder a greater burden of the cost of those benefits? That question suggests that it is the cost, not necessarily the role of the union itself, which is the problem. After all, unions were founded to reduce the disadvantage that single employees face when bargaining with employers. Because so many government employees are union members, collective bargaining is even more important for them.

Ultimately, the benefit of unions is in the impact they have on economic productivity and output. The more productive the union workers become as a result of collective bargaining, the better off the economy will be.

The long-term repercussions of the Wisconsin law have yet to be realized. As a result of this bill, wage increases higher than the rate of inflation for Wisconsin public sector employees must be voted upon. Imagine if you are working for the Wisconsin government, and are able to find a higher-paying job in the private sector. What will you do? If you decide to leave because your options are better elsewhere, then the government must replace you. How will the government find workers to replace you? For some sectors of the government, reduced numbers of workers may mean greater efficiency. For other sectors, though, reduced numbers of government workers may mean reduced services.

Concepts and Summary

The recent level of U.S. immigration is at a historically high level if measured in absolute numbers, but not if measured as a share of population. The overall gains to the U.S. economy from immigration are real but relatively small. However, immigration also causes effects like slightly lower wages for low-skill workers and budget problems for certain state and local governments.

CHAPTER

22 KNOWLEDGE, RISK AND INSURANCE

22.1 IMPERFECT INFORMATION AND ASYMMETRIC INFORMATION PROBLEM

Consider a purchase that many people make at important times in their lives: buying expensive jewelry. In May 1994, Doree Lynn bought an expensive ring from a jeweler in Washington, D.C., which included an emerald that cost $14,500. Several years later, the emerald fractured. Lynn took it to another jeweler who found that cracks in the emerald had been filled with an epoxy resin. Lynn sued the original jeweler in 1997 for selling her a treated emerald without telling her, and won. The case publicized a number of little-known facts about precious stones. Most emeralds have internal flaws, and so they are soaked in clear oil or an epoxy resin to hide the flaws and make the color more deep and clear. Clear oil can leak out over time, and epoxy resin can discolor with age or heat. However, using clear oil or epoxy to "fill" emeralds is completely legal, as long as it is disclosed.

After Doree Lynn's lawsuit, the NBC news show "Dateline" bought emeralds at four prominent jewelry stores in New York City in 1997. All the sales clerks at these stores, unaware that they were being recorded on a hidden camera, said the stones were untreated. When the emeralds were tested at a laboratory, however, it was discovered they had all been treated with oil or epoxy. Emeralds are not the only gemstones that are treated. Diamonds, topaz, and tourmaline are also often irradiated to enhance colors. The general rule is that all treatments to gemstones should be revealed, but often disclosure is not made. As such, many buyers face a situation of **asymmetric information**, where the both parties involved in an economic transaction have an unequal amount of information (one party knows much more than the other).

Many economic transactions are made in a situation of **imperfect information**, where either the buyer, the seller, or both, are less than 100% certain about the qualities of what is being bought and sold. Also, the transaction may be characterized by asymmetric information, in which one party has more information than the other regarding the economic transaction. Let's begin with some examples of how imperfect information complicates transactions in goods, labor, and **financial capital markets.** The presence of imperfect information can easily cause a decline in prices or quantities of products sold. However, buyers and sellers also have incentives to create mechanisms that will allow them to make mutually beneficial transactions even in the face of imperfect information.

If you are unclear about the difference between asymmetric information and imperfect information, read the following Clear It Up feature.

Difference between imperfect and asymmetric information

For a market to reach equilibrium sellers and buyers must have full information about the product's price and quality. If there is limited information, then buyers and sellers may not be able to transact or will possibly make poor decisions.

Imperfect information refers to the situation where buyers and/or sellers do not have all of the necessary information to make an informed decision about the price or quality of a product. The term imperfect information simply means that not all the information necessary to make an informed decision is known to the buyers and/or sellers. Asymmetric information is the condition where one party, either the buyer or the seller, has more information about the quality or price of the product than the other party. In either case (imperfect or asymmetric information) buyers or sellers need remedies to make more informed decisions.

"Lemons" and Other Examples of Imperfect Information

Consider Marvin, who is trying to decide whether to buy a used car. Let's assume that Marvin is truly clueless about what happens inside a car's engine. He is willing to do some background research, like reading Consumer Reports or checking websites that offer information about makes and models of used cars and what they should cost. He might pay a mechanic to inspect the car. Even after devoting some money and time collecting information, however, Marvin still cannot be absolutely sure that he is buying a high-quality used car. He knows that he might buy the car, drive it home, and use it for a few weeks before discovering that car is a "lemon," which is slang for a defective product (especially a car).

Imagine that Marvin shops for a used car and finds two that look very similar in terms of mileage, exterior appearances, and age. One car costs $4,000, while the other car costs $4,600. Which car should Marvin buy?

If Marvin was choosing in a world of perfect information, the answer would be simple: he should buy the cheaper car. But Marvin is operating in a world of imperfect information, where the sellers likely know more about the car's problems than he does, and have an incentive to hide the information. After all, the more problems that are disclosed, the lower the car's selling price.

What should Marvin do? First, he needs to understand that even with imperfect information, prices still reflect information. Typically, used cars are more expensive on some dealer lots because the dealers have a trustworthy reputation to uphold. Those dealers try to fix problems that may not be obvious to their customers, in order to create good word of mouth about their vehicles' long term reliability. The short term benefits of selling their customers a "lemon" could cause a quick collapse in the dealer's reputation and a loss of long term profits. On other lots that are less well-established, one can find cheaper used cars, but the buyer takes on more risk when a dealer's reputation has little at stake. The cheapest cars of all often appear on Craigslist, where the individual seller has no reputation to defend. In sum, cheaper prices do carry more risk, so Marvin should balance his appetite for risk versus the potential headaches of many more unanticipated trips to the repair shop.

Similar problems with imperfect information arise in labor and financial capital markets. Consider Greta, who is applying for a job. Her potential employer, like the used car buyer, is concerned about ending up with a "lemon"—in this case a poor quality employee. The employer will collect information about Greta's academic and work history. In the end, however, a degree of uncertainty will inevitably remain regarding Greta's abilities, which are hard to demonstrate without actually observing her on the job. How can a potential employer screen for certain attributes, such as motivation, timeliness, ability to get along with others, and so on? Employers often look to trade schools and colleges to pre-screen candidates. Employers may not even interview a candidate unless he has a degree and, sometimes, a degree from a particular school. Employers may also view awards, a high grade point average, and other accolades as a signal of hard work, perseverance, and ability. Employers may also seek references for insights into key attributes such as energy level, work ethic, and so on.

How Imperfect Information Can Affect Equilibrium Price and Quantity

The presence of imperfect information can discourage both buyers and sellers from participating in the market. Buyers may become reluctant to participate because they cannot determine the quality of a product. Sellers of high-quality or medium-quality goods may be reluctant to participate, because it is difficult to demonstrate the quality of their goods to buyers—and since buyers cannot determine which goods have higher quality, they are likely to be unwilling to pay a higher price for such goods.

A market with few buyers and few sellers is sometimes referred to as a **thin market**. By contrast, a market with many buyers and sellers is called a **thick market**.

When imperfect information is severe and buyers and sellers are discouraged from participating, markets may become extremely thin as a relatively small number of buyer and sellers attempt to communicate enough information that they can agree on a price.

When Price Mixes with Imperfect Information about Quality

A buyer confronted with imperfect information will often believe that the price being charged reveals something about the quality of the product. For example, a buyer may assume that a gemstone or a used car that costs more must be of higher quality, even though the buyer is not an expert on gemstones. Think of the expensive restaurant where the food must be good because it is so expensive or the shop where the clothes must be stylish because they cost so much, or the gallery where the art must be great, because it costs so much. If you are hiring a lawyer, you might assume that a lawyer who charges $400 per hour must be better than a lawyer who charges $150 per hour. In these cases, price can act as a signal of quality.

When buyers use the market price to draw inferences about the quality of products, then markets may have trouble reaching an equilibrium price and quantity. Imagine a situation where a used car dealer has a lot full of used cars that do not seem to be selling, and so the dealer decides to cut the prices of the cars to sell a greater quantity. In a market with imperfect information, many buyers may assume that the lower price implies low-quality cars. As a result, the lower price may not attract more customers. Conversely, a dealer who raises prices may find that customers assume that the higher price means that cars are of higher quality; as a result of raising prices, the dealer might sell more cars. (Whether or not consumers always behave rationally, as an economist would see it, is the subject of the following Clear It Up feature.)

The idea that higher prices might cause a greater quantity demanded and that lower prices might cause a lower quantity demanded runs exactly counter to the basic model of demand and supply (as outlined in the Demand and Supply chapter). These contrary effects, however, will reach natural limits. At some point, if the price is high enough, the quantity demanded will decline. Conversely, when the price declines far enough, buyers will increasingly find value even if the quality is lower. In addition, information eventually becomes more widely known. An overpriced restaurant that charges more than the quality of its food is worth to many buyers will not last forever.

Is consumer behavior rational?

There is a lot of human behavior out there that mainstream economists have tended to call "irrational" since it is consistently at odds with economists' utility maximizing models. The typical response is for economists to brush these behaviors aside and call them "anomalies" or unexplained quirks.

"If only you knew more economics, you would not be so irrational," is what many mainstream economists seem to be saying. A group known as behavioral economists has challenged this notion, because so much of this so-called "quirky" behavior is extremely common among us. For example, a conventional economist would say that if you lost a $10 bill today, and also got an extra $10 in your paycheck, you should feel perfectly neutral. After all, –$10 + $10 = $0. You are the same financially as you were before. However, behavioral economists have done research that shows many people will feel some negative emotion—anger, frustration, and so forth—after those two things happen. We tend to focus more on the loss than the gain. This is known as "loss aversion," where a $1 loss pains us 2.25 times more than a $1 gain helps us, according to the economists Daniel Kahneman and Amos Tversky in a famous 1979 Econometrica paper. This has implications for investing, as people tend to "overplay" the stock market by reacting more to losses than to gains.

Behavioral economics also tries to explain why people make seemingly irrational decisions in the presence of different situations, or how the decision is "framed." A popular example is outlined here: Imagine you have the opportunity to buy an alarm clock for $20 in Store A. Across the street, you learn, is the exact same clock at Store B for $10. You might say it is worth your time—a five minute walk—to save $10. Now, take a different example: You are in Store A buying a $300 phone. Five minutes away, at Store B, the same phone is $290. You again save $10 by taking a five minute walk. Do you do it?

Surprisingly, it is likely that you would not. Mainstream economists would say "$10 is $10" and that it would be irrational to make a five minute walk for $10 in one case and not the other. However, behavioral economists have pointed out that most of us evaluate outcomes relative to a reference point—here the cost of the product—and think of gains and losses as percentages rather than using actual savings.

Which view is right? Both have their advantages, but behavioral economists have at least shed a light on trying to describe and explain systematic behavior which previously has been dismissed as irrational. If most of us are engaged in some "irrational behavior," perhaps there are deeper underlying reasons for this behavior in the first place.

Mechanisms to Reduce the Risk of Imperfect Information

If you were selling a good like emeralds or used cars where imperfect information is likely to be a problem, how could you reassure possible buyers? If you were buying a good where imperfect information is a problem, what would it take to reassure you? Buyers and sellers in the goods market rely on reputation as well as guarantees, warrantees, and service contracts to assure product quality; in the labor market, occupational licenses and certifications are used to assure competency, while in financial capital market cosigners and collateral are used as insurance against unforeseen, detrimental events.

In the goods market, the seller of a good might offer a **money-back guarantee**, an agreement that functions as a promise of quality. This strategy may be especially important for a company that sells goods through mail-order catalogs or over the web, whose customers cannot see the actual products, because it encourages people to buy something even if they are not certain they want to keep it.

L.L. Bean started using money-back-guarantees in 1911, when the founder stitched waterproof shoe rubbers together with leather shoe tops, and sold them as hunting shoes. He guaranteed satisfaction. However, the stitching came apart and, out of the first batch of 100 pairs that were sold, 90 pairs were returned. L.L. Bean took out a bank loan, repaired all of the shoes, and replaced them. The L.L. Bean reputation for customer satisfaction began to spread. Many firms today offer money-back-guarantees for a few weeks or months, but L.L. Bean offers a complete money-back guarantee. Anything you have bought from L.L. Bean can always be returned, no matter how many years later or what condition the product is in, for a full money-back guarantee.

L.L. Bean has very few stores. Instead, most of its sales are made by mail, telephone, or, now, through their website. For this kind of firm, imperfect information may be an especially difficult problem, because customers cannot see and touch what they are buying. A combination of a money-back guarantee and a reputation for quality can help for a mail-order firm to flourish.

Sellers may offer a **warranty**, which is a promise to fix or replace the good, at least for a certain period of time. The seller may also offer a buyer a chance to buy a **service contract**, where the buyer pays an extra amount and the seller agrees to fix anything that goes wrong for a set time period. Service contracts are often used with large purchases such as cars, appliances and even houses.

Guarantees, warranties, and service contracts are examples of explicit reassurance that sellers provide. In many cases, firms also offer unstated guarantees. For example, some movie theaters might refund the cost of a ticket to a customer who walks out complaining about the show. Likewise, while restaurants do not generally advertise a money-back guarantee or exchange policies, many restaurants allow customers to exchange one dish for another or reduce the price of the bill if the customer is not satisfied.

The rationale for these policies is that firms want repeat customers, who in turn will recommend the business to others; as such, establishing a good reputation is of paramount importance. When buyers know that a firm is concerned about its reputation, they are less likely to worry about receiving a poor-quality product. For example, a well-established grocery store with a good reputation can often charge a higher price than a temporary stand at a local farmer's market, where the buyer may never see the seller again.

Sellers of labor provide information through resumes, recommendations, school transcripts, and examples of their work. Occupational licenses are also used to establish quality in the labor market. Occupational licenses, which are typically issued by government agencies, show that a worker has completed a certain type of education or passed a certain test. Some of the professionals who must hold a license are doctors, teachers, nurses, engineers, accountants, and lawyers. In addition, most states require a license to work as a barber, an embalmer, a dietitian, a massage therapist, a hearing aid dealer, a counselor, an insurance agent, and a real estate broker. Some other jobs require a license in only one state. Minnesota requires a state license to be a field archeologist. North Dakota has a state license for bait retailers. In Louisiana, a state license is needed to be a "stress analyst" and California requires a state license to be a furniture upholsterer. According to a 2013 study from the University of Chicago, about 29% of U.S. workers have jobs that require occupational licenses.

Occupational licenses have their downside as well, as they represent a barrier to entry to certain industries. This makes it more difficult for new entrants to compete with incumbents, which can lead to higher prices and less consumer choice. In industries that require licenses, the government has decided that the additional information provided by licenses outweighs the negative effect on competition.

Are advertisers allowed to benefit from imperfect information?

Many advertisements seem full of imperfect information—at least by what they imply. Driving a certain car, drinking a particular soda, or wearing a certain shoe are all unlikely to bring fashionable friends and fun automatically, if at all. The government rules on advertising, enforced by the **Federal Trade Commission (FTC)**, allow advertising to contain a certain amount of exaggeration about the general delight of using a product. They, however, also demand that if a claim is presented as a fact, it must be true.

Legally, deceptive advertising dates back to the 1950s when Colgate-Palmolive created a television advertisement that seemed to show Rapid Shave shaving cream being spread on sandpaper and then the sand was shaved off the sandpaper. What the television advertisement actually showed was sand sprinkled on Plexiglas—without glue—and then scraped aside by the razor.

In the 1960s, in magazine advertisements for Campbell's vegetable soup, the company was having problems getting an appetizing picture of the soup, because the vegetables kept sinking. So they filled a bowl with marbles and poured the soup over the top, so that the bowl appeared to be crammed with vegetables.

In the late 1980s, the Volvo Company filmed a television advertisement that showed a monster truck driving over cars, crunching their roofs—all except for the Volvo, which did not crush. However, the FTC found in 1991 that the roof of the Volvo used in the filming had been reinforced with an extra steel framework, while the roof supports on the other car brands had been cut.

The Wonder Bread Company ran television advertisements featuring "Professor Wonder," who said that because Wonder Bread contained extra calcium, it would help children's minds work better and improve their memory. The FTC objected, and in 2002 the company agreed to stop running the advertisements.

As can be seen in each of these cases, factual claims about the product's performance are often checked, at least to some extent, by the Federal Trade Commission. Language and images that are exaggerated or ambiguous, but not actually false, are allowed in advertising. Untrue "facts" are not allowed. In any case, an old Latin saying applies when watching advertisements: *Caveat emptor*—that is, "let the buyer beware."

On the buyer's side of the labor market, a standard precaution against hiring a "lemon" of an employee is to specify that the first few months of employment are officially a trial or probationary period, and that the worker can be let go for any reason or no reason after that time. Sometimes workers also receive lower pay during this trial period.

In the financial capital market, before a bank makes a loan, it requires a prospective borrower fill out forms regarding the sources of income; in addition, the bank conducts a credit check on the individual's past borrowing. Another approach is to require a cosigner on a loan; that is, another person or firm who legally pledges to repay some or all of the money if the original borrower does not do so. Yet another approach is to require collateral, often property or equipment that the bank would have a right to seize and sell if the loan is not repaid.

Buyers of goods and services cannot possibly become experts in evaluating the quality of gemstones, used cars, lawyers, and everything else they buy. Employers and lenders cannot be perfectly omniscient about whether possible workers will turn out well or potential borrowers will repay loans on time. But the mechanisms mentioned above can reduce the risks associated with imperfect information so that the buyer and seller are willing to proceed.

Key Concepts and Summary

Many economic transactions are made in a situation of imperfect information, where either the buyer, the seller, or both are less than 100% certain about the qualities of what is being bought and sold. When information about the quality of products is highly imperfect, it may be difficult for a market to exist.

A "lemon" is the name given to a product that turns out, after the purchase, to have low quality. When the seller has more accurate information about the quality of the product than the buyer, the buyer will be hesitant to buy, out of fear of purchasing a "lemon."

Markets have many ways to deal with imperfect information. In goods markets, buyers facing imperfect information about products may depend upon money-back guarantees, warranties, service contracts, and reputation. In labor markets, employers facing imperfect information about potential employees may turn to resumes, recommendations, occupational licenses for certain jobs, and employment for trial periods. In capital markets, lenders facing imperfect information about borrowers may require detailed loan applications and credit checks, cosigners, and collateral.

22.2 INSURANCE AND INACCURATE INFORMATION

Insurance is a method that households and firms use to prevent any single event from having a significant detrimental financial effect. Generally, households or firms with insurance make regular payments, called premiums. The insurance company prices these premiums based on the probability of certain events occurring among a pool of people. Members of the group who then suffer a specified bad experience receive payments from this pool of money.

Many people have several kinds of insurance: health insurance that pays when they receive medical care; car insurance that pays if they are the driver in an automobile accident; house or renter's insurance that pays if possessions are stolen or damaged by fire; and life insurance, which pays for the family if the principal dies. Table 1 lists a set of insurance markets.

Table 1. Some Insurance Markets

Type of Insurance	Who Pays for It?	It Pays Out When . . .
Health insurance	Employers and individuals	Medical expenses are incurred
Life insurance	Employers and individuals	Policyholder dies
Automobile insurance	Individuals	Car is damaged, stolen, or causes damage to others
Property and homeowner's insurance	Homeowners and renters	Dwelling is damaged or burglarized
Liability insurance	Firms and individuals	An injury occurs for which you are partly responsible
Malpractice insurance	Doctors, lawyers, and other professionals	A poor quality of service is provided that causes harm to others

All insurance involves imperfect information in both an obvious way and in a deeper way. At an obvious level, future events cannot be predicted with certainty.

For example, it cannot be known with certainty who will have a car accident, become ill, die, or have his home robbed in the next year. Imperfect information also applies to estimating the risk that something will happen to any individual. It is difficult for an insurance company to estimate the risk that, say, a particular 20-year-old male driver from New York City will have an accident, because even within that group, some drivers will drive more safely than others. Thus, adverse events occur out of a combination of people's characteristics and choices that make the risks higher or lower and then the good or bad luck of what actually happens.

How Insurance Works

A simplified example of automobile insurance might work this way. Suppose that a group of 100 drivers can be divided into three groups. In a given year, 60 of those people have only a few door dings or chipped paint, which costs $100 each. Another 30 of the drivers have medium-sized accidents that cost an average of $1,000 in damages, and 10 of the drivers have large accidents that cost $15,000 in damages. For the moment, let's imagine that at the beginning of any year, there is no way of identifying the drivers who are low-risk, medium-risk, or high-risk. The total damage incurred by car accidents in this group of 100 drivers will be $186,000, that is:

If each of the 100 drivers pays a premium of $1,860 each year, the insurance company will collect the $186,000 that is needed to cover the costs of the accidents that occur.

Since insurance companies have such a large number of clients, they are able to negotiate with providers of health care and other services for lower rates than the individual would be able to get, thus increasing the benefit to consumers of becoming insured and saving the insurance company itself money when it pays out claims.

Insurance companies receive income, as shown in Figure 1, from insurance premiums and investment income. Investment income is derived from investing the funds that insurance companies received in the past but did not pay out as insurance claims in prior years. The insurance company receives a rate of return from investing these funds or reserves. The investments are typically made in fairly safe, liquid (easy to convert into cash) investments, as the insurance companies needs to be able to readily access these funds when a major disaster strikes.

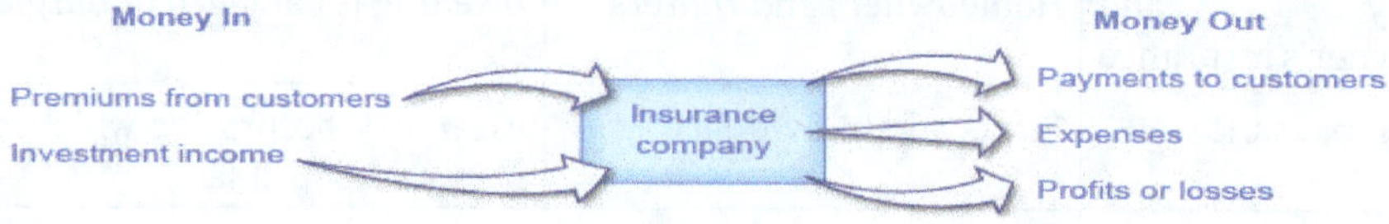

Figure 1. An Insurance Company: What Comes In, What Goes Out. Money flows into an insurance company through premiums and investments and out through the payment of claims and operating expenses.

Government and Social Insurance

Federal and state governments run a number of insurance programs. Some of the programs look much like **private insurance**, in the sense that the members of a group makes steady payments into a fund, and those in the group who suffer an adverse experience receive payments. Other programs protect against risk, but without an explicit fund being set up. Following are some examples.

- **Unemployment insurance**: Employers in every state pay a small amount for unemployment insurance, which goes into a fund that is used to pay benefits to workers for a period of time, usually six months, after they lose their jobs.
- **Pension insurance**: Employers that offer pensions to their retired employees are required by law to pay a small fraction of what they are setting aside for pensions to the Pension Benefit Guarantee Corporation, which is used to pay at least some pension benefits to workers if a company goes bankrupt and cannot pay the pensions it has promised.
- **Deposit insurance**: Banks are required by law to pay a small fraction of their deposits to the Federal Deposit Insurance Corporation, which goes into a fund that is used to pay depositors the value of their bank deposits up to $250,000 (the amount was raised from $100,000 to $250,000 in 2008) if the bank should go bankrupt.
- **Workman's compensation insurance**: Employers are required by law to pay a small percentage of the salaries that they pay into funds, typically run at the state level, that are used to pay benefits to workers who suffer an injury on the job.
- **Retirement insurance**: All workers pay a percentage of their income into Social Security and into Medicare, which then provides income and health care benefits to the elderly. Social Security and Medicare are not literally "insurance" in the sense that those currently contributing to the fund are not eligible for benefits. They function like insurance, however, in the sense that regular payments are made into the programs today in exchange for benefits to be received in the case of a later event—either becoming old or becoming sick when old. Such programs are sometimes called "social insurance."

The major additional costs to insurance companies, other than the payment of claims, are the costs of running a business: the administrative costs of hiring workers, administering accounts, and processing insurance claims. For most insurance companies, the insurance premiums coming in and the claims payments going out are much larger than the amounts earned by investing money or the administrative costs.

Thus, while factors like investment income earned on reserves, administrative costs, and groups with different risks complicate the overall picture, a fundamental law of insurance must hold true: The average person's payments into insurance over time must cover 1) the average person's claims, 2) the costs of running the company, and 3) leave room for the firm's profits. This law can be boiled down to the idea that average premiums and average insurance payouts must be approximately equal.

Risk Groups and Actuarial Fairness

Not all of those who purchase insurance face the same risks. Some people may be more likely, because of genetics or personal habits, to fall sick with certain diseases. Some people may live in an area where car theft or home robbery is more likely than others. Some drivers are safer than others. A risk group can be defined as a group that shares roughly the same risks of an adverse event occurring.

Insurance companies often classify people into risk groups, and charge lower premiums to those with lower risks. If people are not separated into risk groups, then those with low-risk must pay for those with high risks. In the simple example of how car insurance works, given earlier, 60 drivers had very low damage of $100 each, 30 drivers had medium-sized accidents that cost $1,000 each, and 10 of the drivers had large accidents that cost $15,000. If all 100 of these drivers pay the same $1,860, then those with low damages are in effect paying for those with high damages.

If it is possible to classify drivers according to risk group, then each group can be charged according to its expected losses. For example, the insurance company might charge the 60 drivers who seem safest of all $100 apiece, which is the average value of the damages they cause. Then the intermediate group could pay $1,000 apiece and the high-cost group $15,000 each. When the level of insurance premiums that someone pays is equal to the amount that an average person in that risk group would collect in insurance payments, the level of insurance is said to be "actuarially fair."

Classifying people into risk groups can be controversial. For example, if someone had a major automobile accident last year, should that person be classified as a high-risk driver who is likely to have similar accidents in the future, or as a low-risk driver who was just extremely unlucky? The driver is likely to claim to be low-risk, and thus someone who should be in a risk group with those who pay low insurance premiums in the future. The insurance company is likely to believe that, on average, having a major accident is a signal of being a high-risk driver, and thus try to charge this driver higher insurance premiums. The next two sections discuss the two major problems of imperfect information in insurance markets—called moral hazard and adverse selection. Both problems arise from attempts to categorize those purchasing insurance into risk groups.

The Moral Hazard Problem

Moral hazard refers to the case when people engage in riskier behavior with insurance than they would if they did not have insurance. For example, if you have health insurance that covers the cost of visiting the doctor, you may be less likely to take precautions against catching an illness that might require a doctor's visit. If you have car insurance, you will worry less about driving or parking your car in ways that make it more likely to get dented. In another example, a business without insurance might install absolute top-level security and fire sprinkler systems to guard against theft and fire. If it is insured, that same business might only install a minimum level of security and fire sprinkler systems.

Moral hazard cannot be eliminated, but insurance companies have some ways of reducing its effect. Investigations to prevent insurance fraud are one way of reducing the extreme cases of moral hazard. Insurance companies can also monitor certain kinds of behavior; to return to the example from above, they might offer a business a lower rate on property insurance if the business installs a top-level security and fire sprinkler system and has those systems inspected once a year.

Another method to reduce moral hazard is to require the injured party to pay a share of the costs. For example, insurance policies often have **deductibles**, which is an amount that the insurance policyholder must pay out of their own pocket before the insurance coverage starts paying. For example, auto insurance might pay for all losses greater than $500. Health insurance policies often have a **copayment**, in which the policyholder must pay a small amount; for example, a person might have to pay $20 for each doctor visit, and the insurance company would cover the rest. Another method of cost-sharing is **coinsurance**, which means that the insurance company covers a certain percentage of the cost. For example, insurance might pay for 80% of the costs of repairing a home after a fire, but the homeowner would pay the other 20%.

All of these forms of cost-sharing discourage moral hazard, because people know that they will have to pay something out of their own pocket when they make an insurance claim. The effect can be powerful. One prominent study found that when people face moderate deductibles and copayments for their health insurance, they consume about one-third less in medical care than people who have complete insurance and do not pay anything out of pocket, presumably because deductibles and copayments reduce the level of moral hazard. However, those who consumed less health care did not seem to have any difference in health status.

A final way of reducing moral hazard, which is especially applicable to health care, is to focus on the incentives of providers of health care, rather than consumers. Traditionally, most health care in the United States has been provided on a fee-for-service basis, which means that medical care providers are paid for the services they provide and are paid more if they provide additional services. However, in the last decade or so, the structure of healthcare provision has shifted to an emphasis on health maintenance organizations (HMOs). A health maintenance organization (HMO) provides healthcare that receives a fixed amount per person enrolled in the plan—regardless of how many services are provided. In this case, a patient with insurance has an incentive to demand more care, but the healthcare provider, which is receiving only a fixed payment, has an incentive to reduce the moral hazard problem by limiting the quantity of care provided—as long as it will not lead to worse health problems and higher costs later. Today, many doctors are paid with some combination of managed care and fee-for-service; that is, a flat amount per patient, but with additional payments for the treatment of certain health conditions.

Imperfect information is the cause of the moral hazard problem. If an insurance company had perfect information on risk, it could simply raise its premiums every time an insured party engages in riskier behavior. However, an insurance company cannot monitor all the risks that people take all the time and so, even with various checks and cost-sharing, moral hazard will remain a problem.

The Adverse Selection Problem

Adverse selection refers to the problem in which the buyers of insurance have more information about whether they are high-risk or low-risk than the insurance company does. This creates an asymmetric information problem for the insurance company because buyers who are high-risk tend to want to buy more insurance, without letting the insurance company know about their higher risk. For example, someone purchasing health insurance or life insurance probably knows more about their family's health history than an insurer can reasonably find out even with a costly investigation; someone purchasing car insurance may know that they are a high-risk driver who has not yet had a major accident—but it is hard for the insurance company to collect information about how people actually drive.

To understand how adverse selection can strangle an insurance market, recall the situation of 100 drivers who are buying automobile insurance, where 60 drivers had very low damages of $100 each, 30 drivers had medium-sized accidents that cost $1,000 each, and 10 of the drivers had large accidents that cost $15,000. That would equal $186,000 in total payouts by the insurance company. Imagine that, while the insurance company knows the overall size of the losses, it cannot identify the high-risk, medium-risk, and low-risk drivers. However, the drivers themselves know their risk groups. Since there is asymmetric information between the insurance company and the drivers, the insurance company would likely set the price of insurance at $1,860 per year, to cover the average loss (not including the cost of overhead and profit). The result is that those with low risks of only $100 will likely decide not to buy insurance; after all, it makes no sense for them to pay $1,860 per year when they are likely only to experience losses of $100. Those with medium risks of a $1,000 accident will not buy insurance either. So the insurance company ends up only selling insurance for $1,860 to high-risk drivers who will average $15,000 in claims apiece. So the insurance company ends up losing a lot of money. If the insurance company tries to raise its premiums to cover the losses of those with high risks, then those with low or medium risks will be even more discouraged from buying insurance.

Rather than face such a situation of adverse selection, the insurance company may decide not to sell insurance in this market at all. If an insurance market is to exist, then one of two things must happen. First, the insurance company might find some way of separating insurance buyers into risk groups with some degree of accuracy and charging them accordingly, which in practice often means that the insurance company tries not to sell insurance to those who may pose high risks. Or second, those with low risks must be required to buy insurance, even if they have to pay more than the actuarially fair amount for their risk group. The notion that people can be required to purchase insurance raises the issue of government laws and regulations that influence the insurance industry.

U.S. Health Care in an International Context

The United States is the only high-income country in the world where most health insurance is paid for and provided by private firms. Greater government involvement in the provision of health insurance is one possible way of addressing moral hazard and adverse selection problems.

The moral hazard problem with health insurance is that when people have insurance, they will demand higher quantities of health care. In the United States, private healthcare insurance tends to encourage an ever-greater demand for healthcare services, which healthcare providers are happy to fulfill. Table 2 shows that on a per-person basis, U.S. healthcare spending towers above other countries. It should be noted that while healthcare expenditures in the United States are far higher than healthcare expenditures in other countries, the health outcomes in the United States, as measured by life expectancy and lower rates of childhood mortality, tend to be lower. Health outcomes, however, may not be significantly affected by healthcare expenditures. Many studies have shown that a country's health is more closely related to diet, exercise, and genetic factors than to healthcare expenditure. This fact further emphasizes that the United States is spending very large amounts on medical care with little obvious health gain.

In the U.S. health insurance market, the main way of solving this adverse selection problem is that health insurance is often sold through groups based on place of employment, or, under The Affordable Care Act, from a state government sponsored health exchange market. From an insurance company's point of view, selling insurance through an employer mixes together a group of people—some with high risks of future health problems and some with lower risks—and thus reduces the insurance firm's fear of attracting only those who have high risks. However, many small companies do not provide health insurance to their employees, and many lower-paying jobs do not include health insurance. Even after all U.S. government programs that provide health insurance for the elderly and the poor are taken into account, approximately 32 million Americans were without health insurance in 2015. While a government-controlled system can avoid the adverse selection problem entirely by providing at least basic health insurance for all, another option is to mandate that all Americans buy health insurance from some provider by preventing providers from denying individuals based on preexisting conditions. Indeed, this approach was adopted in the Patient Protection and Affordable Care Act, which is discussed later on in this chapter.

Table 2. A Comparison of Healthcare Spending Across Select Countries. (Source: 2010 OECD study and World Fact Book)

Country	Health Care Spending per Person (in 2008)	Male Life Expectancy at Birth, in Years (in 2012)	Female Life Expectancy at Birth, in Years (in 2012)	Male Chance of Dying before Age 5, per 1,000 (in 2012)	Female Chance of Dying before Age 5, per 1,000 (in 2012)
United States	$7,538	76	81	8	7
Germany	$3,737	78	83	4	4
France	$3,696	78	85	4	4
Canada	$4,079	79	84	6	5
United Kingdom	$3,129	78	83	5	4

At its best, the largely private U.S. system of health insurance and healthcare delivery provides an extraordinarily high quality of care, along with generating a seemingly endless parade of life-saving innovations. But the system also struggles to control its high costs and to provide basic medical care to all. Other countries have lower costs and more equal access, but they often struggle to provide rapid access to health care and to offer the near-miracles of the most up-to-date medical care. The challenge is a healthcare system that strikes the right balance between quality, access, and cost.

Government Regulation of Insurance

The U.S. insurance industry is primarily regulated at the state level; indeed, since 1871 there has been a National Association of Insurance Commissioners that brings together these state regulators to exchange information and strategies. The state insurance regulators typically attempt to accomplish two things: to keep the price of insurance low and to make sure that everyone has insurance. These goals, however, can conflict with each other and also become easily entangled in politics.

If insurance premiums are set at actuarially fair levels, so that people end up paying an amount that accurately reflects their risk group, certain people will end up paying a lot. For example, if health insurance companies were trying to cover people who already have a chronic disease like AIDS, or who were elderly, they would charge these groups very high premiums for health insurance, because their expected health care costs are quite high. Women in the age bracket 18–44 consume, on average, about 65% more in health care spending than men. Young male drivers have more car accidents than young female drivers. Thus, actuarially fair insurance would tend to charge young men much more for car insurance than young women. Because people in high-risk groups would find themselves charged so heavily for insurance, they might choose not to buy insurance at all.

State insurance regulators have sometimes reacted by passing rules that attempt to set low premiums for insurance. Over time, however, the fundamental law of insurance must hold: the average amount received by individuals must equal the average amount paid in premiums. When rules are passed to keep premiums low, insurance companies try to avoid insuring any high-risk or even medium-risk parties. If a state legislature passes strict rules requiring insurance companies to sell to everyone at low prices, the insurance companies always have the option of withdrawing from doing business in that state. For example, the insurance regulators in New Jersey are well-known for attempting to keep auto insurance premiums low, and more than 20 different insurance companies stopped doing business in the state in the late 1990s and early 2000s. Similarly, in 2009, State Farm announced that it was withdrawing from selling property insurance in Florida.

In short, government regulators cannot force companies to charge low prices and provide high levels of insurance coverage—and thus take losses—for a sustained period of time. If insurance premiums are going to be set below the actuarially fair level for a certain group, some other group will have to make up the difference. There are two other groups who can make up the difference: taxpayers or other buyers of insurance.

In some industries, the U.S. government has decided free markets will not provide insurance at an affordable price, and so the government pays for it directly. For example, private health insurance is too expensive for many people whose incomes are too low. To combat this, the U.S. government, together with the states, runs the Medicaid program, which provides health care to those with low incomes. Private health insurance also does not work well for the elderly, because their average health care costs can be very high. Thus, the U.S. government started the Medicare program, which provides health insurance to all those over age 65. Other government-funded health-care programs are aimed at military veterans, as an added benefit, and children in families with relatively low incomes.

Another common government intervention in insurance markets is to require that everyone buy certain kinds of insurance. For example, most states legally require car owners to buy auto insurance. Likewise, when a bank loans someone money to buy a home, the person is typically required to have homeowner's insurance, which protects against fire and other physical damage (like hailstorms) to the home. A legal requirement that everyone must buy insurance means that insurance companies do not need to worry that those with low risks will avoid buying insurance. Since insurance companies do not need to fear adverse selection, they can set their prices based on an average for the market, and those with lower risks will, to some extent, end up subsidizing those with higher risks. However, even when laws are passed requiring people to purchase insurance, insurance companies cannot be compelled to sell insurance to everyone who asks—at least not at low cost. Thus, insurance companies will still try to avoid selling insurance to those with high risks whenever possible.

The government cannot pass laws that make the problems of moral hazard and adverse selection disappear, but the government can make political decisions that certain groups should have insurance, even though the private market would not otherwise provide that insurance. Also, the government can impose the costs of that decision on taxpayers or on other buyers of insurance.

The Patient Protection and Affordable Care Act

In March of 2010, President Obama signed into law the **Patient Protection and Affordable Care Act (PPACA)**. This highly contentious law began to be phased in over time starting in October of 2013. The goal of the act is to bring the United States closer to universal coverage. Some of the key features of the plan include:

- Individual mandate: All individuals, who do not receive health care through their employer or through a government program (for example, Medicare), are required to have health insurance or pay a fine. The individual mandate's goal was to reduce the adverse selection problem and keep prices down by requiring all consumers—even the healthiest ones—to have health insurance. Without the need to guard against adverse selection (whereby only the riskiest consumers buy insurance) by raising prices, health insurance companies could provide more reasonable plans to their customers.
- Each state is required to have health insurance exchanges whereby insurance companies compete for business. The goal of the exchanges is to improve competition in the market for health insurance.

- Employer mandate: All employers with more than 50 employees must offer health insurance to their employees.

The Affordable Care Act (ACA) will be funded through additional taxes to include:

- Increase the Medicare tax by 0.9 percent and add a 3.8 percent tax on unearned income for high income taxpayers.
- Charge an annual fee on health insurance providers.
- Impose other taxes such as a 2.3% tax on manufacturers and importers of certain medical devices.

Many people and politicians have sought to overturn the bill. Those that oppose the bill believe it violates an individual's right to choose whether to have insurance or not. In 2012, a number of states challenged the law on the basis that the individual mandate provision is unconstitutional. In June of 2012, the U.S. Supreme Court ruled in a 5–4 decision that the individual mandate is actually a tax, so it is constitutional as the federal government has the right to tax the populace.

Big Deal with Obamacare

What is it that the Affordable Care Act (ACA) will actually do? To begin with, we should note that it is a massively complex law, with a large number of parts, some of which were implemented immediately, and others that will start every year from 2013 through 2020.

As noted in the chapter, people face ever-increasing healthcare costs in the United States. Those with health insurance demand more health care, pushing up the cost. This is one of the problems the ACA is attempting to fix, in part by introducing regulations designed to control increases in healthcare costs. One example is the regulation that caps the amount healthcare providers can spend on administrative costs. Another is a requirement that healthcare providers switch to electronic medical records (EMRs), which will reduce administrative costs.

Another component of the ACA is the requirement that states establish health insurance exchanges, or markets, where people without health insurance, and businesses that do not provide it for their employees, can shop for different insurance plans. Setting up these exchanges reduces the imperfections in the market for insurance and, by adding to the supply of insurance plans, may lead to lower prices if the supply increases more than demand. Also, people who are uninsured tend to use emergency rooms for treatment—the most expensive form of healthcare. Given that there are over 40 million uninsured citizens in the United States, this has contributed significantly to rising costs. Capping administrative costs, requiring the use of EMRs, and establishing health insurance markets for those currently uninsured, are all components of the ACA that are intended to help control increases in healthcare costs.

Over the years, the ranks of the uninsured in the United States have grown as rising prices, designed to offset the problem of distinguishing the high-risk from the low-risk person, have pushed employers and individuals out of the market. Also, insurance companies have increasingly used pre-existing conditions to determine if someone is high risk, and thus they either charge prices based on average costs, or they choose not to insure these groups. This has also contributed to the over 32 million uninsured. The ACA addresses this problem by providing that people with preexisting conditions cannot be denied health insurance.

This presents another selection problem because those with pre-existing conditions are a high-risk group. Taken as a separate group, the law of insurance says they should pay higher prices for insurance. Since they cannot be singled out, prices go up for everyone, and low-risk people leave the group. As the high-risk group gets sicker and more risky, prices go up again, and still more people leave the group, creating an upward spiral in prices. To offset this selection problem, the ACA includes an employer and individual mandate requirement. All businesses and individuals must purchase health insurance.

At the time of this writing, the actual impact of the Patient Protection and Affordable Care Act is still unknown. Due to political opposition and some difficulties with meeting deadlines, several parts of the law have been delayed, and it will be some time before economists are able to collect enough data to determine whether the law has, in fact, increased coverage and lowered costs as was its intent.

Concepts and Summary

Insurance is a way of sharing risk. A group of people pay premiums for insurance against some unpleasant event, and those in the group who actually experience the unpleasant event then receive some compensation. The fundamental law of insurance is that what the average person pays in over time must be very similar to what the average person gets out. In an actuarially fair insurance policy, the premiums that a person pays to the insurance company are the same as the average amount of benefits for a person in that risk group. Moral hazard arises in insurance markets because those who are insured against a risk will have less reason to take steps to avoid the costs from that risk.

Many insurance policies have deductibles, copayments, or coinsurance. A deductible is the maximum amount that the policyholder must pay out-of-pocket before the insurance company pays the rest of the bill. A copayment is a flat fee that an insurance policy-holder must pay before receiving services. Coinsurance requires the policyholder to pay a certain percentage of costs. Deductibles, copayments, and coinsurance reduce moral hazard by requiring the insured party to bear some of the costs before collecting insurance benefits.

In a fee-for-service health financing system, medical care providers are reimbursed according to the cost of services they provide. An alternative method of organizing health care is through health maintenance organizations (HMOs), where medical care providers are reimbursed according to the number of patients they handle, and it is up to the providers to allocate resources between patients who receive more or fewer health care services. Adverse selection arises in insurance markets when insurance buyers know more about the risks they face than does the insurance company. As a result, the insurance company runs the risk that low-risk parties will avoid its insurance because it is too costly for them, while high-risk parties will embrace it because it looks like a good deal to them.

CHAPTER

FINANCIAL MARKETS AND BUSINESS 23

23.1 THE PROCESS BY WHICH BUSINESSES RAISE CAPITAL

Firms often make decisions that involve spending money in the present and expecting to earn profits in the future. Examples include when a firm buys a machine that will last 10 years, or builds a new plant that will last for 30 years, or starts a research and development project. Firms can raise the financial capital they need to pay for such projects in four main ways: (1) from early-stage investors; (2) by reinvesting profits; (3) by borrowing through banks or bonds; and (4) by selling stock. When owners of a business choose sources of financial capital, they also choose how to pay for them.

Early Stage Financial Capital

Firms that are just beginning often have an idea or a prototype for a product or service to sell, but few customers, or even no customers at all, and thus are not earning profits. Such firms face a difficult problem when it comes to raising financial capital: How can a firm that has not yet demonstrated any ability to earn profits pay a rate of return to financial investors?

For many small businesses, the original source of money is the owner of the business. Someone who decides to start a restaurant or a gas station, for instance, might cover the startup costs by dipping into his or her own bank account, or by borrowing money (perhaps using a home as collateral). Alternatively, many cities have a network of well-to-do individuals, known as "angel investors," who will put their own money into small new companies at an early stage of development, in exchange for owning some portion of the firm.

Venture capital firms make financial investments in new companies that are still relatively small in size, but that have potential to grow substantially. These firms gather money from a variety of individual or institutional investors, including banks, institutions like college endowments, insurance companies that hold financial reserves, and corporate pension funds. Venture capital firms do more than just supply money to small startups. They also provide advice on potential products, customers, and key employees. Typically, a venture capital fund invests in a number of firms, and then investors in that fund receive returns according to how the fund as a whole performs.

The amount of money invested in venture capital fluctuates substantially from year to year: as one example, venture capital firms invested more than $48.3 billion in 2014, according to the **National Venture Capital Association.** All early-stage investors realize that the majority of small startup businesses will never hit it big; indeed, many of them will go out of business within a few months or years. They also know that getting in on the ground floor of a few huge successes like a Netflix or an Amazon.com can make up for a lot of failures. Early-stage investors are therefore willing to take large risks in order to be in a position to gain substantial returns on their investment.

Profits as a Source of Financial Capital

If firms are earning profits (their revenues are greater than costs), they can choose to reinvest some of these profits in equipment, structures, and research and development. For many established companies, reinvesting their own profits is one primary source of financial capital. Companies and firms just getting started may have numerous attractive investment opportunities, but few current profits to invest. Even large firms can experience a year or two of earning low profits or even suffering losses, but unless the firm can find a steady and reliable source of financial capital so that it can continue making real investments in tough times, the firm may not survive until better times arrive. Firms often need to find sources of financial capital other than profits.

Borrowing: Banks and Bonds

When a firm has a record of at least earning significant revenues, and better still of earning profits, the firm can make a credible promise to pay interest, and so it becomes possible for the firm to borrow money. Firms have two main methods of borrowing: banks and bonds.

A bank loan for a firm works in much the same way as a loan for an individual who is buying a car or a house. The firm borrows an amount of money and then promises to repay it, including some rate of interest, over a predetermined period of time. If the firm fails to make its loan payments, the bank (or banks) can often take the firm to court and require it to sell its buildings or equipment to make the loan payments.

Another source of financial capital is a bond. A bond is a financial contract: a borrower agrees to repay the amount that was borrowed and also a rate of interest over a period of time in the future. A corporate bond is issued by firms, but bonds are also issued by various levels of government. For example, a municipal bond is issued by cities, a state bond by U.S. states, and a Treasury bond by the federal government through the U.S. Department of the Treasury. A bond specifies an amount that will be borrowed, the interest rate that will be paid, and the time until repayment.

A large company, for example, might issue bonds for $10 million; the firm promises to make interest payments at an annual rate of 8%, or $800,000 per year and then, after 10 years, will repay the $10 million it originally borrowed. When a firm issues bonds, the total amount that is borrowed is divided up. A firm seeks to borrow $50 million by issuing bonds, might actually issue 10,000 bonds of $5,000 each. In this way, an individual investor could, in effect, loan the firm $5,000, or any multiple of that amount. Anyone who owns a bond and receives the interest payments is called a **bondholder**. If a firm issues bonds and fails to make the promised interest payments, the bondholders can take the firm to court and require it to pay, even if the firm needs to raise the money by selling buildings or equipment. However, there is no guarantee the firm will have sufficient assets to pay off the bonds. The bondholders may get back only a portion of what they loaned the firm.

Bank borrowing is more customized than issuing bonds, so it often works better for relatively small firms. The bank can get to know the firm extremely well—often because the bank can monitor sales and expenses quite accurately by looking at deposits and withdrawals. Relatively large and well-known firms often issue bonds instead. They use bonds to raise new financial capital that pays for investments, or to raise capital to pay off old bonds, or to buy other firms. However, the idea that banks are usually used for relatively smaller loans and bonds for larger loans is not an ironclad rule: sometimes groups of banks make large loans and sometimes relatively small and lesser-known firms issue bonds.

Corporate Stock and Public Firms

A corporation is a business that "incorporates"—that is owned by shareholders that have limited liability for the debt of the company but share in its profits (and losses). Corporations may be private or public, and may or may not have stock that is publicly traded. They may raise funds to finance their operations or new investments by raising capital through the sale of stock or the issuance of bonds.

Those who buy the stock become the owners, or shareholders, of the firm. Stock represents ownership of a firm; that is, a person who owns 100% of a company's stock, by definition, owns the entire company. The stock of a company is divided into shares. Corporate giants like IBM, AT&T, Ford, General Electric, Microsoft, Merck, and Exxon all have millions of shares of stock. In most large and well-known firms, no individual owns a majority of the shares of the stock. Instead, large numbers of shareholders—even those who hold thousands of shares—each have only a small slice of the overall ownership of the firm.

When a company is owned by a large number of shareholders, there are three questions to ask:

- How and when does the company get money from the sale of its stock?
- What rate of return does the company promise to pay when it sells stock?
- Who makes decisions in a company owned by a large number of shareholders?

First, a firm receives money from the sale of its stock only when the company sells its own stock to the public (the public includes individuals, mutual funds, insurance companies, and pension funds). A firm's first sale of stock to the public is called an **initial public offering (IPO)**. The IPO is important for two reasons. For one, the IPO, and any stock issued thereafter, such as stock held as treasury stock (shares that a company keeps in their own treasury) or new stock issued later as a secondary offering, provides the funds to repay the early-stage investors, like the angel investors and the venture capital firms. A venture capital firm may have a 40% ownership in the firm. When the firm sells stock, the venture capital firm sells its part ownership of the firm to the public. A second reason for the importance of the IPO is that it provides the established company with financial capital for a substantial expansion of its operations.

Most of the time when corporate stock is bought and sold, however, the firm receives no financial return at all. If you buy shares of stock in General Motors, you almost certainly buy them from the current owner of those shares, and General Motors does not receive any of your money. This pattern should not seem particularly odd. After all, if you buy a house, the current owner gets your money, not the original builder of the house. Similarly, when you buy shares of stock, you are buying a small slice of ownership of the firm from the existing owner—and the firm that originally issued the stock is not a part of this transaction.

Second, when a firm decides to issue stock, it must recognize that investors will expect to receive a rate of return. That rate of return can come in two forms. A firm can make a direct payment to its shareholders, called a **dividend**. Alternatively, a financial investor might buy a share of stock in Wal-Mart for $45 and then later sell that share of stock to someone else for $60, for a gain of $15. The increase in the value of the stock (or of any asset) between when it is bought and when it is sold is called a **capital gain**.

Third: Who makes the decisions about when a firm will issue stock, or pay dividends, or re-invest profits? To understand the answers to these questions, it is useful to separate firms into two groups: private and public.

A private company is owned by the people who run it on a day-to-day basis. A private company can be run by individuals, in which case it is called a sole proprietorship, or it can be run by a group, in which case it is a partnership. A private company can also be a corporation, but with no publicly issued stock. A small law firm run by one person, even if it employs some other lawyers, would be a sole proprietorship. A larger law firm may be owned jointly by its partners. Most private companies are relatively small, but there are some large private corporations, with tens of billions of dollars in annual sales, that do not have publicly issued stock, such as farm products dealer Cargill, the Mars candy company, and the Bechtel engineering and construction firm.

When a firm decides to sell stock, which in turn can be bought and sold by financial investors, it is called a **public company**. Shareholders own a public company. Since the shareholders are a very broad group, often consisting of thousands or even millions of investors, the shareholders vote for a board of directors, who in turn hire top executives to run the firm on a day-to-day basis. The more shares of stock a shareholder owns, the more votes that shareholder is entitled to cast for the company's board of directors.

In theory, the board of directors helps to ensure that the firm is run in the interests of the true owners—the shareholders. However, the top executives who run the firm have a strong voice in choosing the candidates who will be on their board of directors. After all, few shareholders are knowledgeable enough or have enough of a personal incentive to spend energy and money nominating alternative members of the board.

How Firms Choose between Sources of Financial Capital

There are clear patterns in how businesses raise financial capital. These patterns can be explained in terms of imperfect information, which as discussed in Information, Risk, and Insurance, is a situation where buyers and sellers in a market do not both have full and equal information. Those who are actually running a firm will almost always have more information about whether the firm is likely to earn profits in the future than outside investors who provide financial capital.

Any young startup firm is a risk; indeed, some startup firms are only a little more than an idea on paper. The firm's founders inevitably have better information about how hard they are willing to work, and whether the firm is likely to succeed, than anyone else. When the founders put their own money into the firm, they demonstrate a belief in its prospects. At this early stage, angel investors and venture capitalists try to overcome the imperfect information, at least in part, by knowing the managers and their business plan personally and by giving them advice.

Accurate information is sometimes not available because **corporate governance**, the name economists give to the institutions that are supposed to watch over top executives, fails, as the following Clear It Up feature on Lehman Brothers shows.

How did lack of corporate governance lead to the Lehman Brothers failure?

In 2008, Lehman Brothers was the fourth largest U.S. investment bank, with 25,000 employees. The firm had been in business for 164 years. On September 15, 2008, Lehman Brothers filed for Chapter 11 bankruptcy protection. There are many causes of the Lehman Brothers failure. One area of apparent failure was the lack of oversight by the Board of Directors to keep managers from undertaking excessive risk. Part of the oversight failure, according to Tim Geithner's April 10, 2010, testimony to Congress, can be attributed to the Executive Compensation Committee's emphasis on short-term gains without enough consideration of the risks. In addition, according to the court examiner's report, the Lehman Brother's Board of Directors paid too little attention to the details of the operations of Lehman Brothers and also had limited financial service experience.

The board of directors, elected by the shareholders, is supposed to be the first line of corporate governance and oversight for top executives. A second institution of corporate governance is the auditing firm hired to go over the financial records of the company and certify that everything looks reasonable. A third institution of corporate governance is outside investors, especially large shareholders like those who invest large mutual funds or pension funds. In the case of Lehman Brothers, corporate governance failed to provide investors with accurate financial information about the firm's operations.

As a firm becomes at least somewhat established and its strategy appears likely to lead to profits in the near future, knowing the individual managers and their business plans on a personal basis becomes less important, because information has become more widely available regarding the company's products, revenues, costs, and profits. As a result, other outside investors who do not know the managers personally, like bondholders and shareholders, are more willing to provide financial capital to the firm.

At this point, a firm must often choose how to access financial capital. It may choose to borrow from a bank, issue bonds, or issue stock. The great disadvantage of borrowing money from a bank or issuing bonds is that the firm commits to scheduled interest payments, whether or not it has sufficient income. The great advantage of borrowing money is that the firm maintains control of its operations and is not subject to shareholders. Issuing stock involves selling off ownership of the company to the public and becoming responsible to a board of directors and the shareholders.

The benefit of issuing stock is that a small and growing firm increases its visibility in the financial markets and can access large amounts of financial capital for expansion, without worrying about paying this money back. If the firm is successful and profitable, the board of directors will need to decide upon a dividend payout or how to reinvest profits to further grow the company. Issuing and placing stock is expensive, requires the expertise of investment bankers and attorneys, and entails compliance with reporting requirements to shareholders and government agencies, such as the federal Securities and Exchange Commission.

Concepts and Summary

Companies can raise early-stage financial capital in several ways: from their owners' or managers' personal savings, or credit cards and from private investors like angel investors and venture capital firms.

A bond is a financial contract through which a borrower agrees to repay the amount that was borrowed. A bond specifies an amount that will be borrowed, the amounts that will be repaid over time based on the interest rate when the bond is issued, and the time until repayment. Corporate bonds are issued by firms; municipal bonds are issued by cities, state bonds by U.S. states, and Treasury bonds by the federal government through the U.S. Department of the Treasury.

Stock represents ownership of a firm. The stock of a company is divided into shares. A firm receives financial capital when it sells stock to the public. A company's first sale of stock to the public is called the initial public offering (IPO). However, a firm does not receive any funds when one shareholder sells stock in the firm to another investor. The rate of return on stock is received in two forms: dividends and capital gains.

A private company is usually owned by the people who run it on a day-to-day basis, although it can be run by hired managers. A private company owned and run by an individual is called a sole proprietorship, while a firm owned run by a group is called a partnership. When a firm decides to sell stock that can be bought and sold by financial investors, then the firm is owned by its shareholders—who in turn elect a board of directors to hire top day-to-day management—and is called a public company. Corporate governance is the name economists give to the institutions that are supposed to watch over top executives, though it does not always work.

23.2 HOW HOUSEHOLDS PROVIDE CAPITAL FOR THE ECONOMY

The ways in which firms would prefer to raise funds are only half the story of financial markets. The other half is what those households and individuals who supply funds desire, and how they perceive the available choices. The focus of our discussion now shifts from firms on the demand side of financial capital markets to households on the supply side of those markets. The mechanisms for saving available to households can be divided into several categories: deposits in bank accounts; bonds; stocks; money market mutual funds; stock and bond mutual funds; and housing and other tangible assets like owning gold. Each of these investments needs to be analyzed in terms of three factors: (1) the expected rate of return it will pay; (2) the risk that the return will be much lower or higher than expected; and (3) the liquidity of the investment, which refers to how easily money or financial assets can be exchanged for a good or service. We will do this analysis as we discuss each of these investments in the sections below. First, however, we need to understand the difference between expected rate of return, risk, and actual rate of return.

Expected Rate of Return, Risk, and Actual Rate of Return

The expected rate of return refers to how much a project or an investment is expected to return to the investor, either in future interest payments, capital gains, or increased profitability. It is usually the average return over a period of time, usually in years or even decades. Risk measures the uncertainty of that project's profitability. There are several types of risk, including default risk and interest rate risk. Default risk, as its name suggests, is the risk that the borrower fails to pay back the bond. Interest rate risk is the danger that you might buy a long term bond at a 6% interest rate right before market rates suddenly raise, so had you waited, you could have gotten a similar bond that paid 9%. A high-risk investment is one for which a wide range of potential payoffs is reasonably probable. A low-risk investment will have actual returns that are fairly close to its expected rate of return year after year. A high-risk investment will have actual returns that are much higher than the expected rate of return in some months or years and much lower in other months or years. The actual rate of return refers to the total rate of return, including capital gains and interest paid on an investment at the end of a period of time.

Bank Accounts

An intermediary is one who stands between two other parties; for example, a person who arranges a blind date between two other people is one kind of intermediary. In financial capital markets, banks are an example of a **financial intermediary**—that is, an institution that operates between a saver who deposits funds in a bank and a borrower who receives a loan from that bank. When a bank serves as a financial intermediary, unlike the situation with a couple on a blind date, the saver and the borrower never meet. In fact, it is not even possible to make direct connections between those who deposit funds in banks and those who borrow from banks, because all funds deposited end up in one big pool, which is then loaned out.

Figure 1 illustrates the position of banks as a financial intermediary, with a pattern of deposits flowing into a bank and loans flowing out, and then repayment of the loans flowing back to the bank, with interest payments for the original savers.

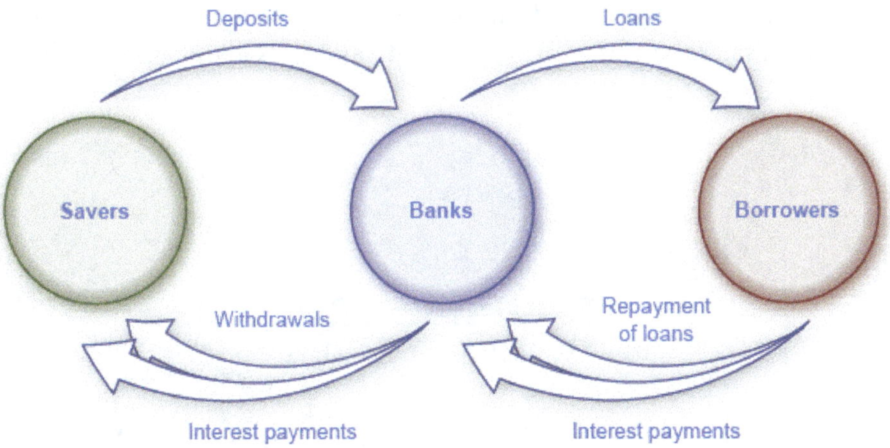

Figure 1. Banks as Financial Intermediaries. Banks are a financial intermediary because they stand between savers and borrowers. Savers place deposits with banks, and then receive interest payments and withdraw money. Borrowers receive loans from banks, and repay the loans with interest.

Banks offer a range of accounts to serve different needs. A checking account typically pays little or no interest, but it facilitates transactions by giving you easy access to your money, either by writing a check or by using a debit card (that is, a card which works like a credit card, except that purchases are immediately deducted from your checking account rather than being billed separately through a credit card company). A savings account typically pays some interest rate, but getting the money typically requires you to make a trip to the bank or an automatic teller machine (or you can access the funds electronically). The lines between checking and savings accounts have blurred in the last couple of decades, as many banks offer checking accounts that will pay an interest rate similar to a savings account if you keep a certain minimum amount in the account, or conversely, offer savings accounts that allow you to write at least a few checks per month.

Another way to deposit savings at a bank is to use a **certificate of deposit (CD)**. With a CD, as it is commonly called, you agree to deposit a certain amount of money, often measured in thousands of dollars, in the account for a stated period of time, typically ranging from a few months to several years. In exchange, the bank agrees to pay a higher interest rate than for a regular savings account. While you can withdraw the money before the allotted time, as the advertisements for CDs always warn, there is "a substantial penalty for early withdrawal."

Figure 2 shows the annual rate of interest paid on a six-month, one-year, and five-year CD since 1984, as reported by Bankrate.com. The interest rates paid by savings accounts are typically a little lower than the CD rate, because financial investors need to receive a slightly higher rate of interest as compensation for promising to leave deposits untouched for a period of time in a CD, and thus giving up some liquidity.

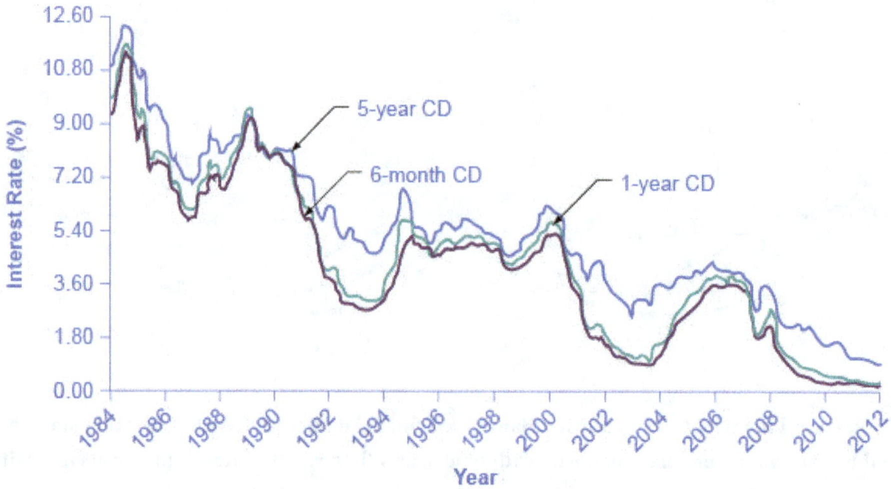

Figure 2. Interest Rates on Six-Month, One-Year, and Five-Year Certificates of Deposit. The interest rates on certificates of deposit have fluctuated over time. The high interest rates of the early 1980s are indicative of the relatively high inflation rate in the United States at that time. Interest rates fluctuate with the business cycle, typically increasing during expansions and decreasing during a recession. Note the steep decline in CD rates since 2008, the beginning of the Great Recession.

The great advantages of bank accounts are that financial investors have very easy access to their money, and also money in bank accounts is extremely safe. In part, this safety arises because a bank account offers more security than keeping a few thousand dollars in the toe of a sock in your underwear drawer. In addition, the Federal Deposit Insurance Corporation (FDIC) protects the savings of the average person. Every bank is required by law to pay a fee to the FDIC, based on the size of its deposits. Then, if a bank should happen to go bankrupt and not be able to repay depositors, the FDIC guarantees that all customers will receive their deposits back up to $250,000.

The bottom line on bank accounts looks like this: low risk means low rate of return but high liquidity.

Bonds

An investor who buys a bond expects to receive a rate of return. However, bonds vary in the rates of return that they offer, according to the riskiness of the borrower. An interest rate can always be divided up into three components (as explained in Choice in a World of Scarcity): compensation for delaying consumption, an adjustment for an inflationary rise in the overall level of prices, and a risk premium that takes the borrower's riskiness into account.

The U.S. government is considered to be an extremely safe borrower, so when the U.S. government issues Treasury bonds, it can pay a relatively low rate of interest. Firms that appear to be safe borrowers, perhaps because of their sheer size or because they have consistently earned profits over time, will still pay a higher interest rate than the U.S. government. Firms that appear to be riskier borrowers, perhaps because they are still growing or their businesses appear shaky, will pay the highest interest rates when they issue bonds. Bonds that offer high interest rates to compensate for their relatively high chance of default are called **high yield bonds** or **junk bonds**. A number of today's well-known firms issued junk bonds in the 1980s when they were starting to grow, including Turner Broadcasting and Microsoft.

A bond issued by the U.S. government or a large corporation may seem to be relatively low risk: after all, the issuer of the bond has promised to make certain payments over time, and except for rare cases of bankruptcy, these payments will be made. If the issuer of a corporate bond fails to make the payments that it owes to its bondholders, the bondholders can require that the company declare bankruptcy, sell off its assets, and pay them as much as it can. Even in the case of junk bonds, a wise investor can reduce the risk by purchasing bonds from a wide range of different companies since, even if a few firms go broke and do not pay, they are not all likely to go bankrupt.

As we noted before, bonds carry an interest rate risk. For example, imagine you decide to buy a 10-year bond that would pay an annual interest rate of 8%. Soon after you buy the bond, interest rates on bonds rise, so that now similar companies are paying an annual rate of 12%. Anyone who buys a bond now can receive annual payments of $120 per year, but since your bond was issued at an interest rate of 8%, you have tied up $1,000 and receive payments of only $80 per year. In the meaningful sense of opportunity cost, you are missing out on the higher payments that you could have received. Furthermore, the amount you should be willing to pay now for future payments can be calculated. To place a present discounted value on a future payment, decide what you would need in the present to equal a certain amount in the future. This calculation will require an interest rate. For example, if the interest rate is 25%, then a payment of $125 a year from now will have a present discounted value of $100—that is, you could take $100 in the present and have $125 in the future. (This is discussed further in the appendix on Present Discounted Value.)

In financial terms, a bond has several parts. A bond is basically an "I owe you" note that is given to an investor in exchange for capital (money). The bond has a face value. This is the amount the borrower agrees to pay the investor at maturity. The bond has a coupon rate or interest rate, which is usually semi-annual, but can be paid at different times throughout the year. (Bonds used to be paper documents with coupons that were clipped and turned in to the bank to receive interest.) The bond has a maturity date when the borrower will pay back its face value as well as its last interest payment. Combining the bond's face value, interest rate, and maturity date, and market interest rates, allows a buyer to compute a bond's present value, which is the most that a buyer would be willing to pay for a given bond. This may or may not be the same as the face value.

The **bond yield** measures the rate of return a bond is expected to pay over time. Bonds are bought not only when they are issued; they are also bought and sold during their lifetimes. When buying a bond that has been around for a few years, investors should know that the interest rate printed on a bond is often not the same as the bond yield, even on new bonds. Read the next Work It Out feature to see how this happens.

Calculating the Bond Yield

You have bought a $1,000 bond whose coupon rate is 8%. To calculate your return or yield, follow these steps:

- Assume the following:
- Consider the risk of the bond. If this bond carries no risk, then it would be safe to assume that the bond will sell for $1,000 when it is issued and pay the purchaser $80 per year until its maturity, at which time the final interest payment will be made and the original $1,000 will be repaid. Now, assume that over time the interest rates prevailing in the economy rise to 12% and that there is now only one year left to this bond's maturity. This makes the bond an unattractive investment, since an investor can find another bond that perhaps pays 12%. To induce the investor to buy the 8% bond, the bond seller will lower its price below its face value of $1,000.
- Calculate the price of the bond when its interest rate is less than the market interest rate. The expected payments from the bond one year from now are $1,080, because in the bond's last year the issuer of the bond will make the final interest payment and then also repay the original $1,000. Given that interest rates are now 12%, you know that you could invest $964 in an alternative investment and receive $1,080 a year from now; that is:

$$\$964(1 + 0.12) = \$1080$$

  Therefore, you will not pay more than $964 for the original $1,000 bond.
- Consider that the investor will receive the $1,000 face value, plus $80 for the last year's interest payment. The yield on the bond will be:

$$(\$1080 - \$964)/\$964 = 12\%$$

- The yield, or total return, means interest payments, plus capital gains. Note that the interest or coupon rate of 8% did not change. When interest rates rise, bonds previously issued at lower interest rates will sell for less than face value. Conversely, when interest rates fall, bonds previously issued at higher interest rates will sell for more than face value.

Figure 3 shows bond yield for two kinds of bonds: 10-year Treasury bonds (which are officially called "notes") and corporate bonds issued by firms that have been given an AAA rating as relatively safe borrowers by Moody's, an independent firm that publishes such ratings. Even though corporate bonds pay a higher interest rate, because firms are riskier borrowers than the federal government, the rates tend to rise and fall together. Treasury bonds typically pay more than bank accounts, and corporate bonds typically pay a higher interest rate than Treasury bonds.

Figure 3. Interest Rates for Corporate Bonds and Ten-Year U.S. Treasury Bonds. The interest rates for corporate bonds and U.S. Treasury bonds (officially "notes") rise and fall together, depending on conditions for borrowers and lenders in financial markets for borrowing. The corporate bonds always pay a higher interest rate, to make up for the higher risk they have of defaulting compared with the U.S. government.

The bottom line for bonds: rate of return—low to moderate, depending on the risk of the borrower; risk—low to moderate, depending on whether interest rates in the economy change substantially after the bond is issued; liquidity—moderate, because the bond needs to be sold before the investor regains the cash.

Stocks

As stated earlier, the rate of return on a financial investment in a share of stock can come in two forms: as dividends paid by the firm and as a capital gain achieved by selling the stock for more than you paid. The range of possible returns from buying stock is mind-bending. Firms can decide to pay dividends or not. A stock price can rise to a multiple of its original price or sink all the way to zero. Even in short periods of time, well-established companies can see large movements in the price of their stock. For example, in July 1, 2011, Netflix stock peaked at $295 per share; one year later, on July 30, 2012, it was at $53.91 per share; in 2015, it had recovered to $414. When Facebook went public, its shares of stock sold for around $40 per share, but in 2015, they were selling for slightly over $83.

The reasons why stock prices fall and rise so abruptly will be discussed below, but first you need to know how we measure stock market performance. There are a number of different ways of measuring the overall performance of the stock market, based on averaging the stock prices of different subsets of companies. Perhaps the best-known measure of the stock markets is the Dow Jones Industrial Average, which is based on the stock prices of 30 large U.S. companies. Another gauge of stock market performance, the Standard & Poor's 500, follows the stock prices of the 500 largest U.S. companies. The Wilshire 5000 tracks the stock prices of essentially all U.S. companies that have stock the public can buy and sell.

Other measures of stock markets focus on where stocks are traded. For example, the New York Stock Exchange monitors the performance of stocks that are traded on that exchange in New York City. The Nasdaq stock market includes about 3,600 stocks, with a concentration of technology stocks. Table 1 lists some of the most commonly cited measures of U.S. and international stock markets.

Table 1. Some Measures of Stock Markets

Measure of the Stock Market	Comments
Dow Jones Industrial Average (DJIA): http://indexes.dowjones.com	Based on 30 large companies from a diverse set of representative industries, chosen by analysts at Dow Jones and Company. The index was started in 1896.
Standard & Poor's 500: http://www.standardandpoors.com	Based on 500 large U.S. firms, chosen by analysts at Standard & Poor's to represent the economy as a whole.
Wilshire 5000: http://www.wilshire.com	Includes essentially all U.S. companies with stock ownership. Despite the name, this index includes about 7,000 firms.
New York Stock Exchange: http://www.nyse.com	The oldest and largest U.S. stock market, dating back to 1792. It trades stocks for 2,800 companies of all sizes. It is located at 18 Broad St. in New York City.
NASDAQ: http://www.nasdaq.com	Founded in 1971 as an electronic stock market, allowing people to buy or sell from many physical locations. It has about 3,600 companies.
FTSE: http://www.ftse.com	Includes the 100 largest companies on the London Stock Exchange. Pronounced "footsie." Originally stood for Financial Times Stock Exchange.
Nikkei: http://www.nikkei.co.jp/nikkeiinfo/en/	Nikkei stands for Nihon Keizai Shimbun, which translates as the Japan Economic Journal, a major business newspaper in Japan. Index includes the 225 largest and most actively traded stocks on the Tokyo Stock Exchange.
DAX: http://www.exchange.de	Tracks 30 of the largest companies on the Frankfurt, Germany, stock exchange. DAX is an abbreviation for Deutscher Aktien Index.

The trend in the stock market is generally up over time, but with some large dips along the way. Figure 4 shows the path of the Standard & Poor's 500 index (which is measured on the left-hand vertical axis) and the Dow Jones Index (which is measured on the right-hand vertical axis). Broad measures of the stock market, like the ones listed here, tend to move together. The S&P 500 Index is the weighted average market capitalization of the firms selected to be in the index. The Dow Jones Industrial Average is the price weighted average of 30 industrial stocks tracked on the New York Stock Exchange.

When the Dow Jones average rises from 5,000 to 10,000, you know that the average price of the stocks in that index has roughly doubled. Figure 4 shows that stock prices did not rise much in the 1970s, but then started a steady climb in the 1980s. From 2000 to 2013, stock prices bounced up and down, but ended up at about the same level.

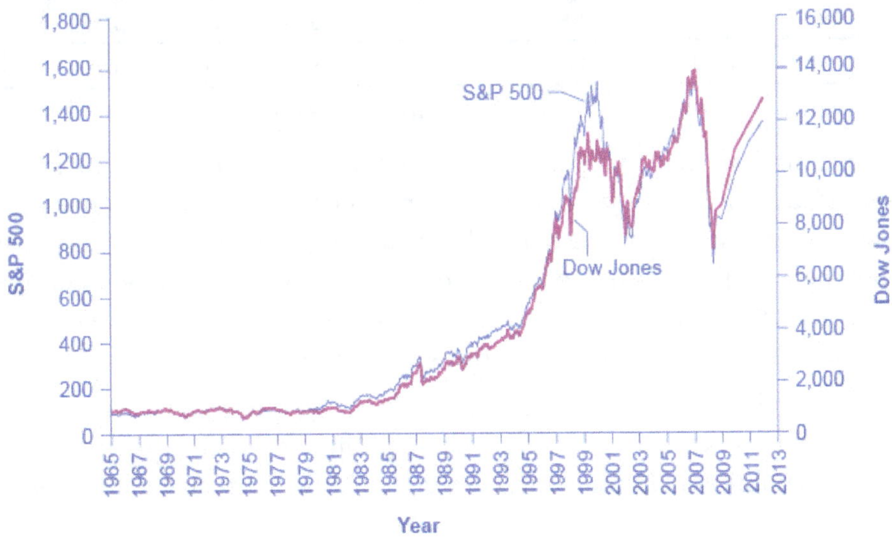

Figure 4. The Dow Jones Industrial Index and the Standard & Poor's 500, 1965–2013. Stock prices rose dramatically from the 1980s up to about 2000. From 2000 to 2013, stock prices bounced up and down, but ended up at about the same level.

Table 2 shows the total annual rate of return an investor would have received from buying the stocks in the S&P 500 index over recent decades. The total return here includes both dividends paid by these companies and also capital gains arising from increases in the value of the stock. (For technical reasons related to how the numbers are calculated, the dividends and capital gains do not add exactly to the total return.) From the 1950s to the 1980s, the average firm paid annual dividends equal to about 4% of the value of its stock. Since the 1990s, dividends have dropped and now often provide a return closer to 1% to 2%. In the 1960s and 1970s, the gap between percent earned on capital gains and dividends was much closer than it has been since the 1980s. In the 1980s and 1990s, however, capital gains were far higher than dividends. In the 2000s, dividends remained low and, while stock prices fluctuated, they ended the decade roughly where they had started.

Table 2. Annual Returns on S&P 500 Stocks, 1950–2012

Period	Total Annual Return	Capital Gains	Dividends
1950–1959	19.25%	13.58%	4.99%
1960–1969	7.78%	4.39%	3.25%
1970–1979	5.88%	1.60%	4.20%
1980–1989	17.55%	12.59%	4.40%
1990–1999	18.21%	15.31%	2.51%
2000–2009	-1.00%	-2.70%	1.70%
2010	15.06%	13.22%	1.84%
2011	2.11%	0.04%	2.07%
2012	16.00%	13.87%	2.13%

The overall pattern is that stocks as a group have provided a high rate of return over extended periods of time, but this return comes with risks. The market value of individual companies can rise and fall substantially, both over short time periods and over the long run. During extended periods of time like the 1970s or the first decade of the 2000s, the overall return on the stock market can be quite modest. The stock market can sometimes fall sharply, as it did in 2008.

The bottom line on investing in stocks is that the rate of return over time will be high, but the risks are also high, especially in the short run; liquidity is also high since stock in publicly held companies can be readily sold for spendable money.

Mutual Funds

Buying stocks or bonds issued by a single company is always somewhat risky. An individual firm may find itself buffeted by unfavorable supply and demand conditions or hurt by unlucky or unwise managerial decisions. Thus, a standard recommendation from financial investors is **diversification**, which means buying stocks or bonds from a wide range of companies. A saver who diversifies is following the old proverb: "Don't put all your eggs in one basket." In any broad group of companies, some firms will do better than expected and some will do worse—but the extremes have a tendency to cancel out extreme increases and decreases in value.

Purchasing a diversified group of the stocks or bonds has gotten easier in the Internet age, but it remains something of a task. To simplify the process, companies offer **mutual funds**, which are organizations that buy a range of stocks or bonds from different companies. The financial investor buys shares of the mutual fund, and then receives a return based on how the fund as a whole performs. In 2012, according to the Investment Company Factbook, about 44% of U.S. households had a financial investment in a mutual fund—including many people who have their retirement savings or pension money invested in this way.

Mutual funds can be focused in certain areas: one mutual fund might invest only in stocks of companies based in Indonesia, or only in bonds issued by large manufacturing companies, or only in stock of biotechnology companies. At the other end of the spectrum, a mutual fund might be quite broad; at the extreme, some mutual funds own a tiny share of every firm in the stock market, and thus the value of the mutual fund will fluctuate with the average of the overall stock market. A mutual fund that seeks only to mimic the overall performance of the market is called an **index fund**.

Diversification can offset some of the risks of individual stocks rising or falling. Even investors who buy an indexed mutual fund designed to mimic some measure of the broad stock market, like the Standard & Poor's 500, had better buckle their seatbelts against some ups and downs, like those the stock market experienced in the first decade of the 2000s. In 2008 average U.S. stock funds declined 38%, reducing the wealth of individuals and households. This steep drop in value hit hardest those who were close to retirement and were counting on their stock funds to supplement retirement income.

The bottom line on investing in mutual funds is that the rate of return over time will be high; the risks are also high, but the risks and returns for an individual mutual fund will be lower than those for an individual stock. As with stocks, liquidity is also high provided the mutual fund or stock index fund is readily traded.

Housing and Other Tangible Assets

Households can also seek a rate of return by purchasing tangible assets, especially housing. About two-thirds of U.S. households own their own home. An owner's equity in a house is the monetary value the owner would have after selling the house and repaying any outstanding bank loans used to buy the house. For example, imagine that you buy a house for $200,000, paying 10% of the price as a down payment and taking out a bank loan for the remaining $180,000. Over time, you pay off some of your bank loan, so that only $100,000 remains, and the value of the house on the market rises to $250,000. At that point, your equity in the home is the value of the home minus the value of the loan outstanding, which is $150,000. For many middle-class Americans, home equity is their single greatest financial asset. The total value of all home equity held by U.S. households was $11.3 trillion at the end of 2015, according to Federal Reserve Data.

Investment in a house is tangibly different from bank accounts, stocks, and bonds because a house offers both a financial and a nonfinancial return. If you buy a house to live in, part of the return on your investment occurs from your consumption of "housing services"—that is, having a place to live. (Of course, if you buy a home and rent it out, you receive rental payments for the housing services you provide, which would offer a financial return.) Buying a house to live in also offers the possibility of a capital gain from selling the house in the future for more than you paid for it. There can, however, be different outcomes, as the Clear It Up on the housing market shows.

Housing prices have usually risen steadily over time; for example, the median sales price for an existing one-family home was $122,900 in 1990, but $294,000 in 2015. Over these 23 years, home prices increased an average of 3.1% per year, which is an average financial return over this time. Figure 5 shows U.S. Census data for the median average sales price of a house in the United States over this time period.

However, the possible capital gains from rising housing prices are riskier than these national price averages. Certain regions of the country or metropolitan areas have seen drops in housing prices over time. The median housing price for the United States as a whole fell almost 7% in 2008 and again in 2009, dropping the median price from $247,900 to $216,700. As of 2015, home values had almost recovered to their pre-recession levels.

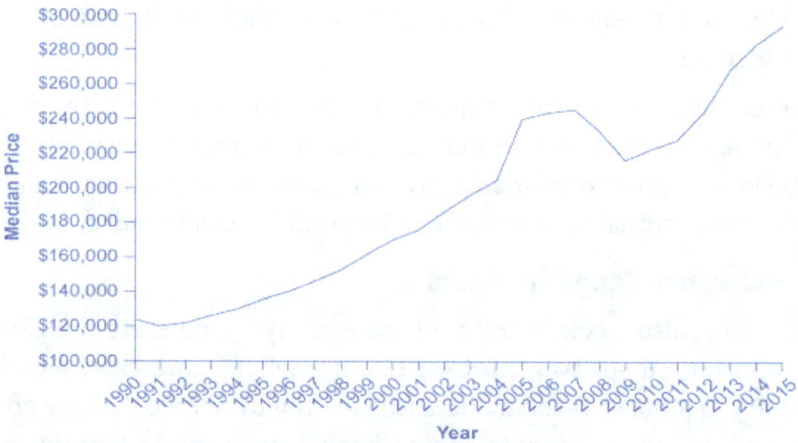

Figure 5. The Median Average Sales Price for New Single-Family Homes, 1990–2015. The median price is the price where half of sales prices are higher and half are lower. The median sales price for an new one-family home was $122,900 in 1990. It rose as high as $248,000 in 2007, before falling to $232,000 in 2008. In 2015, the median sales price was $294,000. Of course, this national figure conceals many local differences, like the areas where housing prices are higher or lower, or how housing prices have risen or fallen at certain times. (Source: U.S. Census)

Investors can also put money into other tangible assets such as gold, silver, and other precious metals, or in duller commodities like sugar, cocoa, coffee, orange juice, oil, and natural gas. The return on these investments derives from the saver's hope of buying low, selling high, and receiving a capital gain. Investing in, say, gold or coffee offers relatively little in the way of nonfinancial benefits to the user (unless the investor likes to caress gold or gaze upon a warehouse full of coffee). Indeed, typically investors in these commodities never even see the physical goods; instead, they sign a contract that takes ownership of a certain quantity of these commodities, which are stored in a warehouse, and later they sell the ownership to someone else. As one example, from 1981 to 2005, the price of gold generally fluctuated between about $300 and $500 per ounce, but then rose sharply to over $1,100 per ounce by early 2010.

A final area of tangible assets are "collectibles" like paintings, fine wine, jewelry, antiques, or even baseball cards. Most collectibles provide returns both in the form of services or of a potentially higher selling price in the future. You can use paintings by hanging them on the wall; jewelry by wearing it; baseball cards by displaying them. You can also hope to sell them someday for more than you paid for them. However, the evidence on prices of collectibles, while scanty, is that while they may go through periods where prices skyrocket for a time, you should not expect to make a higher-than-average rate of return over a sustained period of time from investing in this way.

The bottom line on investing in tangible assets: rate of return—moderate, especially if you can receive nonfinancial benefits from, for example, living in the house; risk—moderate for housing or high if you buy gold or baseball cards; liquidity—low, because it often takes considerable time and energy to sell a house or a piece of fine art and turn your capital gain into cash. The next Clear It Up feature explains the issues in the recent U.S. housing market crisis.

What was all the commotion in the recent U.S. housing market?

The cumulative average growth rate in housing prices from 1981 to 2000 was 5.1%. The price of an average U.S. home then took off from 2003 to 2005, rising at more than 10% per year. No serious analyst believed this rate of growth was sustainable; after all, if housing prices grew at, say, 11% per year over time, the average price of a home would more than double every seven years. However, at the time many serious analysts saw no reason for deep concern. After all, housing prices often change in fits and starts, like all prices, and a price surge for a few years is often followed by prices that are flat or even declining a bit as local markets adjust.

The sharp rise in housing prices was driven by a high level of demand for housing. Interest rates were low, so people were encouraged to borrow money to buy a house. Banks became much more flexible in their lending, making what were called "subprime" loans. Banks loaned money with low, or sometimes no, down payment. They offered loans with very low payments for the first two years, but then much higher payments after that; the idea was that housing prices would keep rising, so the borrower would just refinance the mortgage two years in the future, and thus would not ever have to make the higher payments. Some banks even offered so-called NINJA loans, which meant a loan given even though the borrower had No Income, No Job or Assets.

In retrospect, these loans seem nearly crazy. Many borrowers figured, however, that as long as housing prices kept rising, it made sense to buy. Many lenders used a process called "securitizing," in which they sold their mortgages to financial companies, which put all the mortgages into a big pool, creating large financial securities, and then re-sold these mortgage-backed securities to investors. In this way, the lenders off-loaded the risks of the mortgages to investors. Investors were interested in mortgage-backed securities as they appeared to offer a steady stream of income, provided the mortgages were repaid. Investors relied on the ratings agencies to assess the credit risk associated with the mortgage backed securities. In hindsight, it appears that the credit agencies were far too lenient in their ratings of many of the securitized loans. Bank and financial regulators watched the steady rise in the market for mortgage-backed securities, but saw no reason at the time to intervene.

When housing prices turned down, many households that had borrowed when prices were high found that what they owed the bank was more than their home was worth. Many banks believed that they had diversified by selling their individual loans and instead buying securities based on mortgage loans from all over the country. After all, banks thought back in 2005, the average price of a house had not declined at any time since the Great Depression of the 1930s. These securities based on mortgage loans, however, turned out to be far riskier than expected. The bust in housing prices weakened the finances of both banks and households, and thus helped bring on the Great Recession of 2008–2009.

The Trade-offs between Return and Risk

The discussion of financial investments has emphasized the expected rate of return, the risk, and the liquidity of each investment. Table 3 summarizes these characteristics.

Table 3. Key Characteristics for Financial Investments

Financial Investment	Return	Risk	Liquidity
Checking account	Very low	Very little	Very high
Savings account	Low	Very little	High
Certificate of deposit	Low to medium	Very little	Medium
Stocks	High	Medium to high	Medium
Bonds	Medium	Low to medium	Medium

Financial Investment	Return	Risk	Liquidity
Mutual funds	Medium to high	Medium to high	Medium to high
Housing	Medium	Medium	Low
Gold	Medium	High	Low
Collectibles	Low to medium	High	Low

The household investment choices listed here display a tradeoff between the expected return and the degree of risk involved. Bank accounts have very low risk and very low returns; bonds have higher risk but higher returns; and stocks are riskiest of all but have the potential for still higher returns. In effect, the higher average return compensates for the higher degree of risk. If risky assets like stocks did not also offer a higher average return, then few investors would want them.

This tradeoff between return and risk complicates the task of any financial investor: Is it better to invest safely or to take a risk and go for the high return? Ultimately, choices about risk and return will be based on personal preferences. However, it is often useful to examine risk and return in the context of different time frames.

The high returns of stock market investments refer to a high average return that can be expected over a period of several years or decades. The high risk of such investments refers to the fact that in shorter time frames, from months to a few years, the rate of return may fluctuate a great deal. Thus, a person near retirement age, who already owns a house, may prefer reduced risk and certainty about retirement income. For young workers, just starting to make a reasonably profitable living, it may make sense to put most of their savings for retirement in stocks. Stocks are risky in the short term, to be sure, but when the worker can look forward to several decades during which stock market ups and downs can even out, stocks will typically pay a much higher return over that extended period than will bonds or bank accounts. Thus, tradeoffs between risk and return must be considered in the context of where the investor is in life.

Concepts and Summary

All investments can be categorized according to three key characteristics: average expected return, degree of risk, and liquidity. To get a higher rate of return, an investor must typically accept either more risk or less liquidity. Banks are an example of a financial intermediary, an institution that operates to coordinate supply and demand in the financial capital market. Banks offer a range of accounts, including checking accounts, savings accounts, and certificates of deposit. Under the federal deposit insurance program, banks purchase insurance against the risk of a bank failure.

A typical bond promises the financial investor a series of payments over time, based on the interest rate at the time the bond is issued, and then repayment of what was borrowed. Bonds that offer a high rate of return but also a relatively high chance of defaulting on the payments are called high yield or junk bonds. The bond yield is the rate of return that a bond promises to pay at the time of purchase. Even when bonds make payments based on a fixed rate of interest, they are somewhat risky, because if interest rates rise for the economy as a whole, an investor who owns bonds issued at lower interest rates is now locked into the low rate and suffers a loss.

Changes in the price of a stock depend on changes in expectations about future profits. Investing in any individual firm is somewhat risky, so investors are wise to practice diversification, which means investing in a range of companies. A mutual fund purchases an array of stocks and/or bonds. An investor in the mutual fund then receives a return depending on the overall performance of the investments made by the fund as a whole. A mutual fund that seeks to imitate the overall behavior of the stock market is called an index fund.

Housing and other tangible assets can also be regarded as forms of financial investment, which pay a rate of return in the form of capital gains. Housing can also offer a nonfinancial return—specifically, you can live in it.

23.3 HOW TO GAIN PERSONAL WEALTH

Getting rich may seem straightforward enough. Figure out what companies are going to grow and earn high profits in the future, or figure out what companies are going to become popular for everyone else to buy. Those companies are the ones that will pay high dividends or whose stock price will climb in the future. Then, buy stock in those companies. Presto! Multiply your money!

Why is this path to riches not as easy as it sounds? This module first discusses the problems with picking stocks, and then discusses a more reliable but undeniably duller method of accumulating personal wealth.

Why It Is Hard to Get Rich Quick: The Random Walk Theory

The chief problem with attempting to buy stock in companies that will have higher prices in the future is that many other financial investors are trying to do the same thing. Thus, in attempting to get rich in the stock market, it is no help to identify a company that is going to earn high profits if many other investors have already reached the same conclusion, because the stock price will already be high, based on the expected high level of future profits.

The idea that stock prices are based on expectations about the future has a powerful and unexpected implication. If expectations determine stock price, then shifts in expectations will determine shifts in the stock price. Thus, what matters for predicting whether the stock price of a company will do well is not whether the company will actually earn profits in the future. Instead, you must find a company that is widely believed at present to have poor prospects, but that will actually turn out to be a shining star. Brigades of stock market analysts and individual investors are carrying out such research 24 hours a day.

The fundamental problem with predicting future stock winners is that, by definition, no one can predict the future news that alters expectations about profits. Because stock prices will shift in response to unpredictable future news, these prices will tend to follow what mathematicians call a "random walk with a trend." The "random walk" part means that, on any given day, stock prices are just as likely to rise as to fall. "With a trend" means that over time, the upward steps tend to be larger than the downward steps, so stocks do gradually climb.

If stocks follow a random walk, then not even financial professionals will be able to choose those that will beat the average consistently. While some investment advisers are better than average in any given year, and some even succeed for a number of years in a row, the majority of financial investors do not outguess the market. If we look back over time, it is typically true that half or two-thirds of the mutual funds that attempted to pick stocks which would rise more than the market average actually ended up doing worse than the market average. For the average investor who reads the business pages of the newspaper over a cup of coffee in the morning, the odds of doing better than full-time professionals is not very good at all. Trying to pick the stocks that will gain a great deal in the future is a risky and unlikely way to become rich.

Getting Rich the Slow, Boring Way

Many U.S. citizens can accumulate a large amount of wealth during their lifetimes, if they make two key choices. The first is to complete additional education and training. In 2014, the U.S. Census Bureau reported median earnings for households where the main earner had only a high school degree of $33,124; for those with a two-year associate degree, median earnings were $40,560 and for those with a four-year bachelor's degree, median income was $54,340. Learning is not only good for you, but it pays off financially, too.

The second key choice is to start saving money early in life, and to give the power of compound interest a chance. Imagine that at age 25, you save $3,000 and place that money into an account that you do not touch. In the long run, it is not unreasonable to assume a 7% real annual rate of return (that is, 7% above the rate of inflation) on money invested in a well-diversified stock portfolio. After 40 years, using the formula for compound interest, the original $3,000 investment will have multiplied nearly fifteen fold:

$$3,000(1 + .07)^{40} = \$44,923$$

Having $45,000 does not make you a millionaire. Notice, however, that this tidy sum is the result of saving $3,000 exactly once. Saving that amount every year for several decades—or saving more as income rises—will multiply the total considerably. This type of wealth will not rival the riches of Microsoft CEO Bill Gates, but remember that only half of Americans have any money in mutual funds at all. Accumulating hundreds of thousands of dollars by retirement is a perfectly achievable goal for a well-educated person who starts saving early in life—and that amount of accumulated wealth will put you at or near the top 10% of all American households. The following Work It Out feature shows the difference between simple and compound interest, and the power of compound interest.

Simple and Compound Interest

Simple interest is an interest rate calculation only on the principal amount.

Step 1. Learn the formula for simple interest:

$$Principal \times Rate \times Time = Interest$$

Step 2. Practice using the simple interest formula.

Example 1: $100 Deposit at a simple interest rate of 5% held for one year is:

$$\$100 \times 0.05 \times 1 = \$5$$

Simple interest in this example is $5.

Example 2: $100 Deposit at a simple interest rate of 5% held for three years is:

$$\$100 \times 0.05 \times 3 = \$15$$

Simple interest in this example is $15.

Step 3. Calculate the total future amount using this formula:

$$Total\ future\ amount = principal + interest$$

Step 4. Put the two simple interest formulas together.

$$Total\ future\ amount\ (with\ simple\ interest) = Principal + (Principal \times Rate \times Time)$$

Step 5. Apply the simple interest formula to our three year example.

$$Total\ future\ amount\ (with\ simple\ interest) = \$100 + (\$100 \times 0.05 \times 3) = \$115$$

Compound interest is an interest rate calculation on the principal plus the accumulated interest.

Step 6. To find the compound interest, we determine the difference between the future value and the present value of the principal. This is accomplished as follows:

$$Future\ Value \quad Principal \times (1 + interest\ rate)^{time}$$

$$Compound\ interest \quad Future\ Value - Present\ Value$$

Step 7. Apply this formula to our three-year scenario. Follow the calculations in Table 4.

Table 4

Year 1	
Amount in Bank	$100
Bank Interest Rate	5%
Total	$105
	$100 + ($100 × 0.5)
Year 2	
Amount in Bank	$105
Bank Interest Rate	5%
Total	$110.25
	$105 + ($105 × .05)
Year 3	
Amount in Bank	$110.25
Bank Interest Rate	5%
Total	$115.75
	$110.25 + ($110.25 × .05)
Compound interest	$115.75 – $100 = $15.75

Step 8. Note that, after three years, the total is $115.75. Therefore the total compound interest is $15.75. This is $0.75 more than was obtained with simple interest. While this may not seem like much, keep in mind that we were only working with $100 and over a relatively short time period. Compound interest can make a huge difference with larger sums of money and over longer periods of time.

Getting additional education and saving money early in life obviously will not make you rich overnight. Additional education typically means putting off earning income and living as a student for more years. Saving money often requires choices like driving an older or less expensive car, living in a smaller apartment or buying a smaller house, and making other day-to-day sacrifices. For most people, the tradeoffs for achieving substantial personal wealth will require effort, patience, and sacrifice.

How Capital Markets Transform Financial Flows

Financial capital markets have the power to repackage money as it moves from those who supply financial capital to those who demand it. Banks accept checking account deposits and turn them into long-term loans to companies. Individual firms sell shares of stock and issue bonds to raise capital. Firms make and sell an astonishing array of goods and services, but an investor can receive a return on the company's decisions by buying stock in that company. Stocks and bonds are sold and resold by financial investors to one another. Venture capitalists and angel investors search for promising small companies. Mutual funds combine the stocks and bonds—and thus, indirectly, the products and investments—of many different companies.

In this chapter, we discussed the basic mechanisms of financial markets. (A more advanced course in economics or finance will consider more sophisticated tools.) The fundamentals of those financial capital markets remain the same: Firms are trying to raise financial capital and households are looking for a desirable combination of rate of return, risk, and liquidity. Financial markets are society's mechanisms for bringing together these forces of demand and supply.

The Housing Bubble and the Financial Crisis of 2007

The housing boom and bust in the United States, and the resulting multi-trillion-dollar decline in home equity, started with the fall of home prices starting in 2007. As home values fell, many home prices fell below the amount owed on the mortgage and owners stopped paying and defaulted on their loan. Banks found that their assets (loans) became worthless. Many financial institutions around the world had invested in mortgage-backed securities, or had purchased insurance on mortgage-backed securities. When housing prices collapsed, the value of those financial assets collapsed as well. The asset side of the banks' balance sheets dropped, causing bank failures and bank runs. Around the globe, financial institutions were bankrupted or nearly so. The result was a large decrease in lending and borrowing, referred to as a freezing up of available credit. When credit dries up, the economy is on its knees. The crisis was not limited to the United States. Iceland, Ireland, the United Kingdom, Spain, Portugal, and Greece all had similar housing boom and bust cycles, and similar credit freezes.

If businesses cannot access financial capital, they cannot make physical capital investments. Those investments ultimately lead to job creation. So when credit dried up, businesses invested less, and they ultimately laid off millions of workers. This caused incomes to drop, which caused demand to drop. In turn businesses sold less, so they laid off more workers. Compounding these events, as economic conditions worsened, financial institutions were even less likely to make loans.

To make matters even worse, as businesses sold less, their expected future profit decreased, and this led to a drop in stock prices. Combining all these effects led to major decreases in incomes, demand, consumption, and employment, and to the Great Recession, which in the United States officially lasted from December 2007 to June 2009. During this time, the unemployment rate rose from 5% to a peak of 10.1%. Four years after the recession officially ended, unemployment was still stubbornly high, at 7.6%, and 11.8 million people were still unemployed.

As the world's leading consumer, if the United States goes into recession, it usually drags other countries down with it. The Great Recession was no exception. With few exceptions, U.S. trading partners also entered into recessions of their own, of varying lengths, or suffered slower economic growth. Like the United States, many European countries also gave direct financial assistance, so-called bailouts, to the institutions that make up their financial markets. There was good reason to do this. Financial markets bridge the gap between demanders and suppliers of financial capital. These institutions and markets need to function in order for an economy to invest in new financial capital.

However, much of this bailout money was borrowed, and this borrowed money contributed to another crisis in Europe. Because of the impact on their budgets of the financial crisis and the resulting bailouts, many countries found themselves with unsustainably high deficits. They chose to undertake austerity measures, large decreases in government spending and large tax increases, in order to reduce their deficits. Greece, Ireland, Spain, and Portugal have all had to undertake relatively severe austerity measures. The ramifications of this crisis have spread; the viability of the euro has even been called into question.

Concepts and Summary

It is extremely difficult, even for financial professionals, to predict changes in future expectations and thus to choose the stocks whose price is going to rise in the future. Most Americans can accumulate considerable financial wealth if they follow two rules: complete significant additional education and training after graduating from high school and start saving money early in life.

CHAPTER 24

INTRODUCTION TO PUBLIC ECONOMY

24.1 VOTER PARTICIPATION AND ELECTION COSTS

In U.S. presidential elections over the last few decades, about 55% to 65% of voting-age citizens actually voted, according to the U.S. Census. In congressional elections when there is no presidential race, or in local elections, the turnout is typically lower, often less than half the eligible voters. In other countries, the share of adults who vote is often higher. For example, in national elections since the 1980s in Germany, Spain, and France, about 75% to 80% of those of voting age cast ballots. Even this total falls well short of 100%. Some countries have laws that require voting, among them Australia, Belgium, Italy, Greece, Turkey, Singapore, and most Latin American nations. At the time the United States was founded, voting was mandatory in Virginia, Maryland, Delaware, and Georgia. Even if the law can require people to vote, however, no law can require that each voter cast an informed or a thoughtful vote. Moreover, in the United States and in most countries around the world, the freedom to vote has also typically meant the freedom *not* to vote.

Why do people not vote? Perhaps they do not care too much about who wins, or they are uninformed about who is running, or they do not believe their vote will matter or change their lives in any way. Indeed, these reasons are probably tied together, since people who do not believe their vote matters will not bother to become informed or care who wins. Economists have suggested why a utility-maximizing person might rationally decide not to vote or not to become informed about the election. While a few elections in very small towns may be decided by a single vote, in most elections of any size, the margin of victory is measured in hundreds, thousands, or even millions of votes. A rational voter will recognize that one vote is extremely unlikely to make a difference. This theory of rational ignorance holds that people will not vote if the costs of becoming informed and voting are too high, or they feel their vote will not be decisive in the election.

In a 1957 work, An Economic Theory of Democracy, the economist Anthony Downs stated the problem this way: "It seems probable that for a great many citizens in a democracy, rational behavior excludes any investment whatever in political information per se. No matter how significant a difference between parties is revealed to the rational citizen by his free information, or how uncertain he is about which party to support, he realizes that his vote has almost no chance of influencing the outcome... He will not even utilize all the free information available, since assimilating it takes time." In his classic 1948 novel Walden Two, the psychologist B. F. Skinner puts the issue even more succinctly via one of his characters, who states: "The chance that one man's vote will decide the issue in a national election...is less than the chance that he will be killed on his way to the polls." The following Clear It Up feature explores another aspect of the election process: spending.

How much is too much to spend on an election?

According to a report from *The New York Times*, the 2012 elections for president, Congress, and state and local offices, saw a total of about $5.8 billion spent. The money raised went to the campaigns, including advertising, fundraising, travel, and staff. Many people worry that politicians spend too much time raising money and end up entangled with special interest groups that make major donations. Critics would prefer a system that restricts what candidates can spend, perhaps in exchange for limited public campaign financing or free television advertising time.

How much spending on campaigns is too much? Five billion dollars will buy a lot of potato chips, but in the U.S. economy, which exceeded $16 trillion in 2012, the $5.8 billion spent on political campaigns was about 1/25 of 1% of the overall economy. Here is another way to think about campaign spending. Total government spending programs in 2009, including federal and state governments, was about $5.1 trillion, so the cost of choosing the people who would determine how this money would be spent was about 1/10 of 1% of that. In the context of the enormous U.S. economy, $5.8 billion is not as much money as it sounds. U.S. consumers spend about $2 billion per year on toothpaste and $7 billion on hair care products. In 2008, Proctor and Gamble spent $4.8 billion on advertising. It may not be sensible to believe the United States is going to decide its presidential elections for less than we spend on toothpaste or than Proctor and Gamble spends on advertisements.

Whatever we believe about whether candidates and their parties spend too much or too little on elections, the U.S. Supreme Court has placed limits on how government can limit campaign spending. In a 1976 decision, *Buckley v. Valeo*, the Supreme Court emphasized that the First Amendment to the U.S. Constitution specifies freedom of speech. The federal government and states can offer candidates a voluntary deal in which government makes some public financing available to candidates, but only if the candidates agree to abide by certain spending limits. Of course, candidates can also voluntarily agree to set certain spending limits if they wish. But government cannot forbid people or organizations to raise and spend money above these limits if they choose.

In 2002, Congress passed and President George W. Bush signed into law the Bipartisan Campaign Reform Act (BCRA). The relatively noncontroversial portions of the act strengthen the rules requiring full and speedy disclosure of who contributes money to campaigns. However, some controversial portions of the Act limit the ability of individuals and groups to make certain kinds of political donations and they ban certain kinds of advertising in the months leading up to an election. These bans were called into question after the release of two films: Michael Moore's Fahrenheit 9/11 and Citizens United's Hillary: The Movie. At question was whether each film sought to discredit political candidates for office too close to an election, in violation of the BCRA. Moore's film was found by lower courts not to violate the Act, while Citizens United's was. The fight reached the Supreme Court, as Citizens United v. Federal Election Commission, saying that the First Amendment protects the rights of corporations as well as individuals to donate to political campaigns. The Court ruled, in a 5–4 decision, that the spending limits were unconstitutional. This controversial decision, which essentially allows unlimited contributions by corporations to political action committees, overruled several previous decisions and will likely be revisited in the future, due to the strength of the public reaction. For now, it has resulted in a sharp increase in election spending.

While many U.S. adults do not bother to vote in presidential elections, more than half do. What motivates them? Research on voting behavior has shown that people who are more settled or more "connected" to society tend to vote more frequently. According to the *Washington Post*, more married people vote than single people. Those with a job vote more than the unemployed. Those who have lived longer in a neighborhood are more likely to vote than newcomers. Those who report that they know their neighbors and talk to them are more likely to vote than socially isolated people. Those with a higher income and level of education are also more likely to vote. These factors suggest that politicians are likely to focus more on the interests of married, employed, well-educated people with at least a middle-class level of income than on the interests of other groups. For example, those who vote may tend to be more supportive of financial assistance for the two-year and four-year colleges they expect their children to attend than they are of medical care or public school education aimed at families of the poor and unemployed.

A number of proposals have been offered to encourage greater voter turnout: making it easier to register to vote, keeping the polls open for more hours, or even moving Election Day to the weekend, when fewer people need to worry about jobs or school commitments. However, the changes that have been made do not seem to have caused a long-term upward trend in the number of people voting. After all, casting an informed vote will always impose some costs of time and energy. It is not clear how to strengthen people's feeling of connectedness to society in a way that will lead to a substantial increase in voter turnout. Without greater voter turnout, however, politicians elected by the votes of 60% or fewer of the population may not enact economic policy in the best interests of 100% of the population. Meanwhile, countering a long trend toward making voting easier, many states have recently erected new voting laws that critics say are actually barriers to voting. States have passed laws reducing early voting, restricting groups who are organizing get-out-the-vote efforts, enacted strict photo ID laws, as well as laws that require showing proof of U.S. citizenship. The ACLU argues that while these laws profess to prevent voter fraud, they are in effect making it harder for individuals to cast their vote.

Concepts and Summary

The theory of rational ignorance says voters will recognize that their single vote is extremely unlikely to influence the outcome of an election. As a consequence, they will choose to remain uninformed about issues and not vote. This theory helps explain why voter turnout is so low in the United States.

24.2 POLITICS OF PARTICULAR INTEREST

Many political issues are of intense interest to a relatively small group, as noted above. For example, many U.S. drivers do not much care where the tires for their car were made—they just want good quality as inexpensively as they can get it. In September 2009, President Obama and Congress enacted a tariff (taxes added on imported goods) on tires imported from China that would increase the import price of Chinese tires by 35 percent in its first year, 30 percent in its second year, and 25 percent in its third year. Interestingly, the U.S. companies that make tires did not favor this step, because most of them also import tires from China and other countries. (See Globalization and Protectionism for more on tariffs.) However, the United Steelworkers union, which had seen jobs in the tire industry fall by 5,000 over the previous five years, lobbied fiercely for the tariff to be enacted. With this tariff, the cost of all tires increased significantly. (See the closing Bring It Home feature at the end of this chapter for more information on the tire tariff.)

Special interest groups are groups that are small in number relative to the nation, but quite well organized and focused on a specific issue. A special interest group can pressure legislators to enact public policies that do not benefit society as a whole. Imagine an environmental rule to reduce air pollution that will cost 10 large companies $8 million each, for a total cost of $80 million. The social benefits from enacting this rule provide an average benefit of $10 for every person in the United States, for a total of about $3 trillion. Even though the benefits are far higher than the costs for society as a whole, the 10 companies are likely to lobby much more fiercely to avoid $8 million in costs than the average person is to argue for $10 worth of benefits.

As this example suggests, we can relate the problem of special interests in politics to an issue raised in Environmental Protection and Negative Externalities about economic policy with respect to negative externalities and pollution—the problem called regulatory capture (which we defined in Monopoly and Antitrust Policy). In legislative bodies and agencies that write laws and regulations about how much corporations will pay in taxes, or rules for safety in the workplace, or instructions on how to satisfy environmental regulations, you can be sure the specific industry affected has lobbyists who study every word and every comma. They talk with the legislators who are writing the legislation and suggest alternative wording. They contribute to the campaigns of legislators on the key committees—and may even offer those legislators high-paying jobs after they have left office. As a result, it often turns out that those who are being regulated can exercise considerable influence over the regulators.

In the early 2000s, about 40 million people in the United States were eligible for **Medicare**, a government program that provides health insurance for those 65 and older. On some issues, the elderly are a powerful interest group. They donate money and time to political campaigns, and in the 2012 presidential election, 70% of those over age 65 voted, while just 49% of those aged 18 to 24 cast a ballot, according to the U.S. Census.

In 2003, Congress passed and President George Bush signed into law a substantial expansion of Medicare that helped the elderly to pay for prescription drugs. The prescription drug benefit cost the federal government about $40 billion in 2006, and the Medicare system projects that the annual cost will rise to $121 billion by 2016. The political pressure to pass a prescription drug benefit for Medicare was apparently quite high, while the political pressure to assist the 40 million with no health insurance at all was considerably lower. One reason might be that senior citizens are represented by **AARP**, a well-funded and well-organized lobbying group, while there is no umbrella organization to lobby for those without health insurance.

In the battle over passage of the 2010 Affordable Care Act (ACA), which became known as "Obamacare," there was heavy lobbying on all sides by insurance companies and pharmaceutical companies. However, a lobby group, Health Care for America Now (HCAN), was financed by labor unions and community groups and was organized to offset corporate lobbying. HCAN, spending $60 million dollars, was successful in helping to get the legislation passed which added new regulations on insurance companies and a mandate that all individuals will obtain health insurance by 2014. The following Work It Out feature further explains voter incentives and lobbyist influence.

Paying To Get Your Way

Suppose Congress proposes a tax on carbon emissions for certain factories in a small town of 10,000 people. The tax is estimated to reduce pollution to such an extent that it will benefit each resident by an equivalent of $300. The tax will also reduce profits to the town's two large factories by $1 million each. How much should the factory owners be willing to spend to fight the passage of the tax, and how much should the townspeople be willing to pay to support it? Why is society unlikely to achieve the optimal outcome?

Step 1. The two factory owners each stand to lose $1 million if the tax is passed, so each should be willing to spend up to that amount to prevent the passage of the tax, a combined sum of $2 million. Of course, in the real world, there is no guarantee that lobbying efforts will be successful, so the factory owners may choose to invest an amount that is substantially lower.

Step 2. There are 10,000 townspeople, each standing to benefit by $300 if the tax passes. Theoretically, then, they should be willing to spend up to $3 million (10,000 × $300) to ensure passage. (Again, in the real world with no guarantees of success, they may choose to spend less.)

Step 3. It is costly and difficult for 10,000 people to coordinate in such a way as to influence public policy. Since each person stands to gain only $300, many may feel lobbying is not worth the effort.

Step 4. The two factory owners, however, find it very easy and profitable to coordinate their activities, so they have a greater incentive to do so.

Special interests may develop a close relationship with one political party, so their ability to influence legislation rises and falls as that party moves in or out of power. A special interest may even hurt a political party if it appears to a number of voters that the relationship is too cozy. In a close election, a small group that has been under-represented in the past may find that it can tip the election one way or another—so that group will suddenly receive considerable attention. Democratic institutions produce an ebb and flow of political parties and interests and thus offer both opportunities for special interests and ways of counterbalancing those interests over time.

Identifiable Winners, Anonymous Losers

A number of economic policies produce gains whose beneficiaries are easily identifiable, but costs that are partly or entirely shared by a large number who remain anonymous. A democratic political system probably has a bias toward those who are identifiable.

For example, policies that impose **price controls**—like rent control—may look as if they benefit renters and impose costs only on landlords. However, when landlords then decide to reduce the number of rental units available in the area, a number of people who would have liked to rent an apartment end up living somewhere else because no units were available. These would-be renters have experienced a cost of rent control, but it is hard to identify who they are.

Similarly, policies that block imports will benefit the firms that would have competed with those imports—and workers at those firms—who are likely to be quite visible. Consumers who would have preferred to purchase the imported products, and who thus bear some costs of the protectionist policy, are much less visible.

Specific tax breaks and spending programs also have identifiable winners and impose costs on others who are hard to identify. Special interests are more likely to arise from a group that is easily identifiable, rather than from a group where some of those who suffer may not even recognize they are bearing costs.

Pork Barrels and Logrolling

Politicians have an incentive to ensure that government money is spent in their home state or district, where it will benefit their constituents in a direct and obvious way. Thus, when legislators are negotiating over whether to support a piece of legislation, they commonly ask each other to include **pork-barrel spending**, legislation that benefits mainly a single political district. Pork-barrel spending is another case in which democracy is challenged by concentrated benefits and widely dispersed costs: the benefits of pork-barrel spending are obvious and direct to local voters, while the costs are spread over the entire country. Read the following Clear It Up feature for more information on pork-barrel spending.

How much impact can pork-barrel spending have?

U.S. Senator Robert C. Byrd of West Virginia, who was originally elected to the Senate in 1958 and served until 2010, is widely regarded as one of the masters of pork-barrel politics, directing a steady stream of federal funds to his home state. A journalist once compiled a list of structures in West Virginia at least partly funded by the government and named after Byrd: "the Robert C. Byrd Highway; the Robert C. Byrd Locks and Dam; the Robert C. Byrd Institute; the Robert C. Byrd Life Long Learning Center; the Robert C. Byrd Honors Scholarship Program; the Robert C. Byrd Green Bank Telescope; the Robert C. Byrd Institute for Advanced Flexible Manufacturing; the Robert C. Byrd Federal Courthouse; the Robert C. Byrd Health Sciences Center; the Robert C. Byrd Academic and Technology Center; the Robert C. Byrd United Technical Center; the Robert C. Byrd Federal Building; the Robert C. Byrd Drive; the Robert C. Byrd Hilltop Office Complex; the Robert C. Byrd Library; and the Robert C. Byrd Learning Resource Center; the Robert C. Byrd Rural Health Center." This list does not include government-funded projects in West Virginia that were not named after Byrd. Of course, we would have to analyze each of these expenditures in detail to figure out whether they should be treated as pork-barrel spending or whether they provide widespread benefits that reach beyond West Virginia. At least some of them, or a portion of them, certainly would fall into that category. Because there are currently no term limits for Congressional representatives, those who have been in office longer generally have more power to enact pork-barrel projects.

The amount spent on individual pork-barrel projects is small, but many small projects can add up to a substantial total. A nonprofit watchdog organization, called Citizens against Government Waste, produces an annual report, the Pig Book that attempts to quantify the amount of pork-barrel spending, focusing on items that were requested by only one member of Congress, that were passed into law without any public hearings, or that serve only a local purpose. Whether any specific item qualifies as pork can be controversial, of course, but at least by this measure, pork-barrel spending totaled $2.7 billion in 2014.

Pork-barrel spending can be encouraged by **logrolling**, an action in which all members of a group of legislators agree to vote for a package of otherwise unrelated laws that they individually favor. For example, if one member of the U.S. Congress suggests building a new bridge or hospital in his or her own congressional district, the other members might oppose it. However, if 51% of the legislators come together, they can pass a bill that includes a bridge or hospital for every one of their districts.

As a reflection of this interest of legislators in their own districts, the U.S. government has typically spread out its spending on military bases and weapons programs to congressional districts all across the country. In part, this is done to help create a situation that encourages members of Congress to vote in support of defense spending.

Concepts and Summary

Special interest politics arises when a relatively small group, called a special interest group, each of whose members has a large interest in a political outcome, devotes a lot of time and energy to lobbying for the group's preferred choice. Meanwhile, the large majority, each of whose members has only a small interest in this issue, pays no attention.

Pork-barrel spending is defined as legislation whose benefits are concentrated on a single district while the costs are spread widely over the country. Logrolling refers to a situation in which two or more legislators agree to vote for each other's legislation, which can then encourage pork-barrel spending in many districts.

24.3 PROBLEMS WITH THE DEMOCRATIC SYSTEM OF GOVERNMENT

Most developed countries today have a democratic system of government: citizens express their opinions through votes and those votes affect the direction of the country. The advantage of democracy over other systems is that it allows everyone in a society an equal say and therefore may reduce the possibility of oppression of the masses by a small group of wealthy oligarchs. There is no such thing as a perfect system, and democracy, for all its popularity, is not without its problems, a few of which we will examine here.

Democracy is sometimes summed up (and oversimplified) in two words: "Majority rule." When voters face three or more choices, however, then voting may not always be a useful way of determining what the majority prefers.

As one example, consider an election in a state where 60% of the population is liberal and 40% is conservative. If there are only two candidates, one from each side, and if liberals and conservatives vote in the same 60–40 proportions in which they are represented in the population, then the liberal will win. What if the election ends up including two liberal candidates and one conservative? It is possible that the liberal vote will split and victory will go to the minority party. In this case, the outcome does not reflect the majority's preference.

Does the majority view prevail in the case of sugar quotas? Clearly there are more sugar consumers in the United States than sugar producers, but the U.S. domestic sugar lobby (www.sugarcane.org) has successfully argued for protection against imports since 1789. By law, therefore, U.S. makers of cookies and candies must use 85% domestic sugar in their products. Meanwhile quotas on imported sugar restrict supply and keep the domestic price of sugar up—raising prices for companies that use sugar in the production of their goods and for consumers. The European Union allows sugar imports, and prices there are 40% lower than U.S. sugar prices. Sugar-producing countries in the Caribbean repeatedly protest the U.S. quotas at the World Trade Organization meetings, but each bite of cookie, at present, costs you more than if there were no sugar lobby. This case goes against the theory of the "median" voter in a democracy. The median voter theory argues that politicians will try to match policies to what pleases the median voter preferences. If we think of political positions along a spectrum from left to right, the median voter is in the middle of the spectrum. This theory argues that actual policy will reflect "middle of the road." In the case of sugar lobby politics, the minority, not the median, dominates policy.

Sometimes it is not even clear how to define what the majority opinion might be. Step aside from politics for a moment and think about a choice facing three families (the Ortegas, the Schmidts, and the Alexanders) who are planning to celebrate New Year's Day together. They agree to vote on the menu, choosing from three entrees, and they agree that the majority vote wins. With three families, it seems reasonable that one choice of entree will get a 2–1 majority. What if, however, their vote ends up looking like Table 1?

Clearly, the three families disagree on their first choice. But the problem goes even deeper. Instead of looking at all three choices at once, compare them two at a time. (See Figure 1) In a vote of turkey versus beef, turkey wins by 2–1. In a vote of beef versus lasagna, beef wins 2–1. If turkey beats beef, and beef beats lasagna, then it might seem only logical that turkey must also beat lasagna. However, with the preferences shown, lasagna is preferred to turkey by a 2–1 vote, as well. If lasagna is preferred to turkey, and turkey beats beef, then surely it must be that lasagna also beats beef? Actually, no; beef beats lasagna. In other words, the majority view may not win. Clearly, as any car salesmen will tell you, choices are influenced by the way they are presented.

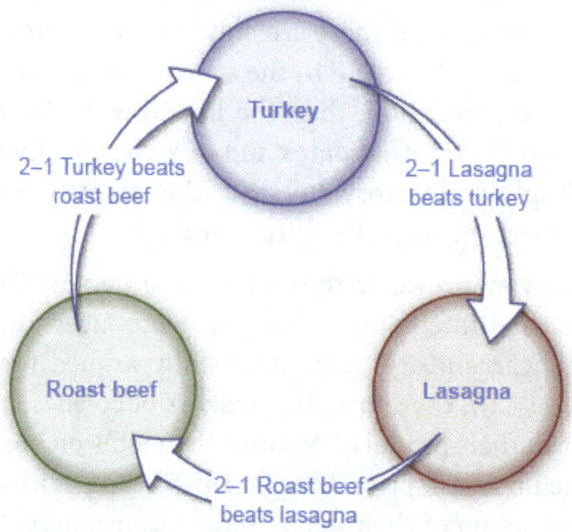

Figure 1. A Voting Cycle. Given these choices, voting will struggle to produce a majority outcome. Turkey is favored over roast beef by 2–1 and roast beef is favored over lasagna by 2–1. If turkey beats roast beef and roast beef beats lasagna, then it might seem that turkey must beat lasagna, too. But given these preferences, lasagna is favored over turkey by 2–1.

Table 1. Circular Preferences

	The Ortega Family	The Schmidt Family	The Alexander Family
First Choice	Turkey	Roast beef	Lasagna
Second Choice	Roast beef	Lasagna	Turkey
Third Choice	Lasagna	Turkey	Roast beef

The situation in which Choice A is preferred by a majority over Choice B, Choice B is preferred by a majority over Choice C, and Choice C is preferred by a majority over Choice A is called a **voting cycle**. It is easy to imagine sets of government choices—say, perhaps the choice between increased defense spending, increased government spending on health care, and a tax cut—in which a voting cycle could occur. The result will be determined by the order in which choices are presented and voted on, not by majority rule, because every choice is both preferred to some alternative and also not preferred to another alternative.

Where Is Government's Self-Correcting Mechanism?

When a firm produces a product no one wants to buy or produces at a higher cost than its competitors, the firm is likely to suffer losses. If it cannot change its ways, it will go out of business. This self-correcting mechanism in the marketplace can have harsh effects on workers or on local economies, but it also puts pressure on firms for good performance.

Government agencies, on the other hand, do not sell their products in a market; they receive tax dollars instead. They are not challenged by competitors as are private-sector firms. If the U.S. Department of Education or the U.S. Department of Defense is doing a poor job, citizens cannot purchase their services from another provider and drive the existing government agencies into bankruptcy. If you are upset that the Internal Revenue Service is slow in sending you a tax refund or seems unable to answer your questions, you cannot decide to pay your income taxes through a different organization. Of course, elected politicians can assign new leaders to government agencies and instruct them to reorganize or to emphasize a different mission. The pressure government faces, however, to change its bureaucracy, to seek greater efficiency, and to improve customer responsiveness is much milder than the threat of being put out of business altogether.

This insight suggests that when government provides goods or services directly, we might expect it to do so with less efficiency than private firms—except in certain cases where the government agency may compete directly with private firms. At the local level, for example, services like garbage collection can be provided by government directly, by private firms under contract to the government, or by a mix of government employees competing with private firms.

A Balanced View of Markets and Government

The British statesman Sir Winston Churchill (1874–1965) once wrote: "No one pretends that democracy is perfect or all-wise. Indeed, it has been said that democracy is the worst form of government except for all of the other forms which have been tried from time to time." In that spirit, the theme of this discussion is certainly not that democratic government should be abandoned. A practical student of public policy needs to recognize that in some cases, like the case of well-organized special interests or pork-barrel legislation, a democratic government may seek to enact economically unwise projects or programs. In other cases, by placing a low priority on the problems of those who are not well organized or who are less likely to vote, the government may fail to act when it could do some good. In these and other cases, there is no automatic reason to believe that government will necessarily make economically sensible choices.

"The true test of a first-rate mind is the ability to hold two contradictory ideas at the same time," wrote the American author F. Scott Fitzgerald (1896–1940). At this point in your study of microeconomics, you should be able to go one better than Fitzgerald and hold three somewhat contradictory ideas about the interrelationship between markets and government in your mind at the same time.

First, markets are extraordinarily useful and flexible institutions through which society can allocate its scarce resources. This idea was introduced with the subjects of international trade and demand and supply in other chapters and reinforced in all the subsequent discussions of how households and firms make decisions.

Second, markets may sometimes produce unwanted results. A short list of the cases in which markets produce unwanted results includes monopoly and other cases of imperfect competition, pollution, poverty and inequality of incomes, discrimination, and failure to provide insurance.

Third, while government may play a useful role in addressing the problems of markets, government action is also imperfect and may not reflect majority views. Economists readily admit that, in settings like monopoly or negative externalities, a potential role exists for government intervention. However, in the real world, it is not enough to point out that government action might be a good idea. Instead, we must have some confidence that the government is likely to identify and carry out the appropriate public policy. To make sensible judgments about economic policy, we must see the strengths and weaknesses of both markets and government. We must not idealize or demonize either unregulated markets or government actions. Instead, consider the actual strengths and weaknesses of real-world markets and real-world governments.

These three insights seldom lead to simple or obvious political conclusions. As the famous British economist **Joan Robinson** wrote some decades ago: "[E]conomic theory, in itself, preaches no doctrines and cannot establish any universally valid laws. It is a method of ordering ideas and formulating questions." The study of economics is neither politically conservative, nor moderate, nor liberal. There are economists who are Democrats, Republicans, libertarians, socialists, and members of every other political group you can name. Of course, conservatives may tend to emphasize the virtues of markets and the limitations of government, while liberals may tend to emphasize the shortcomings of markets and the need for government programs. Such differences only illustrate that the language and terminology of economics is not limited to one set of political beliefs, but can be used by all.

Chinese Tire Tariffs

In April 2009, the union representing U.S. tire manufacturing workers filed a request with the U.S. **International Trade Commission (ITC)**, asking it to investigate tire imports from China. Under U.S. trade law, if imports from a country increase to the point that they cause market disruption in the United States, as determined by the ITC, then it can also recommend a remedy for this market disruption. In this case, the ITC determined that from 2004 to 2008, U.S. tire manufacturers suffered declines in production, financial health, and employment as a direct result of increases in tire imports from China. The ITC recommended that an additional tax be placed on tire imports from China. President Obama and Congress agreed with the ITC recommendation, and in June 2009 tariffs on Chinese tires increased from 4% to 39%.

Why would U.S. consumers buy imported tires from China in the first place? Most likely, because they are cheaper than tires produced domestically or in other countries. Therefore, this tariff increase should cause U.S. consumers to pay higher prices for tires, either because Chinese tires are now more expensive, or because U.S. consumers are pushed by the tariff to buy more expensive tires made by U.S. manufacturers or those from other countries. In the end, this tariff made U.S. consumers pay more for tires.

Was this tariff met with outrage expressed via social media, traditional media, or mass protests? Were there "Occupy Wall Street-type" demonstrations? The answer is a resounding "No." Most U.S. tire consumers were likely unaware of the tariff increase, although they may have noticed the price increase, which was between $4 and $13 depending on the type of tire. Tire consumers are also potential voters. Conceivably, a tax increase, even a small one, might make voters unhappy. However, voters probably realized that it was not worth their time to learn anything about this issue or cast a vote based on it. They probably thought their vote would not matter in determining the outcome of an election or changing this policy.

Estimates of the impact of this tariff show it costs U.S. consumers around $1.11 billion annually. Of this amount, roughly $817 million ends up in the pockets of foreign tire manufacturers other than in China, and the remaining $294 million goes to U.S. tire manufacturers. In other words, the tariff increase on Chinese tires may have saved 1,200 jobs in the domestic tire sector, but it cost 3,700 jobs in other sectors, as consumers had to cut down on their spending because they were paying more for tires. Jobs were actually lost as a result of this tariff. Workers in U.S. tire manufacturing firms earned about $40,000 in 2010. Given the number of jobs saved and the total cost to U.S. consumers, the cost of saving one job amounted to $926,500!

This tariff caused a net decline in U.S. social surplus. (Total surplus is discussed in the Demand and Supply chapter, and tariffs are discussed in the The International Trade and Capital Flows chapter.) Instead of saving jobs, it cost jobs, and those jobs that it saved cost many times more than the people working in them could ever hope to earn. Why would the government do this?

The chapter answers this question by discussing the influence special interest groups have on economic policy. The steelworkers union, whose members make tires, saw more and more of its members lose their jobs as U.S. consumers consumed more and more cheap Chinese tires. By definition, this union is relatively small but well organized, especially compared to tire consumers. It stands to gain much for each of its members, compared to what each tire consumer may have to give up in terms of higher prices. So the steelworkers union (joined by domestic tire manufacturers) has not only the means but the incentive to lobby economic policymakers and lawmakers. Given that U.S. tire consumers are a large and unorganized group, if they even are a group, it is unlikely they will lobby against higher tire tariffs. In the end, lawmakers tend to listen to those who lobby them, even though the results make for bad economic policy.

Concepts and Summary

Majority votes can run into difficulties when more than two choices exist. A voting cycle occurs when, in a situation with at least three choices, choice A is preferred by a majority vote to choice B, choice B is preferred by a majority vote to choice C, and choice C is preferred by a majority vote to choice A. In such a situation, it is impossible to identify what the majority prefers. Another difficulty arises when the vote is so divided that no choice receives a majority.

A practical approach to microeconomic policy will need to take a realistic view of the specific strengths and weaknesses of markets and the specific strengths and weaknesses of government, rather than making the easy but wrong assumption that either the market or government is always beneficial or always harmful.

CHAPTER

MONEY AND THE FIRM'S THEORY 25

25.1 THE BARTER MYTH AND THE METALLIST

In what kind of economy do we live and operate our daily lives? This is not a trivial question. As ideas about how human beings can best organize their resources developed into enlightenment philosophy, a prominent method for expressing what a society free of the feudal constraints would look like involved imaginary stories. Philosophers, such as John Locke, Thomas Hobbes, and Jean-Jacques Rousseau asked their audience to imagine a place called the state of nature to consider possible social outcomes when this place is populated with free individuals. In the state of nature, will chaos, barbarism, or a harmonious stable society result?

In Locke's version, individuals needed to follow two constraints or simple rules in order for a harmonious and stable society to emerge. The first of these constraints is the spoilage constraint. In the state of nature, no individual should collect more food, nuts, and berries than they can consume before they spoil. Second, the prejudice constraint cannot be violated. This constraint is "predicated on the right to subsistence: the privatization of land [can]not disadvantage non-property holders, violating their right to subsistence goods." As long as all those in the state of nature follow these two simple moral constraints, then a harmonious and stable society is argued to emerge. Through the evolution of similar stories, political economist would add their own plot twists and establish the setting for neoclassical economics.

What these imaginary stories have in common is the collective illusion that capitalism or free-market economics grows out of a state of nature. The basic plot and stage for this story remain the same in neoclassical economics. How many of you got dressed and ready for your classes today in the Cartesian plane? Like their enlightenment predecessors' use of the state of nature, the neoclassical story also takes place in a space that is not inhabited by human beings. The mathematical universe of maximization and optimal decisions, like Locke's imagined individuals, aggregates to a harmonious and stable solution. This solution is known as equilibrium in the formalized mathematical models of neoclassical economics. While the technical names and the math provide the neoclassical story with a scientific veneer, the underlying plot remains generally the same as those told over the previous four hundred plus years. A strong characteristic of these stories is their staying power, but a significant cost of such longevity is a lack of analysis regarding the actual economy in which we live and conduct our daily lives.

The economy described by Jean-Baptiste Say[2] and other classical political economists of his era, as well as by modern neoclassical economists, is a barter economy. In a barter economy, goods trade for other goods. If we were to open a barter market in class, students could trade their hats, backpacks, books, shoes, and whatever else they had in their possession with other students. In this scenario, would much trade occur? Generally, the answer would be no. This is because it would be rare that the double coincidence of wants would be solved very often. This means that for trade to occur I must have what you want and you must have what I want. If and only if this is the case will trade occur because trade must make us both better off than we were before the trade took place. To solve this problem and reduce the amount of time individuals would need to spend seeking out solutions to the double coincidence of wants, society spontaneously agrees to accept a commodity as the facilitator of exchange—or at least this is how the story is told from the state of nature and Cartesian plane origins.

The magical device that solves the double coincidence of wants and sets the economy free is money. Commodity money in the form of gold or silver has an **intrinsic value** that can be measured and all parties understand its value. Intrinsic value is a key concept and can be defined as the value the object has in and of itself. This is why precious metals are central to this story, as it is believed gold has value in and of itself. Thus, through this agreement, the transaction costs for all the producers and consumers in this economy are reduced and are therefore better off. This is the story often told by a group of economists known as the **Metallists**, because of the use of precious metals to denote the value of money. We can model money as the facilitator of a barter transaction using the following notation of C for commodity and M for money.

This is likely the story you have heard before, and it is definitely the one told to your parents in their introductory economics courses. As mentioned above, it is an old story. Roots to its origins go as far back as Plato and Aristotle, but the more modern versions are linked to the 16th and 17th-century enlightenment philosophers discussed above. The staying power and continued adherence to this story are heavily reliant upon metal's intrinsic value. If money's value is connected to the weight and quality of metal, then it, just like the gold, silver, or the other goods it trades for, is a commodity. As a commodity, money preserves the barter system. In a barter framework, economists are able to practice **real analysis.**

Real analysis is described by the 20th-century economist Joseph Schumpeter as: [all] the essential phenomena of economic life are capable of being described in terms of goods and services, of decisions about them, and of relations between them. Money enters the picture only in the modest role of a technical device that has been adopted in order to facilitate transactions. This device can no doubt get out of order, and if it does it will indeed produce phenomena that are specifically attributable to its *modus operandi*. But so long as it functions normally, it does not affect the economic process, which behaves in the same way as it would in a barter economy

In other words, economists can study real changes to output, employment, distribution, and growth without addressing money as anything other than a facilitator of exchange, because in the long-run money is neutral. Money does not generate real changes only nominal changes that create short-run disturbances to the stability of economic equilibrium. In other words, it disrupts the *modus operandi* in Schumpeter's quote. By examining money,within the context of modern economic events, it will become clear that the commitment made by neoclassical economics to the Metallist's story is not intended to provide an accurate understanding of history, but is rather an effort to preserve their method of economic analysis and the continued application of optimization techniques and mathematical modeling.

While the barter story is intuitively appealing, especially when described as an economy at a time and place far, far away, difficult questions about value and the role of the state complicate the drama. For instance, when gold or silver was spontaneously accepted as the commodity money, did people just trade nuggets of the metal? Where did coins come from? Who made the coins, and how was their value determined? Then finally, as economies incorporate paper money, how is the value of the currency maintained, especially if it cannot be directly converted into gold or silver? These questions are examples of critical analysis. Rather than accepting the story as given, critical thinking and investigation will help economists and policymakers to develop an understanding of money and its evolution in economic systems.

To address these critical inquiries, let us return to Schumpeter's description. Money's value is as a technical device used in the facilitation of exchanges. Its value is intrinsically derived through a precious metal. In this scenario, it is a commodity like all other commodities. Difficulty only emerges, if it gets out of order. If money's modus operandi extends beyond the facilitator role, then the economy is no longer functioning as a barter system. It is in this capacity, as something more than a technical device that the Chartalist school of thought is introduced here, in the second act.

The complications, regarding money's value, have become increasingly difficult for Medallists to assume away and maintain money's status as a commodity. The most significant of these changes to the global economy has been the development of fiat currency systems that have completely broken monetary systems from the gold standard. An example of fiat money is the U.S. dollar. They are issued by fiat because the issuer will not give us anything other than other dollars in return. It is an inconvertible paper money. The gold standard allowed for the commodity money story to survive the complications associated with the expansions of both credit money lending and paper money, because money remained **convertible** into gold. However, the elimination of the gold standard has ended the convertibility scene and requires a new dialogue. If money cannot be converted into gold, and value is not intrinsically determined, then where does its value come from?

25.2 SMITH, MARX, KEYNES, CHARTALISM AND MODERN MONEY THEORY

The answers to the questions of value raised in the previous section can be found by examining the following two quotes, from arguably the two most significant characters in the history of political economy. The first comes from Adam Smith's *The Wealth of Nations*:

> A prince, who should enact a certain proportion of his taxes be paid in a paper money of a certain kind, might thereby give a certain value to this paper money.

The second quote, similar in theme, comes from Karl Marx's *Capital Vol. I*, and reads:

> The only part of the so-called national wealth that actually enters into the collective possessions of modern peoples is–their national debt. Hence as a necessary consequence, the modern doctrine that a nation becomes the richer the more deeply it is in debt. Public credit becomes the credo of capital. And with the rise of national debt-making, want of faith in the national debt takes the place of the blasphemy against the Holy Ghost, which may not be forgiven.

From these two quotes, the primary difference between the Metallists and Chartalists approaches to understanding money is revealed. Money is not a commodity. Money is, in the words of the legal scholar Friedrich Knapp, a creature of the state.

What may seem to be a subtle difference is in reality substantial. The reorientation of money as a state phenomenon, rather than a market solution to the double coincidence of wants requires a completely different framework for analyzing the economy. The economy can no longer be modeled as a barter system. Real analysis fails to capture the complexity of money, and thus even the existence of general equilibrium itself is called into question. Returning to Schumpeter, if the *modus operandi* of money is not simply a facilitator role, then we must conduct **monetary analysis.** Simply put, this requires the abandonment "of the idea that all essential features of economic life can be represented by a barter-economy model" (Schumpeter 1954).

We can begin to appreciate the difference between the analysis of a barter system and a money economy by applying Marx's notation and modeling of the **circuit of money capital**. This notation is simple and straightforward (see also Chapter 16: "The Megacorp").

$$M \rightarrow C \ldots P \ldots C' \rightarrow M'$$

where the first stage M – C is termed purchase and is followed by the production process P culminating with C' – M' sale. This analysis of the economy is a monetary analysis. Returning to the barter notation, from above, the transaction would look like this.

$$C \rightarrow M \rightarrow C$$

Note, there is no C' in this exchange. This is because the value is generated, not by production or labor, but through the act of exchange. Remember, in the barter economy of the neoclassical school, trade does not occur unless both parties benefit. Value is created through the exchange process and relative prices become the measure of those values (this is also described in Chapter 3 On Values). Where in Marx's model, value is created through the production process and comes from labor.

As you can see, the interpretation of how the economy operates is very different. The predictions of outcomes from market activity are also at odds. In the real analysis of neoclassical economics, markets tend towards equilibrium. Real analysis predicts a stable solution where the quantity demanded is equal to the quantity supplied. However, if the economy is investigated from the monetary analysis perspective, simple solutions do not immediately present themselves, as conflict, business cycles, and crisis are all consistently observed in capitalist economies and central topics of analysis in Marx's theoretical framework.

This is one reason why John Maynard Keynes considered his approach to understanding the economy as *The General Theory of Employment, Interest, and Money*. Similar to Marx, although Keynes denies any Marxian influence, Keynes moves his analysis of the economy beyond the barter system and real analysis and attempts to understand the dynamics of a **monetary production economy**. For Keynes, in a monetary production economy, there is no reason to assume the economy will trend towards full employment equilibrium in the labor market. In fact, given the special properties of money, the economy is more than capable of coming to rest, for long periods of time, at a level of output far below what is necessary to achieve full employment.

Keynes argues that money has two special properties that differentiate it from all other commodities in the economy. The first is that money has a near-zero elasticity of production. This means that, while it might be reasonable to argue that a problem in our local economy is that there is a shortage of money, we cannot go into the business of selling money. So unlike wheat, milk, cars, tables, or any other good or service, as entrepreneurs, we cannot address the unmet demand for money by producing it ourselves. The second of these properties is a near-zero elasticity of substitution. This property relates to the use of money as a means of payment. The state and most private vendors will only accept dollars (in the United States) as a means of payment to satisfy debt obligations. Wow, that is a mouthful, but it simply means that there are very few substitutes for money as a method of payment. The IRS will not take your laptop as payment for your taxes. The gas company is not interested in your tee-shirts to satisfy your bill, they will only accept one thing: cash. As the Wu-Tang Clan so succinctly puts it, C.R.E.A.M. cash rules everything around me.... dollar dollar bill y'all.

Figure 1. $1 Federal Reserve Note

These two special characteristics of money influence a monetary production economy, by incorporating two missing pieces from the real analysis approach of neoclassical economics, uncertainty, and the state. Hence, it is a more "general theory." Let's discuss the state first and then provide a brief discussion of uncertainty. Why can't we produce dollars? Well, this is against the law. By law, the Treasury Department is the only producer of new U.S. dollars. We will elaborate on this in detail in the next section. Second, why won't the state take my laptop? For this let's take a moment to look at the dollar (Figure 1 above). Up in the upper left corner, it says "THIS NOTE IS LEGAL TENDER FOR ALL DEBTS, PUBLIC AND PRIVATE". This means that there is no reason for the state to accept anything else in payment. If you believe that your laptop is of sufficient value to cover your tax obligation, then you must first convert it into cash to pay your tax bill, and this introduces an important concept in Keynes's monetary framework, **liquidity**.

Liquidity is a measure of the costs associated with converting an asset into cash. For example, your savings account is an asset. It is very liquid, but to convert it into cash you need to go to the bank and withdraw the funds. This time and effort is a cost, but these costs are relatively low. An example of an asset that is not generally described as being liquid is a home. The sale and conversion of a home into cash is a time consuming and often expensive process. An asset's liquidity is of great importance for understanding economic volatility and how risk and uncertainty differ.

To describe the value of assets in a monetary production economy, Keynes uses what he describes as the own rate. The own rate is a measure of an asset's economic value and is composed of three parts, the expected return on the asset (q), its carrying costs (c), and the liquidity premium (l). This is displayed mathematically as, own rate = q – c + l.

Returning to the example of a home, the expected return, pre-housing crisis, was strong, based on historical data. A home's carrying costs are not cheap. Maintenance, mortgage payments, property taxes, etc. all push up the carrying costs, but you get to live there and conventional wisdom said that a homes value always increases. The final component is its liquidity premium, which is also related to the expected return. A house in a sellers' market in a good neighborhood might sell quickly, whereas a home next to a newly constructed slaughterhouse might not be so easy to unload.

Thus, people's view of the future plays a critical role in determining the own rate. If the housing market is strong, then it is easy to sell because the expected return is positive and the future seller does not think selling in the future has many risks either. On the other hand, if the market is doing poorly, then the expected return is going down, carrying costs might be increasing, as pickier buyers are demanding more and more repairs, and the liquidity premium is disappearing, as a buyer cannot be found.

This equation can be applied to all sorts of commodities. Give it a try in the exercise section below. Think about a car, stocks, and bonds, or a record collection. These assets all change in own rate based on expectations of the future and how quickly they can be converted into cash. Because it is more difficult to convert assets into cash when markets are unstable and uncertain, people tend to hold onto the one asset that is not negatively impacted. You guessed it: money.

The saving money by an individual in times of uncertainty is problematic for the economy. Keynes argues that this virtuous behavior, from the classical economic perspective, aggregates to difficulties for the macroeconomy as a whole. If you are saving, then, yes, this practice can be beneficial for you, but if we are all saving, then we are not spending and this sends negative signals to investors and business owners. So while individual savings are good, the aggregation of this positive behavior generates adverse economic conditions as a whole. This problem is known as the Paradox of Thrift. This paradox creates difficulties for the neoclassical argument that the aggregation of optimal decisions aggregates to a stable and harmonious society or equilibrium conditions.

If we return to Adam Smith's comments above, we can add the contributions by Marx and Keynes to complete the basic framework for understanding money, not as a commodity in a barter system, but as a social relation in a modern capitalist economy. Remember, the value of money in the Metallist's story is derived intrinsically by a precious metal, but Adam Smith seems to be suggesting that value can be generated by the actions of the Prince. This is a prescient observation by Smith, as modern fiat currencies maintain the value by generating demand through the implementation of a tax or other obligation to the money issuing authority. Therefore, an historical and institutional approach to investigating money reveals fundamentally different dynamics and explanations of the operations of the modern economy. From this interdisciplinary perspective: all economic activity is observed to begin and end with money, money plays this central role because it has special properties, and an authority, such as the state, is responsible for maintaining their currency's value.

By breaking free from the methodological constraints of real analysis, Modern Monetary Theory (MMT) is able to provide insights into economic activity where money serves as more than a contributor to the modus operandi in support of barter. In the next section, money is investigated as a social relation. This social relation can be described as a two-sided balance sheet operation. These relations of credits and debits are ordered in the modern economy by a hierarchical structure. As this institutional structure is outlined below, the coordinating function of money and its role in determining value becomes clear.

25.3 THE MONEY HIERARCHY AND A FALSE DUALITY BETWEEN THE STATE AND THE MARKET

Hyman Minsky once argued that anyone can make money; the real trick is getting people to accept it. For the Metallists, gold or a precious metal's intrinsic value insured money's acceptance as a facilitator of exchange. While simplicity is often a strong characteristic, when it comes to money, a more thorough understanding of money's source of value transforms the relationship between the market and the state. We often think of these two concepts as opposing forces struggling to direct economic activity. From this perspective, one might imagine the market as the strong lead character in pursuit of efficient solutions, and the state as a pesky nemesis taking resources from the market to achieve its own objectives. This plot, however, takes an unexpected twist in Modern Money Theory, as these two characters are revealed to be the same person. The real analysis claims of duality between the state and the market are the product of methodology. The "trick" is not that we accept dollars, but that the true source of their value continues to be largely ignored by economists, policymakers, and the general public.

In 2011, renowned London School of Economics anthropologist David Graeber published a comprehensive examination of the historical origins and development of money, titled Debt: The First 5000 Years. While all 5000 years are interesting, and students are encouraged to explore this exemplary work of scholarship, our focus is limited to the current economic system. This narrow focus will allow us to build upon the above ideas of Marx and Keynes and to develop an understanding of key concepts from MMT. The first of these concepts is the hierarchy of money. From this conceptual framework, we will explore the technostructure of money (see Chapter 16 The Megacorp). The collection of institutions that regulate money's issuance or production is similar to market governance (see Chapter 16 The Megacorp) of business enterprises in that stability is a primary objective. Given the central role of money in economic activity and its origins with the state, the clear delineation between where the market begins and state ends is all but erased.

We begin our analysis with MMT's hierarchy of money. As a social relation, not all money is created equal. For example, by definition as a social relation, you borrowing a shirt from your roommate is a money transaction, as long as you promise to give it back. We call this an IOU. I had a friend in high school that literally carried around a notebook listing all of the people that owed him money (he now works in finance). These records represented promises to pay. For some of those entries, repayment was completed and their name removed, for others, I'm sure they are still in that notebook somewhere in Ol' Johnny Cocktail's archives.

These promises to pay were money transactions. They are two-sided balance sheet operations. Johnny extends credit to his friend; the friend takes on a debt to Johnny. When repayment occurs Johnny's asset, and his friend's liability is terminated. Going back to Hyman Minsky's comment, if one regularly borrows and repays Johnny rapidly, then both parties are willing to accept the terms of the social relation. However, if one does not repay, then future credit extension will not occur. Thus, it takes two to tango. This type of transaction between friends and family are so common, we would not generally describe them as money, because that seems odd. Similarly, borrowing a cup of sugar from your neighbor to make cookies and promising to give some of the cookies in exchange is an informal arrangement, but is still one of credit and debt and thus money. The informality of these transactions makes them difficult to enforce; hence they represent the money social relations at the base of our money hierarchy (Figure 2).

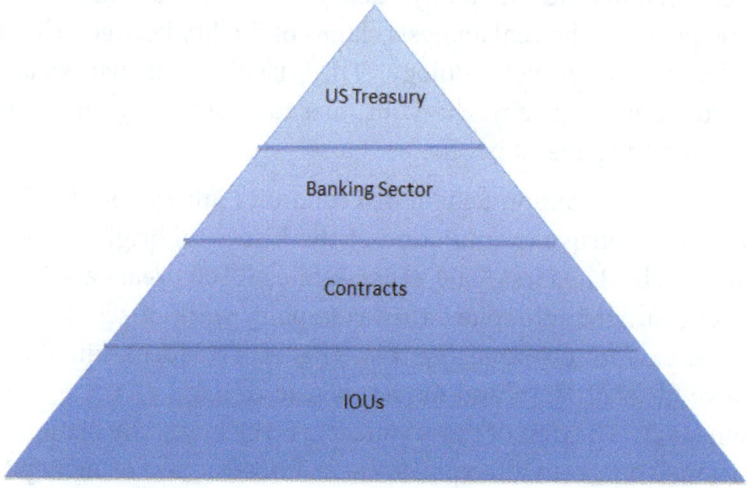

Figure 2. The Money Hierarchy

What differentiates the common and largely unregulated IOU transactions from those that are described as we move up the hierarchy is the institutional formality and enforceability of those social relations. So the second level, contracts, might be promises to pay businesses, such as your network services provider. They promise to provide a service for a year, and you promise to pay a dollar amount for that service. They credit you with service and you pay back your debt. This contract, unlike Johnny's notebook, is legally enforceable in dollars. If you or the network provider breaks your promise legal recourse is available.

Moving on up the hierarchy, we have the financial sector and then the U.S. Treasury at the very top. The formality and institutional structure of the social relations generated by these organizations is what places them at higher levels of this hierarchy. The financial sector is similar to the contracts created below it on the hierarchy, so we will focus our attention on the U.S. Treasury. The U.S. Treasury is unique because by Constitutional Law it is the sole source of new U.S. dollar issue. This institutional reality is one of the most significant aspects of MMT because in stark contrast to the Metallist's story money comes from the state, not the market.

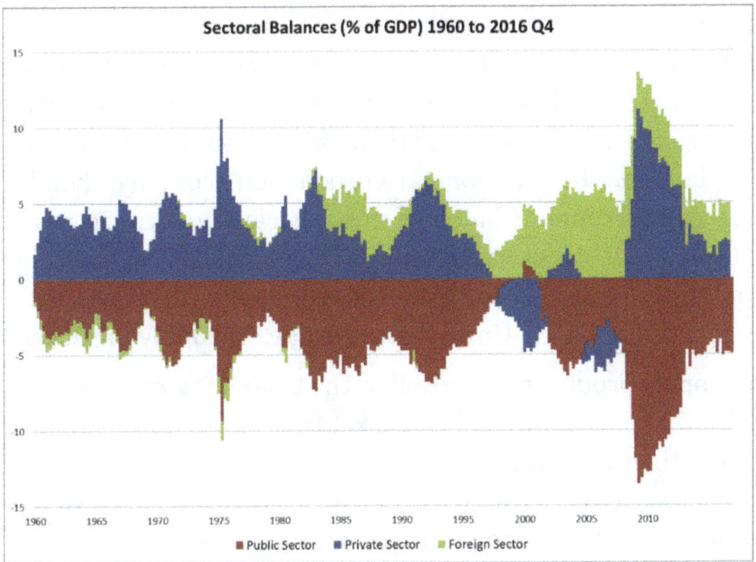

Figure 3. Vividly displays the hierarchy in action. As you can see, as the red line goes into the negative (government deficit), the green line increases (private sector wealth), at a nearly 1:1 ratio. This relationship between public and private spending is described by the accounting identity equation know as sectoral balances.

$$0 = (S - I) + (T - G) + (\text{net exports})$$

This equation states that the balance sheets of the private, public, and international current accounts sectors of the economy sum to zero. If we were to close the economy and only have the public and private sector, then when the private sector spends more than it takes in (deficit spends), the public sector, by accounting identity, runs a surplus. This situation rarely occurs. If we examine Figure 3, we see that in the early 2000s a very brief period of government budget surplus took place, only to be followed by recession and a movement back to state deficits and private surpluses.

Before pressing forward, let's take a moment to summarize the hierarchy of money. Money is a social relation. It is a two-sided balance sheet operation or an IOU. It consists of at least two parties who agree to a credit debit relationship. The hierarchy of money is characterized by the institutional constraints and enforcement of these social relations. At the top of the hierarchy is the issuer of the currency. The currency issued in the United States is the dollar. Rather than the dollar emerging in the market to solve the double coincidence of wants, the dollar comes from the state. This leaves us with the question of value. If there is not a precious metal or intrinsic value to the dollar, then where does its value come from?

Value comes from a promise from the state to accept U.S. dollars as payment for taxes. This promise creates a demand for dollars in the United States. The demand for dollars is what maintains the dollar's value. Thus, MMT argues that taxes drive money. An important question that this raises is how does this impact the value of goods and services produced? Remember in the orthodox approach the prices of goods and services are measures of their relative values as they are traded in a barter system, but if we have a monetary production economy, then how are these activities ' values determined? Much of this was clearly outlined at the enterprise level in the Costs and Prices chapter and further analyzed in the Megacorp. Here we ask the question, how does our perspective on value change when we approach money as an industry with the United States as the monopoly producer?

As the monopoly producer of the dollar, the United States government is not the pesky nemesis taking money from the market to fund its spending. Instead, private markets and the financial industry are provided with the legal authority to create dollar-denominated assets. This process greatly limits what is viewed to have value to activities that generate profits. This mode of utilizing money-issuing authority makes it very difficult for many in the economic system to participate in the dollar economy. Orthodox economics and the Metallist story argues that value creation is best handled by markets, rather than direct state spending. As the monopoly producer of the currency, it is a political decision about how money enters the system and assigns value. Many MMT theorists argue that the values of the community would be better met through a universal program for full employment. This would mean the monopoly producer would take more control over value creation to meet the needs of the public than it currently does.

The sectoral balances relationship between the public and private sector, suggests that there is an intimate relationship between the state and market activities. The approach taken by neoclassical economics suggests an antagonistic relationship based on real analysis. The foundation for this position is that the state must take money from the private sector to spend. The history and an institutional analysis of where money comes from debunk this foundation. If, as Keynes suggests, we live in a monetary production economy and new issue comes from the state, then continuing to approach the market and state as hard duals is likely to continue to leave many outside of the dollar economy in states of unemployment and poverty.

To further examine money's ability to activate value, we will now turn to an examination of local currency systems. Local currency systems are experiments. These experiments are attempting to build an understanding of the power of our most important social technology. Remember, we have defined technology as the application of scientific or organized knowledge of practical tasks. What could be more practical a task than to understand money?

25.4 SOCIAL MONEY AND COMMUNITY CURRENCIES IN LOCAL CURRENCY SYSTEMS

As an alternative to centralized money issue, communities are exploring their own money issuing strategies. There are several types of local currency systems, and we will describe a couple of the most common ones' general characteristics and institutional structures below. One source that outlines the extent to which currency experimentation has grown during the era of neoliberalism is described by the 2012 International Journal of Community Currency Research Special Issue titled "Thirty Years of Community Currencies: A Review of Impacts, Potential and Challenges." This edition contains papers from a two-day academic conference that included scholars from several academic disciplines. Scholars in economics, history, geography, law, sociology, anthropology, and political science, etc. presented research from those disciplines individually and through interdisciplinary methodologies as well. In addition to the diversity of academic perspectives community currencies are attracting, they are also covering diverse political and geographic terrains across the planet. More than 20 different countries were represented at this conference.

One reason that such a diverse set of tools is necessary for studying community currencies is that if the Metallist's story of money is false, then the price mechanism or the invisible hand is not an adequate means of determining value. In *The Picture of Dorian Gray*, Oscar Wilde tells us that; "Nowadays people know the price of everything and the value of nothing." Community currencies are projects that work to allow communities to assign values to activities and goods that central currency schemes are not pricing properly. As such, these activities are experiments. These experiments are guided by general philosophies, such as solidarity and reciprocity. Their philosophies influence goals and the purpose of currency creation, examples include community stability, intergenerational relationship building, and strengthening of territory or stimulating economic activity. From these general goals, communities create real jobs: to promote sustainable production, support the elderly, women's programs, and other civically oriented tasks not being met by the market of fiscal sectors of the economy. Thus, when value is reintroduced into a discussion about the economy, the limited toolset available under real analysis is replaced by a diversity of methodologies from several academic disciplines.

In an effort to organize the analysis of this diverse and growing collection of money systems, three categories of local currency systems have been suggested. The first of these are local currencies are territorial projects. These projects are typically defined by geographic boundaries and are designed to strengthen the area's resilience or development. Second, community currencies are projects developed to address a specific community need. Such needs are usually determined by a group of local actors attempting to emphasize increased wellbeing, empowerment of a repressed group, or support environmental health. The third type is a complementary currency. Complementary currencies are designed to support an economic objective. These systems are generally designed with regard to market principles and work to support activities between production and exchange of goods and services. These types of currency systems are not mutually exclusive in their characteristics. In fact, many take on objectives and characteristics that draw from multiple currency types. One such currency system is the Red del Traque (RT) of Argentina.

Ecologists developed the RT currency system. In this ecological model, the wellbeing of women and families was a primary objective. To accomplish their objective, markets or 'nodos' were set up in economically depressed neighborhoods. These markets used the RT currency system to organize labor efforts and create household stability by encouraging self-production, reducing waste, promoting the resale of household items, providing social welfare labor, and helping to distribute unsold surpluses in local businesses through new trade outlets. Thus, from this description, we could classify the RT in all three of the suggested category types. It is a community currency based on its primary objective. It can also be described as a complementary currency as it facilitated market exchanges, and it targeted particular territories based on economic need, territorial.

By creating a local currency system, many Argentinians who had been abandoned by the peso economy were provided an opportunity to contribute to social activity and find some economic stability. In a sense, Argentinians were able to solve Keynes's elasticity problem. There was a shortage of money in their communities, so they found a creative, socially driven solution to solve the shortage. This local currency system effectively organized available resources and produced outputs that were deemed valuable to the community.

To conclude, money takes on very different roles in our economic system based on the methodology applied to study economic activity. If it is simply the medium of exchange, then the coordination of inputs to produce outputs is the role of individual firms. However, when money is observed in its historical and institutional setting, business enterprises need money to initiate those coordinating functions, as we see in Marx's circuit of money capital. Given this central role in all economic activity, the task of economists and other scholars is to help society create laws and institutions such that money is available to initiate productive value-generating activities because merely assessing value through profits appears to be a woefully inadequate approach.

The French economists Jerome Blanc has published widely in the area of community and complementary currencies.

Georgina Gomez and Bert Helmsing from the Hague in the Netherlands published a very interesting article about the spatial distribution of the RT in Argentina in the 2008 Vol. 36(11) of World Development titled "Selective Spatial Closure and Local Economic Development."

CHAPTER

INTRODUCTION TO INTERNATIONAL TRADE 26

26.1 COMPARATIVE AND ABSOLUTE BENEFIT

The American statesman Benjamin Franklin (1706–1790) once wrote: "No nation was ever ruined by trade." Many economists would express their attitudes toward international trade in an even more positive manner. The evidence that international trade confers overall benefits on economies is pretty strong. Trade has accompanied economic growth in the United States and around the world. Many of the national economies that have shown the most rapid growth in the last few decades—for example, Japan, South Korea, China, and India—have done so by dramatically orienting their economies toward international trade. There is no modern example of a country that has shut itself off from world trade and yet prospered. To understand the benefits of trade, or why we trade in the first place, we need to understand the concepts of comparative and absolute advantage.

In 1817, **David Ricardo**, a businessman, economist, and member of the British Parliament, wrote a treatise called *On the Principles of Political Economy and Taxation.* In this treatise, Ricardo argued that specialization and free trade benefit all trading partners, even those that may be relatively inefficient. To see what he meant, we must be able to distinguish between absolute and comparative advantage.

A country has an absolute advantage in producing a good over another country if it uses fewer resources to produce that good. Absolute advantage can be the result of a country's natural endowment. For example, extracting oil in Saudi Arabia is pretty much just a matter of "drilling a hole." Producing oil in other countries can require considerable exploration and costly technologies for drilling and extraction—if indeed they have any oil at all. The United States has some of the richest farmland in the world, making it easier to grow corn and wheat than in many other countries. Guatemala and Colombia have climates especially suited for growing coffee. Chile and Zambia have some of the world's richest copper mines. As some have argued, "geography is destiny." Chile will provide copper and Guatemala will produce coffee, and they will trade. When each country has a product others need and it can be produced with fewer resources in one country over another, then it is easy to imagine all parties benefitting from trade. However, thinking about trade just in terms of geography and absolute advantage is incomplete. Trade really occurs because of comparative advantage.

Recall from the chapter Choice in a World of Scarcity that a country has a comparative advantage when a good can be produced at a lower cost in terms of other goods. The question each country or company should be asking when it trades is this: "What do we give up to produce this good?" It should be no surprise that the concept of comparative advantage is based on this idea of opportunity cost from Choice in a World of Scarcity. For example, if Zambia focuses its resources on producing copper, its labor, land and financial resources cannot be used to produce other goods such as corn. As a result, Zambia gives up the opportunity to produce corn. How do we quantify the cost in terms of other goods? Simplify the problem and assume that Zambia just needs labor to produce copper and corn. The companies that produce either copper or corn tell you that it takes 10 hours to mine a ton of copper and 20 hours to harvest a bushel of corn. This means the opportunity cost of producing a ton of copper is 2 bushels of corn. The next section develops absolute and comparative advantage in greater detail and relates them to trade.

A Numerical Example of Absolute and Comparative Advantage

Consider a hypothetical world with two countries, Saudi Arabia and the United States, and two products, oil and corn. Further assume that consumers in both countries desire both these goods. These goods are homogeneous, meaning that consumers/producers cannot differentiate between corn or oil from either country. There is only one resource available in both countries, labor hours. Saudi Arabia can produce oil with fewer resources, while the United States can produce corn with fewer resources. Table 1 illustrates the advantages of the two countries, expressed in terms of how many hours it takes to produce one unit of each good.

Table 1. How Many Hours It Takes to Produce Oil and Corn

Country	Oil (hours per barrel)	Corn (hours per bushel)
Saudi Arabia	1	4
United States	2	1

In Table 1, Saudi Arabia has an absolute advantage in the production of oil because it only takes an hour to produce a barrel of oil compared to two hours in the United States. The United States has an absolute advantage in the production of corn.

To simplify, let's say that Saudi Arabia and the United States each have 100 worker hours (see Table 2). We illustrate what each country is capable of producing on its own using a production possibility frontier (PPF) graph, shown in Figure 1. Recall from Choice in a World of Scarcity that the production possibilities frontier shows the maximum amount that each country can produce given its limited resources, in this case workers, and its level of technology.

Table 2. Production Possibilities before Trade

Country	Oil Production using 100 worker hours (barrels)		Corn Production using 100 worker hours (bushels)
Saudi Arabia	100	or	25
United States	50	or	100

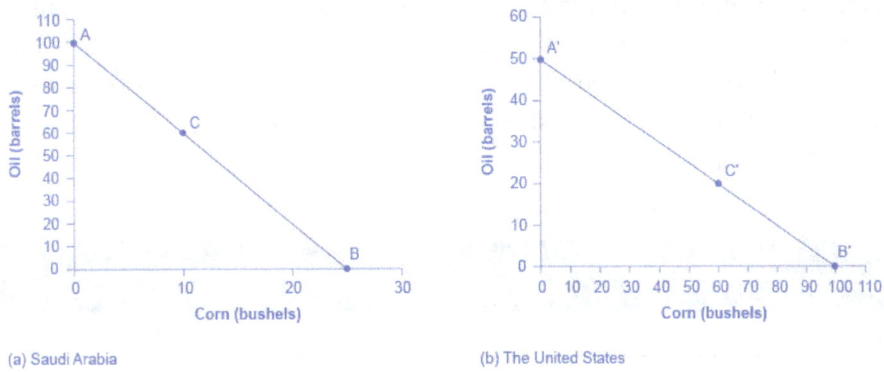

Figure 1. Production Possibilities Frontiers. (a) Saudi Arabia can produce 100 barrels of oil at maximum and zero corn (point A), or 25 bushels of corn and zero oil (point B). It can also produce other combinations of oil and corn if it wants to consume both goods, such as at point C. Here it chooses to produce/consume 60 barrels of oil, leaving 40 work hours that can be allocated to producing 10 bushels of corn, using the data in Table 1. (b) If the United States produces only oil, it can produce, at maximum, 50 barrels and zero corn (point A'), or at the other extreme, it can produce a maximum of 100 bushels of corn and no oil (point B'). Other combinations of both oil and corn are possible, such as point C'. All points above the frontiers are impossible to produce given the current level of resources and technology.

Arguably Saudi and U.S. consumers desire both oil and corn to live. Let's say that before trade occurs, both countries produce and consume at point C or C'. Thus, before trade, the Saudi Arabian economy will devote 60 worker hours to produce oil, as shown in Table 3. Given the information in Table 1, this choice implies that it produces/consumes 60 barrels of oil. With the remaining 40 worker hours, since it needs four hours to produce a bushel of corn, it can produce only 10 bushels. To be at point C', the U.S. economy devotes 40 worker hours to produce 20 barrels of oil and the remaining worker hours can be allocated to produce 60 bushels of corn.

Table 3. Production before Trade

Country	Oil Production (barrels)	Corn Production (bushels)
Saudi Arabia (C)	60	10
United States (C')	20	60
Total World Production	80	70

The slope of the production possibility frontier illustrates the opportunity cost of producing oil in terms of corn. Using all its resources, the United States can produce 50 barrels of oil or 100 bushels of corn. So the opportunity cost of one barrel of oil is two bushels of corn—or the slope is 1/2. Thus, in the U.S. production possibility frontier graph, every increase in oil production of one barrel implies a decrease of two bushels of corn. Saudi Arabia can produce 100 barrels of oil or 25 bushels of corn. The opportunity cost of producing one barrel of oil is the loss of 1/4 of a bushel of corn that Saudi workers could otherwise have produced. In terms of corn, notice that Saudi Arabia gives up the least to produce a barrel of oil. These calculations are summarized in Table 4.

Table 4. Opportunity Cost and Comparative Advantage

Country	Opportunity cost of one unit — Oil (in terms of corn)	Opportunity cost of one unit — Corn (in terms of oil)
Saudi Arabia	¼	4
United States	2	½

Again recall that comparative advantage was defined as the opportunity cost of producing goods. Since Saudi Arabia gives up the least to produce a barrel of oil, (1414 < 22 in Table 4) it has a comparative advantage in oil production. The United States gives up the least to produce a bushel of corn, so it has a comparative advantage in corn production.

In this example, there is symmetry between absolute and comparative advantage. Saudi Arabia needs fewer worker hours to produce oil (absolute advantage, see Table 1), and also gives up the least in terms of other goods to produce oil (comparative advantage, see Table 4). Such symmetry is not always the case, as we will show after we have discussed gains from trade fully. But first, read the following Clear It Up feature to make sure you understand why the PPF line in the graphs is straight.

Can a production possibility frontier be straight?

When you first met the production possibility frontier (PPF) in the chapter on Choice in a World of Scarcity it was drawn with an outward-bending shape. This shape illustrated that as inputs were transferred from producing one good to another—like from education to health services—there were increasing opportunity costs. In the examples in this chapter, the PPFs are drawn as straight lines, which means that opportunity costs are constant. When a marginal unit of labor is transferred away from growing corn and toward producing oil, the decline in the quantity of corn and the increase in the quantity of oil is always the same. In reality this is possible only if the contribution of additional workers to output did not change as the scale of production changed. The linear production possibilities frontier is a less realistic model, but a straight line simplifies calculations. It also illustrates economic themes like absolute and comparative advantage just as clearly.

Gains from Trade

Consider the trading positions of the United States and Saudi Arabia after they have specialized and traded. Before trade, Saudi Arabia produces/consumes 60 barrels of oil and 10 bushels of corn. The United States produces/consumes 20 barrels of oil and 60 bushels of corn. Given their current production levels, if the United States can trade an amount of corn fewer than 60 bushels and receives in exchange an amount of oil greater than 20 barrels, it will gain from trade. With trade, the United States can consume more of both goods than it did without specialization and trade. (Recall that the chapter Welcome to Economics! defined specialization as it applies to workers and firms. Specialization is also used to describe the occurrence when a country shifts resources to focus on producing a good that offers comparative advantage.) Similarly, if Saudi Arabia can trade an amount of oil less than 60 barrels and receive in exchange an amount of corn greater than 10 bushels, it will have more of both goods than it did before specialization and trade. Table 5 illustrates the range of trades that would benefit both sides.

Table 5. The Range of Trades That Benefit Both the United States and Saudi Arabia

The U.S. Economy, after Specialization, Will Benefit If It:	The Saudi Arabian Economy, after Specialization, Will Benefit If It:
Exports no more than 60 bushels of corn	Imports at least 10 bushels of corn
Imports at least 20 barrels of oil	Exports less than 60 barrels of oil

The underlying reason why trade benefits both sides is rooted in the concept of opportunity cost, as the following Clear It Up feature explains. If Saudi Arabia wishes to expand domestic production of corn in a world without international trade, then based on its opportunity costs it must give up four barrels of oil for every one additional bushel of corn. If Saudi Arabia could find a way to give up less than four barrels of oil for an additional bushel of corn (or equivalently, to receive more than one bushel of corn for four barrels of oil), it would be better off.

What are the opportunity costs and gains from trade?

The range of trades that will benefit each country is based on the country's opportunity cost of producing each good. The United States can produce 100 bushels of corn or 50 barrels of oil. For the United States, the opportunity cost of producing one barrel of oil is two bushels of corn. If we divide the numbers above by 50, we get the same ratio: one barrel of oil is equivalent to two bushels of corn, or (100/50 = 2 and 50/50 = 1). In a trade with Saudi Arabia, if the United States is going to give up 100 bushels of corn in exports, it must import at least 50 barrels of oil to be just as well off. Clearly, to gain from trade it needs to be able to gain more than a half barrel of oil for its bushel of corn—or why trade at all?

Recall that David Ricardo argued that if each country specializes in its comparative advantage, it will benefit from trade, and total global output will increase. How can we show gains from trade as a result of comparative advantage and specialization? Table 6 shows the output assuming that each country specializes in its comparative advantage and produces no other good. This is 100% specialization. Specialization leads to an increase in total world production. (Compare the total world production in Table 3 to that in Table 6.)

Table 6. How Specialization Expands Output

Country	Quantity produced after 100% specialization — Oil (barrels)	Quantity produced after 100% specialization — Corn (bushels)
Saudi Arabia	100	0
United States	0	100
Total World Production	100	100

What if we did not have complete specialization, as in Table 6? Would there still be gains from trade? Consider another example, such as when the United States and Saudi Arabia start at C and C', respectively, as shown in Figure 1. Consider what occurs when trade is allowed and the United States exports 20 bushels of corn to Saudi Arabia in exchange for 20 barrels of oil.

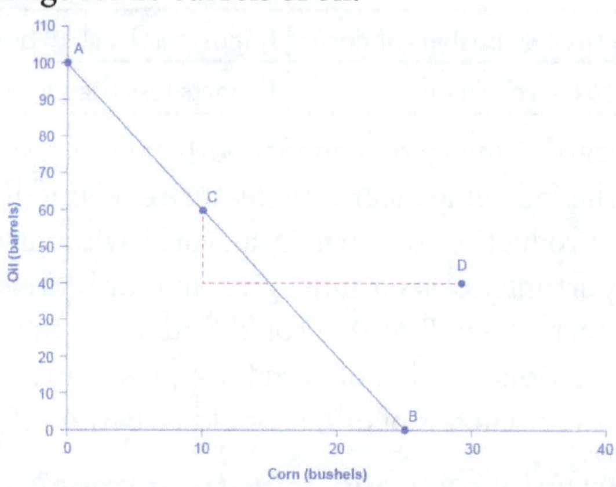

Figure 2. Production Possibilities Frontier in Saudi Arabia. Gains from trade of oil can increase only by achieving less from trade of corn. The opposite is true as well: The more gains from trade of corn, the fewer gains from trade of oil.

Starting at point C, reduce Saudi Oil production by 20 and exchange it for 20 units of corn to reach point D (see Figure 2). Notice that even without 100% specialization, if the "trading price," in this case 20 barrels of oil for 20 bushels of corn, is greater than the country's opportunity cost, the Saudis will gain from trade. Indeed both countries consume more of both goods after specialized production and trade occurs.

Concepts and Summary

A country has an absolute advantage in those products in which it has a productivity edge over other countries; it takes fewer resources to produce a product. A country has a comparative advantage when a good can be produced at a lower cost in terms of other goods. Countries that specialize based on comparative advantage gain from trade.

26.2 IF A COUNTRY HAS AN ABSOLUTE ADVANTAGE IN ALL GOODS, WHAT HAPPENS?

What happens to the possibilities for trade if one country has an absolute advantage in everything? This is typical for high-income countries that often have well-educated workers, technologically advanced equipment, and the most up-to-date production processes. These high-income countries can produce all products with fewer resources than a low-income country. If the high-income country is more productive across the board, will there still be gains from trade? Good students of Ricardo understand that trade is about mutually beneficial exchange. Even when one country has an absolute advantage in all products, trade can still benefit both sides. This is because gains from trade come from specializing in one's comparative advantage.

Production Possibilities and Comparative Advantage

Consider the example of trade between the United States and Mexico described in Table 8. In this example, it takes four U.S. workers to produce 1,000 pairs of shoes, but it takes five Mexican workers to do so. It takes one U.S. worker to produce 1,000 refrigerators, but it takes four Mexican workers to do so. The United States has an absolute advantage in productivity with regard to both shoes and refrigerators; that is, it takes fewer workers in the United States than in Mexico to produce both a given number of shoes and a given number of refrigerators.

Table 8. Resources Needed to Produce Shoes and Refrigerators

Country	Number of Workers needed to produce 1,000 units — Shoes	Number of Workers needed to produce 1,000 units — Refrigerators
United States	4 workers	1 worker
Mexico	5 workers	4 workers

Absolute advantage simply compares the productivity of a worker between countries. It answers the question, "How many inputs do I need to produce shoes in Mexico?" Comparative advantage asks this same question slightly differently. Instead of comparing how many workers it takes to produce a good, it asks, "How much am I giving up to produce this good in this country?" Another way of looking at this is that comparative advantage identifies the good for which the producer's absolute advantage is relatively larger, or where the producer's absolute productivity disadvantage is relatively smaller. The United States can produce 1,000 shoes with four-fifths as many workers as Mexico (four versus five), but it can produce 1,000 refrigerators with only one-quarter as many workers (one versus four). So, the comparative advantage of the United States, where its absolute productivity advantage is relatively greatest, lies with refrigerators, and Mexico's comparative advantage, where its absolute productivity disadvantage is least, is in the production of shoes.

Mutually Beneficial Trade with Comparative Advantage

When nations increase production in their area of comparative advantage and trade with each other, both countries can benefit. Again, the production possibility frontier is a useful tool to visualize this benefit.

Consider a situation where the United States and Mexico each have 40 workers. For example, as Table 9 shows, if the United States divides its labor so that 40 workers are making shoes, then, since it takes four workers in the United States to make 1,000 shoes, a total of 10,000 shoes will be produced. (If four workers can make 1,000 shoes, then 40 workers will make 10,000 shoes). If the 40 workers in the United States are making refrigerators, and each worker can produce 1,000 refrigerators, then a total of 40,000 refrigerators will be produced.

Table 9. Production Possibilities before Trade with Complete Specialization

Country	Shoe Production — using 40 workers		Refrigerator Production — using 40 workers
United States	10,000 shoes	or	40,000 refrigerators
Mexico	8,000 shoes	or	10,000 refrigerators

As always, the slope of the production possibility frontier for each country is the opportunity cost of one refrigerator in terms of foregone shoe production–when labor is transferred from producing the latter to producing the former (see Figure 1).

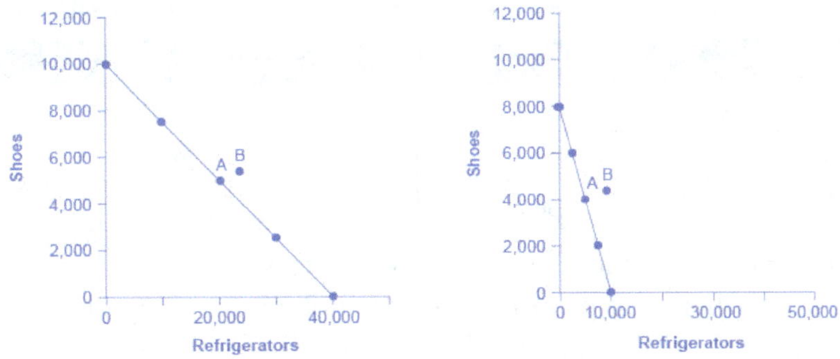

(a) U.S. PPF (40 workers) (b) Mexico PPF (40 workers)

Figure 1. Production Possibility Frontiers. (a) With 40 workers, the United States can produce either 10,000 shoes and zero refrigerators or 40,000 refrigerators and zero shoes. (b) With 40 workers, Mexico can produce a maximum of 8,000 shoes and zero refrigerators, or 10,000 refrigerators and zero shoes. All other points on the production possibility line are possible combinations of the two goods that can be produced given current resources. Point A on both graphs is where the countries start producing and consuming before trade. Point B is where they end up after trade.

Let's say that, in the situation before trade, each nation prefers to produce a combination of shoes and refrigerators that is shown at point A. Table 10 shows the output of each good for each country and the total output for the two countries.

Table 10. Total Production at Point A before Trade

Country	Current Shoe Production	Current Refrigerator Production
United States	5,000	20,000
Mexico	4,000	5,000
Total	9,000	25,000

Continuing with this scenario, each country transfers some amount of labor toward its area of comparative advantage. For example, the United States transfers six workers away from shoes and toward producing refrigerators. As a result, U.S. production of shoes decreases by 1,500 units (6/4 × 1,000), while its production of refrigerators increases by 6,000 (that is, 6/1 × 1,000). Mexico also moves production toward its area of comparative advantage, transferring 10 workers away from refrigerators and toward production of shoes. As a result, production of refrigerators in Mexico falls by 2,500 (10/4 × 1,000), but production of shoes increases by 2,000 pairs (10/5 × 1,000). Notice that when both countries shift production toward each of their comparative advantages (what they are relatively better at), their combined production of both goods rises, as shown in Table 11. The reduction of shoe production by 1,500 pairs in the United States is more than offset by the gain of 2,000 pairs of shoes in Mexico, while the reduction of 2,500 refrigerators in Mexico is more than offset by the additional 6,000 refrigerators produced in the United States.

Table 11. Shifting Production Toward Comparative Advantage Raises Total Output

Country	Shoe Production	Refrigerator Production
United States	3,500	26,000
Mexico	6,000	2,500
Total	9,500	28,500

This numerical example illustrates the remarkable insight of comparative advantage: even when one country has an absolute advantage in all goods and another country has an absolute disadvantage in all goods, both countries can still benefit from trade. Even though the United States has an absolute advantage in producing both refrigerators and shoes, it makes economic sense for it to specialize in the good for which it has a comparative advantage. The United States will export refrigerators and in return import shoes.

How Opportunity Cost Sets the Boundaries of Trade

This example shows that both parties can benefit from specializing in their comparative advantages and trading. By using the opportunity costs in this example, it is possible to identify the range of possible trades that would benefit each country.

Mexico started out, before specialization and trade, producing 4,000 pairs of shoes and 5,000 refrigerators (see Figure 1 and Table 10). Then, in the numerical example given, Mexico shifted production toward its comparative advantage and produced 6,000 pairs of shoes but only 2,500 refrigerators. Thus, if Mexico can export no more than 2,000 pairs of shoes (giving up 2,000 pairs of shoes) in exchange for imports of at least 2,500 refrigerators (a gain of 2,500 refrigerators), it will be able to consume more of both goods than before trade. Mexico will be unambiguously better off. Conversely, the United States started off, before specialization and trade, producing 5,000 pairs of shoes and 20,000 refrigerators. In the example, it then shifted production toward its comparative advantage, producing only 3,500 shoes but 26,000 refrigerators. If the United States can export no more than 6,000 refrigerators in exchange for imports of at least 1,500 pairs of shoes, it will be able to consume more of both goods and will be unambiguously better off.

The range of trades that can benefit both nations is shown in Table 12. For example, a trade where the U.S. exports 4,000 refrigerators to Mexico in exchange for 1,800 pairs of shoes would benefit both sides, in the sense that both countries would be able to consume more of both goods than in a world without trade.

Table 12. The Range of Trades That Benefit Both the United States and Mexico

The U.S. economy, after specialization, will benefit if it:	The Mexican economy, after specialization, will benefit if it:
Exports fewer than 6,000 refrigerators	Imports at least 2,500 refrigerators
Imports at least 1,500 pairs of shoes	Exports no more than 2,000 pairs of shoes

Trade allows each country to take advantage of lower opportunity costs in the other country. If Mexico wants to produce more refrigerators without trade, it must face its domestic opportunity costs and reduce shoe production. If Mexico, instead, produces more shoes and then trades for refrigerators made in the United States, where the opportunity cost of producing refrigerators is lower, Mexico can in effect take advantage of the lower opportunity cost of refrigerators in the United States. Conversely, when the United States specializes in its comparative advantage of refrigerator production and trades for shoes produced in Mexico, international trade allows the United States to take advantage of the lower opportunity cost of shoe production in Mexico.

The theory of comparative advantage explains why countries trade: they have different comparative advantages. It shows that the gains from international trade result from pursuing comparative advantage and producing at a lower opportunity cost. The following Work It Out feature shows how to calculate absolute and comparative advantage and the way to apply them to a country's production.

Calculating Absolute and Comparative Advantage

In Canada a worker can produce 20 barrels of oil or 40 tons of lumber. In Venezuela, a worker can produce 60 barrels of oil or 30 tons of lumber.

Table 13.

Country	Oil (barrels)		Lumber (tons)
Canada	20	or	40
Venezuela	60	or	30

- Who has the absolute advantage in the production of oil or lumber? How can you tell?
- Which country has a comparative advantage in the production of oil?
- Which country has a comparative advantage in producing lumber?
- In this example, is absolute advantage the same as comparative advantage, or not?
- In what product should Canada specialize? In what product should Venezuela specialize?

Step 1. Make a table like Table 13.

Step 2. To calculate absolute advantage, look at the larger of the numbers for each product. One worker in Canada can produce more lumber (40 tons versus 30 tons), so Canada has the absolute advantage in lumber. One worker in Venezuela can produce 60 barrels of oil compared to a worker in Canada who can produce only 20.

Step 3. To calculate comparative advantage, find the opportunity cost of producing one barrel of oil in both countries. The country with the lowest opportunity cost has the comparative advantage. With the same labor time, Canada can produce either 20 barrels of oil or 40 tons of lumber. So in effect, 20 barrels of oil is equivalent to 40 tons of lumber: 20 oil = 40 lumber. Divide both sides of the equation by 20 to calculate the opportunity cost of one barrel of oil in Canada. 20/20 oil = 40/20 lumber. 1 oil = 2 lumber. To produce one additional barrel of oil in Canada has an opportunity cost of 2 lumber. Calculate the same way for Venezuela: 60 oil = 30 lumber. Divide both sides of the equation by 60. One oil in Venezuela has an opportunity cost of 1/2 lumber. Because 1/2 lumber < 2 lumber, Venezuela has the comparative advantage in producing oil.

Step 4. Calculate the opportunity cost of one lumber by reversing the numbers, with lumber on the left side of the equation. In Canada, 40 lumber is equivalent in labor time to 20 barrels of oil: 40 lumber = 20 oil. Divide each side of the equation by 40. The opportunity cost of one lumber is 1/2 oil. In Venezuela, the equivalent labor time will produce 30 lumber or 60 oil: 30 lumber = 60 oil. Divide each side by 30. One lumber has an opportunity cost of two oil. Canada has the lower opportunity cost in producing lumber.

Step 5. In this example, absolute advantage is the same as comparative advantage. Canada has the absolute and comparative advantage in lumber; Venezuela has the absolute and comparative advantage in oil.

Step 6. Canada should specialize in what it has a relative lower opportunity cost, which is lumber, and Venezuela should specialize in oil. Canada will be exporting lumber and importing oil, and Venezuela will be exporting oil and importing lumber.

Comparative Advantage Goes Camping

To build an intuitive understanding of how comparative advantage can benefit all parties, set aside examples that involve national economies for a moment and consider the situation of a group of friends who decide to go camping together. The six friends have a wide range of skills and experiences, but one person in particular, Jethro, has done lots of camping before and is also a great athlete. Jethro has an absolute advantage in all aspects of camping: he is faster at carrying a backpack, gathering firewood, paddling a canoe, setting up tents, making a meal, and washing up. So here is the question: Because Jethro has an absolute productivity advantage in everything, should he do all the work?

Of course not! Even if Jethro is willing to work like a mule while everyone else sits around, he, like most mortals, only has 24 hours in a day. If everyone sits around and waits for Jethro to do everything, not only will Jethro be an unhappy camper, but there will not be much output for his group of six friends to consume. The theory of comparative advantage suggests that everyone will benefit if they figure out their areas of comparative advantage—that is, the area of camping where their productivity disadvantage is least, compared to Jethro. For example, it may be that Jethro is 80% faster at building fires and cooking meals than anyone else, but only 20% faster at gathering firewood and 10% faster at setting up tents. In that case, Jethro should focus on building fires and making meals, and others should attend to the other tasks, each according to where their productivity disadvantage is smallest. If the campers coordinate their efforts according to comparative advantage, they can all gain.

Concepts and Summary

Even when a country has high levels of productivity in all goods, it can still benefit from trade. Gains from trade come about as a result of comparative advantage. By specializing in a good that it gives up the least to produce, a country can produce more and offer that additional output for sale. If other countries specialize in the area of their comparative advantage as well and trade, the highly productive country is able to benefit from a lower opportunity cost of production in other countries.

26.3 INTRA-INDUSTRY TRADE BETWEEN SIMILAR ECONOMIES

Absolute and comparative advantages explain a great deal about patterns of global trade. For example, they help to explain the patterns noted at the start of this chapter, like why you may be eating fresh fruit from Chile or Mexico, or why lower productivity regions like Africa and Latin America are able to sell a substantial proportion of their exports to higher productivity regions like the European Union and North America. Comparative advantage, however, at least at first glance, does not seem especially well-suited to explain other common patterns of international trade.

The Prevalence of Intra-industry Trade between Similar Economies

The theory of comparative advantage suggests that trade should happen between economies with large differences in opportunity costs of production. Roughly half of all world trade involves shipping goods between the fairly similar high-income economies of the United States, Canada, the European Union, Japan, Mexico, and China (see Table 14).

Table 14. Where U.S. Exports Go and U.S. Imports Originate (2015) (Source: https://www.census.gov/foreign-trade/Press-Release/current_press_release/ft900.pdf)

Country	U.S. Exports Go to ...	U.S. Imports Come from ...
European Union	19.0%	21.0%
Canada	22.0%	14.0%
Japan	4.0%	6.0%
Mexico	15.0%	13.0%
China	8.0%	20.0%

Moreover, the theory of comparative advantage suggests that each economy should specialize to a degree in certain products, and then exchange those products. A high proportion of trade, however, is intra-industry trade—that is, trade of goods within the same industry from one country to another. For example, the United States produces and exports autos and imports autos. Table 15 shows some of the largest categories of U.S. exports and imports. In all of these categories, the United States is both a substantial exporter and a substantial importer of goods from the same industry. In 2014, according to the Bureau of Economic Analysis, the United States exported $159 billion worth of autos, and imported $327 billion worth of autos. About 60% of U.S. trade and 60% of European trade is intra-industry trade.

Table 15. Some Intra-Industry U.S. Exports and Imports in 2014 (Source: http://www.bea.gov/newsreleases/international/trade/tradnewsrelease.htm)

Some U.S. Exports	Quantity of Exports ($ billions)	Quantity of Imports ($ billions)
Autos	$146	$327
Food and beverages	$144	$126
Capital goods	$550	$551
Consumer goods	$199	$558
Industrial supplies	$507	$665
Other transportation	$45	$55

Why do similar high-income economies engage in intra-industry trade? What can be the economic benefit of having workers of fairly similar skills making cars, computers, machinery and other products which are then shipped across the oceans to and from the United States, the European Union, and Japan? There are two reasons: (1) The division of labor leads to learning, innovation, and unique skills; and (2) economies of scale.

Gains from Specialization and Learning

Consider the category of machinery, where the U.S. economy has considerable intra-industry trade. Machinery comes in many varieties, so the United States may be exporting machinery for manufacturing with wood, but importing machinery for photographic processing. The underlying reason why a country like the United States, Japan, or Germany produces one kind of machinery rather than another is usually not related to U.S., German, or Japanese firms and workers having generally higher or lower skills. It is just that, in working on very specific and particular products, firms in certain countries develop unique and different skills.

Specialization in the world economy can be very finely split. In fact, recent years have seen a trend in international trade called splitting up the value chain. The value chain describes how a good is produced in stages. As indicated in the beginning of the chapter, the production of the iPhone involves the design and engineering of the phone in the United States, parts supplied from Korea, the assembly of the parts in China, and the advertising and marketing done in the United States. Thanks in large part to improvements in communication technology, sharing information, and transportation, it has become easier to split up the value chain. Instead of production in a single large factory, all of these steps can be split up among different firms operating in different places and even different countries. Because firms split up the value chain, international trade often does not involve whole finished products like automobiles or refrigerators being traded between nations. Instead, it involves shipping more specialized goods like, say, automobile dashboards or the shelving that fits inside refrigerators. Intra-industry trade between similar countries produces economic gains because it allows workers and firms to learn and innovate on particular products—and often to focus on very particular parts of the value chain.

Economies of Scale, Competition, Variety

A second broad reason that intra-industry trade between similar nations produces economic gains involves economies of scale. The concept of economies of scale, as introduced in Cost and Industry Structure, means that as the scale of output goes up, average costs of production decline—at least up to a point. Figure 1 illustrates economies of scale for a plant producing toaster ovens. The horizontal axis of the figure shows the quantity of production by a certain firm or at a certain manufacturing plant. The vertical axis measures the average cost of production. Production plant S produces a small level of output at 30 units and has an average cost of production of \$30 per toaster oven. Plant M produces at a medium level of output at 50 units, and has an average cost of production of \$20 per toaster oven. Plant L produces 150 units of output with an average cost of production of only \$10 per toaster oven. Although plant V can produce 200 units of output, it still has the same unit cost as Plant L.

In this example, a small or medium plant, like S or M, will not be able to compete in the market with a large or a very large plant like L or V, because the firm that operates L or V will be able to produce and sell their output at a lower price. In this example, economies of scale operate up to point L, but beyond point L to V, the additional scale of production does not continue to reduce average costs of production.

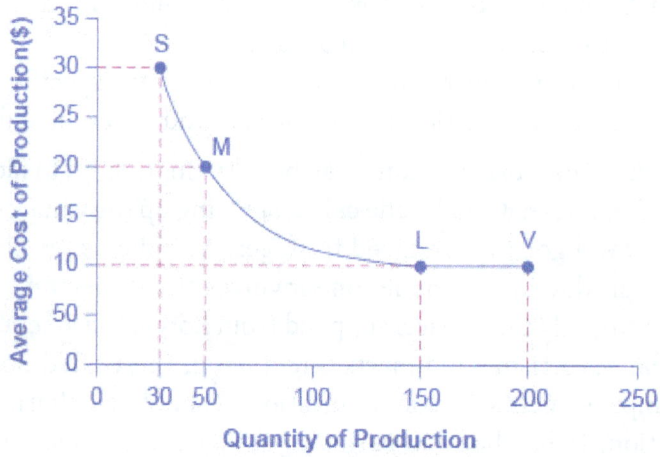

Figure 1. Economies of Scale. Production Plant S, has an average cost of production of $30 per toaster oven. Production plant M has an average cost of production of $20 per toaster oven. Production plant L has an average cost of production of only $10 per toaster oven. Production plant V would still have an average cost of production of $10 per toaster oven. Thus, production plant M can produce toaster ovens more cheaply than plant S because of economies of scale, and plants L or V can produce more cheaply than S or M because of economies of scale. However, the economies of scale end at an output level of 150. Plant V, despite being larger, cannot produce more cheaply on average than plant L.

The concept of economies of scale becomes especially relevant to international trade when it enables one or two large producers to supply the entire country. For example, a single large automobile factory could probably supply all the cars purchased in a smaller economy like the United Kingdom or Belgium in a given year. However, if a country has only one or two large factories producing cars, and no **international trade**, then consumers in that country would have relatively little choice between kinds of cars (other than the color of the paint and other nonessential options). Little or no competition will exist between different car manufacturers.

International trade provides a way to combine the lower average production costs that come from economies of scale and still have competition and variety for consumers. Large automobile factories in different countries can make and sell their products around the world. If the U.S. automobile market was made up of only General Motors, Ford, and Chrysler, the level of competition and consumer choice would be quite a lot lower than when U.S. carmakers must face competition from Toyota, Honda, Suzuki, Fiat, Mitsubishi, Nissan, Volkswagen, Kia, Hyundai, BMW, Subaru, and others. Greater competition brings with it innovation and responsiveness to what consumers want. America's car producers make far better cars now than they did several decades ago, and much of the reason is competitive pressure, especially from East Asian and European carmakers.

Dynamic Comparative Advantage

The sources of gains from intra-industry trade between similar economies—namely, the learning that comes from a high degree of specialization and splitting up the value chain and from economies of scale—do not contradict the earlier theory of comparative advantage. Instead, they help to broaden the concept.

In intra-industry trade, the level of worker productivity is not determined by climate or geography. It is not even determined by the general level of education or skill. Instead, the level of worker productivity is determined by how firms engage in specific learning about specialized products, including taking advantage of economies of scale. In this vision, comparative advantage can be dynamic—that is, it can evolve and change over time as new skills are developed and as the value chain is split up in new ways. This line of thinking also suggests that countries are not destined to have the same comparative advantage forever, but must instead be flexible in response to ongoing changes in comparative advantage.

Concepts and Summary

A large share of global trade happens between high-income economies that are quite similar in having well-educated workers and advanced technology. These countries practice intra-industry trade, in which they import and export the same products at the same time, like cars, machinery, and computers. In the case of intra-industry trade between economies with similar income levels, the gains from trade come from specialized learning in very particular tasks and from economies of scale. Splitting up the value chain means that several stages of producing a good take place in different countries around the world.

26.4 THE ADVANTAGES OF REDUCING INTERNATIONAL TRADE BARRIERS

Tariffs are taxes that governments place on imported goods for a variety of reasons. Some of these reasons include protecting sensitive industries, for humanitarian reasons, and protecting against dumping. Traditionally, tariffs were used simply as a political tool to protect certain vested economic, social, and cultural interests. The World Trade Organization (WTO) is committed to lowering barriers to trade. The world's nations meet through the WTO to negotiate how they can reduce barriers to trade, such as tariffs. WTO negotiations happen in "rounds," where all countries negotiate one agreement to encourage trade, take a year or two off, and then start negotiating a new agreement. The current round of negotiations is called the Doha Round because it was officially launched in Doha, the capital city of Qatar, in November 2001. In 2009, economists from the World Bank summarized recent research and found that the Doha round of negotiations would increase the size of the world economy by $160 billion to $385 billion per year, depending on the precise deal that ended up being negotiated.

In the context of a global economy that currently produces more than $30 trillion of goods and services each year, this amount is not huge: it is an increase of 1% or less. But before dismissing the gains from trade too quickly, it is worth remembering two points.

- First, a gain of a few hundred billion dollars is enough money to deserve attention! Moreover, remember that this increase is not a one-time event; it would persist each year into the future.
- Second, the estimate of gains may be on the low side because some of the gains from trade are not measured especially well in economic statistics. For example, it is difficult to measure the potential advantages to consumers of having a variety of products available and a greater degree of competition among producers. Perhaps the most important unmeasured factor is that trade between countries, especially when firms are splitting up the value chain of production, often involves a transfer of knowledge that can involve skills in production, technology, management, finance, and law.

Low-income countries benefit more from trade than high-income countries do. In some ways, the giant U.S. economy has less need for international trade, because it can already take advantage of internal trade within its economy. However, many smaller national economies around the world, in regions like Latin America, Africa, the Middle East, and Asia, have much more limited possibilities for trade inside their countries or their immediate regions. Without international trade, they may have little ability to benefit from comparative advantage, slicing up the value chain, or economies of scale. Moreover, smaller economies often have fewer competitive firms making goods within their economy, and thus firms have less pressure from other firms to provide the goods and prices that consumers want.

The economic gains from expanding international trade are measured in hundreds of billions of dollars, and the gains from international trade as a whole probably reach well into the trillions of dollars. The potential for gains from trade may be especially high among the smaller and lower-income countries of the world.

From Interpersonal to International Trade

Most people find it easy to believe that they, personally, would not be better off if they tried to grow and process all of their own food, to make all of their own clothes, to build their own cars and houses from scratch, and so on. Instead, we all benefit from living in economies where people and firms can specialize and trade with each other.

The benefits of trade do not stop at national boundaries, either. Earlier we explained that the division of labor could increase output for three reasons: (1) workers with different characteristics can specialize in the types of production where they have a comparative advantage; (2) firms and workers who specialize in a certain product become more productive with learning and practice; and (3) economies of scale. These three reasons apply from the individual and community level right up to the international level. If it makes sense to you that interpersonal, intercommunity, and interstate trade offer economic gains, it should make sense that international trade offers gains, too.

International trade currently involves about $20 trillion worth of goods and services moving around the globe. Any economic force of that size, even if it confers overall benefits, is certain to cause disruption and controversy. This chapter has only made the case that trade brings economic benefits. Other chapters discuss, in detail, the public policy arguments over whether to restrict international trade.

It's Apple's (Global) iPhone

Apple Corporation uses a global platform to produce the iPhone. Now that you understand the concept of comparative advantage, you can see why the engineering and design of the iPhone is done in the United States. The United States has built up a comparative advantage over the years in designing and marketing products, and sacrifices fewer resources to design high-tech devices relative to other countries. China has a comparative advantage in assembling the phone due to its large skilled labor force. Korea has a comparative advantage in producing components. Korea focuses its production by increasing its scale, learning better ways to produce screens and computer chips, and uses innovation to lower average costs of production. Apple, in turn, benefits because it can purchase these quality products at lower prices. Put the global assembly line together and you have the device with which we are all so familiar.

Concepts and Summary

Tariffs are placed on imported goods as a way of protecting sensitive industries, for humanitarian reasons, and for protection against dumping. Traditionally, tariffs were used as a political tool to protect certain vested economic, social, and cultural interests. The WTO has been, and continues to be, a way for nations to meet and negotiate through barriers to trade. The gains of international trade are very large, especially for smaller countries, but are beneficial to all.

CHAPTER 27
GLOBALIZATION AND PROTECTIONISM

INTRODUCTION TO GLOBALIZATION AND PROTECTIONISM

FIgure 1. Flat Screen Competition. The market for flat-panel displays in the United States is huge. The manufacturers of flat screens in the United States must compete against manufacturers from around the world. (Credit: modification of work by "Jemimus"/Flickr Creative Commons)

What's the Downside of Protection?

Governments are motivated to limit and alter market outcomes for political or social ends. While governments can limit the rise in prices of some products, they cannot control how much people want to buy or how much firms are willing to sell. The laws of demand and supply still hold. Trade policy is an example where regulations can redirect economic forces, but it cannot stop them from manifesting themselves elsewhere.

Flat-panel displays, the displays for laptop computers, tablets, and flat screen televisions, are an example of such an enduring principle. In the early 1990s, the vast majority of flat-panel displays used in U.S.-manufactured laptops were imported, primarily from Japan. The small but politically powerful U.S. flat-panel-display industry filed a dumping complaint with the Commerce Department. They argued that Japanese firms were selling displays at "less than fair value," which made it difficult for U.S. firms to compete. This argument for trade protection is referred to as anti-dumping. Other arguments for protection in this complaint included national security. After a preliminary determination by the Commerce Department that the Japanese firms were dumping, the U.S. International Trade Commission imposed a 63% dumping margin (or tax) on the import of flat-panel displays. Was this a successful exercise of U.S. trade policy? See what you think after reading the chapter.

CHAPTER OBJECTIVES

Introduction to Globalization and Protectionism

In this chapter, you will learn about:

- Protectionism: An Indirect Subsidy from Consumers to Producers
- International Trade and Its Effects on Jobs, Wages, and Working Conditions
- Arguments in Support of Restricting Imports
- How Trade Policy Is Enacted: Globally, Regionally, and Nationally
- The Tradeoffs of Trade Policy

The world has become more connected on multiple levels, especially economically. In 1970, imports and exports made up 11% of U.S. GDP, while now they make up 32%. However, the United States, due to its size, is less internationally connected than most countries. For example, according to the World Bank, 97% of Botswana's economic activity is connected to trade. This chapter explores trade policy—the laws and strategies a country uses to regulate international trade. This topic is not without controversy.

As the world has become more globally connected, firms and workers in high-income countries like the United States, Japan, or the nations of the European Union, perceive a competitive threat from firms in medium-income countries like Mexico, China, or South Africa, that have lower costs of living and therefore pay lower wages. Firms and workers in low-income countries fear that they will suffer if they must compete against more productive workers and advanced technology in high-income countries.

On a different tack, some environmentalists worry that multinational firms may evade environmental protection laws by moving their production to countries with loose or nonexistent pollution standards, trading a clean environment for jobs. Some politicians worry that their country may become overly dependent on key imported products, like oil, which in a time of war could threaten national security. All of these fears influence governments to reach the same basic policy conclusion: to protect national interests, whether businesses, jobs, or security, imports of foreign products should be restricted. This chapter analyzes such arguments. First, however, it is essential to learn a few key concepts and understand how the demand and supply model applies to international trade.

27.1 PROTECTIONISM: AN INDIRECT SUBSIDY FROM CONSUMERS TO PRODUCERS

When a government legislates policies to reduce or block international trade it is engaging in **protectionism**. Protectionist policies often seek to shield domestic producers and domestic workers from foreign competition. Protectionism takes three main forms: tariffs, import quotas, and nontariff barriers.

Recall from International Trade that tariffs are taxes imposed on imported goods and services. They make imports more expensive for consumers, discouraging imports. For example, in recent years large, flat-screen televisions imported from China have faced a 5% tariff rate.

Another way to control trade is through **import quotas**, which are numerical limitations on the quantity of products that can be imported. For instance, during the early 1980s, the Reagan Administration imposed a quota on the import of Japanese automobiles. In the 1970s, many developed countries, including the United States, found themselves with declining textile industries. Textile production does not require highly skilled workers, so producers were able to set up lower-cost factories in developing countries. In order to "manage" this loss of jobs and income, the developed countries established an international Multifiber Agreement that essentially divided up the market for textile exports between importers and the remaining domestic producers. The agreement, which ran from 1974 to 2004, specified the exact quota of textile imports that each developed country would accept from each low-income country. A similar story exists for sugar imports into the United States, which are still governed by quotas.

Nontariff barriers are all the other ways that a nation can draw up rules, regulations, inspections, and paperwork to make it more costly or difficult to import products. A rule requiring certain safety standards can limit imports just as effectively as high tariffs or low import quotas, for instance. There are also nontariff barriers in the form of "rules-of-origin" regulations- these rules describe the "Made in Country X" label as the one in which the last substantial change in the product took place. A manufacturer wishing to evade import restrictions may try to change the production process so that the last big change in the product happens in his or her own country. For example, certain textiles are made in the United States, shipped to other countries, combined with textiles made in those other countries to make apparel—and then re-exported back to the United States for a final assembly, to escape paying tariffs or to obtain a "Made in the USA" label.

Despite import quotas, tariffs, and nontariff barriers, the share of apparel sold in the United States that is imported rose from about half in 1999 to about three-quarters today. The U.S. Bureau of Labor Statistics (BLS), estimated the number of U.S. jobs in textiles and apparel fell from 666,360 in 2007 to 385,240 in 2012, a 42% decline. Even more U.S. textile industry jobs would have been lost without tariffs, however, domestic jobs that are saved by import quotas come at a cost. Because textile and apparel protectionism adds to the costs of imports, consumers end up paying billions of dollars more for clothing each year.

When the United States eliminates trade barriers in one area, consumers spend the money they save on that product elsewhere in the economy—so there is no overall loss of jobs for the economy as a whole. Of course, workers in some of the poorest countries of the world who would otherwise have jobs producing textiles, would gain considerably if the United States reduced its barriers to trade in textiles. That said, there are good reasons to be wary about reducing barriers to trade. The 2012 and 2013 Bangladeshi fires in textile factories, which resulted in a horrific loss of life, present complications that our simplified analysis in the chapter will not capture.

Realizing the compromises between nations that come about due to trade policy, many countries came together in 1947 to form the General Agreement on Tariffs and Trade (GATT). (We'll cover the GATT in more detail later in the chapter.) This agreement has since been superseded by the **World Trade Organization (WTO)**, whose membership includes about 150 nations and most of the economies of the world. It is the primary international mechanism through which nations negotiate their trade rules—including rules about tariffs, quotas, and nontariff barriers. The next section examines the results of such protectionism and develops a simple model to show the impact of trade policy.

Demand and Supply Analysis of Protectionism

To the non-economist, restricting imports may appear to be nothing more than taking sales from foreign producers and giving them to domestic producers. Other factors are at work, however, because firms do not operate in a vacuum. Instead, firms sell their products either to consumers or to other firms (if they are business suppliers), who are also affected by the trade barriers. A demand and supply analysis of protectionism shows that it is not just a matter of domestic gains and foreign losses, but a policy that imposes substantial domestic costs as well.

Consider two countries, Brazil and the United States, who produce sugar. Each country has a domestic supply and demand for sugar, as detailed in Table 1 and illustrated in Figure 1. In Brazil, without trade, the equilibrium price of sugar is 12 cents per pound and the equilibrium output is 30 tons. When there is no trade in the United States, the equilibrium price of sugar is 24 cents per pound and the equilibrium quantity is 80 tons. These equilibrium points are labeled with the point E.

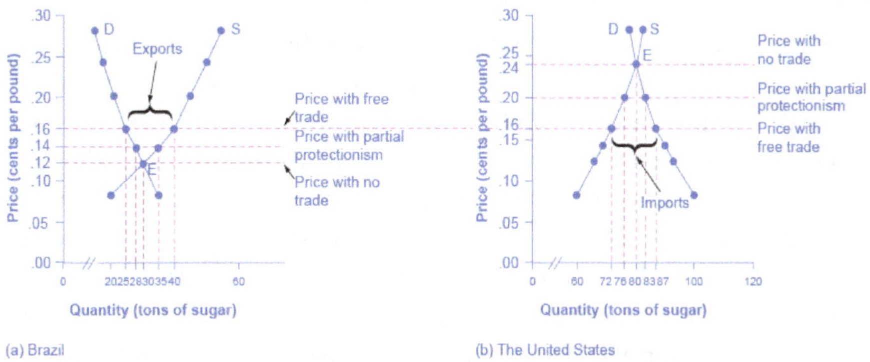

Figure 1. The Sugar Trade between Brazil and the United States. Before trade, the equilibrium price of sugar in Brazil is 12 cents a pound and for 24 cents per pound in the United States. When trade is allowed, businesses will buy cheap sugar in Brazil and sell it in the United States. This will result in higher prices in Brazil and lower prices in the United States. Ignoring transaction costs, prices should converge to 16 cents per pound, with Brazil exporting 15 tons of sugar and the United States importing 15 tons of sugar. If trade is only partly open between the countries, it will lead to an outcome between the free-trade and no-trade possibilities.

Table 1. The Sugar Trade between Brazil and the United States

Price	Brazil: Quantity Supplied (tons)	Brazil: Quantity Demanded (tons)	U.S.: Quantity Supplied (tons)	U.S.: Quantity Demanded (tons)
8 cents	20	35	60	100
12 cents	30	30	66	93
14 cents	35	28	69	90
16 cents	40	25	72	87
20 cents	45	21	76	83
24 cents	50	18	80	80
28 cents	55	15	82	78

If international trade between Brazil and the United States now becomes possible, profit-seeking firms will spot an opportunity: buy sugar cheaply in Brazil, and sell it at a higher price in the United States. As sugar is shipped from Brazil to the United States, the quantity of sugar produced in Brazil will be greater than Brazilian consumption (with the extra production being exported), and the amount produced in the United States will be less than the amount of U.S. consumption (with the extra consumption being imported). Exports to the United States will reduce the supply of sugar in Brazil, raising its price. Imports into the United States will increase the supply of sugar, lowering its price. When the price of sugar is the same in both countries, there is no incentive to trade further. As Figure 1 shows, the equilibrium with trade occurs at a price of 16 cents per pound. At that price, the sugar farmers of Brazil supply a quantity of 40 tons, while the consumers of Brazil buy only 25 tons.

The extra 15 tons of sugar production, shown by the horizontal gap between the demand curve and the supply curve in Brazil, is exported to the United States. In the United States, at a price of 16 cents, the farmers produce a quantity of 72 tons and consumers demand a quantity of 87 tons. The excess demand of 15 tons by American consumers, shown by the horizontal gap between demand and domestic supply at the price of 16 cents, is supplied by imported sugar. Free trade typically results in income distribution effects, but the key is to recognize the overall gains from trade, as shown in Figure 2. Building on the concepts outlined in Demand and Supply and Demand, Supply, and Efficiency in terms of consumer and producer surplus, Figure 2 (a) shows that producers in Brazil gain by selling more sugar at a higher price, while Figure 2 (b) shows consumers in the United States benefit from the lower price and greater availability of sugar. Consumers in Brazil are worse off (compare their no-trade consumer surplus with the free-trade consumer surplus) and U.S. producers of sugar are worse off. There are gains from trade—an increase in social surplus in each country. That is, both the United States and Brazil are better off than they would be without trade. The following Clear It Up feature explains how trade policy can influence low-income countries.

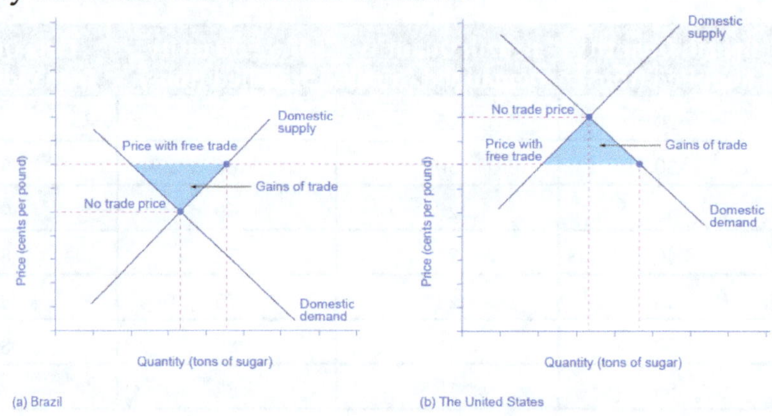

Figure 2. Free Trade of Sugar. Free trade results in gains from trade. Total surplus increases in both countries. However, there are clear income distribution effects.

Why are there low-income countries?

Why are the poor countries of the world poor? There are a number of reasons, but one of them will surprise you: the trade policies of the high-income countries. Following is a stark review of social priorities which has been widely publicized by the international aid organization, **Oxfam International**.

High-income countries of the world—primarily the United States, Canada, countries of the European Union, and Japan—subsidize their domestic farmers collectively by about $360 billion per year. By contrast, the total amount of foreign aid from these same high-income countries to the poor countries of the world is about $70 billion per year, or less than 20% of the farm subsidies. Why does this matter?

It matters because the support of farmers in high-income countries is devastating to the livelihoods of farmers in low-income countries. Even when their climate and land are well-suited to products like cotton, rice, sugar, or milk, farmers in low-income countries find it difficult to compete. Farm subsidies in the high-income countries cause farmers in those countries to increase the amount they produce. This increase in supply drives down world prices of farm products below the costs of production. As Michael Gerson of the Washington Post describes it: "[T]he effects in the cotton-growing regions of West Africa are dramatic . . . keep[ing] millions of Africans on the edge of malnutrition. In some of the poorest countries on Earth, cotton farmers are some of the poorest people, earning about a dollar a day. . . . Who benefits from the current system of subsidies? About 20,000 American cotton producers, with an average annual income of more than $125,000."

As if subsidies were not enough, often, the high-income countries block agricultural exports from low-income countries. In some cases, the situation gets even worse when the governments of high-income countries, having bought and paid for an excess supply of farm products, give away those products in poor countries and drive local farmers out of business altogether.

For example, shipments of excess milk from the European Union to Jamaica have caused great hardship for Jamaican dairy farmers. Shipments of excess rice from the United States to Haiti drove thousands of low-income rice farmers in Haiti out of business. The opportunity costs of protectionism are not paid just by domestic consumers, but also by foreign producers—and for many agricultural products, those foreign producers are the world's poor.

Now, let's look at what happens with **protectionism**. U.S. sugar farmers are likely to argue that, if only they could be protected from sugar imported from Brazil, the United States would have higher domestic sugar production, more jobs in the sugar industry, and American sugar farmers would receive a higher price. If the United States government sets a high-enough tariff on imported sugar, or sets an import quota at zero, the result will be that the quantity of sugar traded between countries could be reduced to zero, and the prices in each country will return to the levels before trade was allowed.

Blocking only some trade is also possible. Suppose that the United States passed a sugar import quota of seven tons. The United States will import no more than seven tons of sugar, which means that Brazil can export no more than seven tons of sugar to the United States. As a result, the price of sugar in the United States will be 20 cents, which is the price where the quantity demanded is seven tons greater than the domestic quantity supplied. Conversely, if Brazil can export only seven tons of sugar, then the price of sugar in Brazil will be 14 cents per pound, which is the price where the domestic quantity supplied in Brazil is seven tons greater than domestic demand.

In general, when a country sets a low or medium tariff or import quota, the equilibrium price and quantity will be somewhere between no trade and completely free trade. The following Work It Out explores the impact of these trade barriers.

Effects of Trade Barriers

Let's look carefully at the effects of tariffs or quotas. If the U.S. government imposes a tariff or quota sufficient to eliminate trade with Brazil, two things occur: U.S. consumers pay a higher price and therefore buy a smaller quantity of sugar. U.S. producers obtain a higher price so they sell a larger quantity of sugar. The effects of a tariff on producers and consumers in the United States can be measured using two concepts developed in Demand, Supply, and Efficiency: **consumer surplus** and **producer surplus.**

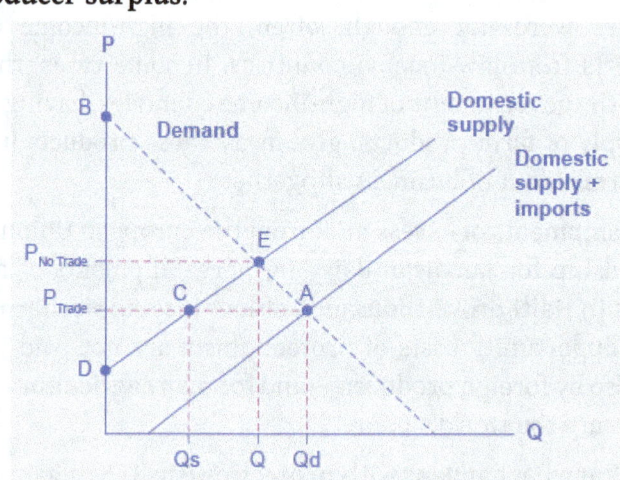

Figure 3. U.S. Sugar Supply and Demand. When there is free trade, the equilibrium is at point A. When there is no trade, the equilibrium is at point E.

Step 1. Look at Figure 3, which shows a hypothetical version of the demand and supply of sugar in the United States.

Step 2. Note that the sugar market is in equilibrium at point A where Domestic Quantity Demanded (Qd) = Quantity Supplied (Domestic Qs + Imports from Brazil) at a price of P_{Trade} when there is free trade.

Step 3. Note, also, that imports are equal to the distance between points C and A.

Step 4. Recall that consumer surplus is the value a consumer gets beyond what they paid for when they buy a product. Graphically, it is the area under a demand curve but above the price. In this case, the consumer surplus in the United States is the area of the triangle formed by the points P_{Trade}, A, and B.

Step 5. Recall, also, that producer surplus is another name for profit—it is the income producers get above the cost of production, which is shown by the supply curve here. In this case, the producer surplus with trade is the area of the triangle formed by the points P_{trade}, C, and D.

Step 6. Suppose that the barriers to trade are imposed, imports are excluded, and the price rises to $P_{NoTrade}$. Look what happens to producer surplus and consumer surplus. At the higher price, the domestic quantity supplied increases from Qs to Q at point E. Because producers are selling more quantity at a higher price, the producer surplus increases to the area of the triangle $P_{NoTrade}$, E, and D.

Step 7. Compare the areas of the two triangles and you will see the increase in the producer surplus.

Step 8. Examine the consumer surplus. Consumers are now paying a higher price to get a lower quantity (Q instead of Qd). Their consumer surplus shrinks to the area of the triangle $P_{NoTrade}$, E, and B.

Step 9. Determine the net effect. The producer surplus increases by the area P_{trade}, C, E, $P_{NoTrade}$. The loss of consumer surplus, however, is larger. It is the area P_{trade}, A, E, $P_{NoTrade}$. In other words, consumers lose more than producers gain as a result of the trade barriers and the United States has a lower social surplus.

Who Benefits and Who Pays?

Using the demand and supply model, consider the impact of protectionism on producers and consumers in each of the two countries. For protected producers like U.S. sugar farmers, restricting imports is clearly positive. Without a need to face imported products, these producers are able to sell more, at a higher price. For consumers in the country with the protected good, in this case U.S. sugar consumers, restricting imports is clearly negative. They end up buying a lower quantity of the good and paying a higher price for what they do buy, compared to the equilibrium price and quantity without trade. The following Clear It Up feature considers why a country might outsource jobs even for a domestic product.

Why are Life Savers, an American product, not made in America?

Life Savers, the hard candy with the hole in the middle, were invented in 1912 by Clarence Crane in Cleveland, Ohio. Starting in the late 1960s and for 35 years afterward, 46 billion Life Savers a year, in 200 million rolls, were produced by a plant in Holland, Michigan. But in 2002, the Kraft Company announced that the Michigan plant would be closed and Life Saver production moved across the border to Montreal, Canada.

One reason is that Canadian workers are paid slightly less, especially in healthcare and insurance costs that are not linked to employment there. Another main reason is that the United States government keeps the price of sugar high for the benefit of sugar farmers, with a combination of a government price floor program and strict quotas on imported sugar. According to the Coalition for Sugar Reform, from 2009 to 2012, the price of refined sugar in the United States ranged from 64% to 92% higher than the world price. Life Saver production uses over 100 tons of sugar each day, because the candies are 95% sugar.

A number of other candy companies have also reduced U.S. production and expanded foreign production. Indeed, from 1997 to 2011, some 127,000 jobs in the sugar-using industries, or more than seven times the total employment in sugar production, were eliminated. While the candy industry is especially affected by the cost of sugar, the costs are spread more broadly. U.S. consumers pay roughly $1 billion per year in higher food prices because of elevated sugar costs. Meanwhile, sugar producers in low-income countries are driven out of business. Because of the sugar subsidies to domestic producers and the quotas on imports, they cannot sell their output profitably, or at all, in the United States market.

The fact that protectionism pushes up prices for consumers in the country enacting such protectionism is not always acknowledged openly, but it is not disputed. After all, if protectionism did not benefit domestic producers, there would not be much point in enacting such policies in the first place. Protectionism is simply a method of requiring consumers to subsidize producers. The subsidy is indirect, since it is paid by consumers through higher prices, rather than a direct subsidy paid by the government with money collected from taxpayers. But protectionism works like a subsidy, nonetheless. The American satirist Ambrose Bierce defined "tariff" this way in his 1911 book, *The Devil's Dictionary*: "Tariff, n. A scale of taxes on imports, designed to protect the domestic producer against the greed of his consumer."

The effect of protectionism on producers and consumers in the foreign country is complex. When an import quota is used to impose partial protectionism, the sugar producers of Brazil receive a lower price for the sugar they sell in Brazil—but a higher price for the sugar they are allowed to export to the United States. Indeed, notice that some of the burden of protectionism, paid by domestic consumers, ends up in the hands of foreign producers in this case. Brazilian sugar consumers seem to benefit from U.S. protectionism, because it reduces the price of sugar that they pay. On the other hand, at least some of these Brazilian sugar consumers also work as sugar farmers, so their incomes and jobs are reduced by protectionism. Moreover, if trade between the countries vanishes, Brazilian consumers would miss out on better prices for imported goods—which do not appear in our single-market example of sugar protectionism.

The effects of protectionism on foreign countries notwithstanding, protectionism requires domestic consumers of a product (consumers may include either households or other firms) to pay higher prices to benefit domestic producers of that product. In addition, when a country enacts protectionism, it loses the economic gains it would have been able to achieve through a combination of comparative advantage, specialized learning, and economies of scale, concepts discussed in International Trade.

Key Concepts and Summary

There are three tools for restricting the flow of trade: tariffs, import quotas, and nontariff barriers. When a country places limitations on imports from abroad, regardless of whether it uses tariffs, quotas, or nontariff barriers, it is said to be practicing protectionism. Protectionism will raise the price of the protected good in the domestic market, which causes domestic consumers to pay more, but domestic producers to earn more.

27.2 INTERNATIONAL TRADE AND ITS EFFECTS ON JOBS, WAGES, AND WORKING CONDITIONS

In theory at least, imports might injure workers in several different ways: fewer jobs, lower wages, or poor working conditions. Let's consider these in turn.

Fewer Jobs?

In the early 1990s, the United States was negotiating the North American Free Trade Agreement (NAFTA) with Mexico, an agreement that reduced tariffs, import quotas, and nontariff barriers to trade between the United States, Mexico, and Canada. H. Ross Perot, a 1992 candidate for U.S. president, claimed, in prominent campaign arguments, that if the United States expanded trade with Mexico, there would be a "giant sucking sound" as U.S. employers relocated to Mexico to take advantage of lower wages. After all, average wages in Mexico were, at that time, about one-eighth of those in the United States. NAFTA passed Congress, President Bill Clinton signed it into law, and it took effect in 1995. For the next six years, the United States economy had some of the most rapid job growth and low unemployment in its history. Those who feared that open trade with Mexico would lead to a dramatic decrease in jobs were proven wrong.

This result was no surprise to economists. After all, the trend toward globalization has been going on for decades, not just since NAFTA. If trade did reduce the number of available jobs, then the United States should have been seeing a steady loss of jobs for decades. While the United States economy does experience rises and falls in unemployment rates—according to the Bureau of Labor Statistics, from spring 2008 to late 2009, the unemployment rate rose from 4.4% to 10%; it has since fallen back to 5.5% in spring 2015—the number of jobs is not falling over extended periods of time. The number of U.S. jobs rose from 71 million in 1970 to 138 million in 2012.

Protectionism certainly saves jobs in the specific industry being protected but, for two reasons, it costs jobs in other unprotected industries. First, if consumers are paying higher prices to the protected industry, they inevitably have less money to spend on goods from other industries, and so jobs are lost in those other industries. Second, if the protected product is sold to other firms, so that other firms must now pay a higher price for a key input, then those firms will lose sales to foreign producers who do not need to pay the higher price. Lost sales translate into lost jobs. The hidden opportunity cost of using protectionism to save jobs in one industry is jobs sacrificed in other industries. This is why the United States International Trade Commission, in its study of barriers to trade, predicts that reducing trade barriers would not lead to an overall loss of jobs. Protectionism reshuffles jobs from industries without import protections to industries that are protected from imports, but it does not create more jobs.

Moreover, the costs of saving jobs through protectionism can be very high. A number of different studies have attempted to estimate the cost to consumers in higher prices per job saved through protectionism. Table 2 shows a sample of results, compiled by economists at the Federal Reserve Bank of Dallas. Saving a job through protectionism typically costs much more than the actual worker's salary. For example, a study published in 2002 compiled evidence that using protectionism to save an average job in the textile and apparel industry would cost $199,000 per job saved. In other words, those workers could have been paid $100,000 per year to be unemployed and the cost would only be half of what it is to keep them working in the textile and apparel industry. This result is not unique to textiles and apparel.

Table 2. Cost to U.S. Consumers of Saving a Job through Protectionism (Source: Federal Reserve Bank of Dallas)

Industry Protected with Import Tariffs or Quotas	Annual Cost per Job Saved
Sugar	$826,000
Polyethylene resins	$812,000
Dairy products	$685,000
Frozen concentrated orange juice	$635,000

Ball bearings	$603,000
Machine tools	$479,000
Women's handbags	$263,000
Glassware	$247,000
Apparel and textiles	$199,000
Rubber footwear	$168,000
Women's nonathletic footwear	$139,000

Why does it cost so much to save jobs through protectionism? The basic reason is that not all of the extra money paid by consumers because of tariffs or quotas goes to save jobs. For example, if tariffs are imposed on steel imports so that buyers of steel pay a higher price, U.S. steel companies earn greater profits, buy more equipment, pay bigger bonuses to managers, give pay raises to existing employees—and also avoid firing some additional workers. Only part of the higher price of protected steel goes toward saving jobs. Also, when an industry is protected, the economy as a whole loses the benefits of playing to its comparative advantage—in other words, producing what it is best at. So, part of the higher price that consumers pay for protected goods is lost economic efficiency, which can be measured as another deadweight loss, like that discussed in Labor and Financial Markets.

There's a bumper sticker that speaks to the threat some U.S. workers feel from imported products: "Buy American—Save U.S. Jobs." If the car were being driven by an economist, the sticker might declare: "Block Imports—Save Jobs for Some Americans, Lose Jobs for Other Americans, and Also Pay High Prices."

Trade and Wages

Even if trade does not reduce the number of jobs, it could affect wages. Here, it is important to separate issues about the average level of wages from issues about whether the wages of certain workers may be helped or hurt by trade.

Because trade raises the amount that an economy can produce by letting firms and workers play to their comparative advantage, trade will also cause the average level of wages in an economy to rise. Workers who can produce more will be more desirable to employers, which will shift the demand for their labor out to the right, and increase wages in the labor market. By contrast, barriers to trade will reduce the average level of wages in an economy.

However, even if trade increases the overall wage level, it will still benefit some workers and hurt others. Workers in industries that are confronted by competition from imported products may find that demand for their labor decreases and shifts back to the left, so that their wages decline with a rise in international trade. Conversely, workers in industries that benefit from selling in global markets may find that demand for their labor shifts out to the right, so that trade raises their wages.

One concern is that while globalization may be benefiting high-skilled, high-wage workers in the United States, it may also impose costs on low-skilled, low-wage workers. After all, high-skilled U.S. workers presumably benefit from increased sales of sophisticated products like computers, machinery, and pharmaceuticals in which the United States has a comparative advantage. Meanwhile, low-skilled U.S. workers must now compete against extremely low-wage workers worldwide for making simpler products like toys and clothing. As a result, the wages of low-skilled U.S. workers are likely to fall. There are, however, a number of reasons to believe that while globalization has helped some U.S. industries and hurt others, it has not focused its negative impact on the wages of low-skilled Americans. First, about half of U.S. trade is intra-industry trade. That means the U.S. trades similar goods with other high-wage economies like Canada, Japan, Germany, and the United Kingdom. For instance, in 2014 the U.S. exported over 2 million cars, from all the major automakers, and also imported several million cars from other countries.

Most U.S. workers in these industries have above-average skills and wages—and many of them do quite well in the world of globalization. Some evidence suggested that intra-industry trade between similar countries had a small impact on domestic workers but later evidence indicates that it all depends on how flexible the labor market is. In other words, the key is how flexible workers are in finding jobs in different industries. Trade on low-wage workers depends a lot on the structure of labor markets and indirect effects felt in other parts of the economy. For example, in the United States and the United Kingdom, because labor market frictions are low, the impact of trade on low income workers is small.

Second, many low-skilled U.S. workers hold service jobs that cannot be replaced by imports from low-wage countries. For example, lawn care services or moving and hauling services or hotel maids cannot be imported from countries long distances away like China or Bangladesh. Competition from imported products is not the primary determinant of their wages.

Finally, while the focus of the discussion here is on wages, it is worth pointing out that low-wage U.S. workers suffer due to protectionism in all the industries—even those that they do not work in the U.S. For example, food and clothing are protected industries. These low-wage workers therefore pay higher prices for these basic necessities and as such their dollar stretches over fewer goods.

The benefits and costs of increased trade in terms of its effect on wages are not distributed evenly across the economy. However, the growth of international trade has helped to raise the productivity of U.S. workers as a whole—and thus helped to raise the average level of wages.

Labor Standards and Working Conditions

Workers in many low-income countries around the world labor under conditions that would be illegal for a worker in the United States. Workers in countries like China, Thailand, Brazil, South Africa, and Poland are often paid less than the United States **minimum wage**. For example, in the United States, the minimum wage is $7.25 per hour; a typical wage in many low-income countries might be more like $7.25 per day, or often much less. Moreover, working conditions in low-income countries may be extremely unpleasant, or even unsafe. In the worst cases, production may involve the labor of small children or even workers who are treated nearly like slaves. These concerns over standards of foreign labor do not affect most of U.S. trade, which is intra-industry and carried out with other high-income countries that have labor standards similar to the United States, but it is, nonetheless, morally and economically important.

In thinking about labor standards in other countries, it is important to draw some distinctions between what is truly unacceptable and what is painful to think about. Most people, economists included, have little difficulty with the idea that production by six-year-olds confined in factories or by slave labor is morally unacceptable. They would support aggressive efforts to eliminate such practices—including shutting out imported products made with such labor. Many cases, however, are less clear-cut. An opinion article in the New York Times several years ago described the case of Ahmed Zia, a 14-year-old boy from Pakistan. He earned $2 per day working in a carpet factory. He dropped out of school in second grade. Should the United States and other countries refuse to purchase rugs made by Ahmed and his co-workers? If the carpet factories were to close, the likely alternative job for Ahmed is farm work, and as Ahmed says of his carpet-weaving job: "This makes much more money and is more comfortable."

Other workers may have even less attractive alternative jobs, perhaps scavenging garbage or prostitution. The real problem for Ahmed and many others in low-income countries is not that globalization has made their lives worse, but rather that they have so few good life alternatives. The United States went through similar situations during the nineteenth and early twentieth centuries.

In closing, there is some irony when the United States government or U.S. citizens take issue with labor standards in low-income countries, because the United States is not a world leader in government laws to protect employees. In Western European countries and Canada, all citizens are guaranteed some form of national healthcare by the government; the United States does not offer such a guarantee but has moved in the direction of universal health insurance coverage under the recent Affordable Care Act. Many European workers receive six weeks or more of paid vacation per year; in the United States, vacations are often one to three weeks per year. If European countries accused the United States of using unfair labor standards to make U.S. products cheaply, and announced that they would shut out all U.S. imports until the United States adopted guaranteed national healthcare, added more national holidays, and doubled vacation time, Americans would be outraged. Yet when U.S. protectionists start talking about restricting imports from poor countries because of low wage levels and poor working conditions, they are making a very similar argument. This is not to say that labor conditions in low-income countries are not an important issue. They are. However, linking labor conditions in low-income countries to trade deflects the emphasis from the real question to ask: "What are acceptable and enforceable minimum labor standards and protections to have the world over?"

Key Concepts and Summary

As international trade increases, it contributes to a shift in jobs away from industries where that economy does not have a comparative advantage and toward industries where it does have a comparative advantage. The degree to which trade affects labor markets has a lot to do with the structure of the labor market in that country and the adjustment process in other industries. Global trade should raise the average level of wages by increasing productivity. However, this increase in average wages may include both gains to workers in certain jobs and industries and losses to others.

In thinking about labor practices in low-income countries, it is useful to draw a line between what is unpleasant to think about and what is morally objectionable. For example, low wages and long working hours in poor countries are unpleasant to think about, but for people in low-income parts of the world, it may well be the best option open to them. Practices like child labor and forced labor are morally objectionable and many countries refuse to import products made using these practices.

27.3 ARGUMENTS IN SUPPORT OF RESTRICTING IMPORTS

As previously noted, protectionism requires domestic consumers of a product to pay higher prices to benefit domestic producers of that product. Countries that institute protectionist policies lose the economic gains achieved through a combination of comparative advantage, specialized learning, and economies of scale. With these overall costs in mind, let us now consider, one by one, a number of arguments that support restricting imports.

The Infant Industry Argument

Imagine Bhutan wants to start its own computer industry, but it has no computer firms that can produce at a low enough price and high enough quality to compete in world markets. However, Bhutanese politicians, business leaders, and workers hope that if the local industry had a chance to get established, before it needed to face international competition, then a domestic company or group of companies could develop the skills, management, technology, and economies of scale that it needs to become a successful profit-earning domestic industry. Thus, the infant industry argument for protectionism is to block imports for a limited time, to give the infant industry time to mature, before it starts competing on equal terms in the global economy. (Revisit Macroeconomic Policy Around the World for more information on the infant industry argument.)

The infant industry argument is theoretically possible, even sensible: give an industry a short-term indirect subsidy through protection, and then reap the long-term economic benefits of having a vibrant, healthy industry. Implementation, however, is tricky. In many countries, infant industries have gone from babyhood to senility and obsolescence without ever having reached the profitable maturity stage. Meanwhile, the protectionism that was supposed to be short-term often took a very long time to be repealed.

As one example, Brazil treated its computer industry as an infant industry from the late 1970s until about 1990. In an attempt to establish its computer industry in the global economy, Brazil largely barred imports of computer products for several decades. This policy guaranteed increased sales for Brazilian computers. However, by the mid-1980s, due to lack of international competition, Brazil had a backward and out-of-date industry, typically lagging behind world standards for price and performance by three to five years—a long time in this fast-moving industry. After more than a decade, during which Brazilian consumers and industries that would have benefited from up-to-date computers paid the costs and Brazil's computer industry never competed effectively on world markets, Brazil phased out its infant industry policy for the computer industry.

Protectionism for infant industries always imposes costs on domestic users of the product, and typically has provided little benefit in the form of stronger, competitive industries. However, several countries in East Asia offer an exception. Japan, Korea, Thailand, and other countries in this region have sometimes provided a package of indirect and direct subsidies targeted at certain industries, including protection from foreign competition and government loans at interest rates below the market equilibrium. In Japan and Korea, for example, subsidies helped get their domestic steel and auto industries up and running.

Why did the infant industry policy of protectionism and other subsidies work fairly well in East Asia? A study by the World Bank in the early 1990s offered three guidelines to countries thinking about infant industry protection:

- Do not hand out protectionism and other subsidies to all industries, but focus on a few industries where your country has a realistic chance to be a world-class producer.
- Be very hesitant about using protectionism in areas like computers, where many other industries rely on having the best products available, because it is not useful to help one industry by imposing high costs on many other industries.
- Have clear guidelines for when the infant industry policy will end.

In Korea in the 1970s and 1980s, a common practice was to link protectionism and subsidies to export sales in global markets. If export sales rose, then the infant industry had succeeded and the protectionism could be phased out. If export sales did not rise, then the infant industry policy had failed and the protectionism could be phased out. Either way, the protectionism would be temporary.

Following these rules is easier said than done. Politics often intrudes, both in choosing which industries will receive the benefits of being treated as "infants" and when to phase out import restrictions and other subsidies. Also, if the government of a country wishes to impose costs on its citizens so that it can provide subsidies to a few key industries, it has many tools for doing so: direct government payments, loans, targeted tax reductions, government support of research and development of new technologies, and so on. In other words, protectionism is not the only or even the best way to support key industries.

The Anti-Dumping Argument

Dumping refers to selling goods below their cost of production. Anti-dumping laws block imports that are sold below the cost of production by imposing tariffs that increase the price of these imports to reflect their cost of production. Since dumping is not allowed under the rules of the World Trade Organization (WTO), nations that believe they are on the receiving end of dumped goods can file a complaint with the WTO. Anti-dumping complaints have risen in recent years, from about 100 cases per year in the late 1980s to about 200 new cases each year by the late 2000s. Note that dumping cases are countercyclical. During recessions, case filings increase. During economic booms, case filings go down. Individual countries have also frequently started their own anti-dumping investigations. The U.S. government has dozens of anti-dumping orders in place from past investigations. In 2009, for example, some U.S. imports that were under anti-dumping orders included pasta from Turkey, steel pipe fittings from Thailand, pressure-sensitive plastic tape from Italy, preserved mushrooms and lined paper products from India, and cut-to-length carbon steel and non-frozen apple juice concentrate from China.

Why Might Dumping Occur?

Why would foreign firms export a product at less than its cost of production—which presumably means taking a loss? This question has two possible answers, one innocent and one more sinister.

The innocent explanation is that market prices are set by demand and supply, not by the cost of production. Perhaps demand for a product shifts back to the left or supply shifts out to the right, which drives the market price to low levels—even below the cost of production. When a local store has a going-out-of-business sale, for example, it may sell goods at below the cost of production. If international companies find that there is excess supply of steel or computer chips or machine tools that is driving the market price down below their cost of production—this may be the market in action.

The sinister explanation is that dumping is part of a long-term strategy. Foreign firms sell goods at prices below the cost of production for a short period of time, and when they have driven out the domestic U.S. competition, they then raise prices. This scenario is sometimes called predatory pricing, which is discussed in the Monopoly chapter.

Should Anti-Dumping Cases Be Limited?

Anti-dumping cases pose two questions. How much sense do they make in economic theory? How much sense do they make as practical policy?

In terms of economic theory, the case for anti-dumping laws is weak. In a market governed by demand and supply, the government does not guarantee that firms will be able to make a profit. After all, low prices are difficult for producers, but benefit consumers. Moreover, although there are plenty of cases in which foreign producers have driven out domestic firms, there are zero documented cases in which the foreign producers then jacked up prices. Instead, foreign producers typically continue competing hard against each other and providing low prices to consumers. In short, it is difficult to find evidence of predatory pricing by foreign firms exporting to the United States.

Even if one could make a case that the government should sometimes enact anti-dumping rules in the short term, and then allow free trade to resume shortly thereafter, there is a growing concern that anti-dumping investigations often involve more politics than careful analysis. The U.S. Commerce Department is charged with calculating the appropriate "cost of production," which can be as much an art as a science.

For example, if a company built a new factory two years ago, should part of the factory's cost be counted in this year's cost of production? When a company is in a country where prices are controlled by the government, like China for example, how can one measure the true cost of production? When a domestic industry complains loudly enough, government regulators seem very likely to find that unfair dumping has occurred. Indeed, a common pattern has arisen where a domestic industry files an anti-dumping complaint, the governments meet and negotiate a reduction in imports, and then the domestic producers drop the anti-dumping suit. In such cases, anti-dumping cases often appear to be little more than a cover story for imposing tariffs or import quotas.

In the 1980s, almost all of the anti-dumping cases were initiated by the United States, Canada, the European Union, Australia, and New Zealand. By the 2000s, countries like Argentina, Brazil, South Korea, South Africa, Mexico, and India were filing the majority of the anti-dumping cases before the WTO. As the number of anti-dumping cases has increased, and as countries such as the United States and the European Union feel targeted by the anti-dumping actions of others, the WTO may well propose some additional guidelines to limit the reach of anti-dumping laws.

The Environmental Protection Argument

The potential for global trade to affect the environment has become controversial. A president of the Sierra Club, an environmental lobbying organization, once wrote: "The consequences of globalization for the environment are not good. ... Globalization, if we are lucky, will raise average incomes enough to pay for cleaning up some of the mess that we have made. But before we get there, globalization could also destroy enough of the planet's basic biological and physical systems that prospects for life itself will be radically compromised."

If free trade meant the destruction of life itself, then even economists would convert to protectionism! While globalization—and economic activity of all kinds—can pose environmental dangers, it seems quite possible that, with the appropriate safeguards in place, the environmental impacts of trade can be minimized. In some cases, trade may even bring environmental benefits.

In general, high-income countries such as the United States, Canada, Japan, and the nations of the European Union have relatively strict environmental standards. In contrast, middle- and low-income countries like Brazil, Nigeria, India, and China have lower environmental standards. The general view of the governments of such countries is that environmental protection is a luxury: as soon as their people have enough to eat, decent healthcare, and longer life expectancies, then they will spend more money on sewage treatment plants, scrubbers to reduce air pollution from factory smokestacks, national parks to protect wildlife, and so on.

This gap in environmental standards between high-income and low-income countries raises two worrisome possibilities in a world of increasing global trade: the "race to the bottom" scenario and the question of how quickly environmental standards will improve in low-income countries.

The Race to the Bottom Scenario

The race to the bottom scenario of global environmental degradation runs like this. Profit-seeking multinational companies shift their production from countries with strong environmental standards to countries with weak standards, thus reducing their costs and increasing their profits. Faced with such behavior, countries reduce their environmental standards to attract multinational firms, which, after all, provide jobs and economic clout. As a result, global production becomes concentrated in countries where it can pollute the most and environmental laws everywhere "race to the bottom."

Although the race-to-the-bottom scenario sounds plausible, it does not appear to describe reality. In fact, the financial incentive for firms to shift production to poor countries to take advantage of their weaker environmental rules does not seem especially powerful. When firms decide where to locate a new factory, they look at many different factors: the costs of labor and financial capital; whether the location is close to a reliable suppliers of the inputs that they need; whether the location is close to customers; the quality of transportation, communications, and electrical power networks; the level of taxes; and the competence and honesty of the local government. The cost of environmental regulations is a factor, too, but typically environmental costs are no more than 1 to 2% of the costs faced by a large industrial plant. The other factors that determine location are much more important to these companies than trying to skimp on environmental protection costs.

When an international company does choose to build a plant in a low-income country with lax environmental laws, it typically builds a plant similar to those that it operates in high-income countries with stricter environmental standards. Part of the reason for this decision is that designing an industrial plant is a complex and costly task, and so if a plant works well in a high-income country, companies prefer to use the same design everywhere. Also, companies realize that if they create an environmental disaster in a low-income country, it is likely to cost them a substantial amount of money in paying for damages, lost trust, and reduced sales—by building up-to-date plants everywhere they minimize such risks. As a result of these factors, foreign-owned plants in low-income countries often have a better record of compliance with environmental laws than do locally-owned plants.

Pressuring Low-Income Countries for Higher Environmental Standards

In some cases, the issue is not so much whether globalization will pressure low-income countries to reduce their environmental standards, but instead whether the threat of blocking international trade can pressure these countries into adopting stronger standards. For example, restrictions on ivory imports in high-income countries, along with stronger government efforts to catch elephant poachers, have been credited with helping to reduce the illegal poaching of elephants in certain African countries.

However, it would be highly undemocratic for the well-fed citizens of high-income countries to attempt to dictate to the ill-fed citizens of low-income countries what domestic policies and priorities they must adopt, or how they should balance environmental goals against other priorities for their citizens. Furthermore, if high-income countries want stronger environmental standards in low-income countries, they have many options other than the threat of protectionism. For example, high-income countries could pay for anti-pollution equipment in low-income countries, or could help to pay for national parks. High-income countries could help pay for and carry out the scientific and economic studies that would help environmentalists in low-income countries to make a more persuasive case for the economic benefits of protecting the environment.

After all, environmental protection is vital to two industries of key importance in many low-income countries—agriculture and tourism. Environmental advocates can set up standards for labeling products, like "this tuna caught in a net that kept dolphins safe" or "this product made only with wood not taken from rainforests," so that consumer pressure can reinforce environmentalist values. These values are also reinforced by the United Nations, which sponsors treaties to address issues such as climate change and global warming, the preservation of biodiversity, the spread of deserts, and the environmental health of the seabed. Countries that share a national border or are within a region often sign environmental agreements about air and water rights, too. The WTO is also becoming more aware of environmental issues and more careful about ensuring that increases in trade do not inflict environmental damage.

Finally, it should be noted that these concerns about the race to the bottom or pressuring low-income countries for more strict environmental standards do not apply very well to the roughly half of all U.S. trade that occurs with other high-income countries. Indeed, many European countries have stricter environmental standards in certain industries than the United States.

The Unsafe Consumer Products Argument

One argument for shutting out certain imported products is that they are unsafe for consumers. Indeed, consumer rights groups have sometimes warned that the World Trade Organization would require nations to reduce their health and safety standards for imported products. However, the WTO explains its current agreement on the subject in this way: "It allows countries to set their own standards." But it also says "regulations must be based on science. . . . And they should not arbitrarily or unjustifiably discriminate between countries where identical or similar conditions prevail." Thus, for example, under WTO rules it is perfectly legitimate for the United States to pass laws requiring that all food products or cars sold in the United States meet certain safety standards approved by the United States government, whether or not other countries choose to pass similar standards. However, such standards must have some scientific basis. It is improper to impose one set of health and safety standards for domestically produced goods but a different set of standards for imports, or one set of standards for imports from Europe and a different set of standards for imports from Latin America.

In 2007, Mattel recalled nearly two million toys imported from China due to concerns about high levels of lead in the paint, as well as some loose parts. It is unclear if other toys were subject to similar standards. More recently, in 2013, Japan blocked imports of U.S. wheat because of concerns that genetically modified (GMO) wheat might be included in the shipments. The science on the impact of GMOs on health is still developing.

The National Interest Argument

Some argue that a nation should not depend too heavily on other countries for supplies of certain key products, such as oil, or for special materials or technologies that might have national security applications. On closer consideration, this argument for protectionism proves rather weak.

As an example, in the United States, oil provides about 40% of all the energy and 32% of the oil used in the United States economy is imported. Several times in the last few decades, when disruptions in the Middle East have shifted the supply curve of oil back to the left and sharply raised the price, the effects have been felt across the United States economy. This is not, however, a very convincing argument for restricting imports of oil. If the United States needs to be protected from a possible cutoff of foreign oil, then a more reasonable strategy would be to import 100% of the petroleum supply now, and save U.S. domestic oil resources for when or if the foreign supply is cut off. It might also be useful to import extra oil and put it into a stockpile for use in an emergency, as the United States government did by starting a Strategic Petroleum Reserve in 1977. Moreover, it may be necessary to discourage people from using oil, and to start a high-powered program to seek out alternatives to oil. A straightforward way to do this would be to raise taxes on oil. What's more, it makes no sense to argue that because oil is highly important to the United States economy, then the United States should shut out oil imports and use up its domestic supplies of oil more quickly. U.S. domestic production of oil is increasing. Shale oil is adding to domestic supply using fracking extraction techniques.

Whether or not to limit certain kinds of imports of key technologies or materials that might be important to national security and weapons systems is a slightly different issue. If weapons' builders are not confident that they can continue to obtain a key product in wartime, they might decide to avoid designing weapons that use this key product, or they can go ahead and design the weapons and stockpile enough of the key high-tech components or materials to last through an armed conflict. Indeed, there is a U.S. Defense National Stockpile Center that has built up reserves of many materials, from aluminum oxides, antimony, and bauxite to tungsten, vegetable tannin extracts, and zinc (although many of these stockpiles have been reduced and sold in recent years). Think every country is pro-trade? How about the U.S.? The following Clear it Up might surprise you.

How does the United States really feel about expanding trade?

How do people around the world feel about expanding trade between nations? In summer 2007, the Pew Foundation surveyed 45,000 people in 47 countries. One of the questions asked about opinions on growing trade ties between countries. Table 3 shows the percentages who answered either "very good" or "somewhat good" for some of countries surveyed.

For those who think of the United States as the world's leading supporter of expanding trade, the survey results may be perplexing. When adding up the shares of those who say that growing trade ties between countries is "very good" or "somewhat good," Americans had the least favorable attitude toward increasing globalization, while the Chinese and South Africans ranked highest. In fact, among the 47 countries surveyed, the United States ranked by far the lowest on this measure, followed by Egypt, Italy, and Argentina.

Table 3. The Status of Growing Trade Ties between Countries (Source: http://www.pewglobal.org/files/pdf/258.pdf)

Country	Very Good	Somewhat Good	Total
China	38%	53%	91%
South Africa	42%	43%	87%
South Korea	24%	62%	86%
Germany	30%	55%	85%
Canada	29%	53%	82%
United Kingdom	28%	50%	78%
Mexico	22%	55%	77%
Brazil	13%	59%	72%
Japan	17%	55%	72%
United States	14%	45%	59%

One final reason why economists often treat the **national interest argument** skeptically is that almost any product can be touted by lobbyists and politicians as vital to national security. In 1954, the United States became worried that it was importing half of the wool required for military uniforms, so it declared wool and mohair to be "strategic materials" and began to give subsidies to wool and mohair farmers. Although wool was removed from the official list of "strategic" materials in 1960, the subsidies for mohair continued for almost 40 years until they were repealed in 1993, and then were reinstated in 2002. All too often, the national interest argument has become an excuse for handing out the indirect subsidy of protectionism to certain industries or companies. After all, decisions about what constitutes a key strategic material are made by politicians, not nonpartisan analysts.

Key Concepts and Summary

There are a number of arguments that support restricting imports. These arguments are based around industry and competition, environmental concerns, and issues of safety and security.

The infant industry argument for protectionism is that small domestic industries need to be temporarily nurtured and protected from foreign competition for a time so that they can grow into strong competitors. In some cases, notably in East Asia, this approach has worked. Often, however, the infant industries never grow up. On the other hand, arguments against dumping (which is setting prices below the cost of production to drive competitors out of the market), often simply seem to be a convenient excuse for imposing protectionism.

Low-income countries typically have lower environmental standards than high-income countries because they are more worried about immediate basics such as food, education, and healthcare. However, except for a small number of extreme cases, shutting off trade seems unlikely to be an effective method of pursuing a cleaner environment.

Finally, there are arguments involving safety and security. Under the rules of the World Trade Organization, countries are allowed to set whatever standards for product safety they wish, but the standards must be the same for domestic products as for imported products and there must be a scientific basis for the standard. The national interest argument for protectionism holds that it is unwise to import certain key products because if the nation becomes dependent on key imported supplies, it could be vulnerable to a cutoff. However, it is often wiser to stockpile resources and to use foreign supplies when available, rather than preemptively restricting foreign supplies so as not to become dependent on them.

27.4 HOW TRADE POLICY IS ENACTED: GLOBALLY, REGIONALLY, AND NATIONALLY

These public policy arguments about how nations should react to globalization and trade are fought out at several levels: at the global level through the World Trade Organization and through regional trade agreements between pairs or groups of countries.

The World Trade Organization

The World Trade Organization (WTO) was officially born in 1995, but its history is much longer. In the years after the Great Depression and World War II, there was a worldwide push to build institutions that would tie the nations of the world together. The United Nations officially came into existence in 1945. The World Bank, which assists the poorest people in the world, and the International Monetary Fund, which addresses issues raised by international financial transactions, were both created in 1946. The third planned organization was to be an International Trade Organization, which would manage international trade. The United Nations was unable to agree to this. Instead, the General Agreement on Tariffs and Trade (GATT), was established in 1947 to provide a forum in which nations could come together to negotiate reductions in tariffs and other barriers to trade. In 1995, the GATT was transformed into the WTO.

The GATT process was to negotiate an agreement to reduce barriers to trade, sign that agreement, pause for a while, and then start negotiating the next agreement. The rounds of talks in the GATT, and now the WTO, are shown in Table 6. Notice that the early rounds of GATT talks took a relatively short time, included a small number of countries, and focused almost entirely on reducing tariffs. Since the 1970s, however, rounds of trade talks have taken years, included a large number of countries, and an ever-broadening range of issues.

Table 6. The Negotiating Rounds of GATT and the World Trade Organization

Year	Place or Name of Round	Main Subjects	Number of Countries Involved
1947	Geneva	Tariff reduction	23
1949	Annecy	Tariff reduction	13
1951	Torquay	Tariff reduction	38
1956	Geneva	Tariff reduction	26
1960–61	Dillon round	Tariff reduction	26
1964–67	Kennedy round	Tariffs, anti-dumping measures	62
1973–79	Tokyo round	Tariffs, nontariff barriers	102

Year	Place or Name of Round	Main Subjects	Number of Countries Involved
1986–94	Uruguay round	Tariffs, nontariff barriers, services, intellectual property, dispute settlement, textiles, agriculture, creation of WTO	123
2001–	Doha round	Agriculture, services, intellectual property, competition, investment, environment, dispute settlement	147

The sluggish pace of GATT negotiations led to an old joke that GATT really stood for Gentleman's Agreement to Talk and Talk. The slow pace of international trade talks, however, is understandable, even sensible. Having dozens of nations agree to any treaty is a lengthy process. GATT often set up separate trading rules for certain industries, like agriculture, and separate trading rules for certain countries, like the low-income countries. There were rules, exceptions to rules, opportunities to opt out of rules, and precise wording to be fought over in every case. Like the GATT before it, the WTO is not a world government, with power to impose its decisions on others. The total staff of the WTO in 2014 is 640 people and its annual budget (as of 2014) is \$197 million, which makes it smaller in size than many large universities.

Regional Trading Agreements

There are different types of economic integration across the globe, ranging from **free trade agreements**, in which participants allow each other's imports without tariffs or quotas, to **common markets**, in which participants have a common external trade policy as well as free trade within the group, to full **economic unions**, in which, in addition to a common market, monetary and fiscal policies are coordinated. Many nations belong both to the World Trade Organization and to regional trading agreements.

The best known of these regional trading agreements is the **European Union**. In the years after World War II, leaders of several European nations reasoned that if they could tie their economies together more closely, they might be more likely to avoid another devastating war. Their efforts began with a free trade association, evolved into a common market, and then transformed into what is now a full economic union, known as the European Union. The EU, as it is often called, has a number of goals. For example, in the early 2000s it introduced a common currency for Europe, the euro, and phased out most of the former national forms of money like the German mark and the French franc, though a few have retained their own currency. Another key element of the union is to eliminate barriers to the mobility of goods, labor, and capital across Europe.

For the United States, perhaps the best-known regional trading agreement is the **North American Free Trade Agreement (NAFTA)**. The United States also participates in some less-prominent regional trading agreements, like the Caribbean Basin Initiative, which offers reduced tariffs for imports from these countries, and a free trade agreement with Israel.

The world has seen a flood of regional trading agreements in recent years. About 100 such agreements are now in place. A few of the more prominent ones are listed in Table 7. Some are just agreements to continue talking; others set specific goals for reducing tariffs, import quotas, and nontariff barriers. One economist described the current trade treaties as a "spaghetti bowl," which is what a map with lines connecting all the countries with trade treaties looks like.

There is concern among economists who favor free trade that some of these regional agreements may promise free trade, but actually act as a way for the countries within the regional agreement to try to limit trade from anywhere else. In some cases, the regional trade agreements may even conflict with the broader agreements of the World Trade Organization.

Table 7. Some Regional Trade Agreements

Trade Agreements	Participating Countries
Asia Pacific Economic Cooperation (APEC)	Australia, Brunei, Canada, Chile, People's Republic of China, Hong Kong, China, Indonesia, Japan, Republic of Korea, Malaysia, Mexico, New Zealand, Papua New Guinea, Peru, Philippines, Russia, Singapore, Chinese Taipei, Thailand, United States, Vietnam
European Union (EU)	Austria, Belgium, Bulgaria, Cyprus, Czech Republic, Denmark, Estonia, Finland, France, Germany, Greece, Hungary, Ireland, Italy, Latvia, Lithuania, Luxembourg, Malta, Netherlands, Poland, Portugal, Romania, Slovakia, Slovenia, Spain, Sweden, United Kingdom
North America Free Trade Agreement (NAFTA)	Canada, Mexico, United States
Latin American Integration Association (LAIA)	Argentina, Bolivia, Brazil, Chile, Columbia, Ecuador, Mexico, Paraguay, Peru, Uruguay, Venezuela
Association of Southeast Asian Nations (ASEAN)	Brunei, Cambodia, Indonesia, Laos, Malaysia, Myanmar, Philippines, Singapore, Thailand, Vietnam
Southern African Development Community (SADC)	Angola, Botswana, Congo, Lesotho, Malawi, Mauritius, Mozambique, Namibia, Seychelles, South Africa, Swaziland, Tanzania, Zambia, Zimbabwe

Trade Policy at the National Level

Yet another dimension of trade policy, along with international and regional trade agreements, happens at the national level. The United States, for example, imposes import quotas on sugar, because of a fear that such imports would drive down the price of sugar and thus injure domestic sugar producers. One of the jobs of the United States Department of Commerce is to determine if imports from other countries are being dumped. The United States International Trade Commission—a government agency—determines whether domestic industries have been substantially injured by the dumping, and if so, the president can impose tariffs that are intended to offset the unfairly low price.

In the arena of trade policy, the battle often seems to be between national laws that increase protectionism and international agreements that try to reduce protectionism, like the WTO. Why would a country pass laws or negotiate agreements to shut out certain foreign products, like sugar or textiles, while simultaneously negotiating to reduce trade barriers in general? One plausible answer is that international trade agreements offer a method for countries to restrain their own special interests. A member of Congress can say to an industry lobbying for tariffs or quotas on imports: "Sure would like to help you, but that pesky WTO agreement just won't let me."

If consumers are the biggest losers from trade, why do they not fight back? The quick answer is because it is easier to organize a small group of people around a narrow interest versus a large group that has diffuse interests. This is a question about trade policy theory. Visit this website and read the article by Jonathan Rauch.

Long-Term Trends in Barriers to Trade

In newspaper headlines, trade policy appears mostly as disputes and acrimony. Countries are almost constantly threatening to challenge the "unfair" trading practices of other nations. Cases are brought to the dispute settlement procedures of the WTO, the European Union, NAFTA, and other regional trading agreements. Politicians in national legislatures, goaded on by lobbyists, often threaten to pass bills that will "establish a fair playing field" or "prevent unfair trade"—although most such bills seek to accomplish these high-sounding goals by placing more restrictions on trade. Protesters in the streets may object to specific trade rules or to the entire practice of international trade.

Through all the controversy, the general trend in the last 60 years is clearly toward lower barriers to trade. The average level of tariffs on imported products charged by industrialized countries was 40% in 1946. By 1990, after decades of GATT negotiations, it was down to less than 5%. Indeed, one of the reasons that GATT negotiations shifted from focusing on tariff reduction in the early rounds to a broader agenda was that tariffs had been reduced so dramatically there was not much more to do in that area. U.S. tariffs have followed this general pattern: After rising sharply during the Great Depression, tariffs dropped off to less than 2% by the end of the century. Although measures of import quotas and nontariff barriers are less exact than those for tariffs, they generally appear to be at lower levels, too.

Thus, the last half-century has seen both a dramatic reduction in government-created barriers to trade, such as tariffs, import quotas, and nontariff barriers, and also a number of technological developments that have made international trade easier, like advances in transportation, communication, and information management. The result has been the powerful surge of international trade.

Key Concepts and Summary

Trade policy is determined at many different levels: administrative agencies within government, laws passed by the legislature, regional negotiations between a small group of nations (sometimes just two), and global negotiations through the World Trade Organization. During the second half of the twentieth century, trade barriers have, in general, declined quite substantially in the United States economy and in the global economy. One reason why countries sign international trade agreements to commit themselves to free trade is to give themselves protection against their own special interests. When an industry lobbies for protection from foreign producers, politicians can point out that, because of the trade treaty, their hands are tied.

27.5 THE TRADEOFFS OF TRADE POLICY

Economists readily acknowledge that international trade is not all sunshine, roses, and happy endings. Over time, the average person gains from international trade, both as a worker who has greater productivity and higher wages because of the benefits of specialization and comparative advantage, and as a consumer who can benefit from shopping all over the world for a greater variety of quality products at attractive prices. The "average person," however, is hypothetical, not real—representing a mix of those who have done very well, those who have done all right, and those who have done poorly. It is a legitimate concern of public policy to focus not just on the average or on the success stories, but also on those have not been so fortunate. Workers in other countries, the environment, and prospects for new industries and materials that might be of key importance to the national economy are also all legitimate issues.

The common belief among economists is that it is better to embrace the gains from trade, and then deal with the costs and tradeoffs with other policy tools, than it is to cut off trade to avoid the costs and tradeoffs.

To gain a better intuitive understanding for this argument, consider a hypothetical American company called Technotron. Technotron invents a new scientific technology that allows the firm to increase the output and quality of its goods with a smaller number of workers at a lower cost. As a result of this technology, other U.S. firms in this industry will lose money and will also have to lay off workers—and some of the competing firms will even go bankrupt. Should the United States government protect the existing firms and their employees by making it illegal for Technotron to use its new technology? Most people who live in market-oriented economies would oppose trying to block better products that lower the cost of services. Certainly, there is a case for society providing temporary support and assistance for those who find themselves without work. Many would argue for government support of programs that encourage retraining and acquiring additional skills. Government might also support research and development efforts, so that other firms may find ways of outdoing Technotron. Blocking the new technology altogether, however, seems like a mistake. After all, few people would advocate giving up electricity because it caused so much disruption to the kerosene and candle business. Few would suggest holding back on improvements in medical technology because they might cause companies selling leeches and snake oil to lose money. In short, most people view disruptions due to technological change as a necessary cost that is worth bearing.

Now, imagine that Technotron's new "technology" is as simple as this: the company imports what it sells from another country. In other words, think of foreign trade as a type of innovative technology. The objective situation is now exactly the same as before. Because of Technotron's new technology—which in this case is importing goods from another county—other firms in this industry will lose money and lay off workers. Just as it would have been inappropriate and ultimately foolish to respond to the disruptions of new scientific technology by trying to shut it down, it would be inappropriate and ultimately foolish to respond to the disruptions of **international trade** by trying to restrict trade.

Some workers and firms will suffer because of international trade. In a living, breathing market-oriented economy, some workers and firms will always be experiencing disruptions, for a wide variety of reasons. Corporate management can be better or worse. Workers for a certain firm can be more productive or less. Tough domestic competitors can create just as much disruption as tough foreign competitors. Sometimes a new product is a hit with consumers; sometimes it is a flop. Sometimes a company is blessed by a run of good luck or stricken with a run of bad luck. For some firms, international trade will offer great opportunities for expanding productivity and jobs; for other firms, trade will impose stress and pain. The disruption caused by international trade is not fundamentally different from all the other disruptions caused by the other workings of a market economy.

In other words, the economic analysis of free trade does not rely on a belief that foreign trade is not disruptive or does not pose tradeoffs; indeed, the story of Technotron begins with a particular **disruptive market change**—a new technology—that causes real tradeoffs. In thinking about the disruptions of foreign trade, or any of the other possible costs and tradeoffs of foreign trade discussed in this chapter, the best public policy solutions typically do not involve protectionism, but instead involve finding ways for public policy to address the particular issues, while still allowing the benefits of international trade to occur.

What's the Downside of Protection?

The domestic flat-panel display industry employed many workers before the ITC imposed the dumping margin tax. Flat-panel displays make up a significant portion of the cost of producing laptop computers—as much as 50%. Therefore, the antidumping tax would substantially increase the cost, and thus the price, of U.S.-manufactured laptops. As a result of the ITC's decision, Apple moved its domestic manufacturing plant for Macintosh computers to Ireland (where it had an existing plant). Toshiba shut down its U.S. manufacturing plant for laptops. And IBM cancelled plans to open a laptop manufacturing plant in North Carolina, instead deciding to expand production at its plant in Japan. In this case, rather than having the desired effect of protecting U.S. interests and giving domestic manufacturing an advantage over items manufactured elsewhere, it had the unintended effect of driving the manufacturing completely out of the country. Many people lost their jobs and most flat-panel display production now occurs in countries other than the United States.

Key Concepts and Summary

International trade certainly has income distribution effects. This is hardly surprising. All domestic or international competitive market forces are disruptive. They cause companies and industries to rise and fall. Government has a role to play in cushioning workers against the disruptions of the market. However, just as it would be unwise in the long term to clamp down on new technology and other causes of disruption in domestic markets, it would be unwise to clamp down on foreign trade. In both cases, the disruption brings with it economic benefits.

CHAPTER

28 THE GLOBALIZATION AND TRADE ECONOMICS: A PLURALISTIC APPROACH

28.1 THE ORTHODOX STORY OF TRADE: A SYNOPSIS

If ever there was a sacrosanct idea within orthodox economic thought, it is the belief, faith even, that orthodox economists have regarding the merits and benefits of economic actors being free to trade. The basis for the orthodox economists' faith has much to do with the theoretical explanation orthodox economists utilize to explain how trade works and why it is beneficial. Consider the ideas presented in the chapter entitled **International Trade**.

As presented, orthodox economics organizes its free trade story around several assumptions. The assumptions are designed to constrain the scope of the analysis so as to simplify the story. In the typical introductory textbook presentation, orthodox economists utilize production possibilities frontiers to depict their story.

In support of the production possibilities frontier presentation, orthodox economists apply eight assumptions. The following represents the eight, most common, assumptions.

- Two producers
- Two products
- Fixed resources.
- Fixed technology.
- Full resource utilization.
- Zero transactions costs
- No external costs or benefits
- Autarky

Let's take a moment to reflect upon these assumptions and what they mean. For starters, it is typically to assume that the two producers in the model will be countries. Within the two countries, only two products will be produced. Each country will have a fixed number of resources available to produce those products. Limited resources will subsequently limit the amount of production of the two products that is possible within the two countries. Additionally, the fixed technology assumption further limits the extent of possible production. Given the limits to production, all resources and technology are assumed to be used, fully utilized, meaning that production will take place at some point on the production possibilities frontier. Once products are produced, if the two countries seek to trade with one another, there will be no transactions costs associated with trade. Transactions costs are costs such as the legal costs of creating contracts or the transportation costs associated with shipping a product from one part of the world to another. In addition to no transactions costs, external costs or benefits are assumed to be absent. As a reminder, external costs or benefits are the possible spillover effects that occur as a result of economic activity such as production or consumption. As one can imagine, because trade requires transportation, the social costs associated with the wastes generated by transportation are very real. However, for the sake of simplicity, the model assumes the costs and/or benefits of externalities are zero. Finally, autarky means that each producer is self-sufficient. Self-sufficient producers do not require trade in order to survive. If trade is a luxury rather than a necessity, then when trade occurs it is voluntary trade and only to the benefit of the trading partners.

Given the model's assumptions, the orthodox free trade story then showcases three essential components to the trade story. First, the initial step in facilitating trade is for producers to identify their comparative advantage. Recall, comparative advantage means that producers are capable of producing some product(s) at a lower opportunity cost than another producer is capable of producing the same product(s). As a producer, regardless of whether the producer is an individual, firm, or nation, as long as the producer is producing the product at a lower opportunity cost than the other producer, the producer with the lower opportunity cost has a comparative advantage. The second step in the trade story is the specialization of production. Upon identifying its comparative advantage, orthodox economics argues that a producer should specialize in the production of the product that which it has a comparative advantage. Specialization means that a producer should direct their available resources toward the production of a specific product. The third component of the trade story is, trade. Specialized producers, producing a product of which they have a comparative advantage, should now seek to identify trading partners that are also specialized producers of desirable products.

1	→	2	→	3
Producer		Producer Specializes in		Trade with
Identifies its		the Production		other Producers
Comparative		of the Comparatively		of other
Advantage		Advantageous Product		Products

The Benefits of Trade

Orthodox economics sees the outcomes of trade as having predominantly positive impacts for the economic well-being of those people participating in the trade. Trade is deemed beneficial for several reasons. Orthodox economics concludes that trade will not only stimulate economic growth, increase efficiency, and enhance economic development, but that trade is also the best path toward pursuing those goals.

The story of growth is relatively straightforward. The economic growth, when examined more specifically, such as in the case of international trade as producers get access to consumers beyond their domestic borders, the number of available consumers should grow. In the face of a larger potential consumer market place, domestic producers will seek to expand their productive capacities, otherwise known as growth, in order to produce more in an effort to take advantage of having more potential consumers.

The story of efficiency is less obvious, but is still relatively straightforward, particularly if viewed through the lens of international trade. In an international trade environment, producers that may have otherwise been subject to their own country's domestic competition, are now confronted by international competition. Given more competition, producers are forced to seek ever more efficient ways to produce products or risk being driven out of business. More trade equates to more competition and, through the eyes of an orthodox economist,

Finally, in the case of the economic development story, the relationship between trade and development is a bit murky but still evident. By focusing on the specialized production product(s) that producers are comparatively good at producing, the total amount of available products should grow. As two or more parties trade, each producer's relative abundance of production becomes available to more people to be consumed. Essentially, with the growth of products comes an increased ability to meet people's wants. As more wants are met, facilitated by trade, the sum total of utility grows for all and everyone is made better off. In this case, economic development is being defined as raised living standards by virtue of access to consumer products.

28.2 A CRITICAL EXAMINATION OF THE ORTHODOX DEPICTION OF FREE TRADE

Within the discipline of economics not all economists agree with the rather rosy picture presented by orthodox economists in their defense of free trade. Critiques of the orthodox free trade story tend to focus on two areas. Some heterodox economists emphasize what they see as the theoretical failures of the orthodox story, namely its disassociation with the "real world." Other heterodox economists focus their criticisms toward the orthodoxy's depiction of the outcomes of trade, particularly the orthodoxy's conclusion that trade stimulates economic growth and economic development

Upon examination it can be argued that both paths of criticism really represent the two different sides of the same coin. For example, if the theoretical model presented by orthodox economics is, in fact, inaccurate because it is in some way divorced of "real world" context, then the theoretical conclusions drawn by the theory will likely also be flawed. Looked at the other way, if "real world" evidence points to outcomes different from the outcomes predicted or perceived by orthodox economics, then it stands to reason that the theoretical model utilized to predict outcomes is failing in some capacity.

In the following sub-sections each of the two critical paths will be explored. The careful reader will note that the two paths frequently intersect.

Technical Critiques: The Orthodox Model is Poorly Constructed

In this section of the chapter we will explore the model imperfections approach to critiquing the orthodox presentation of free trade. The model imperfections critique is, essentially, a failure of the techniques employed by orthodox economists. There are two main types of model imperfections.

- Type One – Mild
- Type Two – More Severe to Very Severe

For Type I critics of the orthodox economic free trade story, the shortcomings associated with the orthodox economic presentation of free trade is strictly the result of a failure of technique, but not necessarily a failure of the overall theory. In other words, the theory does generalize to the real world, but due to model imperfections such as the model's choice of assumptions being overly simplified, the model is unable to fully capture actual real world circumstances. The degree of seriousness associated with these critiques can be classified as mild.

For Type II critics, the model imperfections critique represents a much more serious indictment of the standard orthodox free trade story. In this case, comparative advantage, specialization, and trade does not actually generalize well to the real world. The socially positive results that are depicted in the orthodox theoretical presentation, when these imperfections are accounted for, will not emerge. In other words, because the real world will, and does, contain imperfections that do not conform to the orthodox economic model, the orthodox theoretical presentation will often deviate from actual events in the real world causing the model to blatantly misrepresent the benefits of trade. Importantly, with modifications designed to correct the imperfections, the model can be corrected enough so as to reflect conditions in the real world.

A Note on the Failure of Technique

A failure of technique means that by making alterations to the choice of assumptions, the comparative advantage story can be modified to present theoretical outcomes that are more accurate to the real world. As a general rule the changes in assumptions are applied on an ad hoc basis, meaning that assumptions are altered from situation to situation. The goal becomes to modify assumptions in order to reflect phenomena experienced in the actual global economy. The modification of assumptions suggests that there are limits to the usefulness of the techniques utilized within orthodox economic theory to explain.

Type I Model Imperfections

The following represent examples of instances in which the restrictive features of the assumptions do not provide a "real world" depiction, but also do not fundamentally undermine the free trade story.

Exclusion of Transactions Costs

In constructing their theoretical presentation of international trade, orthodox economics excludes transactions costs. Transactions costs include factors such as transportation, legal, and communications costs. As one can imagine, in the actual world in which we live the trade of products will seemingly always include significant transaction costs. When transactions costs are included some trades that would have otherwise been beneficial will not be worthwhile as the costs associated with making the trade become too high to justify the trade. While this critique certainly does point to instances in which some trades will not happen as would be the case in the standard orthodox trade story, the critique is not a deal breaker as most of the orthodox trade story remains intact.

Non-Linear Production Possibilities Frontiers

Production possibilities curves are not linear (straight line) but rather concave (bowed outward). A bowed outward PPF reflects the principle of increasing opportunity cost. Increasing opportunity cost implies that as a nation moves closer and closer to specializing in the production of one good or one type of good, the opportunity cost of specialization will rise. For example, for countries producing agricultural commodities, there tend to be land or ecology limits on their productive capacity. As a result, to specialize in an agricultural product and then expanding production in an agricultural producing sector may cause there to be an increase in the average cost of production due to declining productivity associated with the diseconomies of scale that accompanies introduction of less and less fertile land.

Since the free trade story is told on the basis of comparative advantage such that a nation produces those goods that require a low opportunity cost of production, if opportunity costs are changing (specifically, rising), then production of a good that may have a low opportunity cost at one point, may have a significantly higher opportunity cost after specialization. The following table illustrates this point.

		CANADA	
SILVER (OUNCES)	0	500,000	600,000
LUMBER (BOARD – FEET)	1,000,000	500,000	0
	1l : 1S	1l : 0.2S	
		1S : 1L	1S : 5L
		MEXICO	
SILVER (OUNCES)	0	40,000	80,000
LUMBER (BOARD – FEET)	80,000	50,000	0
	1L : 1.33S	1L : 0.8S	
		1S : 0.75L	1S : 1.25L

The ratios in red illustrate the lowest opportunity costs of production for both Canada and Mexico. For Canada, the numbers indicate that they have a comparative advantage in producing lumber because they can produce 1 unit of lumber at the expense of only 0.2 units of silver. Canada's comparative advantage outcome emerges when Canadian production changes from 0 lumber and 600,000 silver to 500,000 lumber and 500,000 silver. For Mexico, the numbers indicate that they have a comparative advantage in producing silver because they are capable of producing 1 unit of silver for 0.75 units of lumber. Mexico's comparative advantage emerges when Mexican production changes from 0 silver and 80,000 lumber to 40,000 silver and 40,000 lumber.

According to the logic of orthodox economic theory, now that the Canadian and Mexican comparative advantages have been identified, with Canada having the advantage in lumber and Mexico the advantage in silver, Mexico and Canada should then specialize and trade. Specialization means that Canada should now only produce lumber, moving their production outcome to 0 silver and 1,000,000 lumber while Mexico should now only produce silver, moving their production to 0 lumber and 80,000 silver. It is at this point that a problem appears. Once each country specializes, what was a comparative advantage dissolves into a comparative disadvantage.

Examining the table, as a result of the principle of increasing opportunity cost, the opportunity cost in silver of specializing in lumber increases as Canada moves to maximum lumber production becoming a 1 lumber to 1 silver ratio. Mexico experiences as similar problem except theirs is the problem of a rising opportunity cost associated with forgone lumber. For Mexico the ratio changes to 1 silver for 1.25 lumber (which is also 1 lumber for 0.8 silver). In fact, as is demonstrated by this table, once the country's specialize, each country now has a comparative advantage in the opposite product from what it previously had a comparative advantage. Post-specialization, Mexico is now capable of producing lumber at a lower opportunity cost than Canada and Canada is now able to produce silver at a lower opportunity cost than Mexico. Clearly the orthodox economic story does not fit this circumstance. This is not to say that free trade necessarily breaks down as a result of this scenario, but it does demonstrate that in a more realistic setting, specialization and trade are not appropriate. In fact, one thing the table clearly demonstrates is that both countries are better off producing a combination, a diversity, of products. At this point, based on a diversity of products produced, if the countries trade, then trade will allow both countries to acquire even more of the respective product that they do not have a comparative advantage in producing.

Type II Model Imperfections

The following examples provide an overview of some of the Type II imperfections that appear to generate a divide between real, actual, world circumstances and the orthodox economic trade story. Each imperfection represents a more fundamental challenge to the orthodox model of trade than did the Type I imperfections. As such, the imperfections are presented from least significant to most significant in terms of their implications for the orthodox model.

Specialization and Economic Vulnerability

Any time production becomes highly specialized, the producer confronts potential risks. Here are two potential risks associated with specialization.

- Any country that chooses to completely specialize in the production of one product runs the risk of a decline in the market for the specialized good. For example, consider a circumstance in which consumers lose interest in the product. In this case market demand declines and the country specializing in the production of this product will necessarily suffers significant economic damage.
- Any country that specializes in the production of an agricultural good, beyond losses in consumer demand also face production risks. A change in weather or a natural disaster has the potential to completely undermine the economy of the nation(s) producing the single agricultural product and devastate an economy.

In either of the above stated situations, the orthodox economic advice of specialization and trade has the potential to cause negative, not positive effects, for the participants. Clearly there are potentially economically devastating risks associated with a program of rigid specialization.

Although the issue of risks does present a more pressing critique of the standard orthodox free trade story, because potential risks are not definite risks, absent the emergence of these events, the orthodox free trade story is still applicable. Additionally, if the above stated risks are a concern, one can argue that the orthodox model can alter its assumptions to acknowledge heightened risks and, subsequently, advocate for more diversified economies. Diversified economies can still trade and, within the orthodox economic story, these economies would still be encouraged to open their borders to the free flow of products.

Specialization and Less than Full Employment

While the orthodox economic free trade story presents the idea that trade may produce increases in available goods and services to the trading partners, as a nation or nations specializes the industries suffering from a comparative disadvantage will, ultimately, displace laborers. Because the losses in one industry may not be fully compensated in another industry or industries, more laborers may be displaced than necessarily employed, thus causing unemployment.

An example of the above situation, consider the trading situation of two countries where one country has an abundance of labor and the other country has an abundance of capital (tools, equipment, machinery). In the country that tends to have an abundance of labor the firms within that country would tend to use a lot of labor, and less capital, for their production. In the country that tends to have an abundance of capital, the firms within the capital intensive country will tend to use a lot of capital, rather than labor, in their production processes.

According to orthodox economic theory, in identifying their respective comparative advantages, the labor intensive country would determine that it has a comparative advantage in producing products that require a lot of labor while the capital intensive country would find that it has an advantage in producing products that require a lot of tools, equipment and machinery. The challenge that emerges in this situation is that not all firms in the capital intensive country will be capital intensive producers, some will be labor intensive producers. The labor intensive firms in the capital intensive country will discover that they are at a comparative disadvantage against labor intensive producers from the labor intensive country. The resulting outcome will be that the labor intensive firms, with an abundance of labor, from the capital intensive country, will begin laying off workers. At the same time, while the capital intensive firms in the capital intensive country will likely grow and expand with trade, thus hiring more laborers, it is likely that their hiring will be less than the number of layoffs from the labor intensive firms. In summary, because the firm using a lot of machines tends to use capital rather than labor for its production the number of laborers it absorbs will likely be less than the number of workers the labor intensive firm fires. The overall outcome would be a rise in unemployment in the capital intensive country.

In this instance, the increase in unemployment being described would imply that trading countries will frequently not be operating at their maximum point of productive possibilities. The notion of less than full employment is a concept that is, more often than not, the case across the entire global economy. The evidence of less than full employment is overwhelming. For example, over the last three decades (as global free trade policies and agreements have expanded, not contracted) unemployment rates across countries identified as economically advanced and developed (countries such as the United States, Canada, Japan, Germany, France, the United Kingdom, Australia, Sweden, and others), unemployment rates have ranged from between a low of 3% to as high as 25%. Additionally, in the rest of world, where the majority of the global population resides the absolute number of unemployed or underemployed laborers exceeds 1 billion people. Clearly less than full employment is the norm, not the exception.

A less than full employment outcome undermines the standard orthodox free trade story because countries at less than full employment can produce more of any two products while opportunity costs are zero. In the case of less than full employment, determine a comparative advantage is impossible because both products reflect the lowest possible opportunity cost, zero. In a circumstance such as this, the orthodox free trade story is not capable of explaining the very real world situation of trade under conditions of less than full employment. Correcting the model to account for this imperfection would require that the model assume that an action will be taken to push the economy back to full employment. Such actions could include government (public) policy measures designed to alleviate the unemployment that emerges as a result of trade. Even for many orthodox economists acknowledging the less than full employment scenario is a justification for government action to mitigate the negative consequences associated with trade.

28.3 CHALLENGING FUNCTIONALITY: A MORE PENETRATING CRITICISM

Whereas the model imperfections critiques often cite the idea that the orthodox theory, while too simple, still provides an approximation of the real world. More radical critiques of the orthodox free trade story argue that not only does the orthodox story not generalize to the actual world in which we live, but that the model also cannot be modified to explain certain events or phenomena. For many more radical economists the usefulness of any economic model is how well it can explain the basic functioning of the economy. Failure to account for the actual functional behavior of the economy cannot be corrected by ad hoc assumptions. Instead, what is required, is an altogether different theoretical structure.

The following critiques reflect functional limitations associated with the orthodox trade story. Functional limitations imply the failure of theory to adequately explain events relevant to the real world. Perhaps the theory is simply too narrow in scope and fails to account for other important economic considerations, such as economic growth or economic development. For example, the whole point of the orthodox comparative advantage story is to demonstrate trade between two countries improves the overall economic plight of both countries. Paradoxically, even as the immediate exchange benefits appear, the same theory can be utilized to also explain why the long term economic growth within both economies may be harmed as a result of free trade. In other words, trade is shown to make countries both better off and worse off? How is this possible? The answer is that it is probably not possible, therefore the functional usefulness of the orthodox economic trade story is called into question.

Three Counties and Three Products

Perhaps no example of the limits to the applicability of the orthodox free trade story is more direct than the curious situation of three countries and three products. Given three countries and three commodities, it is not obvious that each country will have a clear lowest opportunity cost product to produce. Absent a clear comparative advantage, what does a country do? If a country doesn't have a comparative advantage does it produce nothing? Does it produce all three products? Can the country without a comparative advantage refuse to engage in trade? Should the country just export its entire population, put up a border wall, and stop functioning? The orthodox presentation of the trade story cannot answer any of these questions. The absence of comparative advantage is the absence of a theoretical explanation.

Clearly this issue of three countries and three products is not the exception, but rather the rule. In the actual world where we there are over 200 hundred countries in the world and, potentially, millions of products. The comparative advantage story is not at all relevant to the actual world, and this proves to be a drastic failure of the orthodox economic model.

Consider the table below:

	COLOMBIA	SCOTLAND	PERU
COFFEE	100	10	30
WOOL	50	40	30
SOYBEANS	60	20	30
	1C : .5W	1C : 4W	1C : 1W
	1C : .6S	1C : 2S	1C : 1S
	1W : 2C	1W : .25C	1W : 1C
	1W : 1.2S	1W : .5S	1W : 1S
	1S : 1.67C	1S : .5C	1S : 1C
	1S : .83W	1S : 2W	1S : 1W

The table represents a scenario in which there are three countries and three products. In the above table, one country will not have a comparative advantage in producing any of the products. The numbers and letters highlighted in red indicate the comparison between two products and the point of lowest opportunity cost production which, recall, is the basis for comparative advantage. For example, as can be seen above, Colombia has a comparative advantage in producing coffee relative to both wool and soybeans. In the case of coffee to wool, every 1 unit of coffee produced requires that Colombia foregoes producing ½ unit of wool. In the case of coffee to soybeans, for every 1 unit of coffee produced 3/5 of a unit of soybeans are foregone. No other producer of coffee can produce coffee at such a low opportunity cost. The reader should note, Colombia also has a comparative advantage in producing soybeans relative to wool, while Scotland has a comparative advantage in producing wool to soybeans and wool to coffee as well as soybeans to coffee. At no point does Peru ever have a comparative advantage. So what should Peru do? The answers really are not remotely obvious with possible solutions becoming increasingly complex. Consider just one possible scenario.

In one scenario, it can be argued that the only viable product that Peru could specialize in producing is soybeans. After all, because Colombia has a comparative advantage in coffee to wool and coffee to soybeans, and its coffee to wool ratio is better than its soybeans to wool ratio, Colombia may find it desirable to specialize in coffee production. Additionally, because Scotland has a comparative advantage in wool to coffee and wool to soybeans, and its wool to coffee ratio is better than its wool to soybeans ratio, Scotland may find it desirable to specialize in wool production. In this case, Peru could, theoretically specialize in soybean production as neither Colombia nor Scotland are producing soybeans but the residents of those countries may want to consume soybeans so Colombia and Scotland could then trade for soybeans and, as Peru is the only soybean producer, Colombia and Scotland would be forced to trade with Peru.

The trouble with the Peru specializing in soybeans scenario is that it wouldn't take Colombia and Scotland too long to realize that they are each better off producing some soybeans for themselves, because each can produce soybeans at a lower opportunity cost than can Peru. For example, if Colombia produced coffee and traded with Peru for Soybeans, the minimum price that Peru could charge Colombia for the soybeans would be 1 unit of soybeans for 1 unit of coffee. If Scotland decided to produce some soybeans to trade with Colombia for coffee, the minimum price Scotland could charge Colombia for soybeans is 1 unit of soybeans for a ½ unit of coffee. In this case Peru would simply not be able to compete with Scotland's price. The same circumstance emerges with Scotland trading wool for soybeans with Peru. The lowest price Peru can charge Scotland for 1 unit of soybeans is 1 unit of wool. If Colombia decided to produce some soybeans to trade with Scotland for wool, the lowest price Colombia could charge is 1 soybean for .83 wool. Peru is, once again, not price competitive and Scotland and Colombia are better off trading with one another for soybeans than they would be trading with Peru for soybeans.

Comparative Advantage and Constant Returns to Scale

The comparative advantage story is based on an assumption of constant returns to scale. As a reminder, constant returns to scale implies that as a productive process grows, the returns in total output generated grows proportionally to the expansion of the productive process. In other words, if a production process doubles in size, then the amount of productive output will also double. The constant returns to scale concept is closely tied to the linear production possibilities frontier concept discussed above. After all, if a production possibilities frontier is linear, and all productive inputs double, then the production possibilities frontier will shift outward proportionally, remaining parallel to the previous production possibilities frontier. The essential point to be grasped here is this, constant returns to scale imply that as production of one product increases

The challenge associated with the concept of constant returns to scale is, what happens if returns to scale are not constant for producers? Orthodox economic theory provides a theoretical foundation for the idea that sometimes production processes experience increasing returns to scale. As a reminder, increasing returns to scale implies that as a production process expands, the associated increase in production expands by more than the growth of the production process. In other words, as a production process doubles its size it will more than double its output yielding a declining average total cost for the output as more output is produced.

Under conditions of increasing returns to scale in production, the country that is the first to produce a commodity will develop a comparative advantage in the production of the commodity. The reason why the first producer of the product will have the comparative advantage is because as that country increases its production of the product, its costs of doing so will decline making it difficult for another country to compete with the first country to produce the product. In other words, one country will have a head start that other countries will not be able to competitively overcome. Presumably, where increasing returns to scale hold for production processes, the first producer of any product will have a competitive advantage over all producers. In this situation, one country could come to dominate production throughout many industries leaving other countries to produce a limited range of other products.

Of course, where increasing returns to scale applies the thought that one country can dominate production may not be acceptable to other countries, particularly for countries attempting to develop economically. The implication is that countries need to protect their industries until those industries have increased their production to the point of increasing returns to scale and, thus, declining average costs of production emerge. Only when a producer has achieved low enough average total costs will it be able to compete effectively in global markets.

Absolute Costs are more Important than Factor Endowments

One theme that emerged above when describing model imperfections is the notion that due to **factor endowments**, some countries are going to be more prone to a greater loss of employment from specialization and trade than would other countries. The basis for the less than full employment argument was a byproduct of the concept of factor endowments. The concept of **factor endowments** is an idea that argues a country's comparative advantage may be influenced by which factors of production the country has an abundance of and which are relatively scarce. A country is said to be factor endowed when it has a relative abundance of a given factor of production. When a country has an abundance of a factor of production, orthodox economics argues that the country will tend to produce products whose production processes are organized to require a lot of the factor of which the country has an abundance. Due to the relative low cost of the abundant factor, the country will likely have a comparative advantage in producing the product that which they have an abundance of the factor of production. So, for example, a country with an abundance of land will likely produce agricultural products as land is the relatively low cost factor of production that the country is more abundantly endowed.

Taken further, the factor endowment story goes so far as to argue that production processes will be modified to adjust to a country's factor abundance and factor scarcity. For orthodox economics what this means is that if a country has an abundance of capital, then the products it produces will utilize an abundance of capital even if the same product can be produced elsewhere with an abundance of labor. Should labor be the factor of production that a country is relatively well endowed, then production processes will be modified to include more labor and less capital, and so on, and so forth.

Certainly, for some types of production, the factor endowment story will be relevant, which also makes the idea of a less than fully employed economy, as argued in the sub-section above, also relevant. However, what happens when the product and the production process are inextricably linked? It is not at all uncommon for a production process to require the same combination of land, labor, and capital, regardless of where production takes place. So even if a country has a large supply of labor, and relatively cheap labor, this does not mean that firms will suddenly change their production processes to take advantage of the cheap factor endowment. An example of this concept can be seen with a company like Boeing. Boeing produces commercial and military aircraft. The production processes require a significant amount of technological know- how, with capital and labor being very specialized and highly skilled. Furthermore, the capital and technology employed in the production of an airplane are very expensive. It is also a well- known fact that Boeing produces airplanes in the United States and China. In comparison to one-another, the United States has an abundance of capital and China has an abundance of labor. If factor endowments were relevant, Boeing would produce its aircraft differently in China than in the United States. In China, Boeing would use more labor and in the United States Boeing would use more capital. In fact, Boeing uses the same combination of capital and labor in its production processes regardless of location of production. The advantage to producing in China is, then, some reductions in absolute labor costs. In this scenario, absolute costs are far more important than some vague notion of opportunity cost. Furthermore, the labor cost reduction is not, however, necessarily significant because the overall costs of producing airplanes tend to be more closely tied to capital, due to the advanced capital and technology used in production, as opposed to overall labor costs. As such, if all of the other costs, such as transportation costs, are not favorable, then it may not be cost effective to produce airplanes in China as opposed to the United States. Either way, absolute costs, not opportunity costs, are often times the most important determinant of what is produced and where it will be produced.

Markets are not Static

So much of the orthodox free trade story seems to be built on a model that yields a surprising lack of choices for producers. After all a country is deemed to be endowed with an allotment of land, labor, and capital, and among those three factors of production the choice of what is produced is determined by which products can be produced at the lowest opportunity cost of production. In this scenario, the country does not choose its initial endowments of factors of production nor, at that point, is the country really making a choice as to what products to produce as the opportunity cost of production will depend on the country's endowment of factors of production relatively to all other countries' endowments of factors of production. In essence, any country is relegated to being at the mercy of global circumstances and global markets.

Being at the mercy of the market is an awfully risky proposition for many countries. A country better hope that what it specializes to produce and then trade will always be a desirable commodity. Unfortunately for many countries, the reality of global markets, where new technologies and changes in tastes and preferences arise on a regular basis, often times causes countries to suffer significant economic hardship and economic development setbacks.

But, are countries and their economies really at the mercy of a global market? If history is a guide, the answer to this question appears to be unequivocally, no. Many students evaluating the factor endowment story outlined above might, for example, question why a given country would accept its factor endowment position? After all, factor endowments such as labor and capital are not, over time, static. Given time, populations tend to grow and countries will find that their allotment of capital stock will also tend to grow. It is not as though the United States was endowed with capital stock from some divine being and, as a result, is a capital intensive country. Any country could, presumably, develop a capital intensive economy. If so desired, countries have the power to influence where capital stock accumulates and toward what end that capital stock can and should be used. Under conditions such as this it appears as though countries have the power to direct their place in the global economy.

Among advanced developed economies there are countless examples of industrial planning and trade protections, essentially market manipulations, being utilized to promote domestic economic objectives and steer a country's economic place in the global economy. In the 18th and 19th centuries countries such as Great Britain and the United States both utilized trade restrictions in an effort to support the development of domestic, high value added, industries, particularly manufacturing. Into and throughout the 20th century, the United States as well as countries such as Germany, Japan, and South Korea have all also utilized trade restrictions and industrial planning policies. In the case of post-World War 2 Japan and Germany, trade restrictions and planning policies were utilized to allow domestic industries that had been destroyed during the war to re-establish themselves in their respective domestic markets. By the 1970s, the protective policies utilized by Japan and Germany allowed both countries to engage in international export of products such as automobiles and electronics, stimulating an export-led growth model. An export-led growth model is the idea that a country can use trade surpluses, exporting more products than they import, to boost domestic economic activity, generate economic development, and improve the country's international competitiveness in the global economy.

Not to be left out, other countries, particularly in Asia, also recognized the benefit of export-led economic growth. South Korea, as one of the Asian Tigers, used trade protections to bolster and create a domestic electronics and automobile industry. Over time South Korean producers such as Samsung in electronics as well as Hyundai and Kia in the automobile industry have become internationally competitive and internationally recognizable producers. Another example is China. The Chinese economy, through use of targeted industrial planning, trade restrictions, and currency adjustments, has utilized an export-led growth model. China has run consistent trade surpluses with the countries within the European Union as well as the United States. The results, since China's "Great Opening Up" in 1978, which began under then Chinese leader Deng Xiaoping, have been an economic boon for China. In the nearly forty years since 1978, China has experienced consistent annualized growth rates of 7-10%.

A Note on China's Inclusion in the World Trade Organization

As of December 11, 2001, China has been a member of the World Trade Organization (WTO). As noted by the policy think tank, the Economic Policy Institute (EPI), China's inclusion in the WTO has not been benign in terms of economic consequences. An EPI study suggests that 2001 and 2013, China's export-led growth model and subsequent trade surpluses with the United States (or U.S. trade deficits with China) has caused the United States to lose 3.2 million jobs, including 2.4 million job losses in the manufacturing sector.

28.4 ANOTHER WAY TO PRESENT INTERNATIONAL TRADE: PATH DEPENDENCY

Given the critiques outlined above, many progressive and radical (heterodox) economists believe that the orthodox economic free trade theory is chronically incapable of addressing important, real world, concerns. Because of its failure to explain real world conditions, the orthodox model is also incapable of suggesting policy approaches that may be helpful in correcting many of the problems that emerge when trade between countries expands and grows. For example, in the orthodox world of free trade, any, and all, trade protections are perceived as inefficient and costly. As a result, if the real world provides evidence of the effectiveness of trade restrictions, a story built on the benefits of free trade cannot and will not be functionally applicable. Using the free trade story in this regard would generate inaccurate analyses, failing to recognize that trade protections have had historic usefulness toward assisting an economy's economic development. In this instance, the free trade story is of no practical/functional use. What is needed, instead, is a different theory of how trade works. A sound theory of regarding trade should be able to demonstrate how trade restrictions may stimulate more economic growth and/or improve a country's economic development prospects.

Because theorists outside of the orthodoxy view the orthodox economic trade story as being impossibly limited in its real world applications, heterodox economists generally begin their trade story from a different perspective. For many heterodox economists, in the real world, specialization and trade are **path dependent**. Path dependence means that history matters. A given country's productive situation is the byproduct of past circumstances, past decision making (with respect to domestic economic choices as well as the country's place in the global economy). Further a country's economic development, it's future productive possibilities and future economic position in the global economy, depends on the choices it makes in the present.

To follow the logic of comparative advantage, a country identifies its comparative advantage, specializes and then trades. So if agricultural products are the only products that a country has a comparative advantage producing, then the country will specialize in the production of agricultural products only and then trade for the other non-agriculture products that are desired. In response to this scenario, heterodox economists ask, for how long does a country only produce agricultural products? After all, from an economic development standpoint it is well known that there is not a single advanced developed economy that only produces agricultural products. In fact, the production of products in all advanced developed economies are overwhelming diverse.

Economic Development and the Case for Conscious Diversification

The United States is widely recognized for having one of the most diverse economies in the world. U.S. based firms produce agricultural products, light and heavy manufactured products, industrial products, pharmaceutical products, and so on and so forth. Aside from no longer being de-stabilized due to weather volatility or changes in consumer tastes and preferences, a diversified economy can better endure overall market volatility because some sectors may grow when others contract. Additionally, as markets change, as new technologies emerge, a diversified economy is better apt to be able to find uses for new technologies and integrate those technologies into their economy. As a result, in the path-dependency-trade-story, diversification, rather than simple specialization and trade, is encouraged because diversification is an economic development strategy. Importantly, as is noted by the critiques provided above, *diversification cannot be achieved by comparative advantage and a free trade environment.*

By evaluating trade through a lens of path dependency, heterodox economists are able to correct for some of real world limitations associated with the orthodox free trade story. For example, the very nature of path dependency requires strategic thinking and public policy planning on the part of countries and their governments. Countries will often target industries for protection from international competition because they see an industry as generating a high-value added, high income, and significant employment outcome for their economy. The automobile industry is an example of industry where countries have been apt to enact policies to encourage both domestic production as well as foreign direct investment into the production of automobiles. Countries such as Azerbaijan, Egypt, and Malaysia all have developing internal domestic automobile producers. Additionally, China is currently the world's largest producer and consumer of automobiles with production being generated by a large number of foreign firms such as Volkswagen and General Motors as well as the domestic Chinese producer, Geely. The benefit of having a viable domestic automobile industry is that automobiles are one of the highest value added mass-consumed products in the world. If a country can produce automobiles to meet even just some of its internal consumer demand for automobiles, then the country will be retaining valuable domestic expenditures in the form of valuable domestic income.

Finally, a path dependency approach to examining trade between countries empowers the heterodox economist to understand why some countries have had more relative success than others with respect to economic development. By thinking of trade as a result of path dependency, the role of trade restrictions, industrial planning, and targeted competition can reveal to the theorist tactics and approaches that have successful enhanced economic development or, alternatively stifled economic development. As a result, the fact that advanced developed economies have a history of managed trade, rather than free trade, can be understood as strategic decision making. Undoubtedly, advanced developed economies owe some of their economic position to the strategic trade choices that they made in the past. Furthermore, the recent success of a country like China can also be explained as being related to the strategic, State planned and managed, trade decisions that the Chinese government has implemented. Finally, the path dependency approach can also be utilized to explain why persistent free trade policies have also been use to undermine the economic development of many countries, exacerbating persistent inequalities between countries.

GLOSSARY

A

Accounting Profit: total revenues minus explicit costs, including depreciation

Acquisition: when one firm purchases another

Additional external cost: additional costs incurred by third parties outside the production process when a unit of output is produced

Adverse selection: when groups with inherently higher risks than the average person seek out insurance, thus straining the insurance system

Affirmative action: active efforts by government or businesses that give special rights to minorities in hiring, promotion, or access to education to make up for past discrimination

Allocative Efficiency: producing the optimal quantity of some output; the quantity where the marginal benefit to society of one more unit just equals the marginal cost

Allocative Efficiency: when the mix of goods being produced represents the mix that society most desires

Anti-dumping laws: laws that block imports sold below the cost of production and impose tariffs that would increase the price of these imports to reflect their cost of production

Antitrust Laws: laws that give government the power to block certain mergers, and even in some cases to break up large firms into smaller ones

Asymmetric information: a situation where the seller or the buyer has more information than the other regarding the quality of the item being sold

Average profit: profit divided by the quantity of output produced; profit margin

Average total cost: total cost divided by the quantity of output

Average variable cost: variable cost divided by the quantity of output

B

Backward-Bending Supply Curve For Labor: the situation when high-wage people can earn so much that they respond to a still-higher wage by working fewer hours

Barriers To Entry: the legal, technological, or market forces that may discourage or prevent potential competitors from entering a market

Behavioral Economics: a branch of economics that seeks to enrich the understanding of decision-making by integrating the insights of psychology and by investigating how given dollar amounts can mean different things to individuals depending on the situation.

Biodiversity: the full spectrum of animal and plant genetic material

Budget Constraint : all possible consumption combinations of goods that someone can afford, given the prices of goods, when all income is spent; the boundary of the opportunity set

Budget constraint line: shows the possible combinations of two goods that are affordable given a consumer's limited income

Bundling: a situation in which multiple products are sold as one

C

CAPABILITY: the availability of functionings coupled with the ability of the individual to achieve a combination of functionings

Cardinal utility: the idea that the utility a consumer assigns to a product is objective and, therefore, quantifiably measurable

Cartel: a group of firms that collude to produce the monopoly output and sell at the monopoly price

ceteris paribus: other things being equal

Circular Flow Diagram: a diagram that views the economy as consisting of households and firms interacting in a goods and services market and a labor market.

Coinsurance: when an insurance policyholder pays a percentage of a loss, and the insurance company pays the remaining cost

Collateral: something valuable—often property or equipment—that a lender would have a right to seize and sell if the loan is not repaid

Collective bargaining: negotiations between unions and a firm or firms

Collusion: when firms act together to reduce output and keep prices high

Command Economy: an economy where economic decisions are passed down from government authority and where resources are owned by the government.

Command-And-Control Regulation: laws that specify allowable quantities of pollution and that also may detail which pollution-control technologies must be used

Common market: economic agreement between countries to allow free trade in goods, services, labor, and financial capital between members while having a common external trade policy

Comparative Advantage: when a country can produce a good at a lower cost in terms of other goods; or, when a country has a lower opportunity cost of production

complements: goods that are often used together so that consumption of one good tends to enhance consumption of the other

Concentration ratio: an early tool to measure the degree of monopoly power in an industry; measures what share of the total sales in the industry are accounted for by the largest firms, typically the top **Four to Eight Firms:** four-firm concentration ratio the percentage of the total sales in the industry that are accounted for by the largest four firms

Constant returns to scale: expanding all inputs proportionately does not change the average cost of production

Consumer equilibrium: when the ratio of the prices of goods is equal to the ratio of the marginal utilities (point at which the consumer can get the most satisfaction)

Consumer Surplus: the extra benefit consumers receive from buying a good or service, measured by what the individuals would have been willing to pay minus the amount that they actually paid

Copayment: when an insurance policyholder must pay a small amount for each service, before insurance covers the rest

COPYRIGHT: a form of legal protection to prevent copying, for commercial purposes, original works of authorship, including books and music

Cosigner: another person or firm who legally pledges to repay some or all of the money on a loan if the original borrower does not do so

Cost-plus regulation: when regulators permit a regulated firm to cover its costs and to make a normal level of profit

Cross-price elasticity of demand: the percentage change in the quantity of good A that is demanded as a result of a percentage change in good B

D

Deadweight Loss: the loss in social surplus that occurs when a market produces an inefficient quantity

Deductible: an amount that the insurance policyholders must pay out of their own pocket before the insurance coverage pays anything

Demand Curve: a graphic representation of the relationship between price and quantity demanded of a certain good or service, with quantity on the horizontal axis and the price on the vertical axis

Demand Schedule: a table that shows a range of prices for a certain good or service and the quantity demanded at each price

Demand: the relationship between price and the quantity demanded of a certain good or service

Deregulation: removing government controls over setting prices and quantities in certain industries

Differentiated product: a product that is perceived by consumers as distinctive in some way

Diminishing marginal utility: the common pattern that each marginal unit of a good consumed provides less of an addition to utility than the previous unit

Discrimination: actions based on the belief that members of a certain group or groups are in some way inferior solely because of a factor such as race, gender, or religion

Diseconomies of scale: the long-run average cost of producing each individual unit increases as total output increases

Disruptive market change: innovative new product or production technology which disrupts the status quo in a market, leading the innovators to earn more income and profits and the other firms to lose income and profits, unless they can come up with their own innovations

Division of Labor: the way in which the work required to produce a good or service is divided into tasks performed by different workers.

Dumping: selling internationally traded goods below their cost of production

Duopoly: an oligopoly with only two firms

E

Earned income tax credit (EITC): a method of assisting the working poor through the tax system

Ecological Economics: a heterodox school of economic thought that situates the economy as a subordinate structure within the natural environment

Economic profit: total revenues minus total costs (explicit plus implicit costs)

Economic Surplus: see social surplus

Economic union: economic agreement between countries to allow free trade between members, a common external trade policy, and coordinated monetary and fiscal policies

Economics: the study of how humans make choices under conditions of scarcity .

Economies of Scale: when the average cost of producing each individual unit declines as total output increases

Effective Income Tax: percentage of total taxes paid divided by total income

Elastic Demand: when the elasticity of demand is greater than one, indicating a high responsiveness of quantity demanded or supplied to changes in price

Elastic Supply: when the elasticity of either supply is greater than one, indicating a high responsiveness of quantity demanded or supplied to changes in price

Elasticity of savings: the percentage change in the quantity of savings divided by the percentage change in interest rates

Elasticity: an economics concept that measures responsiveness of one variable to changes in another variable

Entry: the long-run process of firms entering an industry in response to industry profits

Equilibrium Price: the price where quantity demanded is equal to quantity supplied

Equilibrium Quantity: the quantity at which quantity demanded and quantity supplied are equal for a certain price level

Equilibrium: the situation where quantity demanded is equal to the quantity supplied; the combination of price and quantity where there is no economic pressure from surpluses or shortages that would cause price or quantity to change

Estate tax: a tax imposed on the value of an inheritance

Excess Demand: at the existing price, the quantity demanded exceeds the quantity supplied; also called a shortage

Excess Supply: at the existing price, quantity supplied exceeds the quantity demanded; also called a surplus

Exclusive dealing: an agreement that a dealer will sell only products from one manufacturer

Exit: the long-run process of firms reducing production and shutting down in response to industry **losses:** long-run equilibrium

Explicit costs: out-of-pocket costs for a firm, for example, payments for wages and salaries, rent, or materials

Exploitation: the idea that a producer or producers of a product receive compensation that is less than the value of what the producer or producers contributed to the production process

Export-led growth model: the idea that a country can use trade surpluses, exporting more products than they import, to boost domestic economic activity, generate economic development, and improve the country's international competitiveness in the global economy

Exports: products (goods and services) made domestically and sold abroad.

Externality: a market exchange that affects a third party who is outside or "external" to the exchange; sometimes called a "spillover"

F

Factor Endowments: a country's comparative advantage may be influenced by which factors of production the country has an abundance of and which are relatively scarce

Factors of production: the combination of labor, materials, and machinery that is used to produce goods and services; also called inputs

Fee-for-service: when medical care providers are paid according to the services they provide

FIRM: an organization that combines inputs of labor, capital, land, and raw or finished component materials to produce outputs.

Fiscal Policy: economic policies that involve government spending and taxes.

Fixed cost: expenditure that must be made before production starts and that does not change regardless of the level of production

Free and common socage: a system of land tenure in the American colonies which included perpetual ownership, transmissible to heirs, free disposal of property, alienability

Free rider: those who want others to pay for the public good and then plan to use the good themselves; if many people act as free riders, the public good may never be provided

Free Trade Agreement: economic agreement between countries to allow free trade between members

Functionings: a state of being for an individual as well as the collection of all things an individual can be doing

Fungible: the idea that units of a good, such as dollars, ounces of gold, or barrels of oil are capable of mutual substitution with each other and carry equal value to the individual.

G

Game theory: a branch of mathematics often used by economists that analyzes situations in which players must make decisions and then receive payoffs based on what decisions the other players make

GENERAL AGREEMENT ON TARIFFS AND TRADE (GATT): forum in which nations could come together to negotiate reductions in tariffs and other barriers to trade; the precursor to the World Trade Organization

Globalization: the trend in which buying and selling in markets have increasingly crossed national borders.

Goods and Services Market: a market in which firms are sellers of what they produce and households are buyers.

GROSS DOMESTIC PRODUCT (GDP): measure of the size of total production in an economy.

H

Health Maintenance Organization (Hmo): an organization that provides health care and is paid a fixed amount per person enrolled in the plan—regardless of how many services are provided

Herfindahl-Hirschman Index (HHI): approach to measuring market concentration by adding the square of the market share of each firm in the industry

I

Imperfect information: a situation where either the buyer or the seller, or both, are uncertain about the qualities of what is being bought and sold

Imperfectly competitive: firms and organizations that fall between the extremes of monopoly and perfect competition

Implicit costs: opportunity cost of resources already owned by the firm and used in business, for example, expanding a factory onto land already owned

Import quotas: numerical limits on the quantity of products that can be imported

Imports: products (goods and services) made abroad and then sold domestically.

INCOME EFFECT: a higher price means that, in effect, the buying power of income has been reduced, even though actual income has not changed; always happens simultaneously with a substitution effect

Income inequality: when one group receives a disproportionate share of total income or wealth than others

Income: a flow of money received, often measured on a monthly or an annual basis

Inelastic Demand: when the elasticity of demand is less than one, indicating that a 1 percent increase in price paid by the consumer leads to less than a 1 percent change in purchases (and vice versa); this indicates a low responsiveness by consumers to price changes

Inelastic Supply: when the elasticity of supply is less than one, indicating that a 1 percent increase in price paid to the firm will result in a less than 1 percent increase in production by the firm; this indicates a low responsiveness of the firm to price increases (and vice versa if prices drop)

Inferior good: a good in which the quantity demanded falls as income rises, and in which quantity demanded rises and income falls

Inputs: the combination of labor, materials, and machinery that is used to produce goods and services; also called factors of production

Insurance: method of protecting a person from financial loss, whereby policy holders make regular payments to an insurance entity; the insurance firm then remunerates a group member who suffers significant financial damage from an event covered by the policy

Intangible value: the value of a business enterprise over and above the value of its tangible assets

Intellectual property: the body of law including patents, trademarks, copyrights, and trade secret law that protect the right of inventors to produce and sell their inventions

Intellectual property: the body of law including patents, trademarks, copyrights, and trade secret law that protect the right of inventors to produce and sell their inventions

Interest Rate: the "price" of borrowing in the financial market; a rate of return on an investment

International Externalities: externalities that cross national borders and that cannot be resolved by a single nation acting alone

Invisible Handp: idea that self-interested behavior by individuals can lead to positive social outcomes

K

Kinked demand curve: a perceived demand curve that arises when competing oligopoly firms commit to match price cuts, but not price increases

L

Labor Market: the market in which households sell their labor as workers to business firms or other employers.

Labor union: an organization of workers that negotiates with employers over wages and working conditions

Law of Demand: the common relationship that a higher price leads to a lower quantity demanded of a certain good or service and a lower price leads to a higher quantity demanded, while all other variables are held constant

Law of Diminishing Marginal Utility: as we consume more of a good or service, the utility we get from additional units of the good or service tend to become smaller than what we received from earlier units

Law of Diminishing Returns: as additional increments of resources are added to producing a good or service, the marginal benefit from those additional increments will decline

Law of Supply: the common relationship that a higher price leads to a greater quantity supplied and a lower price leads to a lower quantity supplied, while all other variables are held constant

Legal monopoly: legal prohibitions against competition, such as regulated monopolies and intellectual property protection

Long-run average cost (LRAC) curve: shows the lowest possible average cost of production, allowing all the inputs to production to vary so that the firm is choosing its production technology

LORENZ CURVE: a graph that compares the cumulative income actually received to a perfectly equal **distribution of income:** it shows the share of population on the horizontal axis and the cumulative percentage of total income received on the vertical axis

M

Macroeconomics: the branch of economics that focuses on broad issues such as growth, unemployment, inflation, and trade balance.

Marginal Analysis: examination of decisions on the margin, meaning a little more or a little less from the status quo

Marginal cost: the additional cost of producing one more unit

Marginal Profit: profit of one more unit of output, computed as marginal revenue minus marginal cost

Marginal revenue: the additional revenue gained from selling one more unit

Marginal utility per dollar: the additional satisfaction gained from purchasing a good given the price of the product; MU/Price

Marginal utility: the additional utility provided by one additional unit of consumption

Market Economy: an economy where economic decisions are decentralized, resources are owned by private individuals, and businesses supply goods and services based on demand

Market failure: When the market on its own does not allocate resources efficiently in a way that balances social costs and benefits; externalities are one example of a market failure

Market share: the percentage of total sales in the market

Market: interaction between potential buyers and sellers; a combination of demand and supply

Marketable permit program: a permit that allows a firm to emit a certain amount of pollution; firms with more permits than pollution can sell the remaining permits to other firms

Medicaid: a federal–state joint program enacted in 1965 that provides medical insurance for certain (not all) low-income people, including the near-poor as well as those below the poverty line, and focusing on low-income families with children, the low-income elderly, and the disabled

Merger: when two formerly separate firms combine to become a single firm

Microeconomics: the branch of economics that focuses on actions of particular agents within the economy, like households, workers, and business firms.

Minimum resale price maintenance agreement: an agreement that requires a dealer who buys from a manufacturer to sell for at least a certain minimum price

Minimum Wage: a price floor that makes it illegal for an employer to pay employees less than a certain hourly rate

Model: see theory.

Monetary Policy: policy that involves altering the level of interest rates, the availability of credit in the economy, and the extent of borrowing.

Money-back guarantee: a promise that the buyer's money will be refunded under certain conditions

Monopolistic Competition: many firms competing to sell similar but differentiated products

Monopoly: a situation in which one firm produces all of the output in a market

Moral hazard: when people have insurance against a certain event, they are less likely to guard against that event occurring

N

National interest argument: the argument that there are compelling national interests against depending on key imports from other nations

Natural Monopoly: conomic conditions in the industry, for example, economies of scale or control of a critical resource, that limit effective competition

Near-poor: those who have incomes just above the poverty line

Need: something that is necessary for a human being to sustain basic physical and psychological health

Negative Externalities: situations in which economic activities create unaccounted for costs that impact third parties, or those people who are not directly involved in the economic activity

Negative externality: a situation where a third party, outside the transaction, suffers from a market transaction by others

Nonexcludable: when it is costly or impossible to exclude someone from using the good, and thus hard to charge for it

Nonrivalrous: even when one person uses the good, others can also use it

Nontariff barriers: ways a nation can draw up rules, regulations, inspections, and paperwork to make it more costly or difficult to import products

Normal good: a good in which the quantity demanded rises as income rises, and in which quantity demanded falls as income falls

Normative Statement: statement which describes how the world should be

O

Occupational license: licenses issued by government agencies, which indicate that a worker has completed a certain type of education or passed a certain test

Oligopoly: when a few large firms have all or most of the sales in an industry

Opportunity Cost: measures cost by what is given up in exchange; opportunity cost measures the value of the forgone alternative

Opportunity Set: all possible combinations of consumption that someone can afford given the prices of goods and the individual's income

Ordinal utility: the idea that the utility that a consumer assigns to a product is subjective, in the mind of the consumer, and is, therefore, not directly quantifiably measurable

P

Pareto optimality (the Pareto criterion): when economic outcomes are such that there is no way to make any one or many people better off without making any one person or many worse off

Patent: a government rule that gives the inventor the exclusive legal right to make, use, or sell the invention for a limited time

Pollution charge: a tax imposed on the quantity of pollution that a firm emits; also called a pollution tax

Positive externalities: beneficial spillovers to a third party or parties

Positive externality: a situation where a third party, outside the transaction, benefits from a market transaction by others

Positive Statement: statement which describes the world as it is

Poverty line: the specific amount of income needed for a basic standard of living

Poverty rate: percentage of the population living below the poverty line

Poverty Trap: antipoverty programs set up so that government benefits decline substantially as people earn more income—as a result, working provides little financial gain

Poverty: the situation of being below a certain level of income needed for a basic standard of living

Predatory pricing: when an existing firm uses sharp but temporary price cuts to discourage new competition

Premium: payment made to an insurance company

Price cap regulation: when the regulator sets a price that a firm cannot exceed over the next few years

Price Ceiling: a legal maximum price

Price Control: government laws to regulate prices instead of letting market forces determine prices

Price Elasticity Of Demand: percentage change in the quantity *demanded* of a good or service divided the percentage change in price

Price Elasticity Of Supply: percentage change in the quantity *supplied* divided by the percentage change in price

Price Elasticity: the relationship between the percent change in price resulting in a corresponding percentage change in the quantity demanded or supplied

Price Floor: a legal minimum price

Price: what a buyer pays for a unit of the specific good or service

Prisoner's Dilemma: a game in which the gains from cooperation are larger than the rewards from pursuing self-interest

Private benefits: the dollar value of all benefits of a new product or process invented by a company that can be captured by the investing company

Private Enterprise: system where the means of production (resources and businesses) are owned and operated by private individuals or groups of private individuals

Private enterprise: the ownership of businesses by private individuals

Private rates of return: when the estimated rates of return go primarily to an individual; for example, earning interest on a savings account

Producer Surplus: the extra benefit producers receive from selling a good or service, measured by the price the producer actually received minus the price the producer would have been willing to accept

Production Possibilities Frontier (Ppf): a diagram that shows the productively efficient combinations of two products that an economy can produce given the resources it has available.

Production technologies: alternative methods of combining inputs to produce output

Production: the process of combining inputs to produce outputs, ideally of a value greater than the value of the inputs

Productive Efficiency: when it is impossible to produce more of one good (or service) without decreasing the quantity produced of another good (or service)

Progressive tax system: a tax system in which the rich pay a higher percentage of their income in taxes, rather than a higher absolute amount

Property Rights: the legal rights of ownership on which others are not allowed to infringe without paying compensation

Protectionism: government policies to reduce or block imports

Public good: good that is nonexcludable and nonrivalrous, and thus is difficult for market producers to sell to individual consumers

Q

Quantity Demanded: the total number of units of a good or service consumers are willing to purchase at a given price

Quantity Supplied: the total number of units of a good or service producers are willing to sell at a given price

Quintile: dividing a group into fifths, a method often used to look at distribution of income

R

Race To The Bottom: when production locates in countries with the lowest environmental (or other) standards, putting pressure on all countries to reduce their environmental standards

Redistribution: taking income from those with higher incomes and providing income to those with lower incomes

Regulatory Capture: when the firms supposedly being regulated end up playing a large role in setting the regulations that they will follow and as a result, they "capture" the people doing the regulation, usually through the promise of a job in that "regulated" industry once their term in government has ended.

Restrictive practices: practices that reduce competition but that do not involve outright agreements between firms to raise prices or to reduce the quantity produced

Revenue: income from selling a firm's product; defined as price times quantity sold

Risk group: a group that shares roughly the same risks of an adverse event occurring

S

Safety net: the group of government programs that provide assistance to the poor and the near-poor

Scarcity: when human wants for goods and services exceed the available supply.

Service contract: the buyer pays an extra amount and the seller agrees to fix anything specified in the contract that goes wrong for a set time period

Shift in demand: when a change in some economic factor (other than price) causes a different quantity to be demanded at every price

Shortage: at the existing price, the quantity demanded exceeds the quantity supplied; also called excess demand

Short-run average cost (SRAC) curve: the average total cost curve in the short term; shows the total of the average fixed costs and the average variable costs

Shutdown point: level of output where the marginal cost curve intersects the average variable cost curve at the minimum point of AVC; if the price is below this point, the firm should shut down immediately

Social benefits: the dollar value of all benefits of a new product or process invented by a company that can be captured by other firms and by society as a whole

Social costs: costs that include both the private costs incurred by firms and also additional costs incurred by third parties outside the production process, like costs of pollution

Social rate of return: when the estimated rates of return go primarily to society; for example, providing free education

Social Surplus: the sum of consumer surplus and producer surplus

Specialization: when workers or firms focus on particular tasks for which they are well-suited within the overall production process.

Spillover: see externality

Substitute: a good that can replace another to some extent, so that greater consumption of one good can mean less of the other

Substitution Effect: when a price changes, consumers have an incentive to consume less of the good with a relatively higher price and more of the good with a relatively lower price; always happens simultaneously with an income effect

Sunk Costs: costs that are made in the past and cannot be recovered

Supplemental Nutrition Assistance Program (SNAP): a federally funded program, started in 1964, in which each month poor people receive SNAP cards they can use to buy food

Supply Curve: a line that shows the relationship between price and quantity supplied on a graph, with quantity supplied on the horizontal axis and price on the vertical axis

Supply Schedule: a table that shows a range of prices for a good or service and the quantity supplied at each price

Supply: the relationship between price and the quantity supplied of a certain good or service

Surplus: at the existing price, quantity supplied exceeds the quantity demanded; also called excess supply

T

Theory: a representation of an object or situation that is simplified while including enough of the key features to help us understand the object or situation.

Total cost: the sum of fixed and variable costs of production

Total Surplus: see social surplus

Total utility: satisfaction derived from consumer choices

Trade Secrets: methods of production kept secret by the producing firm

Trademark: an identifying symbol or name for a particular good and can only be used by the firm that registered that trademark

Traditional Economy: typically an agricultural economy where things are done the same as they have **Always Been Done:** underground economy: a market where the buyers and sellers make transactions in violation of one or more government regulations

Tying sales: a situation where a customer is allowed to buy one product only if the customer also buys another product

U

Unitary Elasticity: when the calculated elasticity is equal to one indicating that a change in the price of the good or service results in a proportional change in the quantity demanded or supplied.

Use-Value: the idea that the value of an object is based on how useful the product is to the consumer. Products have an intrinsic value to their consumers

Usury Laws: laws that impose an upper limit on the interest rate that lenders can charge

Utility: satisfaction, usefulness, or value one obtains from consuming goods and services

V

Variable cost: cost of production that increases with the quantity produced

W

Wage elasticity of labor supply: the percentage change in hours worked divided by the percentage change in wages

Want: something that is desired, but also not necessary for an individual to live and function in a society

Warranty: a promise to fix or replace the good for a certain period of time

Wealth: the sum of the value of all assets, including money in bank accounts, financial investments, a pension fund, and the value of a home

World Trade Organization (WTO): organization that seeks to negotiate reductions in barriers to trade and to adjudicate complaints about violations of international trade policy; successor to the General Agreement on Tariffs and Trade (GATT)

REFERENCES

Aboukhadijeh, Feross. "Chapter 20: Girding for War – The North and the South, 1861-1865." StudyNotes, Inc. Accessed July 7, 2013. http://www.apstudynotes.org/us-history/outlines/chapter-20-girding-for-war-the-north-and-the-south-1861-1865/.

AFL-CIO. "Training and Apprenticeships." http://www.aflcio.org/Learn-About-Unions/Training-and-Apprenticeships.

American Community Survey. 2012. "School Enrollment and Work Status: 2011." Accessed April 13, 2015. http://www.census.gov/prod/2013pubs/acsbr11-14.pdf.

Anderson, Deborah J., Melissa Binder, and Kate Krause. "The Motherhood Wage Penalty Revisited: Experience, Heterogeneity, Work Effort, and Work-Schedule Flexibility." Industrial and Labor Relations Review. no. 2 (2003): 273–294. http://www2.econ.iastate.edu/classes/econ321/orazem/anderson_motherhood-penalty.pdf.

Arias, Omar and Walter W. McMahon. "Dynamic Rates of Return to Education in the U.S." Economics of Education Review. 20, 2001. 121–138.

Austin, Algernon. "The Unfinished March: An Overview." Economic Policy Institute. Last modified June 18, 2013. http://www.epi.org/publication/unfinished-march-overview/.

Bertrand, Marianne, and Sendhil Mullainathan. "Are Emily and Greg More Employable Than Lakisha and Jamal? A Field Experiment on Labor Market Discrimination." American Economic Review. no. 4 (2004): 991-1013. https://www.aeaweb.org/articles.php?doi=10.1257/0002828042002561&fnd=s.

Biography.com. 2015. "Alan Turing." Accessed April 1, 2015. http://www.biography.com/people/alan-turing-9512017.

Bishop, Todd. 2014. "Microsoft Exec Admits New Reality: Market Share No Longer 90% — It's 14%."GeekWire. Accessed March 27, 2015. http://www.geekwire.com/2014/microsoft-exec-admits-new-reality-market-share-longer-90-14/.

Blau, Francine D., and Laurence M. Kahn. "The Gender Pay Gap: Have Women Gone as Far as They Can?" Academy of Management Perspectives. no. 1 (2007): 7–23. 10.5465/AMP.2007.24286161.

Board of Governors of the Federal Reserve System. "Research Resources: Survey of Consumer Finances." Last modified December 13, 2013. http://www.federalreserve.gov/econresdata/scf/scfindex.htm.

British Parliament. "(28 August 1833). Slavery Abolition Act 1833; Section LXIV." Accessed July 2013. http://www.pdavis.nl/Legis_07.htm.

Bureau of Labor Statistics, U.S. Department of Labor. 2015. "Median Weekly Earnings by Educational Attainment in 2014." Accessed March 27, 2015. http://www.bls.gov/opub/ted/2015/median-weekly-earnings-by-education-gender-race-and-ethnicity-in-2014.htm.

Bureau of Labor Statistics, U.S. Department of Labor. 2015. "The Employment Situation—February 2015." Accessed March 27, 2015. http://www.bls.gov/news.release/pdf/empsit.pdf.

Bureau of Labor Statistics. "Data Retrieval: Employment, Hours, and Earnings (CES)." Last modified February 1, 2013. http://www.bls.gov/webapps/legacy/cesbtab1.htm.

Bureau of Labor Statistics. "Industries at a Glance." Accessed December 31, 2013. http://www.bls.gov/iag/.

Canty Media. 2015. "The World: Life Expectancy (2015) – Top 100+." Accessed April 1, 2015. http://www.geoba.se/population.php?pc=world&type=15.

Card, David, and Alan B. Kruger. "Trends in Relative Black–White Earnings Revisited (Working Paper #310)." Princeton University and the National Bureau of Economic Research. December 1992. http://harris.princeton.edu/pubs/pdfs/310.pdf.

Catan, T., & Dezember, R. "Kinder-El Paso Merger to Face Antitrust Scrutiny," Wall Street Journal. October 19, 2011.

Center on Budget and Policy Priorities. 2015. "Policy Basics: Where Do Our Federal Tax Dollars Go?" Accessed April 1, 2015. http://www.cbpp.org/cms/?fa=view&id=1258.

Central Intelligence Agency. "The World Factbook." https://www.cia.gov/library/publications/the-world-factbook/index.html.

Central Intelligence Agency. "The World Factbook." https://www.cia.gov/library/publications/the-world-factbook/index.html.

Clark, John Bates. Essentials of Economic Theory: As Applied to Modern Problems of Industry and Public Policy. New York: A. M. Kelley, 1907, 501.

Clune, Michael S. "The Fiscal Impacts of Immigrants: A California Case Study." In The Immigration Debate: Studies on the Economic, Demographic, and Fiscal Effects of Immigration, edited by James P. Smith and Barry Edmonston. Washington, DC: National Academy Press, 1998, 120–182. http://www.nap.edu/openbook.php?record_id=5985&page=120.

Collins, A. "Tallgrass Energy to Acquire Kinder Morgan Assets for $1.8B." The Middle Market, Accessed August 2013. http://www.themiddlemarket.com/news/tallgrass-energy-to-acquire-kinder-morgan-assets-for-1-point-8-billion-232862-1.html.

Congressional Budget Office. "The Distribution of Household Income and Federal Taxes, 2008 and 2009." Last modified July 10, 2012. http://www.cbo.gov/publication/43373.

Congressional Budget Office. 2015. "The Effects of Potential Cuts in SNAP Spending on Households With Different Amounts of Income." Accessed April 13, 2015. https://www.cbo.gov/publication/49978.

Conoco Phillips. "Why Natural Gas." Accessed August 2013. http://www.powerincooperation.com/en/pages/useful.html?gclid=COXg7rH3hrgCFWlp7AodtkgA3g.

Consumer Reports. "Consumer Reports.org." http://www.consumerreports.org/cro/index.htm.

Costanza, Robert, and Lisa Wainger. "No Accounting For Nature: How Conventional Economics Distorts the Value of Things." The Washington Post. September 2, 1990.

CreditCards.com. 2013. http://www.creditcards.com/credit-card-news/credit-card-industry-facts-personal-debt-statistics-1276.php.

Dattel, E. (nd). "Cotton and the Civil War." Mississippi Historical Society. Accessed July 2013. http:/mshistorynow.mdah.state.ms.us/articles/291/cotton-and-the-civil-war.

De la Merced, M. (2012, August 20). "Kinder Morgan to Sell Assets to Tallgrass for $1.8 Billion." The New York Times. August 20, 2012.

Dhillon, Kiran. 2015. "Why Are U.S. Oil Imports Falling?" Time.com. Accessed April 1, 2015. http://time.com/67163/why-are-u-s-oil-imports-falling/.

Donovan, Theresa. Jurist. "Federal Judge Rejects Class Status in Wal-Mart Discrimination Suit." Last modified August 5, 2013. http://jurist.org/paperchase/2013/08/federal-judge-rejects-class-status-in-wal-mart-discrimination-suit.php.

E.Helpman,andO.Itskhoki,"LabourMarketRigidities,TradeandUnemployment," The Review of Economic Studies, 77. 3 (2010): 1100-1137.

Ebeling,Ashlea.2014."IRSAnnounces2015EstateAndGiftTaxLimits."Forbes.Accessed March 16, 2015. http://www.forbes.com/sites/ashleaebeling/2014/10/30/irs-announces-2015-estate-and-gift-tax-limits/.

eMarketer.com. 2014. "Total US Ad Spending to See Largest Increase Since 2004: Mobile advertising leads growth; will surpass radio, magazines and newspapers this year. Accessed March 12, 2015. http://www.emarketer.com/Article/Total-US-Ad-Spending-See-Largest-Increase-Since-2004/1010982.

Environmental Protection Agency. "2006 Pay-As-You-Throw Programs." Accessed December 20, 2013. http://www.epa.gov/epawaste/conserve/tools/payt/states/06comm.htm.

European Commission: Agriculture and Rural Development. 2013. "Overview of the CAP Reform: 2014-2024." Accessed April 13, 205. http://ec.europa.eu/agriculture/cap-post-2013/.

European Union. "Durban Conference Delivers Breakthrough for Climate." Press release. December 11, 2012. Accessed December 19, 2013. http://europa.eu/rapid/press-release_MEMO-11-895_en.htm?locale=en.

Falk, Gene. Congressional Research Service. "The Temporary Assistance for Needy Families (TANF) Block Grant: Responses to Frequently Asked Questions." Last modified October 17, 2013. http://www.fas.org/sgp/crs/misc/RL32760.pdf.

Federal Register: The Daily Journal of the United States Government. "State Median Income Estimates for a Four-Person Household: Notice of the Federal Fiscal Year (FFY) 2013 State Median Income Estimates for Use Under the Low Income Home Energy Assistance Program (LIHEAP)." Last modified March 15, 2012. https://www.federalregister.gov/articles/2012/03/15/2012-6220/state-median-income-estimates-for-a-four-person-household-notice-of-the-federal-fiscal-year-ffy-2013#t-1.

Federal Trade Commission. "About the Federal Trade Commission." Accessed October 17, 2013. http://www.ftc.gov/ftc/about.shtm.

Federal Trade Commission. "About the Federal Trade Commission." Last modified October 17, 2013. http://www.ftc.gov/ftc/about.shtm.

Frank, Robert H., and Philip J. Cook. The Winner-Take-All Society. New York: Martin Kessler Books at The Free Press, 1995.

Gagnon, M. A. (2013). Corruption of pharmaceutical markets: Addressing the misalignment of financial incentives and public health. The Journal of Law, Medicine & Ethics, 41(3), 571-580.

Gagnon, M. A. and J. Lexchin. (2008), "The Cost of Pushing Pills: A New Estimate of Pharmaceutical Promotion Expenditures in the United States," PLoSMedicine, 5(1), 29-33.

Garling, Caleb. "S.F. plane crash: Reporting, emotions on social media," The San Francisco Chronicle. July 7, 2013. http://www.sfgate.com/news/article/S-F-plane-crash-Reporting-emotions-on-social-4651639.php.

Gartner. 2015. "Gartner Says Tablet Sales Continue to Be Slow in 2015." Accessed March 12, 2015. http://www.gartner.com/newsroom/id/2954317.

Grogan, David. 2015. "Federal Judge Finds AmEx's Anti-Steering Rule Violates Antitrust Law." American Booksellers Association. Accessed March 12, 2015. http://www.bookweb.org/news/federal-judge-finds-amex%E2%80%99s-anti-steering-rule-violates-antitrust-law.

Harris, Elizabeth A. "Labor Panel Finds Illegal Punishments at Walmart." The New York Times, November 18, 2013. http://www.nytimes.com/2013/11/19/business/labor-panel-finds-illegal-punishments-at-walmart.html?_r=1&.

Henry J. Kaiser Family Foundation, The. "Health Reform: Summary of the Affordable care Act." Last modified April 25, 2013. http://kff.org/health-reform/fact-sheet/summary-of-new-health-reform-law/.

Holden, Sarah, and Daniel Schrass. 2012. "The rose of IRAs in U.S Households' Saving for Retirement, 2012." ICI Research Perspective 18.8 (2012). http://www.ici.org/pdf/per18-08.pdf.

Huang, Chye-Ching, and Nathaniel Frentz. "Myths and Realities About the Estate Tax." Center on Budget and Policy Priorities. Last modified August 29, 2013. http://www.cbpp.org/files/estatetaxmyths.pdf.

Huffington Post. 2015. "HUFFPOLLSTER: Poll Shows Uptick In Obamacare Favorable Rating." Accessed April 1, 2015. http://www.huffingtonpost.com/2015/03/19/affordable-care-act-fav_n_6900938.html.

Hyclak, Thomas, Geraint Johnes, and Robert Thornton. Fundamentals of Labor Economics. Boston: Houghton Mifflin Company, 2005.

Institute of Education Sciences: National Center for Education Statistics. "Fast Facts: Degrees Conferred by Sex and Race." http://nces.ed.gov/fastfacts/display.asp?id=72.

Irvine, Jessica. "Social Networking Sites are Factories of Modern Ideas." The Sydney Morning Herald. November 25, 2011.http://www.smh.com.au/federal-politics/society-and-culture/social-networking-sites-are-factories-of-modern-ideas-20111124-1nwy3.html#ixzz2YZhPYeME.

Johnson, Oscar William. "Back on Track: Earth Day Success Story; The Chattanooga Choo-Choo No Longer Spews Foul Air." Sports Illustrated. April 30, 1990. http://www.si.com/vault/1990/04/30/121923/back-on-track-earth-day-success-story-the-chattanooga-choo-choo-no-longer-spews-foul-air.

Kahn, C. "Kinder Morgan to Buy El Paso Corp. for $20.7B." USA Today. October 17, 2011.

Kahneman, Daniel and Amos Tversky. "Prospect Theory: An Analysis of Decision under Risk."Econometrica 47.2 (March 1979) 263-291.

Kahneman, Daniel, and Amos Tversky. "Prospect Theory: An Analysis of Decision under Risk." Econometrica. 47, no. 2 (1979): 263-291. http://www.princeton.edu/~kahneman/docs/Publications/prospect_theory.pdf.

Kantar Media. "Our Insights: Infographic—U.S. Advertising Year End Trends Report 2012." Accessed October 17, 2013. http://kantarmedia.us/insight-center/reports/infographic-us-advertising-year-end-trends-report-2012.

Kinder Morgan. (2013). "Investor Information." Accessed August 2013. http://www.kindermorgan.com/investor/.

Kohut, Andrew, Richard Wike, and Juliana Horowitz. "The Pew Global Attitudes Project." Pew Research Center. Last modified October 4, 2007. http://www.pewglobal.org/files/pdf/258.pdf.

Kolesnikova, Natalia A., and Yang Liu. Federal Reserve Bank of St. Louis: The Regional Economist. "Gender Wage Gap May Be Much Smaller Than Most Think." Last modified October 2011. http://www.stlouisfed.org/publications/re/articles/?id=2160.

Kristof, Nicholas. "Let Them Sweat." The New York Times, June 25, 2002. http://www.nytimes.com/2002/06/25/opinion/let-them-sweat.html.

Landsburg, Steven E. The Armchair Economist: Economics and Everyday Life. New York: The Free Press. 2012. specifically Section IV: How Markets Work.

Library of Congress. "Congressional Research Service." http://www.loc.gov/crsinfo/about/.

Luhby, Tami. 2014. "Income is on the rise . . . finally!" Accessed April 10, 2015. http://money.cnn.com/2014/08/20/news/economy/median-income/.

Lutz, Hannah. 2015. "U.S. Auto Exports Hit Record in 2014." Automotive News. Accessed April 1, 2015. http://www.autonews.com/article/20150206/OEM01/150209875/u.s.-auto-exports-hit-record-in-2014.

M.J. Melitz, and D. Trefler. "Gains from Trade when Firms Matter." The Journal of Economic Perspectives, 26.2 (2012): 91-118.

Massachusetts Historical Society. "The Coming of the American Revolution 1764-1776: The Boston Tea Party." Retrieved from http://www.masshist.org/revolution/teaparty.php.

Massachusetts Historical Society. "Whereas our Nation." The Massachusetts Gazette, p. 2. Accessed July 2013 http://www.masshist.org/revolution/image-viewer.php?old=1&item_id=457&img_step=1&nmask=1&mode=large.

McMahon, Walter. Education and Development: Measuring the Social Benefits. Oxford: Oxford University Press, 2000.

Meyer, Ali. 2015. "56,023,000: Record Number of Women Not in Labor Force." CNSNews.com. Accessed March 16, 2015. http://cnsnews.com/news/article/ali-meyer/56023000-record-number-women-not-labor-force.

National Association of Insurance Commissioners. "National Association of Insurance Commissioners & The Center for Insurance Policy and Research." http://www.naic.org/.

National Center for Educational Statistics. "Digest of Education Statistics." (2008 and 2010). Accessed December 11, 2013. nces.ed.gov.

National Center for Environmental Economics (NCEE). "Frequently Asked Questions on Mortality Risk Valuation." United States Environmental Protection Agency. Accessed December 19, 2013. http://yosemite.epa.gov/ee/epa/eed.nsf/pages/MortalityRiskValuation.html#whatvalue World Tourism Organization, "Tourism 2020 Vision." Accessed December 19, 2013. http://www.world-tourism.org/market_research/facts/market_trends.htm.

National Chicken Council. 2015. "Per Capita Consumption of Poultry and Livestock, 1965 to Estimated 2015, in Pounds." Accessed April 13, 2015. http://www.nationalchickencouncil.org/about-the-industry/statistics/per-capita-consumption-of-poultry-and-livestock-1965-to-estimated-2012-in-pounds/.

National Institute of Health. 2015. "Global Competitiveness—The Importance of U.S. Leadership in Science and Innovation for the Future of Our Economy and Our Health." Accessed April 1, 2015. http://www.nih.gov/about/impact/impact_global.pdf.

National Science Foundation. 2013. "U.S. R&D Spending Resumes Growth in 2010 and 2011 but Still Lags Behind the Pace of Expansion of the National Economy." Accessed April 1, 2015. http://www.nsf.gov/statistics/infbrief/nsf13313/.

Nhan, Doris. "Census: More in U.S. Report Nontraditional Households." National Journal. Last modified May 1, 2012. http://www.nationaljournal.com/thenextamerica/demographics/census-more-in-u-s-report-nontraditional-households-20120430.

OECD. "The Organisation for Economic Co-operation and Development (OECD)." http://www.oecd.org/about/.

Office of Management and Budget. "Fiscal Year 2013 Historical Tables: Budget of the U.S. Government." http://www.whitehouse.gov/sites/default/files/omb/budget/fy2013/assets/hist.pdf.

Office of the United States Trade Representative. "U.S. Trade Representative Froman Announces FY 2014 WTO Tariff-Rate Quota Allocations for Raw Cane Sugar, Refined and Specialty Sugar and Sugar-Containing Products."Accessed January 6, 2014. http://www.ustr.gov/about-us/press-office/press-releases/2013/september/WTO-trq-for-sugar.

Orshansky, Mollie. "Children of the Poor." Social Security Bulletin. 26 no. 7 (1963): 3–13. http://www.ssa.gov/policy/docs/ssb/v26n7/v26n7p3.pdf.

Oxfam International. Accessed January 6, 2014. http://www.oxfam.org/.

Pelegrin, William. 2015. "Judge Overrules Antitrust Case Against Google , Says Setting Default Search Engines Is Fair." Digital Trends. Accessed March 12, 2015. http://www.digitaltrends.com/mobile/judge-tosses-out-google-antitrust-lawsuit/.

Pew Research Center. "Pew Research: Center for the People & the Press." http://www.people-press.org/.

Pew Research Center. 2015. "Social Networking Fact Sheet." Accessed March 11, 2015. http://www.pewinternet.org/fact-sheets/social-networking-fact-sheet/.

Podmolik, Mary Ellen. "HUD Finds Housing Discrimination 'Hidden' But Prevalent." Chicago Tribune: Business, June 12, 2013. http://articles.chicagotribune.com/2013-06-12/business/ct-biz-0612-housing-discrimination-20130612_1_renters-testers-chicago-area.

Psacharopoulos, George. "Returns to Investment in Education: A Global Update." World Development 22, 1994. 1325–1343.

Radford, R. A. "The Economic Organisation of a P.O.W. Camp." Economica. no. 48 (1945): 189-201. http://www.jstor.org/stable/2550133.

Rasmussen Reports, LLC. "Rasmussen Reports." http://www.rasmussenreports.com/.

Rauch, J. "Was Mancur Olson Wrong?" The American, February 15, 2013. http://www.american.com/archive/2013/february/was-mancur-olson-wrong.

Robbins, Lionel. An Essay on the Nature and Significance of Economic Science. London: Macmillan. 1932.

Rogowsky, Mark. 2014. "There'd Be No Wireless Wars Without The Blocked T-Mobile Merger, So Where Does That Leave Comcast-TWC?" Forbes.com. Accessed

March 12, 2015. http://www.forbes.com/sites/markrogowsky/2014/08/27/t-mobile-and-sprint-continue-to-battle-thanks-to-the-government/.

Ryan, Dave. "New Report Shows Benefits of 1990 Clean Air Amendments Outweigh Costs by Four-to-One Margin," press release, November 16, 1999. United States Environmental Protection Agency. Accessed December 19, 2013. http://www.epa.gov/oar/sect812/r-140.html.

Salientes-Narisma, Corrie. "Samsung Shift to Innovative Devices Pay Off." Inquirer Technology. Accessed May 15, 2013. http://technology.inquirer.net/23831/samsungs-shift-to-innovative-devices-pays-off.

Smith, Adam. "Of Restraints upon the Importation from Foreign Countries." In The Wealth of Nations. London: Methuen & Co., 1904, first pub 1776), I.V. 2.9.

Smith, Adam. "Of the Propriety of Action." In The Theory of Moral Sentiments. London: A. Millar, 1759, 1.

Smith, James P. "Immigration Reform." Rand Corporation: Rand Review. http://www.rand.org/pubs/periodicals/rand-review/issues/2012/fall/leadership/immigration-reform.html.

Spreen, Thomas Luke. United States Department of Labor: Bureau of Labor Statistics. "Recent College Graduates in the U.S. Labor Force: Data from the Current Population Survey." Monthly Labor Review (February, 2013). http://www.bls.gov/opub/mlr/2013/02/art1full.pdf .

Statistica.com. 2015. "Number of Restaurants in the United States from 2011 to 2014." Accessed March 27, 2015. http://www.statista.com/statistics/244616/number-of-qsr-fsr-chain-independent-restaurants-in-the-us/.

Tax Policy Center: Urban Institute and Brookings Institution. "The Tax Policy Briefing Book: Taxation and the Family: What is the Earned Income Tax Credit?" http://www.taxpolicycenter.org/briefing-book/key-elements/family/eitc.cfm.

Thaler, Richard H. "Shifting Our Retirement Savings into Automatic." The New York Times, April 6, 2013. http://www.nytimes.com/2013/04/07/business/an-automatic-solution-for-the-retirement-savings-problem.html?pagewanted=all.

Thaler, Richard H., and Sendhil Mullainathan. "The Concise Encyclopedia of Economics: Behavioral Economics." Library of Economics and Liberty. http://www.econlib.org/library/Enc/BehavioralEconomics.html.

The Federal Trade Commission. n.d. "The Federal Trade Commission's (FTC) Mission." Accessed March 27, 2015. https://www.ftc.gov/system/files/documents/reports/2014-one-page-ftc-performance-snapshot/150218fy14snapshot.pdf.

The Heritage Foundation. 2015. "2015 Index of Economic Freedom." Accessed March 11, 2015. http://www.heritage.org/index/ranking.

The United States Department of Justice. "Antitrust Division." Accessed October 17, 2013. http://www.justice.gov/atr/.

The Wall Street Journal. 2015. "Auto Sales." Accessed April 10, 2015. http://online.wsj.com/mdc/public/page/2_3022-autosales.html.

The World Bank Group. 2015. "World Data Bank." Accessed March 30, 2014. http://databank.worldbank.org/data/.

The World Bank. "Data: Poverty Headcount Ratio at $1.25 a Day (PPP) (% of Population)." http://data.worldbank.org/indicator/SI.POV.DDAY.

The World Bank. "Merchandise trade (% of GDP)." Accessed January 4, 2014. http://data.worldbank.org/indicator/TG.VAL.TOTL.GD.ZS.

Turner, Margery Austin, Rob Santos, Diane K. Levy, Doug Wissoker, Claudia Aranda, Rob Pitingolo, and The Urban Institute. "Housing Discrimination Against Racial and Ethnic Minorities 2012." U.S. Department of Housing and Urban Development. Last modified June 2013. http://www.huduser.org/Publications/pdf/HUD-514_HDS2012.pdf.

U.S. Bureau of Labor Statistics. 2015. "Consumer Expenditures in 2013." Accessed March 11, 2015. http://www.bls.gov/cex/csxann13.pdf.

U.S. Bureau of Labor Statistics. 2015. "Employer Costs for Employee Compensation—December 2014." Accessed March 11, 2015. http://www.bls.gov/news.release/pdf/ecec.pdf.

U.S. Bureau of Labor Statistics. 2015. "Labor Force Statistics from the Current Population Survey." Accessed March 11, 2015. http://www.bls.gov/cps/cpsaat22.htm.

U.S. Bureau of Labor Statistics: BLS Reports. "Report 1040: Women in the Labor Force: A Databook." Last modified March 26, 2013. http://www.bls.gov/cps/wlf-databook-2012.pdf.

U.S. Bureau of Labor Statistics: BLS Reports. 2014. "Women in the Labor Force: A Databook (Report 1052)." Accessed April 13, 2015. http://www.bls.gov/opub/reports/cps/women-in-the-labor-force-a-databook-2014.pdf.

U.S. Department of Commerce: United States Census Bureau. "American FactFinder." http://factfinder2.census.gov/faces/nav/jsf/pages/index.xhtml.

U.S. Department of Commerce: United States Census Bureau. "Current Population Survey (CPS): CPS Table Creator." http://www.census.gov/cps/data/cpstablecreator.html.

U.S. Department of Commerce: United States Census Bureau. "Income: Table H-2. Share of Aggregate Income Received by Each Fifth and Top 5 Percent of Households." http://www.census.gov/hhes/www/income/data/historical/household/.

U.S. Department of Commerce: United States Census Bureau. "Income: Table F-6. Regions—Families (All Races) by Median and Mean Income." http://www.census.gov/hhes/www/income/data/historical/families/.

U.S. Department of Commerce: United States Census Bureau. "Poverty: Poverty Thresholds." Last modified 2012. http://www.census.gov/hhes/www/poverty/data/threshld/.

U.S. Department of Health & Human Services. 2015. "2015 Poverty Guidelines." Accessed April 10, 2015. http://www.medicaid.gov/medicaid-chip-program-information/by-topics/eligibility/downloads/2015-federal-poverty-level-charts.pdf.

U.S. Department of Health & Human Services. 2015. "Information on Poverty and Income Statistics: A Summary of 2014 Current Population Survey Data." Accessed April 13, 2015. http://aspe.hhs.gov/hsp/14/povertyandincomeest/ib_poverty2014.pdf.

U.S. Department of Homeland Security: Office of Immigration Statistics. "2011 Yearbook of Immigration Statistics." September 2012. http://www.dhs.gov/sites/default/files/publications/immigration-statistics/yearbook/2011/ois_yb_2011.pdf.

U.S. Energy Information Administration (a). "Natural Gas Consumption by End User." Accessed May 31, 2013. http://www.eia.gov/dnav/ng/ng_cons_sum_dcu_nus_a.htm.

U.S. Energy Information Administration (b). "Natural Gas Prices." Accessed June 28, 2013. http://www.eia.gov/dnav/ng/ng_pri_sum_dcu_nus_a.htm.

U.S. Energy Information Administration. "Total Energy: Monthly Energy Review." U.S. Department of Energy. Accessed December 19, 2013. http://www.eia.gov/total0energy/data/monthly/.

U.S. Equal Employment Opportunity Commission, "Walmart to Pay More than $11.7 Million to Settle EEOC Sex Discrimination Suit." Last modified March 1, 2010. http://www.eeoc.gov/eeoc/newsroom/release/3-1-10.cfm.

U.S. Patent and Trademark Office. 2015. "U.S. Patent Statistics: Calendar Years 1963–2014." Accessed April 10, 2015. http://www.uspto.gov/web/offices/ac/ido/oeip/taf/us_stat.pdf.

UNESCO Institute for Statistics. "Statistics in Brief / Profiles" Accessed August 2013. http://stats.uis.unesco.org/unesco/TableViewer/document.aspx?ReportId=121 &IF_Language=en&BR_Country=5580.

United Auto Workers (UAW). "About: Who We Are." http://www.uaw.org/page/who-we-are.

United for Medical Research. "Profiles of Prosperity: How NIH-Supported Research Is Fueling Private Sector Growth and Innovation." Introduction. Accessed January 2014. http://www.unitedformedicalresearch.com/wp-content/uploads/2013/07/UMR_ProsperityReport_071913a.pdf.

United States Census Bureau. 2014. "2013 Highlights." Accessed April 13, 2015. http://www.census.gov/hhes/www/poverty/about/overview/.

United States Census Bureau. 2014. "Historical Income Tables: Households: Table H-2 Share of Aggregate Income Received by Each Fifth and Top 5% of Income. All Races." Accessed April 13, 2015. http://www.census.gov/hhes/www/income/data/historical/household/.

United States Census Bureau. 2014. "Table 1. Educational Attainment of the Population 18 Years and Over, by Age, Sex, Race, and Hispanic Origin: 2014." Accessed April 13, 2015. http://www.census.gov/hhes/socdemo/education/data/cps/2014/tables.html.

United States Department of Commerce. "About the Department of Commerce." Accessed January 6, 2014. http://www.commerce.gov/about-department-commerce.

United States Department of Labor, Bureau of Labor Statistics. 2015. "Economic News; Union Members Summary." Accessed April 13, 2015. http://www.bls.gov/news.release/union2.nr0.htm.

United States Department of Labor. Bureau of Labor Statistics. 2015. "Employment Situation Summary." Accessed April 1, 2015. http://www.bls.gov/news.release/empsit.nr0.htm.

United States Department of Labor: Bureau of Labor Statistics. "Economic News Release: Union Members Summary." Last modified January 23, 2013. http://www.bls.gov/news.release/union2.nr0.htm.

United States Department of Labor: Bureau of Labor Statistics. "News Release: Usual Weekly Earnings of Wage and Salary Workers (Third Quarter 2013)." November 1, 2013. http://www.bls.gov/news.release/pdf/wkyeng.pdf.

United States Department of the Treasury. "Research and Experimentation Tax Credit." Accessed November 2013. http://www.treasury.gov/press-center/news/Pages/investing-in-us-competitiveness.aspx.

United States Department of Transportation. "Total Passengers on U.S Airlines and Foreign Airlines U.S. Flights Increased 1.3% in 2012 from 2011." Accessed October 2013. http://www.rita.dot.gov/bts/press_releases/bts016_13

United States International Trade Commission. "About the USITC." Accessed January 6, 2014. http://www.usitc.gov/press_room/about_usitc.htm.

USA Today. 2015. "Uninsured Rates Drop Dramatically under Obamacare." Accessed April 1, 2015. http://www.usatoday.com/story/news/nation/2015/03/16/uninsured-rates-drop-sharply-under-obamacare/24852325/.

Viscusi, Kip W. Fatal Tradeoffs: Public and Private Responsibilities for Risk. New York: Oxford University Press, 1995.

Warner, Judith. 2014. "Fact Sheet: The Women's Leadership Gap: Women's Leadership by the Numbers." Center for American Progress. Accessed March 16, 2015. https://www.americanprogress.org/issues/women/report/2014/03/07/85457/fact-sheet-the-womens-leadership-gap/.

Weinberger, Catherine J., and Lois Joy. "The Relative Earnings of Black College Graduates, 1980–2001." In Race and Economic Opportunity in the 21st Century, edited by Marlene Kim. New York: Routledge, 2007. http://www.econ.ucsb.edu/~weinberg/grads.pdf.

Wessel, David. "Saudi Arabia Fears $40-a-Barrel Oil, Too." The Wall Street Journal. May 27, 2004, p. 42. http://online.wsj.com/news/articles/SB108561000087822300.

Williamson, Lisa. "US Labor Market in 2012." Bureau of Labor Statistics. Accessed December 1, 2013. http://www.bls.gov/opub/mlr/2013/03/art1full.pdf.

World Trade Organization. 2014. "Annual Report 2014." Accessed April 1, 2015. https://www.wto.org/english/res_e/booksp_e/anrep_e/anrep14_chap10_e.pdf.

INDEX

www.ingramcontent.com/pod-product-compliance
Lightning Source LLC
LaVergne TN
LVHW062223200926
848484LV00006B/1459